This gracefully written, deeply researched, and subtly argued volume illumines a strangely under-studied topic: the conjunction of the rise of electronic mass communications, the emergence of two radio celebrities from dramatically different traditions, and their role in the reception of historic Christian faith in mid-twentieth-century America. Of evangelicals such as Charles Fuller, Billy Graham, and Aimee McPherson, we already know a fair amount. But by focusing on ministries of Fulton J. Sheen and Walter A. Maier, this truly path-breaking volume opens new avenues in our understanding of American religious history."

Grant Wacker, Gilbert T. Rowe Distinguished Professor Emeritus of Christian History at Duke Divinity School

"As a son of radio pioneer Dr. Walter A. Maier of *The Lutheran Hour*, I thought I had ferreted out all the details of his remarkable life, but I was mistaken. Farney found significant material that I should have. You can imagine my delight at reading this fresh information! Pairing Maier with the equally pioneering Fulton Sheen makes sense, since both were radio forces who brought high skills and erudition to their presentations. Sheen went on to enjoy success in television, whereas Maier's death in 1950, just at the start of that new communications medium, prevented what doubtless would have been an equal success, though without the magisterial purple cape. To keep the comparisons fair, Farney principally covers only the radio Sheen in these pages. Anyone born in the Depression 1930s or wartime 1940s will be able to hear two familiar voices as they read."

Paul L. Maier, Russel H. Seibert Professor of Ancient History Emeritus, Western Michigan University

"Nearly nineteen centuries after Paul of Tarsus took up his stylus and wax tablet to connect with the far-flung believers around the Mediterranean, Monsignor Sheen and Reverend Maier used the cutting-edge technology of their day to bring the message of Jesus Christ to new ears. It will be many years before we see the effects (for good or for ill) of the current media on the life of the church, but Professor Farney's engaging work transports us back to the very beginning of the technological age. With the invention of radio, Sheen and Maier could take our Lord's command to 'go out to all nations' to a new level—all from a single microphone in the comfort of a sound booth! They were true pioneers—new apostles of a new evangelization that is still just beginning to bear fruit. I highly recommend this book not just as a historical glimpse back but also as a sign of what may yet be to come. May it inspire a new generation to take up the Lord's Great Commission using every tool at their disposal."

Daniel R. Jenky, CSC, bishop of the Catholic Diocese of Peoria, Illinois

"In *Ministers of a New Medium*, Kirk Farney offers a penetrating assessment of the mid-twentieth-century relationship between Christian ministry and media. His insightful study demands the careful attention of the church and students of US Christianity. Furthermore, it challenges the Christian community to reflect critically on the possibilities that new media offers in the twenty-first century for the propagation of the gospel."

Theon E. Hill, associate professor of communication at Wheaton College

"This dual biography offers compelling portraits of Fulton J. Sheen and Walter A. Maier, each of whom had a rare ability to both cultivate and communicate theological insights. Pairing these media sensations—one Catholic, one Lutheran—allows Farney to tell a story about religion and radio in American culture that is even broader and more interesting than the sum of its parts. In an age when many lament the corrosive effect of new media on faith and morals, the efforts of Sheen and Maier to harness emerging technologies in service of their respective faith traditions offer not only an interesting story about America's past but also a measure of hope for its future."

Kathleen Sprows Cummings, director of the Cushwa Center for the Study of American Catholicism, University of Notre Dame, and author of *A Saint of Our Own: How the Quest for a Holy Hero Helped Catholics Become American*

"Despite being truly dead ends, past theological modernism and today's postmodernism have captured popular culture. No longer in the comfortable center of 'Christian' America, biblical Christianity can glean from Bishop Sheen and Dr. Maier how to be missional in our troubled times with the word that rings true in people's lives. A relevant book for today. Thank you, Dr. Farney!"

Dale A. Meyer, former speaker on *The Lutheran Hour* and president emeritus and professor emeritus, Concordia Seminary

"When Gutenberg invented his printing press, the book he printed was the Bible. In the great awakenings in the eighteenth century, John Wesley and fellow evangelicals produced so many Bibles, sermons, and all sorts of pamphlets, he was called 'the father of the religious paperback.' Evangelists like D. L. Moody and Billy Graham leveraged the architectural advancement of great arenas for their evangelistic meetings, while more recently megachurches take advantage of the interstate highway system that allows people to travel quickly to gather in their auditoriums. But it may be that the use of the radio by Christians represents the most powerful way technology has been used to influence the masses, and two of the most influential voices were Bishop Sheen and Walter Maier. Read this to be informed of an important era in Christian history and to be inspired to utilize technology in our time for Christ."

Ed Stetzer, executive director of the Wheaton College Billy Graham Center and dean of the School of Mission, Ministry, and Leadership

"In the most uncertain of times, Maier and Sheen indiscriminately sowed radio programs that unapologetically chose theological content, rather than shtick or sensationalism, in order to inform and inspire anyone who would listen. This engaging volume not only sheds light on the rich historical evidence related to the groundbreaking radio ministries of Maier and Sheen but also corrects much of what is assumed about the surprising successes of *The Lutheran Hour* and *The Catholic Hour*. A welcome publication in an age that attempts to reduce any explanation of lasting significance to either personality or method."

Daniel N. Harmelink, executive director of the Concordia Historical Institute, Saint Louis, Missouri

"This carefully researched and elegantly written study examines two major figures for US Catholics and Lutherans in the twentieth century: radio preachers who entered millions of homes with eloquent and sophisticated pastoral and theological teaching. Fulton Sheen and Walter Maier both deserve closer attention on their own, and comparing them yields new insights into the history of American Christianity. Yet given the profound changes that have occurred in Christian media globally since their day, especially with the explosion of Pentecostal media in bewildering variety, these earlier seminal figures, here carefully analyzed, create possibilities for future comparative studies. These two cases, here compared across various registers, invite future research that could distinguish truly innovative religious media production and dissemination from those merely iterative, for example, in the financing and organization of media production, the crafting of messages from theological and other perspectives, and the practices operative in the creation of listening/watching/perceiving publics who 'tune in' to Christian media."

Paul Kollman, CSC, University of Notre Dame, Department of Theology

"Two Christian leaders, Roman Catholic Fulton Sheen and Lutheran Walter A. Maier, both of whom served in what might be considered traditional denominations, helped draw their ethnic traditions into the American religious mainstream through their adoption and advocacy for the use of new media and technology. Seeing radio as a God-given tool in service of the proclamation of the gospel, they also helped transform the shape and practice of the larger Christian community. In *Ministers of a New Medium* Kirk Farney tells this remarkable story in a way that draws the reader deeply into the lives of the aforementioned men, along with the development and functioning of their radio programs: Sheen's *The Catholic Hour* and Maier's *The Lutheran Hour*. Working on the bleeding edge of technological development, Maier and Sheen helped transform the twentieth-century church by using their 'golden mouths' and 'ethereal pulpits' to become 'pastors of the airwaves' with the result that, perhaps unknowingly, they were transforming the very nature of what it means to be the church and how that church may express itself."

Lawrence R. Rast Jr., president and professor of American church history at Concordia Theological Seminary in Fort Wayne, Indiana

"Using the latest media technology to teach the Bible in ways that shape the surrounding culture is as old as the Protestant Reformation and as relevant as the latest theology podcast. In this well-written and theologically astute history, Kirk Farney takes us back to the golden age of radio, when the extraordinarily influential ministries of Walter Maier (*The Lutheran Hour*) and Fulton Sheen (*The Catholic Hour*) entered millions of American homes over the airwaves. Dr. Farney shows how these two religious broadcasters adapted their message to a new medium and addressed the pressing spiritual, theological, and sometimes political issues of the twentieth century. His account does more than bring these two radio personalities alive; it focuses a sharp lens on important technological, cultural, and ecclesiastical trends in American history."

Philip Ryken, president of Wheaton College

"*Ministers of a New Medium* offers a fascinating look at how Dr. Fulton J. Sheen and our own broadcast pioneer Dr. Walter A. Maier leveraged the new medium of radio to share the gospel with Americans who were desperately seeking an outlet during troubled times. By offering meticulous details gathered through countless hours of research, Kirk D. Farney parallels the lives and teachings of these groundbreaking religious leaders and traces the overwhelming challenges that each faced and overcame to become a top radio personality of his era. By grasping the significance of using radio for evangelism to the masses, Dr. Maier's vision and persistence paved the way for a global ministry that today not only provides *The Lutheran Hour* as the longest-running Christian radio program in history but utilizes emerging technologies to share Christ's love with tens of millions of people in more than sixty countries."

Kurt Buchholz, president and CEO of Lutheran Hour Ministries

"In examining two pioneers in religious broadcasting, Fulton J. Sheen and Walter A. Maier, Kirk Farney provides an excellent study of religion and media in mid-twentieth-century America. Farney pays close attention to their theological orientations as well as their influence on culture and society. This book is an important contribution to the history of Christianity in the United States."

Mark A. Granquist, Lloyd and Annelotte Svendsbye Professor of the History of Christianity at Luther Seminary in St Paul, Minnesota

"Kirk Farney's work of history will inspire your creativity. Our current technological revolution is not without precedent. Christians seeking to navigate today's communication environment will find the genius of Sheen and Maier to be instructive. These preaching pioneers used radio, the emerging medium of their day, to develop and sustain the theological appetite of Americans. Reading this book prompted me to ask, How must orthodox Christians once again use our contemporary emerging media to respond to the timeless spiritual crises of incivility, rootlessness, and restlessness?"

John Arthur Nunes, senior fellow at the Center for Religion, Culture, and Democracy

"Kirk Farney has given us a gift. What a storyteller! As he spins his yarns about Maier and Sheen, two great radio evangelists, he tells us about our country, the impact of mass media, the church, and ourselves. I appreciated his meticulous research, readable prose, and sense of humor, and so will you. Thank you, Kirk!"

Mark Jeske, pastor of St. Marcus Lutheran Church in Milwaukee, Wisconsin, and principal speaker and author for the Time of Grace Ministry from 2000–2018

MINISTERS
OF A NEW
MEDIUM

KIRK D. FARNEY

ON THE AIR

Ministers of a

NEW
MEDIUM

BROADCASTING THEOLOGY in the RADIO MINISTRIES of
FULTON J. SHEEN *and* WALTER A. MAIER

Foreword by MARK A. NOLL

iVp
Academic

An imprint of InterVarsity Press
Downers Grove, Illinois

InterVarsity Press
P.O. Box 1400, Downers Grove, IL 60515-1426
ivpress.com
email@ivpress.com

InterVarsity Press® is the book-publishing division of InterVarsity Christian Fellowship/USA®, a movement of
students and faculty active on campus at hundreds of universities, colleges, and schools of nursing in the United
States of America, and a member movement of the International Fellowship of Evangelical Students. For information
about local and regional activities, visit intervarsity.org.

Scripture quotations marked NRSV are from the New Revised Standard Version Bible, copyright © 1989 National
Council of the Churches of Christ in the United States of America. Used by permission. All rights reserved worldwide.

Scriptures marked KJV are from the King James Version, public domain.

Quotations from Walter A. Maier's published sermons are used by permission from International Lutheran Laymen's
League, all rights reserved.

The publisher cannot verify the accuracy or functionality of website URLs used in this book beyond the date
of publication.

Cover design and image composite: David Fassett
Interior design: Daniel van Loon
Image: © Image courtesy of Concordia Historical Institute, St. Louis, Missouri

ISBN 978-1-5140-0322-0 (print)
ISBN 978-1-5140-0323-7 (digital)

Printed in the United States of America ∞

InterVarsity Press is committed to ecological stewardship and to the conservation of natural resources
in all our operations. This book was printed using sustainably sourced paper.

Library of Congress Cataloging-in-Publication Data
A catalog record for this book is available from the Library of Congress.

P	25	24	23	22	21	20	19	18	17	16	15	14	13	12	11	10	9	8	7	6	5	4	3	2	1
Y	41	40	39	38	37	36	35	34	33	32	31	30	29	28	27	26	25	24	23	22

To Cheryl, Erin, and Mitch

CONTENTS

FOREWORD

MARK A. NOLL

READERS OF THIS DEEPLY researched and skillfully written book are in for two surprises. The first reveals the remarkable national popularity of two radio preachers during the years when that medium became a fixture in American households. Monsignor Dr. Fulton Sheen, the featured speaker on NBC's *Catholic Hour*, and the Rev. Dr. Walter Maier, of the self-funded *The Lutheran Hour*, became media stars in the era that also saw Jack Benny, Edward R. Murrow, Fibber McGee & Molly, Kate Smith, and Bing Crosby emerge as household names. Amazingly, if judged by mail received, general name recognition, and, in the case of Maier, successful fund raising, these radio preachers may have even outshone the other media stars of their era. Kirk Farney's illuminating account provides the best kind of detailed information on the multi-dimensional savvy that propelled the *Catholic Hour* and *The Lutheran Hour*—but also the many practical and logistical difficulties that Maier and Sheen overcame to become not just "Ministers of a New Medium," but masters of that medium.

The second surprise is just as noteworthy, for Sheen and Maier were not simply popular. They were also popular as supremely well-educated speakers, unabashed advocates of classical Christian teaching, and confident representatives of relatively marginalized denominations. Unlike some radio preachers of their era and many thereafter, Sheen and Maier did not dumb down, sensationalize, or pander. Although they communicated through accessible language and well-chosen anecdotes, they did not hide the fact of their superior learning. Instead, they devoted this learning and their skill as communicators to preaching the main doctrines of classical Christian orthodoxy. The chapters in the book devoted to the preached theology of the two amount to extended expositions of the Christian creeds. The message they broadcast, in other words, was not watered-down.

Walter Maier's Lutheranism and Fulton Sheen's Catholicism made their radio careers even more remarkable. Sheen became a radio fixture only a few years after a surge of anti-Catholic sentiment greeted candidate Al Smith, who in 1928 campaigned as the first Catholic nominee for president from a major political party (he was a Democrat). Opposition resulting from Protestant fears and the belief that Catholicism equated to anti-democratic authority would survive well past the years treated in this book. Yet, with a captivating speaking style and a message effectively communicating main Christian teachings, Sheen sailed calmly by the nation's hereditary anti-Catholic disposition.

Prior to Maier, American Lutheranism was less a threat than an unknown quantity. Lutherans had enjoyed a secure place in pockets of the American landscape since the colonial period. But their identification as the church of German and Scandinavian immigrants set them apart, as did a theology that retained elements of the sixteenth-century Reformation other American Protestants had left behind. In addition, the traumas of the First World War had inspired intense anti-German reactions in areas of the country where most German descendants (and also Lutherans) lived. Yet Maier negotiated whatever hesitations listeners might have had about a Lutheran voice as skillfully as Sheen did for the greater suspicions about heeding a Catholic.

Ministers of a New Medium illuminates early radio history, makes a welcome addition to the American history of Christianity, and brings two larger-than-life personalities into sharper focus. From its pages readers will come away with historical and biographical insights, but also two sturdy and edifying expressions of the Christian faith itself.

ACKNOWLEDGMENTS

THE NUMBER OF INDIVIDUALS who contributed to the conception, research, writing, and publication of this book, both directly and indirectly, is significant and I am deeply grateful to every one of them. Certain contributors, however, deserve special mention. First and foremost is Mark Noll. Mark welcomed me to the University of Notre Dame in 2008, as I left a twenty-six-year career in global banking to pursue PhD studies full-time. He served as a mentor, adviser, and coach as I completed my studies and wrote my dissertation, the latter of which provides the foundational text of this book. Mark has since provided steady encouragement and guidance as I refined my manuscript and secured the appropriate publisher. Most importantly, he continues to be a cherished conversation partner and friend.

I appreciate the professionalism and support of the staff of IVP Academic. Jon Boyd, academic editorial director, saw merit in this project and provided editorial wisdom, constructive advice, and timely positivity along the way. I am grateful for his patience and humor through it all. Additionally, I am thankful for Rebecca Carhart, who skillfully shepherded this project from draft to publication.

Several knowledgeable archivists enabled me to complete the necessary research for this book. I am especially indebted to Mark Bliese and Daniel Harmelink of Concordia Historical Institute, to Sister Connie Derby, RSM, of the Roman Catholic Diocese of Rochester, to Gerry Perschbacher of Lutheran Hour Ministries, and to Keith Call and Bob Shuster of the Buswell Library Archives & Special Collections, Wheaton College.

A special thanks is due another outstanding scholar who also happens to be the son of one of this book's subjects. Paul Maier, professor emeritus of ancient history at Western Michigan University, repeatedly and graciously responded to my inquiries in person, by email, and via telephone. In addition to invaluable information, he offered kind words of encouragement.

I am grateful to my colleagues at Wheaton College for their support, especially our trustees, fellow members of the senior administrative cabinet, the management team that I have the privilege to lead, and members of our faculty. I am particularly appreciative of President Phil Ryken's encouragement that I complete this project and continue other scholarly pursuits, understanding that my administrative responsibilities can easily consume each day. Additionally, I cannot adequately express my thanks to my administrative assistant, Lynn Wartsbaugh, for her helpful efforts in reading and rereading the manuscript, catching errors and typos, suggesting edits, confirming citations, and properly formatting, all the while guarding my office door during periods when I needed to work on this book without interruption.

I thank God for my parents, Roger and Janet Farney, who nurtured my love of learning, and for my sister, Shannon Bushman, who is always there for me. Finally, and with no small amount of emotion, I wish to express my heartful thanks to my wife, Cheryl, and my children, Erin and Mitch. This book is an outgrowth of their love, inspiration, prayer, and patience, in more ways than they know.

ABBREVIATIONS

CH   Catholic Hour
CHI   Concordia Historical Institute
CUA   Catholic University of America
FJS   Fulton J. Sheen
LCMS   Lutheran Church–Missouri Synod
LLL   Lutheran Laymen's League
MBS   Mutual Broadcasting System
NCCM   National Council of Catholic Men
TLH   The Lutheran Hour
WAM   Walter A. Maier

Chapter One

GOLDEN MOUTHS, ETHEREAL PULPITS

If then eye hath not seen, nor ear heard, nor hath it entered into the
heart of man to imagine what good things are prepared for those who
love God, from where . . . shall we be able to come to the knowledge
of these things? Listen a moment and you will hear him answer.

St. John Chrysostom

Turn your radio on . . . and glory share . . . get in
touch with God . . . turn your radio on.

Albert Brumley, "Turn Your Radio On"

On Sunday, October 26, 1924—a "perfect Indian summer day"—the cornerstone was laid for the facilities of the new campus of Concordia Seminary in Clayton, Missouri. Special trains brought enthusiastic Lutherans from around the Midwest to witness the celebratory afternoon, and to lift their voices in a rousing rendition of "A Mighty Fortress Is Our God." Coinciding with this new birth of one of America's largest seminaries that day was the maiden voyage on the nation's airwaves of Lutheran radio station KFUO, which introduced itself to the listening public by broadcasting the seminary proceedings. Concordia's sober, scholarly president, Francis Pieper, stood before newfangled microphones and began to address the physical and ethereal attendees *in Latin*.[1] As the bowtie-clad churchman spoke of Christ's status as the "true cornerstone of the church," an "immense" biplane flew over the campus. Pieper paused his speech and raised his eyes, along with those of the thousands present, to marvel at the display of gravity-defying technology.[2] The epiphanic confluence of ancient Scripture, medieval language, Reformation theology, and modern innovation was not lost on the terra firma–bound spectators. In recapping this moment, the lay periodical *The Lutheran Witness* observed, "A conjunction of a living past with the vibrant present . . . could not have been more perfectly symbolized." The German language periodical, *Der Lutheraner*, provided this succinct summation: "Times change, and we change with them. But God's Word remains forever."[3]

While the observers comprehended the symbolic intersection of modernity and the "faith which was once delivered unto the saints" (Jude 3 KJV), they could not have known the impact this intersection was about to have. Radio and religion would soon emerge as a match seemingly made in heaven. The faith "once delivered unto the saints" could now be delivered to the living rooms of saints and sinners alike, over broadcast towers sprouting up across the land. And millions were ready to listen.

Two learned clergymen and academics, a Catholic priest and a Lutheran minister, led among those who embraced this opportunity to spread the Gospel of Jesus Christ over the airwaves. They did so with remarkable success. Through weekly broadcasts from coast to coast they attained household name status. Those names were Fulton J. Sheen and Walter A. Maier.

---

[1] In that radio transmissions were broadcast invisibly through the air (the heavens, if you will), they were characterized as traversing or manipulating the "ether," especially during radio's Golden Age—thus, the term *ethereal*.

[2] Estimates of the attendees of this event on the new Concordia Seminary campus varied from 12,000 to 20,000. See "Laying of Corner-Stone, Concordia Seminary," *The Lutheran Witness* 43, no. 23 (November 4, 1924), 396.

[3] "Laying of Corner-Stone," 396-97; "A Memorable Day for Our Concordia Seminary in St. Louis," *Der Lutheraner* 80, no. 23 (November 11, 1924), 394-95. (I am grateful to Andrew Hansen for his assistance in translating this text.) *Concordia Seminary: 175th Anniversary Special Edition (1839–2014)*, September 2014, 11-12; www.concordiahistoricalinstitute.org/today-in-history /tih1026/.

In February 1940, the diocesan newspaper of New Orleans, *Catholic Action of the South*, referred to Monsignor Fulton J. Sheen, the popular radio priest of the *Catholic Hour* (CH) radio program, as "the John Chrysostom of the US airwaves."[4] Three years later, *Time* magazine labeled Reverend Walter A. Maier, the dynamic radio preacher of *The Lutheran Hour* (TLH) broadcast, the "Chrysostom of American Lutheranism." (As a courtesy to their less histori-cally minded readers, *Time*'s editors did provide a footnote explaining who this renowned fourth-century Christian preacher was.[5]) Such praise was not uncommon for these two powerful preachers whose "golden mouths" spoke every week over the airwaves of the nation and much of the world.[6] Through radio, both had gained considerable fame, rivaling not just that of other major religious leaders, but of entertainers and politicians as well. Both enjoyed the loyalty of millions of listeners, who formed audiences comparable in size to those of "popular" radio programs. While stylistically different, both preached with urgency and conviction. Both had attained uncommon erudition, yet delivered sermons that touched the common man and woman. Both saw Christian commitment as a central component of the American way of life and the key to the country's well-being. And both espoused a version of Chris-tianity that reflected conservative orthodoxy and tradition, yet with an ecu-menical openness uncommon at the time in their respective denominations.

Those denominational affiliations are a key component in making the stories of Walter Maier and Fulton Sheen so noteworthy, and invite more thorough analysis. That Americans experiencing the Great Depression, then a world war, followed by the war's aftermath and the rise of communism, would have listened to hopeful Christian messages on the radio is not dif-ficult to understand. But that two of the most popular radio preachers would have come from the Roman Catholic Church and the Lutheran Church–Missouri Synod (LCMS) would have been less predictable, given the reli-gious environment of the time.

When CH was launched in 1930, the Catholic Church represented the largest denomination in the United States, with over twenty million members.

---

[4]Kathleen Riley Fields, "Bishop Fulton J. Sheen: An American Catholic Response to the Twentieth Century" (PhD diss., University of Notre Dame, 1988), 108, 137.

[5]"Lutherans," *Time*, October 18, 1943, 46, 49.

[6]"Chrysostom," or *Chrysostomos*, means "Golden Mouthed" in Greek.

Yet anti-Catholic prejudice was widespread, as had been demonstrated by bitter opposition to Democratic Presidential Candidate Al Smith just two years earlier. What is more, many in the American non-Catholic majority viewed Catholicism as the religion of the suspect, ethnically disadvantaged, immigrant population that had come ashore in the latter nineteenth century. Historian Martin Marty has noted that in such an environment "moderates throughout the nation were no less disturbed than [Ku Klux] Klansmen about the threat that America would go Catholic."[7] Notwithstanding the uncharitable views non-Catholics expressed toward the less-than-fully American papists, many of them warmed quickly to Monsignor Sheen and tuned in just like their Catholic neighbors—much to the surprise of network executives and social observers.

The LCMS was one of several Lutheran bodies in America when TLH went on the air—also in 1930. At this time, there were roughly four million Lutherans in the United States, found in twenty-one different denominational bodies.[8] With membership in excess of one million, the LCMS was one of the largest of these Lutheran groups. Yet it was obviously modest in relative size and resources, and even more modest in attracting attention. Though the Lutherans did not elicit the hostility that Catholics endured, they were often viewed as an aloof ethnic enclave, given their sectarian German and Scandinavian ways.[9] Fellow citizens had displayed especially discomforting levels of distrust toward German-Americans, of which Lutherans were a sizable component, during World War I.[10] Demonstrable German-American loyalty during that conflict and subsequent conscious efforts to "Americanize" had broken down some of the previous prejudices, bringing Lutherans more fully into the American mainstream. However, Missouri Synod Lutherans remained in a state of semi-isolation of their own construction, primarily because they doggedly maintained theological commitments that avoided any semblance of "unionism" (a form of ecumenism)

---

[7]Quoted in James Hennesey, *American Catholics: A History of the Roman Catholic Community in the United States* (New York: Oxford University Press, 1981), 237.

[8]Mark A. Noll, *A History of Christianity in the United States and Canada* (Grand Rapids: Eerdmans, 1992), 462.

[9]For a succinct description of the historical marginalization of American Lutheranism, see Mark A. Noll, "The Lutheran Difference," *First Things* 20 (February 1992), 31-40.

[10]See Frederick C. Luebke, *Bonds of Loyalty: German Americans and World War I* (DeKalb, IL: Northern Illinois University Press, 1974), especially chapters 7 and 8.

or syncretism.[11] Yet from this small, easily ignored denomination came Walter Maier and his engaging radio preaching. Like Sheen, he would enjoy the embrace of millions who tuned in. Like Sheen, he would attract listeners across the spectrum of denominational and religious affiliations. And, like Sheen, he would attain a level of recognition, and even celebrity, that many secular competitors within popular culture coveted.

In the anxiety-laden conditions of economic depression, war, and post-bellum change, radio offered Americans a welcome escape. The antics of Lum and Abner, the adventures of the Lone Ranger, the wisecracks of Fred Allen, the tense sleuthing of the Shadow, all provided diversionary transport to fictional places for the masses tuning in. The round trip to such locales, however, took only thirty minutes or less, after which listeners again faced their daily realities. For millions, that task was made less arduous by having a relationship with the God who was the source of their reality. Fulton Sheen and Walter Maier went to their microphones to create and nurture these relationships. Both individual and communal religion flourished in the radio congregations they created. Historian Tona Hangen summarizes, "Religious radio, then, also served as a meeting place, a shared and sacred space that fulfilled the desire for personal connection." It was "a *vox populi* in every sense of the word."[12] Maier's and Sheen's mastery at making these connections produced audiences that dwarfed many other religious broadcasts and rivaled those of the most popular secular programming. In short, religious radio and two of its most successful broadcasters are integral components of radio history; they belong anywhere but on the periphery.

The purpose of this book is to more fully understand their success and to argue for its significance. It will focus on the radio careers of Maier and Sheen, though with sufficient context provided for their respective Lutheran and Catholic identities. It will describe how they gained national airwave access and the challenges they faced in retaining that access. It will discuss the style and content of their preaching, while relating that preaching to the roles Sheen and Maier played in the emerging mass culture created by radio,

---

[11]Martin E. Marty, *Pilgrims in Their Own Land: 500 Years of Religion in America* (New York: Penguin Group, 1985), 367-68.

[12]Tona J. Hangen, "Speaking of God, Listening for Grace: Christian Radio and Its Audiences," in *Radio Cultures: The Sound Medium in American Life,* ed. Michael C. Keith (New York: Peter Lang, 2008), 135.

especially network radio. It will endeavor to understand the receptivity of radio audiences to the messages of these two purveyors of divine wisdom. Finally, it will assess the impact of their radio ministries on their respective denominations and the broader Christian world.

Fulton Sheen and Walter Maier were extraordinary, gifted men. Both were "Type A" personalities, very busy in the vineyard of the Lord. While Maier was more proactive in pushing a gospel radio agenda in the 1920s, both men embraced the opportunities radio presented when they entered network airwaves in 1930. Before they excelled in radio, both had proven themselves as solid thinkers and effective communicators for other purposes. Though their speaking styles differed, each possessed eloquence that inspired listeners. Each drew on education, intellect, and wit. Both possessed firm theological convictions that they expressed forthrightly. Their ability to enlist respected language and thought from traditional Christianity in such a way as to engage contemporary issues proved enduringly popular.

Yet effective as they were personally in communicating a strong message, it is important in understanding their place in American cultural history to recognize that both Maier and Sheen were in the right place at the right time. The emergence of mass culture offered both opportunity and peril, and the stakes were high. As radio historian Jason Loviglio summarizes, "The struggle over the ideological valence of 'the people'" played out in the "development of mass media in this dawning era of mass culture."[13] Historian David Kennedy has written that the medium of radio "swiftly developed into an electronic floodgate through which flowed a one-way tide of mass cultural products that began to swamp the values and manners and tastes of once-isolated localities."[14] As Americans experienced this deluge, the messages they heard and the intimacy they perceived while listening to Sheen's and Maier's "old-time religion" provided a degree of comfort and continuity that should be recognized by historians seeking a well-rounded understanding of this era. The Catholic priest from Peoria played well in Peoria. So did the Lutheran pastor from Boston. Their surprising success, in turn, lent an unexpected

---

[13]Jason Loviglio, "*Vox Pop*: Network Radio and the Voice of the People," *Radio Reader: Essays in the Cultural History of Radio*, ed. Michele Hilmes and Jason Loviglio (New York: Routledge, 2002), 90.

[14]David M. Kennedy, *Freedom from Fear: The American People in Depression and War, 1929–1945* (New York: Oxford University Press, 2005), 228.

respect to their denominations. Such matters are difficult to quantify, but it is almost inconceivable that the acceptance of either Lutherans or Catholics in the broader American society would have advanced as rapidly as it did from the 1920s onward without the effectiveness of these radio preachers.

As the chairman of the Lutheran Laymen's League (LLL) Radio Committee, H. J. Fitzpatrick, chirped at the beginning of his address to the 1943 LLL convention, "Nothing succeeds like success!"[15] Both Sheen and Maier were walking and talking proofs of this axiom. They indeed succeeded in manifold ways. In their own minds and given their own religious commitments, Sheen and Maier, who would have disagreed between themselves on a number of theological points, nonetheless would have agreed on this one: that the only "success" of lasting worth was a soul won for Christ. Surprisingly, however, in the social turbulence of the 1930s and 1940s and the dawn of America's radio culture, the religious success that both preachers sought translated also into an extraordinary and unexpected popular success with the American listening public.

IMPLICATIONS

In concentrating on these two figures, this book illuminates many broader features of American society in the 1930s and 1940s. One issue concerns how Walter Maier and Fulton Sheen fit in the radio landscape of that period. The book will examine how their listening audiences compared in size to other audiences for network radio programming, the nature of their program content, and how this compared to the content of other popular radio programs. It seeks clues as to whether the CH and TLH were perceived as entertainment or preaching and worship. Additionally, it will explore how the celebrity status attained by Maier and Sheen compared to that of other radio personalities.

A broader issue is the presence of religion on the radio from the early days of broadcasting through the 1940s. It is important to understand who the players were on network religious radio during this key period. This book will examine the different means by which network preachers, including Sheen and Maier, gained and retained access to network airwaves, and will

---

[15]H. J. Fitzpatrick, "Report on the Tenth Anniversary Lutheran Hour to the Lutheran Laymen's League Convention, July 9–11, 1943," Lutheran Hour Archives, St. Louis. TLH has operated under the auspices of the LLL since 1930—an arrangement brokered by Walter Maier.

describe the setup for putting TLH and the CH on the air. It will also probe Sheen's and Maier's respective listener bases and the nature of their responses to the radio priest and pastor.

The fact that Maier and Sheen were so successful also reveals much about the culture and religion of the United States during a prolonged period of national calamity—the Great Depression, World War II, and the beginning of the Cold War. Such success raises the question of whether the common belief that organized religion declined during the Depression is, in fact, accurate. This study will also explore Sheen's and Maier's roles in the fundamentalist/modernist controversy within the church, the academy, and society. It will be important to gain an understanding of how the intimacy that audiences perceived with radio personalities allowed Maier and Sheen to fulfill a genuinely pastoral function for individual listeners. Additionally, though Sheen and Maier generally eschewed politics in their preaching, it is important to consider how much their commentary on the economic crisis, the war effort, and the evils of "godless communism," contributed to the state of American "civil religion." Finally, the book provides analysis of how the popularity of Maier and Sheen contributed to greater ecumenism and religious tolerance.

In order to explain how the radio careers of Sheen and Maier worked in this period, it is imperative to understand exactly what they did on the radio. This book attempts to re-create their respective preaching styles, and survey the biblical, theological, pastoral, and topical content of their radio messages. It is especially interesting to see how two men, who had achieved remarkable levels of education, and lived and taught in academic settings, were so adept at engaging their knowledge in ways that reached the average person. A thorough examination of the rarefied theology they preached is required if we are to fully comprehend what their audiences found compelling, and gain a greater understanding of this era of American history as it unfolded.

Finally, this analysis must explore the important denominational aspects of Sheen's and Maier's radio ministries. It will recount what distinctly Catholic and Lutheran elements were contained in their respective CH and TLH messages. In an era when identification with one's own denomination was more pronounced than today, Maier's and Sheen's ability to attract listeners from across the religious/denominational spectrum is significant and must be examined. In turn, it must be recognized that their respective programs brought Lutheranism and Catholicism from the perceived periphery of American Christianity to more mainstream positions. This book will also explore what kind of support and opposition were given to Maier and Sheen by their respective denominational leadership, as well as how the "average" Catholic reacted to the success of Sheen and the "average" Lutheran reacted to the success of Maier.

HISTORICAL TREATMENT

Even for historians with the benefit of hindsight, it has long been conventional wisdom that the Depression either radicalized religion, or undercut the stature of mainline churches.[16] In addition, scholarly convention has held that well past the 1940s American Lutherans remained largely unrecognized and American Catholics remained a source of considerable suspicion. Yet with Sheen and Maier something quite different was going on.

Their huge popularity calls into question historiographical judgments that either ignore Maier, Sheen, and much of religious radio, or assess their roles as peripheral. Beginning in the 1990s, long-overdue scholarly attention has been directed toward radio—its history, content, and cultural impact.[17] Yet even though religion had been a significant part of broadcast programming from commercial radio's birth, its treatment in the emerging scholarship has been inadequate. Few have recognized that "it is . . . possible to see religious broadcasting" as a critical "site of the struggle over the cultural ascendancy of religion in modernity."[18] While a handful of historians have focused specifically on religious radio,[19] most either fail to mention religious content entirely, imply that it was a fringe component, or pay attention only to the more sensational religious radio personalities (e.g., Father Charles Coughlin, Aimee Semple McPherson).

---

[16]For examples, see Sydney E. Ahlstrom, *A Religious History of the American People*, 2nd ed. (New Haven, CT: Yale University Press, 2004), chapters 53 and 54; Robert T. Handy, "The American Religious Depression, 1925–1935," *Church History* 29, no. 1 (March 1960): 3-16.

[17]For a brief summary of radio's historical treatment, see Michele Hilmes, "Rethinking Radio," in Hilmes and Loviglio, *Radio Reader*, 1-19.

[18]Stewart M. Hoover and Douglas K. Wagner, "History and Policy in American Broadcast Treatment of Religion," *Media, Culture & Society* 19, no. 1 (1997): 13.

[19]Helpful historical treatments of Christian radio have been authored by Tona J. Hangen, Quentin J. Schultze, Joel A. Carpenter, Mark Ward Sr., and Bob Lochte, to name a few. Their works will be cited at various places in this book.

In addition to correcting these historiographical shortcomings regarding Maier's and Sheen's religious and cultural significance, this book will also explore their success in light of recent scholarship addressing how radio was "heard" by those tuning in during this period. As network radio in particular stimulated the emergence of mass culture, it also produced a "sense of intimacy" at multiple levels. Isolation was not an uncommon state of existence for people in the early twentieth century. Network radio provided listeners a sense of belonging to a larger community.[20] Mass communication meant mass shared experience, as thousands of citizens came together to form a single audience for popular programs, yet did so primarily in their own personal or familial space. In short, radio created broader community while respecting privacy.

But even as listeners perceived new, substantive communal bonds through shared radio experiences, homogenization of the populace did not occur, as social critics feared. Rather, the voices coming out of radio boxes actually gave audience members a heightened sense of individual empowerment. Every time a radio announcer or personality asked audience members to do something (e.g., try a product, "stay tuned"), listeners sensed that they mattered beyond the walls of their homes. Such personal appeals, coupled with the familiar sound of popular personalities' voices, produced another level of felt intimacy—that between individual listeners and the person to whom such voices belonged. Listeners considered their favorite radio personalities to be trusted friends, with whom they often shared personal opinions (via correspondence), and on whom they projected broad expertise on numerous topics, regardless of whether the broadcaster actually possessed such expertise.[21]

---

[20]Michele Hilmes, *Radio Voices: American Broadcasting, 1922–1952* (Minneapolis: University of Minnesota Press, 1997), 23.

[21]Bruce Lenthall, *Radio's America: The Great Depression and the Rise of Modern Mass Culture* (Chicago: University of Chicago Press, 2007), 64-76. See also Douglas B. Craig, *Fireside Politics: Radio and Political Culture in the United States, 1920–1940* (Baltimore: Johns Hopkins University Press, 2000), especially chapters 7 and 8; Lawrence W. Levine and Cornelia R. Levine, *The Fireside Conversations: America Responds to FDR During the Great Depression* (Berkeley: University of California Press, 2010); Jason Loviglio, *Radio's Intimate Public: Network Broadcasting and Mass-Mediated Democracy* (Minneapolis: University of Minnesota Press, 2005); Robert J. Brown, *Manipulating the Ether: The Power of Broadcast Radio in Thirties America* (Jefferson, NC: McFarland and Company, 1998), 222-23; Derek Vaillant, "'Your Voice Came In Last Night . . . but I Thought It Sounded a Little Scared:' Rural Radio Listening and 'Talking Back' During the Progressive

Recent historical study of radio's ability to draw early listeners into a perceived community, of the even deeper perceptions of intimacy between listeners and radio personalities, of the free agency listeners considered themselves to wield, and of the authoritative deference afforded radio celebrities, may provide significant explanatory power for the success of Fulton Sheen and Walter Maier, as well as confirmation of their importance in the lives of their listeners.

The Shape of This Study

Maier and Sheen aggressively employed the technological and cultural forces of the emerging medium of radio as far-reaching preaching platforms. Listeners across the country, of varying religious affiliations and commitments, embraced their brand of conservative orthodox Christianity, notwithstanding its Lutheran and Catholic packaging. They listened to these ethereal pastors with a remarkable level of perceived intimacy, despite an environment of religious turmoil (modernist/fundamentalist) and within conditions of political and economic upheaval. In short, this is a story of a complex confluence of historical factors. Thus, while this study will focus primarily on cultural and religious history, underlying elements of political, economic, theological, ecclesiastical, and intellectual history are also brought into the conversation.

The next chapter sets the stage by describing the development of radio as a powerful medium of popular communication in the 1930s and 1940s. While attending to the specific role of religious broadcasting in this new medium, it does so while considering networks, the new medium's cultural impact, and what historians have called the "Golden Age of radio." The third and fourth chapters turn to Maier, Sheen, and their "Hours." The biographical sketches in these chapters emphasize the similarities and differences in their youthful formation, formal education, careers as ordained religious leaders, and then their entry into radio. Similar comparisons are also drawn for the Catholic and Lutheran involvement in their programming, in how they funded the programs, and the opportunities and obstacles they

---

Era in Wisconsin, 1920–1932," in Hilmes and Loviglio, *Radio Reader*, 63-111; Kristine M. Mc-Cusker, "'Dear Radio Friend': Listener Mail and the *National Barn Dance*, 1931–1941," *American Studies* 39, no. 2 (Summer 1998): 173-95.

faced along the way. The fifth chapter examines in depth the format of their landmark programs, the way each prepared for a broadcast, and the characteristics of their delivery. From printed and archival sources, as well as from contemporary accounts and surviving recordings of their broadcasts, it is possible to reconstruct how the studios from which they broadcast were set up, how Sheen and Maier prepared and delivered sermons, other elements of each week's programs, and what sort of theological content their radio sermons featured.

Two substantial chapters follow with full treatment of the homiletic content of their programs, described first in foundational theological terms and then in what the broadcasters asked of their listeners by way of personal response. It is important to understand that millions of listeners willingly tuned in, week after week, to hear *what* Sheen and Maier had to say, and one cannot fully understand their impact, their audience, or the times in which they preached without a thorough unpacking of their messages.

Finally, the book ends by considering the evidence for treating Maier and Sheen, in their activity on national radio, as deserving more salience in historical accounts, both religious and cultural, of this turbulent period. Factors like the number of stations carrying their broadcasts, the huge volume of correspondence they received, the personal engagement of listeners and correspondents, their prominence in multiple arenas of national discourse, their broad respect within general religious circles, and their celebrity status off the air, all point to the significance of what Sheen and Maier accomplished on the radio. This last chapter and the brief epilogue also come back to the question of how these radio preachers shaped Lutheranism and Catholicism in the unfolding of American and ecclesiastical history.

Chapter Two

MEDIUM BECOMES LARGE

AMERICAN RADIO IN THE 1930S AND 1940S

When they say "The Radio" they don't mean a cabinet, an electronic

phenomenon, or a man in a studio, they refer to a pervading and

somewhat godlike presence which has come into their lives and homes.

E. B. WHITE, "SABBATH MORN"

IN 1927, H. G. Wells penned a series of articles for the *New York Times* titled "The Way the World Is Going." In the April 3 installment, Wells reviewed radio broadcasting—a cultural force still in its infancy. The Brit did not like what he heard coming through the airwaves. In his judgment, radio suffered from a paucity of high-quality entertainment, substantive exchange of ideas, and stimulating information. Listeners would soon dwindle to only "very sedentary persons living in badly lighted houses or otherwise unable to read . . . who have no capacity nor opportunity for thought or conversation. . . . I am afraid . . . that the future of broadcasting is like the future of crossword puzzles and Oxford trousers, a very trivial future." He concluded that soon "the whole broadcasting industry will begin to dry up."[1]

---

[1] H. G. Wells, "Mr. Wells Bombards the Broadcaster," *New York Times*, April 3, 1927, 3, 16.

The following year, the *Times* quoted Wells's opinion on the future of religion. While he acknowledged that religion may have had its place in society, he judged that "the old faiths have become unconvincing, unsubstantial and insincere."[2]

The dissatisfied prognosticator was wrong—on both counts. Drs. Maier and Sheen were about to prove him so.

In our present, noise-saturated age, the disquieting impact of something so seemingly old-fashioned as radio might be easy to depreciate. Yet broadcast radio not only disrupted the stillness of early twentieth-century American life, it profoundly changed it at individual, familial, communal, and ultimately, national levels. In short, radio transformed US culture. It did so with stunning rapidity and striking thoroughness, in ways both anticipated and unanticipated. There is no denying that when the bucolic, agricultural concept of broadcasting was applied to the emergent technological means of radio, the yields were manifold.

On November 2, 1920, Westinghouse's newly licensed radio station, KDKA in Pittsburgh, went on the air announcing the results of the Harding-Cox presidential election. It was estimated that the listener tally was only between five hundred and a thousand, but the following morning callers to Westinghouse's switchboard asked how to acquire radios.[3] From that start, KDKA began regular daily programming, and commercial broadcasting was born. Reaction by new broadcasters and new radio listeners was swift. Additional broadcasting stations went on the air the following year, and more than five hundred new stations began operations in 1922. Expenditures by Americans buying radio parts and sets soared, totaling $60 million in 1922, $136 million in 1923, and $358 million in 1924. Sales shifted from radio components to complete radio sets, as purchaser profiles broadened from technical experimenters to more common enthusiasts.[4] Newspapers and magazines began covering the rapidly rising interest in radio, some of which

---

[2]"New Book by Wells Sums Up His Utopia," *New York Times*, September 6, 1928.
[3]Anthony Rudel, *Hello, Everybody! The Dawn of American Radio* (Orlando: Harcourt, 2008), 35.
[4]Erik Barnouw, *A Tower in Babel: A History of Broadcasting in the United States to 1933* (New York: Oxford University Press, 1966), 4, 125.

came into being for the sole purpose of monitoring this new medium, which stoked interest even further.[5]

In early 1922, Secretary of Commerce Herbert Hoover referred to the meteoric interest in radio as "one of the most astonishing things that have come under my observation of American life." In one of the periodical articles that quoted the Commerce Secretary, the editors noted, "The present popularity of the wireless telephone began with the establishment of powerful 'broadcasting' stations which send out a regular daily program." For those bewildered by the new craze, the article recapped the progression of the medium:

> For a time interest in the wireless telephone was confined to a few sapient scientists who talked a jargon that failed to arouse any enthusiasm with the ordinary mortal. Then the small boy suddenly discovered that he could have a world of fun with a "radio" telephone. Presently the small boy's elders became interested. Men, women, and children caught the wireless fever.[6]

At this same time, the *New York Times* reported, "In twelve months radio phoning has become the most popular amusement in America."[7]

While the increase in radio ownership and activity was indeed significant, especially in relation to its starting point, the *Times* overstated the relative situation. In 1924, American radio ownership had climbed to three million radio sets, at a time when the total United States population was estimated at 114 million.[8] Although both broadcasting endeavors and radio listeners increased throughout the 1920s, it was not until the mid-1930s that radio "became a pervasive influence in American life."[9] By 1936, Americans owned thirty-three million radio sets, while the aggregate population stood at 128 million. In 1940, a population of 132 million owned fifty million radios.[10]

---

[5]Susan J. Douglas, *Inventing American Broadcasting: 1899–1922* (Baltimore: Johns Hopkins University Press, 1987), 303-6.

[6]"Astonishing Growth of the Radiotelephone," *The Literary Digest* 73, no. 3 (April 15, 1922). For the modern reader, it should be pointed out that the terms *wireless*, *wireless telephone*, *radio phone*, and *radio telephone* were early twentieth-century terms for radios.

[7]As quoted in Douglas, *Inventing American Broadcasting*, 303.

[8]See David Holbrook Culbert, *News for Everyman: Radio and Foreign Affairs in Thirties America* (Westport, CT: Greenwood, 1976), 15; Population data source: US Census Bureau.

[9]Robert J. Brown, *Manipulating the Ether: The Power of Broadcast Radio in Thirties America* (Jefferson, NC: McFarland and Company, 1998), 2.

[10]Culbert, *News for Everyman*, 15.

As for radio ownership by household, the number moved from 40 percent of families at the start of the 1930s to nearly 90 percent by the close of the decade. Radio historian Bruce Lenthall contextualizes this statistic: "In 1940 more families had radios than had cars, telephones, electricity, or plumbing."[11] Average daily listening exceeded four and a half hours.[12]

The well-known sociological studies by Robert Lynd and Helen Lynd reflected radio's shift from a peripheral activity to its mainstream role over this period. In their 1924–1925 survey of "Middletown," little attention was directed to radio. The Lynds tallied that radio ownership ranged from 6 percent to 12 percent of households in Middletown, but noted that "the place of radio in relation to . . . other leisure habits is not wholly clear." While they explained that "this new tool is rolling back the horizons of Middletown," they noted competition for residents' attention: "[Radio] is wedging its way with the movie, the automobile, and other new tools into the twisted mass of habits that are living for the 38,000 people" of the town. As an interesting aside, anticipating a growing role for broadcast orators, the Lynds added that radio was "beginning to take over that function of . . . trips by the trainload . . . to hear a noted speaker."[13]

When the Lynds returned to Middletown in 1935, radio required more attention. "Everywhere the blare of radios was more pervasive than in 1925," they observed. "If a comparative time count were available, it would probably be found that the area of leisure where change in time spent has been greatest . . . is listening to the radio." In addition to its entertainment value, they noted that radio had become an important player in the "daily news dissemination field." The Lynds noticed in particular the importance of radio during dire economic times: "Not only has radio ownership in Middletown increased greatly . . . but people have clung tenaciously to their radios in the depression."[14]

---

[11]Bruce Lenthall, *Radio's America: The Great Depression and the Rise of Modern Mass Culture* (Chicago: University of Chicago Press, 2007), 12.

[12]Alice Goldfarb Marquis, *Hopes and Ashes: The Birth of Modern Times* (New York: Free Press, 1986), 41.

[13]Robert S. Lynd and Helen Merrell Lynd, *Middletown: A Study in Modern American Culture* (New York: Harcourt Brace, 1929), 269-71. The Lynds presented "Middletown" (Muncie, Indiana) as a typical small American city.

[14]Robert S. Lynd and Helen Merrell Lynd, *Middletown in Transition: A Study in Cultural Conflicts* (New York: Harcourt Brace Jovanovich, 1937), 144, 263-64, 386. The Lynds also noted that Middletown had a local broadcasting station that was part of a national broadcasting network. They assessed that this radio station "operates in two directions." First, "Like the movies and the

In fact, radio thrived during the Great Depression, at least in part, because it was a ready source of information in calamitous times, and a relatively inexpensive source of entertainment for individuals and entire families.

Radio's central place in America's culture did not wane as the 1930s ended. As the threat of war loomed, only to become a global reality that the United States could not sidestep, radio provided even more urgent information than it had during the Depression, often from the very locales where conflict and crises were occurring. Even frightening news was apparently less frightening than no news or old news. Still, although broadcast news as a percentage of programming time increased from 7 percent prior to the war to 20 percent near its end, entertainment programs constituted the largest component of air time. (The relative level of news content decreased after World War II, but remained an important part of broadcast programming.) In 1942, the US government ordered the cessation of the manufacture of radio receivers due to more urgent needs for manufacturing and materials relating to the war effort. As a result, the sale of new radios dropped from 13 million in 1941 to less than 4.5 million in 1942. For the remainder of the war, sales would only reach a few hundred thousand per year. Nonetheless, nearly 90 percent of homes had radios, and 6 million automobiles were equipped with them by 1946. Home ownership of radios averaged 1.5 sets per household throughout the war. That number would increase to 2.1 average sets per household by 1950.[15] Even as war restrictions halted radio production in the early 1940s, and as television began to gain traction in American homes in the late 1940s, homes with radios rose every year throughout the decade. Additionally, by the end of 1950, radios were found in 18 million automobiles.[16] To put this last figure in perspective, according to the US Department of Transportation, 43.8 million registered cars were on the country's roads in 1950.[17]

---

national press services in the local newspapers, it carries people away from localism and gives them direct access to the more popular stereotypes in national life." Second, "In the other direction, the local station operates to bind together an increasingly large and diversified city" (264).

[15]Robert L. Hilliard and Michael C. Keith, *The Broadcast Century and Beyond: A Biography of American Broadcasting*, 5th ed. (Burlington, MA: Focal Press, 2010), 91, 95, 98, 101, 104, 106, 120.

[16]Jim Ramsburg, *Network Radio Ratings, 1932–1953: A History of Prime Time Programs Through the Ratings of Nielson, Crossley and Hooper* (Jefferson, NC: McFarland & Company, 2012), 141, 151, 160, 171, 182.

[17]See "State Motor Vehicle Registrations, by Years, 1900–1995," US Department of Transportation, Office of Highway Policy Information, www.fhwa.dot.gov/ohim/summary95/mv200.pdf.

NETWORKS

On November 15, 1926, the National Broadcasting Company (NBC) went on the air over twenty-two stations, with an extravagant, four-hour broadcast from New York's Waldorf-Astoria hotel. Affiliates were located from Portland to Chicago to Kansas City to St. Louis to Washington. The program featured top talent, including Will Rogers, the New York Symphony, and a number of dance bands.[18] It was estimated that two million listeners tuned into this inaugural network broadcast.[19] Depending on one's perspective, NBC transported listeners from around the country to the Waldorf's famed ballroom, or transported dozens of top performers into private parlors and remote cottages across the land. Either way, national network broadcasting was now a formative component of the nation's ether way. While local and regional broadcasts would remain a substantive part of American radio culture, the role of national networks would drive the medium on a number of fronts, not least of which would be religious broadcasting.

Media scholar Michele Hilmes notes that the significance of *National* in NBC's name is seldom given adequate attention. "The name itself," she explains, "lays out . . . not only how NBC came to be but also how broadcasting emerged as one of our primary engines of cultural production around the world." Highlighting NBC's impact on the country as a whole, Hilmes states, "When RCA announced the formation of its new radio 'chain' in 1926, it introduced the first medium that could, through its local stations, connect the scattered and disparate communities of a vast nation *simultaneously* and address the nation as a whole. Thus radio could become a powerful means of creating and defining a national public, sorely needed in those nation-building years between the two world wars."[20]

---

[18]Ramsburg, *Network Radio Ratings*, 9; Jim Cox, *American Radio Networks: A History* (Jefferson, NC: McFarland and Company, 2009), 21.

[19]Edward D. Berkowitz, *Mass Appeal: The Formative Age of the Movies, Radio, and TV* (New York: Cambridge University Press, 2010), 43.

[20]Michele Hilmes, "NBC and the Network Idea: Defining the 'American System,'" in *NBC: America's Network*, ed. Michele Hilmes (Berkeley: University of California Press, 2007), 7. The reference to RCA (Radio Corporation of America) was due to its being the largest shareholder (50 percent) of NBC at the time of the latter's incorporation. In 1930, RCA bought out GE's and Westinghouse's interests making NBC a wholly owned subsidiary. See Ramsburg, *Network Radio Ratings*, 9; Cox, *American Radio Networks*, 14-15.

Network broadcasting, often referred to as "chain broadcasting," moved forward in the following year in two significant ways. First, on New Year's Day of 1927, NBC launched a second, distinct network with six initial affiliates. This second network was labeled the "NBC Blue Network," while the first chain became known as "NBC Red Network." NBC continued to grow both networks, as well as sell programming to independent stations, with hookups to the West Coast being established in 1928. By 1937, it had thirty-three Blue affiliates, thirty Red affiliates, and forty-eight independent stations that put some Red or Blue programming on the air. In the early 1940s, the federal government forced NBC to divest of the Blue network for antitrust purposes. NBC Blue effectively became the ABC (American Broadcasting Company) radio network. By the time of this corporate break-up, NBC had ninety-two Blue outlets, seventy-four Red affiliates, and fifty-nine independents that used some NBC programming.[21]

The second network development of 1927 was the founding of the Columbia Broadcasting System (CBS)—the country's third radio chain. Premiering on Sunday, September 18, as the Columbia Phonograph Broadcasting System, this network began with sixteen affiliates, the initial anchor of which was in Newark (later New York). The locations of its stations included Boston in the east, Detroit in the north, Council Bluffs in the Midwest, and St. Louis in the south.[22] Within a couple of years, CBS would add affiliates on the West Coast, becoming the second truly national network. CBS proved to be a legitimate competitor with NBC, adding affiliates at an impressive pace. By 1933, CBS-linked stations totaled ninety-one, having surpassed NBC's number of affiliates in 1931. While the two would continue battling each other for the title of the largest network, NBC eventually surpassed CBS by a substantial margin, until the government forced NBC to spin off its Blue network.[23]

In October 1934, the network landscape broadened yet again, as four well-established broadcasting stations joined forces to form a new type of network.

---

[21]Cox, *American Radio Networks*, 21, 25, 54, 89-91. Through the period in which NBC had two networks, it ran most of its more popular programming on the Red network, while second-tier talent and more erudite programming aired on the Blue network. (Both featured religious broadcasting.)

[22]Jim Cox, *This Day in Network Radio: A Daily Calendar of Births, Deaths, Debuts, Cancellations, and Other Events in Broadcasting History* (Jefferson, NC: McFarland and Company, 2008), 171.

[23]Cox, *American Radio Networks*, 53-54.

WOR-Newark, WLW-Cincinnati, WXYZ-Detroit, and WGN-Chicago formed the Mutual Broadcasting System (MBS), incorporated in Illinois. The self-identified "network for all America" was designed to be a different type of network than NBC and CBS.[24] There would be no central MBS studio or network performers. Rather, in "mutual" fashion, all programming was to be produced by individual member stations and shared with the broader network. Broadcasting scholar Michael Socolow summarizes Mutual's founding concept: "It would be primarily a program exchange and syndication service for the four stations (and, later, others who joined). . . . It would essentially take America's best *local* programming and *nationalize* it" (emphasis added).[25] While such programming was seldom on par with that of the other major networks, MBS affiliates produced popular news, daytime programming, and major sportscasts, along with a handful of prime time gems.[26]

By the end of 1936, MBS had added affiliates that made it a true national operation. Citing substantial barriers to entry in national broadcasting, *Time* magazine observed that Mutual had "accomplished what radiomen have long held improbable: a fourth coast-to-coast network."[27] In 1939, early radio scholar Gleason L. Archer marveled, "Having surveyed monumental difficulties that beset both NBC and CBS in their first years of operation it is little short of astounding to contemplate the brief but triumphant history of the Mutual Broadcasting System."[28] MBS continued attracting affiliate stations and regional chains, growing from four original stations in 1934 to 160 outlets in 1940. By 1942, MBS boasted more affiliates than any other American network, with the competitive breakdown as follows: MBS: 191, NBC Red: 136, NBC Blue: 116, CBS: 115. While many Mutual affiliates were low-power local and regional stations, by the late 1940s it had amassed over five hundred outlets.[29]

[24]Cox, *American Radio Networks*, 72.

[25]Michael J. Socolow, "'Always in Friendly Competition:' NBC and CBS in the First Decade of National Broadcasting," in Hilmes, *NBC: America's Network*, 36.

[26]Ramsburg, *Network Radio Ratings*, 40-41; Cox, *American Radio Networks*, 73, 81-83. One such Mutual gem was the *Lone Ranger*, originating from Detroit's WXYZ, which some have identified as a driving factor in the network's formation. See Gerald Nachman, *Raised on Radio* (Berkeley: University of California Press, 1998), 196-203.

[27]As quoted in Cox, *American Radio Networks*, 72.

[28]Gleason L. Archer, *Big Business and Radio* (New York: American Historical Company, 1939), 407.

[29]Cox, *American Radio Networks*, 77, 79.

Titus Moody, one of the fictional neighbors on radio's *Allen's Alley,* responding to a question from Fred Allen about what he thought of radio, deadpanned, "I don't hold with furniture that talks."[30] Mr. Moody was out of step with most of America in this judgment, and the very reason was the network program on which he participated, not to mention numerous other network offerings of equal popularity. With all due respect to local broadcasters and the substantive roles they played in their communities, the fact is that networks offered programming that incorporated wider variety and higher quality. In fact, one of the reasons so many stations across the country eagerly joined networks was to offload the burden of coming up with high-quality on-air content.[31] Major networks were a key causal factor as "listening to the radio became America's national indoor pastime."[32] "The advent of the network," notes one media historian, "turned the radio into one of the glamorous household appliances of the so-called new era in the 1920s."[33] Another asserts, "The development of broadcasting networks (or chains) . . . contributed more to the quality of American radio than any other structural innovation."[34]

National networks knew that their survivability and profitability depended on attracting as broad an audience as possible. Therefore, the best programming and the best talent were required. Networks added and modified program content, performers, formats, and relative weighting in a constant attempt to grow audiences, often in collaboration with advertisers and their agencies. Situation comedies and variety shows, inspired by vaudeville, generated early, large network followings. Musical programs, ranging from crooners to classical, soon gained loyal listeners, followed by dramatic productions. As mentioned, news reports and commentaries increased substantially as World War II approached and actualized.[35]

---

[30]*Ken Burns America Collection: Empire of the Air; The Men Who Made Radio,* produced by Ken Burns, Morgan Wesson, and Tom Lewis (Public Broadcasting Service, 1991), 120 minutes, DVD.

[31]Susan Smulyan, "The Rise of the Radio Network System: Technological and Cultural Influences on the Structure of American Broadcasting," *Prospects: An Annual of American Cultural Studies* 11 (1987): 105-15; Alexander Russo, *Points on the Dial: Golden Age Radio Beyond the Networks* (Durham, NC: Duke University Press, 2010), 22, 29.

[32]Nachman, *Raised on Radio,* 9.

[33]Berkowitz, *Mass Appeal,* 44.

[34]Lawrence W. Lichty and Malachi C. Topping, *American Broadcasting: A Source Book on the History of Radio and Television* (New York: Hastings House, 1975), 157.

[35]Thomas Allen Greenfield, *Radio: A Reference Guide* (Westport, CT: Greenwood, 1989), 4; Lichty and Topping, *American Broadcasting,* 301-7.

The breadth of network programming during the so-called Golden Age of radio of the 1930s and 1940s was truly remarkable. In 1958, Ohio State University's Harrison B. Summers compiled a thirty-year history of network radio programming. He listed "all programs ten minutes in length or longer, presented on either a sponsored or on a cooperative sponsorship basis, which were parts of regular program series—as well as all of the important or moderately important sustaining programs." Summers provided the sponsor, program information (length, day, and time), network, and ratings, when available (e.g., Hooper, Nielson). What is striking is that "to aid . . . the reader" in understanding the "general nature" and "relative proportions" of program types, Summers felt it necessary to group programs in thirty to forty-plus classifications, depending on the offerings of each radio season. Even then, the diligent professor fretted that his classifications might have a "serious shortcoming" and "errors" due to less-than-complete information on the program content of more obscure shows.[36] While admitting that classifications are often inadequate, radio historian Jim Cox provides "nine genres that aired in the peak of chain radio." Cox focuses on major entertainment shows, and provides brief descriptions of popular examples of each genre. While acknowledging their presence, he says little about categories like sports, public affairs discussions, gossip, and religion. Nonetheless, groupings and examples provide an instructive glimpse at the networks' programming panorama: audience participation (e.g., *Art Linkletter's House Party, Truth or Consequences*), personality-driven comedy (e.g., *The Edgar Bergen and Charlie McCarthy Show, The Jack Benny Program*), situation comedy (e.g., *Baby Snooks, Fibber McGee & Molly*), drama anthology (e.g., *Lux Radio Theater, The Mercury Theater of the Air*), juvenile adventure (e.g., *The Green Hornet, Jack Armstrong—the All-American Boy*), music (e.g., *The Kate Smith Show, The Metropolitan Opera*), mystery anthology (e.g., *The Whistler, Suspense*), vocational/avocational sleuths (e.g., *Mr. Keen—Tracer of Lost Persons, The Shadow*), and soap opera (e.g., *Ma Perkins, Perry Mason*).[37]

---

[36]Harrison B. Summers, *A Thirty-Year History of Programs Carried on National Radio Networks in the United States, 1926–1956* (Salem, NH: Ayer, 1986), 1-6. "Sustaining programs" were those that were given air time free of charge by the networks.

[37]Cox, *American Radio Networks*, 139-68.

While the entertainment provided by network broadcasts was valued highly by listeners, informational components of national broadcasts provided trusted enlightenment on a variety of subjects, including news, sports, and religion. The relative composition of network programming changed with listener tastes, current events, cultural shifts, network and sponsor experimentation, and performer creativity. Using four broad categories of programming, tables 1 and 2 provide a breakdown of network time allotments over the 1930s and 1940s. In addition to programming shifts, the volume of total network programming to affiliates was dynamic.

Table 1. Breakdown of Network Evening Programming by Category[38]

TYPE	1931	1937	1940	1943	1946	1949
Variety (excluding musical variety)	14%	24%	18%	17%	12%	13%
Music	56%	31%	25%	23%	21%	18%
Drama	15%	23%	23%	24%	30%	35%
Talk	15%	22%	34%	36%	37%	34%
News and Commentary (subset of "Talk" total)	4.2%	9.0%	12.4%	17.0%	16.8%	11.7%
Religious (subset of "Talk" total)	4.5%	1.3%	1.1%	2.9%	1.1%	0.7%
Number of Quarter Hours of Evening Network Programming per Week	310	378	453	383	459	427

In that much of religious broadcasting occurred on Sundays during daytime hours, it is also worth noting the percentages during these same years (table 2).

Table 2. Network Weekend Daytime Programming[39]

TYPE	1931	1937	1940	1943	1946	1949
Religious Programming as a Percentage of Total Network Programming	22.2%	9.3%	10.1%	17.1%	11.9%	11.6%
Number of Quarter Hours of Daytime Network Programming per Weekend	54	129	148	129	193	171

---

[38]For supporting data, see Lichty and Topping, *American Broadcasting*, 429.
[39]Lichty and Topping, *American Broadcasting*, 431.

The networks filled their microphones with fresh, relevant, and stimulating content, and auditors across the land turned their dials to network
stations. By the mid-1930s, 88 percent of all radio listeners preferred network
programming over that offered by broadcasters unaffiliated with a
network—a preference that continued through the following decade.[40] By
1945, two-thirds of all stations in the United States had joined one of the four
national networks. Although local and regional programming, both on
network affiliates (during daily periods when network programming was
not available) and independent stations, provided more community-specific
content, rural and urban listeners demonstrated similar appetites for
network programs.[41]

In a 1945 survey by the National Opinion Research Center of the University of Denver, completed at the request of the National Association of
Broadcasters, the esteem achieved by radio was remarkable. Surveyors interviewed over three thousand citizens from all regions of the country,
meant to represent "a cross-section of the US adult population." Respondents were asked to appraise five major elements of their communities—
newspapers, schools, churches, local government, and radio—on whether
the job they were doing was excellent, good, fair, or poor. Radio scored the
highest, with 82 percent of those interviewed rating it "excellent" or "good."
Churches ranked second, with 76 percent rating them "excellent" or "good."
Providing another data point on certain things never changing, local government scored the poorest.[42] Though the survey admittedly discussed
radio perceptions in general, these results obviously reflect attitudes
toward *network* radio in a significant way, given listeners' preference for
network programming.[43]

---

[40]Cox, *American Radio Networks*, 5.
[41]Steve Craig, *Out of the Dark: A History of Radio and Rural America* (Tuscaloosa: University of
Alabama Press, 2009), 43-45.
[42]Paul L. Lazarsfeld, *The People Look at Radio: Report on a Survey Conducted by the National Opinion Research Center* (Chapel Hill: University of North Carolina Press, 1946), vii, 5-6, 93-98. The
survey included men and women, all adult age groups, all economic levels (though highly
wealthy represented only 2 percent of those interviewed), all education levels, and the full range
of community sizes. 88.3 percent of respondents had working radios when contacted, compared
to the national average at that time of 91 percent.
[43]Notwithstanding the leading role of networks during the 1930s and 1940s, the broadcasting
landscape, which included local and regional stations, was more complex than is often

CULTURAL IMPACT

By embracing radio so quickly and incorporating it into daily life so thoroughly, Americans allowed their culture to be changed in profound ways. Before examining Fulton Sheen's and Walter Maier's religious roles in broadcasting, it is important to step back and explore the most important cultural shifts brought about by radio. Broadcast radio truly birthed "mass" culture. It instantly shrank how listeners perceived their regions, country, and ultimately world. In addition to reducing distances, it reduced time. As one observer states, "The new medium of radio was to the printing press what the telephone had been to the letter: it allowed immediacy."[44] Mass communication created powerful shared experiences, just as it threatened to produce a homogenized, manipulated society. Finally, since radio came into its own during the Great Depression, and matured during a devastating world war, it is also worthwhile to look specifically at how it was used and received as a persuasive tool—especially in politics. These key cultural topics are critical to fully understanding the force and longevity of Maier's and Sheen's radio ministries. It also should be acknowledged that the impact of the development of the aforementioned broad variety of programming, the increasing commercialization of radio broadcasts, the resulting rise of consumerism, and the expanded receptivity to new technology would prove significant to the country's culture.

SHRINKING COUNTRY, SHRINKING WORLD

In our current age of instant global communications, via a variety of media, it is difficult to appreciate fully the isolation experienced by common citizens as recently as the early twentieth century. Though automobiles were shortening the distances between communities, communities still had limited interactions with one another, especially outside their immediate region. In more rural areas, isolation within one's home or within a small group of neighbors was the norm. While newspapers may have provided information on regional, national, and international events, happenings in

---

recognized. For fresh examinations of this complexity, see Russo, *Points of the Dial*, and Craig, *Out of the Dark*.

[44]Tom Lewis, "'A Godlike Presence': The Impact of Radio on the 1920s and 1930s," *OAH Magazine of History* 6, no. 4 (Spring 1992): 26.

Louisville could feel nearly as distant as those in Berlin. As a consequence, when a rancher in Montana or a shopkeeper in Los Angeles or a housewife in Baton Rouge tuned into a broadcast from a Chicago night club or a New York ballroom, the world was perceived instantly as a smaller place. What is more, radio provided listeners a sense of belonging to a larger community— a sense previously absent or vague at best. In 1924, one writer described the "Social Destiny of Radio" this way:

> Look at a map of the United States . . . and try to conjure up a picture of what radio broadcasting will eventually mean to hundreds of little towns that are set down in type so small that it can hardly be read. How unrelated they seem! Then picture the tens of thousands of homes in the cities, the valleys, along the rivers, homes not noted at all on the map. These little towns, these un-marked homes in vast countries seem disconnected. It is only an idea that holds them together,—the idea that they form part of a territory called "our country." . . . If these little towns and villages so remote from one another, so nationally related and yet physically so unrelated, could be made to acquire a sense of intimacy . . . this is exactly what radio is bringing about.[45]

The shared experience of radio, especially after the establishment of na-tionwide networks in the mid-1920s, produced the beginnings of American mass culture. For many, the prospects of a society brought together through the airwaves held great promise. Radio would unite the nation in new and healthy ways. A 1922 *Collier's* columnist promised, "Through the radio-phone, if we choose to use it so, all isolation can be destroyed. . . . The ra-diophone can spread culture everywhere and give everyone a chance and the impulse to use his brains." In turn, radio would do more "than any other agency in spreading mutual understanding to all sections of the country, to unifying our thoughts, ideals, and purposes, to making us a strong and well-knit people."[46] A 1926 article in *Radio Age* specifically highlighted ra-dio's impact on the nation's farmers: "Radio recognizes no snow blockades, is not averse to penetrating the lowly log cabin, is immune to the blasts of winter, is unafraid of darkness, and robs isolation of its terrors."[47]

---

[45]As quoted in Michele Hilmes, *Radio Voices: American Broadcasting, 1922-1952* (Minneapolis: University of Minnesota Press, 1997), 23.

[46]Stanley Frost, "Radio Dreams That Can Come True," *Colliers* 69, no. 23 (June 10, 1922): 18.

[47]As quoted in Susan Smulyan, "Early Broadcasting and Radio Audiences," in *The Hayloft Gang: The Story of the National Barn Dance*, ed. Chad Berry (Urbana: University of Illinois Press, 2008), 120.

Notwithstanding such enthusiasm, others saw danger lurking as they contemplated the potential "homogenizing" of the American mind. Perhaps "everyone" might indeed "use his brains," but only so far as they were distracted by intellectually anemic entertainment, or uncritically absorbed what they were told to think. As historian Bruce Lenthall has explained, once listeners came to "accept the notion of mass communication . . . the meaning of 'to communicate' came to emphasize 'to make common' more than 'to share' or 'to exchange.'"[48]

Two particularly vocal critics of the emerging mass culture were the conservative economist William Orton, and the Marxist journalist James Rorty. Revealing an elitist mindset and "a faith in the virtue of high culture," Orton held that "high culture" and "mass culture" could not coexist, especially on the airwaves. He claimed that programs were crafted to thirteen-year-old minds, threatening to bring mass thought to that level. A "dumbing down" of radio content to a least common denominator would dilute desirable individualism and reduce the populace to the status of what a rather grumpy *Harper's Magazine* editorialist termed "radiots." Rorty, by contrast, was more concerned with the potential for radio to exercise undue control over the masses, especially within the political realm. This consternation was particularly acute given the relative concentration of radio broadcasting ownership in major corporate hands, and the potential influence of seated politicians in regulating what could be broadcast. The worry was that if corporate powers controlled the leading vehicle of public expression, "most Americans would find the value of freedom of speech replaced by the freedom to listen," summarizes Lenthall. As the 1930s progressed, all Rorty and his allies had to do was point to rising fascism in Europe to add credibility to their alarm.[49]

---

[48]Bruce Lenthall, *Radio's America: The Great Depression and the Rise of Modern Mass Culture* (Chicago: University of Chicago Press, 2007), 7.

[49]See Lenthall, *Radio's America*, 17-39; Alice Goldfarb Marquis, "Written on the Wind: The Impact of Radio During the 1930s," *Journal of Contemporary History* 19, no. 3 (July 1984): 389. See also Bruce Lenthall, "Critical Reception: Public Intellectuals Decry Depression-Era Radio, Mass Culture, and Modern America," in *Radio Reader: Essays in the Cultural History of Radio*, ed. Michele Hilmes and Jason Loviglio (New York: Routledge, 2002), 41-62.

PERSONAL APPROPRIATION OF MASS COMMUNICATION

Notwithstanding such concerns, Americans handled the new medium with more independence and control than critics anticipated. To a great extent, Radio Corporation of America (RCA) president and NBC founder David Sarnoff's optimistic prophecy was becoming reality, as "the broad highway of ether" served to "open to all matters of public interest, regardless of race, creed, color, or political party," thereby furthering the "zealously guarded prerogative of the American people" to "form their own opinions, reach their own conclusions, and set their own standards of taste."[50] In short, radio created "a new common fund of experience and information that was democratic in its touch-of-the-dial accessibility."[51] The common experience of listening to programs to which thousands of others across the country were tuning in, yet doing so in the privacy of one's own home or automobile, "temporarily merged" the public and private into what one historian has dubbed an "intimate public."[52] The voices coming out of receivers actually gave listeners a sense of empowerment. As announcers implored Americans to tune into future broadcasts, or to purchase a sponsoring company's product, or write in for special offers and provide feedback, the listeners perceived that their voices mattered.[53] And indeed they did, in a collective manner at least, as corporate ownership of radio stations and corporate sponsorship of programming sought to maximize audience size (and proportionate profit) and keep listeners tuning in.

Radio devotees vested those speaking over the airwaves with considerable authority, especially when they dealt with serious matters. A 1947 article on the social impact of radio noted, "If there is one single function that American radio has performed well it is the generally fair and accurate handling of straight news, which has built up a high degree of public confidence." The author explained that a nationwide survey had discovered that 81 percent of respondents expressed the belief that radio stations were fair

---

[50]Marquis, "Written on the Wind," 385; David Sarnoff, *Looking Ahead: The Papers of David Sarnoff* (New York: McGraw-Hill, 1968), 71.

[51]Amy Henderson, *On the Air: Pioneers of American Broadcasting* (Washington: Smithsonian Institution, 1988), 34.

[52]Jason Loviglio, *Radio's Intimate Public: Network Broadcasting and Mass-Mediated Democracy* (Minneapolis: University of Minnesota Press, 2005), xv.

[53]For superb and persuasive treatment of this phenomenon, see chapter 2, "Radio's Listeners: Personalizing Mass Culture," in Lenthall, *Radio's America*, 53-81.

in giving both sides of an argument, while only 39 percent found newspapers trustworthy in this regard. He concluded that this disparity in trust "was unfounded," since "most stations get their news from the same press associations that supply the newspapers."[54] While this writer raised a valid point, his article demonstrated the power of radio. The sound of sincere, resonant, familiar voices speaking in a well-chosen, yet accessible vocabulary, at predictable intervals, over extended periods of time (often years), gave listeners a sense of confidence that the information coming through their loudspeakers was reliable—and reliable in ways that the printed word could not match.

Whether in disseminating serious information or providing entertainment, perceived intimacy was a key to radio's impact. Historian Alice Goldfarb Marquis comments, "Since its early days radio had evoked an intimate relationship with the listener; the receiver was part of the furniture in the listener's home, and its disembodied voice made him feel that it was speaking directly to him."[55] The intimacy was personal, but often familial as well, as households gathered around the radio set in the evening hours. Media historian Susan Douglas states that the "intimacy of this experience" remained "vivid," explaining that "listeners had a deeply private, personal bond with radio." She adds, "Listening to radio . . . forged powerful connections between people's inner, thinking selves and other selves, other voices, from quite faraway places."[56] "Radio was life-size," notes writer Gerald Nachman, "not bigger than life, like the movies, or smaller than life, like television." He goes on to say that "radio's celebrated 'intimacy'" and "power to charm lay also in the vast net (as in network) it first spread over the country, literally linking Americans to each other through a coast-to-coast web."[57] Historian Elena Razlogova explains, "Network programs, from President Franklin Delano Roosevelt to the man-in-the-street program *Vox Pop*, constructed a national public at the same time as they encouraged intimate relationships between broadcasters and listeners," creating "expectations of

---

[54]Kenneth G. Bartlett, "Social Impact of the Radio," *Annals of the American Academy of Political and Social Science* 250 (March 1947): 89-97.

[55]Marquis, *Hopes and Ashes*, 29.

[56]Susan Douglas, *Listening In: Radio and the American Imagination* (Minneapolis: University of Minnesota Press, 2004), 5, 31.

[57]Nachman, *Raised on Radio*, 7.

reciprocity in network radio."[58] Steve Craig points out that "radio helped convince . . . people that they were not alone in their struggles but part of a nation that was working together."[59] In effect, private radio listening created a sense of intimacy, while at the same time the "mass" nature of such communications contributed to a sense of greater community and shared experience. Historian Jason Loviglio summarizes, "Network radio in the 1930s and 1940s amplified the importance of these 'blurred' social spaces; in the middle distance opening up between publicity and intimacy."[60]

In addition to the very act of choosing the programs to which they listened, the most salient way that listeners asserted their voices was by active letter writing to stations, networks, shows, performers, and sponsors. While many listeners needed little encouragement to interact with the voices coming through their boxes, "those voices and the producers behind them worked hard to encourage listener mail."[61] In fact, prior to more sophisticated rating measures, correspondence volume served as an early gauge of the reach of various programming.[62] By 1931, two-thirds of all radio programs on NBC explicitly requested listeners to write in.[63] To encourage the more recalcitrant, programs offered contests, club memberships, and premiums (inexpensive gifts or souvenirs) to those who sent letters. (In 1939, for instance, 71 percent of NBC's commercially sponsored shows offered such premiums.) It would be easy to assume that such incentives were the primary driver behind letter writing, and that the letters sent were shallow in content. Such was not the case. Interestingly, as common citizens deemed it their right to send letters to radio programs, they became

---

[58]Elena Razlogova, *The Listener's Voice: Early Radio and the American Public* (Philadelphia: University of Pennsylvania Press, 2011), 56.

[59]Craig, *Out of the Dark*, 1.

[60]Loviglio, *Radio's Intimate Public*, xv.

[61]Lenthall, *Radio's America*, 62.

[62]While correspondence volume was an important indicator of the public's listening habits, it was an imperfect measure at best. More scientific rating methodologies were needed and statistical analysis firms responded as early as 1930. Personal interviews, telephone surveys, listener "diaries," and meter devices signaled the increasing sophistication which would be applied to the monitoring of listener habits. For background on the initial phases of rating research, see James G. Webster and Lawrence W. Lichty, *Ratings Analysis: Theory and Practice* (Hillsdale, NJ: Lawrence Erlbaum Associates, 1991), 69-79; and Hugh Malcolm Beville Jr., *Audience Ratings: Radio, Television, Cable* (Hillsdale, NJ: Lawrence Erlbaum Associates, 1988), 7-26. Ratings for Maier and Sheen will be discussed further in chapter 8.

[63]Loviglio, *Radio's Intimate Public*, xxiv.

more comfortable writing to other public figures. Correspondence to entertainers, journalists, politicians, and others "skyrocketed" during this period.[64] In an unexpected way, radio not only invited the voices of its listeners into its own realm, but it also prompted them to raise their voices in other areas of interest or concern.

A 1932 *New York Times Magazine* article observed, "The mail room in a big broadcasting station is the most amazing exhibit in the whole radio show. . . . It is a human document in endless volumes, an orgy of . . . old-fashioned letter writing."[65] Five years later, a writer for the *Literary Digest* marveled that so many Americans "fill the mail-pouches of broadcasters day after day." He claimed that during the previous year 10 percent of "the country's population wrote to some broadcasting station." The article went on to explain that NBC maintained regional "staffs of expert correspondents, statisticians, library researchers, mail-boys, stenographers and sorters, all adding considerably to network overhead," so as to respond to "the widest range of subjects . . . covered by the letter-writers." The piece concluded by providing multiple excerpts of letters, including an appeal for a husband by an eighteen-year-old woman, a promise from an excited father to raise his newborn baby "on the radio," a grateful word from an elderly shut-in who appreciated all of the "worlds" radio opened to her after her friend gave her a "tiny radio," an annoyed "stenographer and Sunday-school teacher" who blamed "dumb" radio programs for preventing her minister from proposing to her, and a request for information on where to rent a tuxedo for a four-year-old boy.[66]

As an outgrowth of perceived intimacy between listeners and the voices they heard, it was common that correspondence directed specifically to radio personalities, stations, and sponsors covered a variety of topics and was often quite personal. The familiar sound of popular personalities' voices transformed such people into the role of trusted friends. Listeners sought information and even personal advice from such "ethereal friends,"

---

[64]Lenthall, *Radio's America*, 62. See also Lawrence W. Levine and Cornelia R. Levine, *The Fireside Conversations: America Responds to FDR During the Great Depression* (Berkeley: University of California Press, 2010), 4-12.

[65]As quoted in Levine and Levine, *Fireside Conversations*, 4.

[66]"Fan Mail: Letters Are More Bread and Butter to Stars of the Microphone," *The Literary Digest* 123, no. 21 (May 22, 1937): 20-22.

on whom they projected broad expertise which they may or may not have had. Many extended invitations to radio personalities to stop by their homes, should he or she pass through their towns. Their letters also provided lively commentary on numerous topics, including news stories, program storylines, sponsor products, and so on.[67] Listeners were generous even with feedback on the sound of announcers' voices, sometimes quite critically.[68]

The closeness listeners felt to their favorite personalities and characters could also be expressed with genuine affection and concern. In addition to enthusiastic fan mail praising a personality's cleverness, or singing talent, or sincerity, fans would sometimes send "premiums" of their own. For example, when popular radio comedian Eddie Cantor on his fortieth birthday mentioned his shirt and socks sizes on the air, fans sent him fifteen thousand appropriately sized birthday presents. Listener interaction, however, also could reveal an odd melding in their conceptions of reality and fantasy. Concerned fans would write letters of advice to fictional characters about their fictional lives. When it was mentioned in the course of an *Amos 'n' Andy* episode that their taxi company needed a typewriter, 1,880 listeners sent typewriters to NBC, though they presumably understood that Amos, Andy, and their company were all fictional. In one particularly striking example of mixed realities, one Massachusetts fan of the *Story of Mary Marlin* serial drama wrote the program to complain about the decision to change an actress playing the lead character, and in the same letter suggested a doctor that he hoped could cure the blindness of another character.[69] Lenthall observes, "The implications are palpable: even an imaginary character might be a friend, and in a fictional plot, might feel like a part of a listener's world." He goes on to quote a female listener from New Hampshire, who wrote to a program, "You are not giving us a fairy story. . . . You are giving us Life."[70]

---

[67] Lenthall, *Radio's America*, 64-76.

[68] See Derek Vaillant, "'Your Voice Came In Last Night . . . but I Thought It Sounded a Little Scared:' Rural Radio Listening and 'Talking Back' During the Progressive Era in Wisconsin, 1920–1932," in Hilmes and Loviglio, *Radio Reader*, 63-111; for additional examination of the very personal nature of radio correspondence, see Kristine M. McCusker, "'Dear Radio Friend': Listener Mail and the *National Barn Dance*, 1931–1941," *American Studies* 39, no. 2 (Summer 1998): 173-95.

[69] Lenthall, *Radio's America*, 70-72.

[70] Lenthall, *Radio's America*, 71.

The uncertain grasp of radio reality came to the fore on a national basis on October 30, 1938. On that Sunday evening, CBS's *Mercury Theater on the Air* broadcast "War of the Worlds," by H. G. Wells. By the forty-fifth minute into this sixty-minute dramatization of a Martian invasion and human annihilation, much of the US populace was in a panic because they thought the broadcast was reporting a real event. The manipulative devices of director Orson Welles explain some of this reaction. The first part of the program featured simulated news bulletins on the attack, tying the story to real places, with the first invasion placed in New Jersey. The announcer's panicky voice sounded "eerily" like that of Herbert Morrison, the news reporter who had covered the *Hindenberg* disaster over the airwaves the year before. That actual tragedy had occurred in New Jersey as well. Other authoritative voices were included in the broadcast, one of which was similar to President Franklin Roosevelt's. Additionally, CBS later estimated that 42 percent of those who mistook the program for actual news had tuned into the program after it had begun and had missed the initial *Mercury Theater* announcements.[71] Contemporary pundits fretted about the effects that radio's mass culture was having on the American mind. One of the most vocal was radio commentator and newspaper columnist Dorothy Thompson. Three days after this broadcast she wrote that only a "deep-seated public gullibility" could account for "a few effective voices, accompanied by sound effects . . . convinc[ing] masses of people of a totally unreasonable and completely fantastic proposition as to create a nationwide panic." Americans needed a "spark of skepticism," especially with regard to what they heard on the radio, in which they had invested unreasonable credibility.[72]

In retrospect, some have speculated that the willingness of listeners to believe what should seem unbelievable had more to do with the "general atmosphere of uncertainty" through which Americans had been living. The 1930s had produced years of stagnating economic depression, numerous natural and human-made catastrophes, the rise of fascism in Europe, and the specter of impending war. What is more, as citizens experienced or witnessed these events, they had grown accustomed to radio

---

[71]See Nachman, *Raised on Radio*, 438-47; and Brown, *Manipulating the Ether*, 197-239.
[72]Brown, *Manipulating the Ether*, 222-23.

providing a calming voice and authoritative reassurance (especially via FDR's "Fireside Chats").[73] Thus, the radio's announcement of death and destruction courtesy of blitzkrieging Martians was easier to believe than what now seems reasonable. Regardless, Americans would listen to ethereal voices and navigate radio's mass culture with more caution thereafter. The point is that the power of messages coming through radio sets had reached remarkable heights in the barely ten years since the establishment of national networks.

ETHEREAL FIRESIDES AND THE BODY POLITIC

Speaking of radio in the 1930s and 1940s, historian David Goodman notes, "Radio seemed to many Americans at the time a profoundly democratic technology."[74] It was "democratic" due to broad accessibility across regions and social classes, and as an instrument enabling civic leaders to speak directly to the citizenry. From the evening in 1920 when KDKA-Pittsburgh announced the results of the Warren Harding-James Cox presidential contest in the first commercial broadcast, politics and radio would be forever linked.[75] Though Harding and his successor, Calvin Coolidge, both used radio to address the American people, Herbert Hoover was the first president to embrace the use of airwaves, which he did during the early years of the Great Depression. While Hoover was generally viewed as a strong orator, he was more effective when seen rather than just heard. In the wake of the Great Crash, he gave twenty-seven national radio addresses in 1930 alone.[76] The pervasively bad news regarding the economy, combined with Hoover's rather ponderous, academic messages, produced a less than warm reception. Additionally, evidencing the new priorities of the emerging radio culture, listeners responded angrily when Hoover ignored his allotted "on air" time limits, thus preventing them from hearing their favorite entertainment shows. Finally, during this period entertainment radio and politics began to interact, as comedian/commentators like Will

---

[73]Brown, *Manipulating the Ether*, 233-36.

[74]David Goodman, *Radio's Civic Ambition: American Broadcasting and Democracy in the 1930s* (New York: Oxford University Press, 2011), xvi.

[75]Harding's subsequent inauguration would be the first covered by a live radio broadcast. See Rudel, *Hello, Everybody!*, 109-10.

[76]Lenthall, *Radio's America*, 88.

Rogers repeatedly criticized Washington politicians, heaping particular scorn on the president.[77]

It was not until the soothing voice and down-to-earth rhetoric of Franklin Roosevelt came over the air that citizens truly welcomed radio as a source of political information. Avoiding the overexposure Hoover brought on himself, FDR limited his famed Fireside Chats to thirty over the course of his presidency.[78] The first Fireside Chat, broadcast on March 12, 1933, set the tone for FDR's future communiques. In a calm, confident, conversational manner, Roosevelt began, "I want to talk to the people of the United States about banking." He went on to explain in laymen's terms the general workings of the banking system, why a bank "holiday" had been necessary, and to request that listeners have confidence in and utilize their community banks for the sake of the entire economy.[79]

Notwithstanding the "mass" nature of these radio addresses, listeners experienced a closeness to their government, an understanding of the events shaping their lives, and a sense of empowerment like never before. Listeners felt that Roosevelt was speaking directly to them. One appreciative letter writer expressed a common sentiment: "It is almost beyond belief that the President has a heart to heart talk with his people over the radio. . . . I heartily approve of your getting into personal touch with 'your people.'"[80]

The presumption of intimacy went in both directions. At the end of his first Fireside Chat, Roosevelt implied an instantaneous sense of audience response: "It has been wonderful to me to catch the note of confidence from all over the country." Listeners sometimes wrote to the president as he was speaking in conversational style, as when one female citizen wrote, "Excuse me while I laugh at the joke you just made."[81] Though some commentators, especially FDR's political opponents, expressed angst over his potential

---

[77]Lenthall, *Radio's America*, 88; and Rudel, *Hello, Everybody!*, 269-71, 296, 300-302.

[78]Obviously, the occasions of national "Fireside Chats" were not the only times that Roosevelt would have been heard over the airwaves, but they were his primary means of explaining policy, commenting on current events, and providing general assurances to an anxious public.

[79]For access to an online audio recording of the first Fireside Chat, see Franklin D. Roosevelt, "First Fireside Chat," March 12, 1933, American Rhetoric, www.americanrhetoric.com/speeches /fdrfirstfiresidechat.html. For text, see Franklin D. Roosevelt, *Fireside Chats: Radio Addresses to the American People 1933–1944* (St. Petersburg, FL: Red and Black, 2008), 5-10.

[80]As quoted in Lenthall, *Radio's America*, 93.

[81]See Loviglio, *Radio's Intimate Public*, 13.

propagandistic abuse of the popular medium, many thought that such information flow gave democratic participants greater awareness of current
events enabling them to hold their leaders more accountable.[82] After all,
Hoover had spoken over the airwaves frequently and the voters, holding him
accountable for a stalled economy, voted him out of office.

As the Depression dragged on, radio writers and performers continued
to incorporate this topic into their scripts, especially on comedy shows. This
occurred in serial programs as well as one-off variety shows. In one noteworthy example, in an *Amos 'n' Andy* show during the FDR-declared bank
holiday, "Amos" provided a comical explanation of the banking crisis and
expressed confidence in the banks. Freeman Gosden and Charles Correll,
the actors who played the comedy's lead characters, observed, "People believed Amos . . . and soon we got a letter from President Roosevelt thanking
us."[83] (This broadcast had not been requested by or coordinated with the
White House.) While the quantitative impact of *Amos 'n' Andy* on banking
deposits is impossible to know, this positive reaction to Amos's reassurance
is remarkable on two levels. First, we again see a blending of the fictional
world of radio drama and the real world of real Americans. This would
appear to be the outgrowth of multiple stable voices creating a growing
sense of actual stability, rather than an exhibition of listener gullibility.
Second, the idea that even some white Americans would respond positively
to financial advice from a fictional, uneducated black man, given the visible
prejudices of the time, demonstrates the power of radio to break down previous societal barriers. (It is worth noting that in 1931, a newspaper article
named Amos 'n' Andy, along with Will Rogers, Charles Lindbergh, and
boxer Gene Tunney, as the country's "public gods.") The reality is that radio's
presence in, and radio's treatment of, the Great Depression provided comic
relief, a shared experience, and a stabilizing force for a society that could
have easily become more turbulent.[84]

---

[82]For a brief overview of how networks wrestled with pressure from political leaders and airtime
access, see Douglas B. Craig, *Fireside Politics: Radio and Political Culture in the United States,
1920–1940* (Baltimore: Johns Hopkins University Press, 2000), 124-31.

[83]Arthur Frank Wertheim, "Relieving Social Tensions: Radio Comedy and the Great Depression,"
Journal of Popular Culture 10, no. 3 (Winter 1976): 504.

[84]For excellent general analysis of the calming role of radio comedy in the Great Depression, see
Wertheim, "Relieving Social Tensions," 501-19. To better understand the appeal of *Amos 'n' Andy*,
arguably the most popular radio show of all time, see Elizabeth McLeod, *The Original Amos 'n'*

RELIGIOUS RADIO

On the first Sunday of 1921, pioneering radio station KDKA in Pittsburgh broadcast worship services of the Calvary Episcopal Church. KDKA management, which had launched commercial radio just two months earlier, thought that providing its few listeners with the first broadcast of a church service would be a good publicity move. With KDKA engineers—one Catholic and one Jewish—near the pulpit donning choir robes, the sounds of the entire service were beamed over the winter air. The broadcast "went over splendidly" as indicated by the positive response the station and the church received, thereby confirming their hunch. One correspondent, a shut-in in Massachusetts, wrote to say that "she could scarcely believe her ears when the organ music and choir sounded," and that the "voice of the pastor thrilled me as few things have in the long suffering years. . . . At the end [I] felt at peace with the world, 'the peace that passeth all understanding.'"[85] Religious broadcasting was born and it would grow up quickly.

Interestingly, while many details of the service were recorded, accounts differ as to who actually preached the sermon. Some claim that senior pastor Edwin J. van Etten embraced the technological opportunity and delivered the New Year's homily. Others claim that van Etten was leery of the technology and asked his associate pastor, Lewis B. Whittemore, to preach that evening. While van Etten himself later took credit for leading the service, recalling a number of specific details from that evening, the pertinent church bulletin lists Whittemore as the presiding pastor and homilist. Regardless of which pastor spoke on January 2, van Etten did preach on the radio thereafter, and KDKA continued to broadcast Calvary Episcopal's services through 1962.[86]

Andy: Freeman Gosden, Charles Correll and the 1928–1943 Radio Serial (Jefferson, NC: McFarland & Company, 2005), 7-126. Notwithstanding the popularity of *Amos 'n' Andy* among both black and white audiences, it would eventually become controversial as civil rights leaders feared its affirmation of black stereotypes. See McLeod, *Original Amos 'n' Andy*, 127-61. See also *Amos 'n' Andy: Anatomy of a Controversy*, executive producer Michael R. Avery, 48 minutes (Scott Entertainment, 1983), DVD.

[85]See Gleason L. Archer, *History of Radio to 1926* (New York: American Historical Society, 1938), 211, 213; Tona J. Hangen, *Redeeming the Dial: Radio, Religion, & Popular Culture in America* (Chapel Hill: University of North Carolina Press, 2002), 21-22; Mark Ward Sr., *Air of Salvation: The Story of Christian Broadcasting* (Grand Rapids, MI: Baker Books, 1994), 23-25; the excerpt from correspondence can be found in Spencer Miller Jr., "Radio and Religion," *Annals of the American Academy of Political Science* 177 (January 1935): 135-36.

[86]Accounts naming van Etten as the first radio preacher include Miller, "Radio and Religion," 135-40; an oft-quoted, unattributed November 1938 article titled "How Radio Religion Began:

As the idea of religious broadcasting quickly caught on, in December of that year the Church of the Covenant of Washington, DC pursued and received the first radio broadcast license issued to a religious organization. Months later, Calvary Baptist Church, one of New York City's oldest congregations, began its radio broadcasts. Expressing the hopefulness of many radio preachers who would follow, the church's pastor, the Reverend John Roach Stratton, declared, "I shall try to continue doing my part . . . tearing down the strongholds of Satan, and I hope that our radio system will prove so efficient that when I twist the Devil's tail in New York, his squawk will be heard across the continent."[87] By 1923, ten ecclesiastically related organizations had stations up and running. According to the Federal Radio Commission, sixty Christian radio licenses had been issued by 1928, most of which were granted to evangelically minded churches. To put this into perspective, there were 732 broadcasting stations in operation in 1927. While many religious broadcasters would later shut down due to regulatory complications and funding problems during the Great Depression, religious broadcasting (almost all of which was Christian) had established itself as a substantive, lasting component of American airwaves.[88]

The appetite for radio programming increased dramatically during the remainder of the 1920s, as more Americans embraced the medium. While some preachers had access to religious radio stations, more of them appeared on commercial outlets. As media scholar Quentin Schultze observes,

---

The First Church Broadcast, The Wood and the Sword," reprinted in pamphlet form by Calvary Episcopal Church; Vincent Edwards, "The First Church Broadcast," *Christian Advocate* 12 (November 14, 1968), 12. Accounts naming Whittemore as the first radio preacher include Ben Armstrong, *The Electric Church* (Nashville: Thomas Nelson Inc., 1979), 19-20; Dennis N. Voskuil, "Reaching Out: Mainline Protestantism and the Media," in *Between the Times: The Travail of the Protestant Establishment in America, 1900–1960*, ed. William R. Hutchison (New York: Cambridge University Press, 1989), 81; Ward, *Air of Salvation*, 23-25; the aforementioned pamphlet, "How Radio Religion Began," published by Calvary Episcopal Church, states that Calvary's "service bulletin and other sources" indicate that Whittemore was the first radio sermonizer. (Calvary Episcopal Church archives, Pittsburgh, box W3, file 20). In February 2011, I interviewed Calvary Episcopal's archivist, Susie Wolfe. She expressed both frustration and bemusement that her church proudly displays a plaque commemorating the first religious broadcast, but cannot conclusively identify the presiding pastor.

[87]As quoted in Bob Lochte, *Christian Radio: The Growth of a Mainstream Broadcasting Force* (Jefferson, NC: McFarland & Company, 2005), 21.

[88]Lochte, *Christian Radio*, 21-25; Barnouw, *Tower in Babel*, 209; Dennis N. Voskuil, "The Power of the Air: Evangelicals and the Rise of Religious Broadcasting," in *American Evangelicals and the Mass Media*, ed. Quentin J. Schultze (Grand Rapids, MI: Zondervan, 1990), 71-74.

the limited number of Christian radio stations was effectively "a blessing in disguise" to many preachers seeking to share the gospel, since the commercial stations they were forced to use often had more powerful signals and larger audiences than their religious-only counterparts. Most commercial stations were open to airing Christian broadcasts, either on a sustaining time basis to "serve the public interest," or as paid programming. Though it would not stay at this relative level, by 1932 more than 8 percent of all radio programming in the United States was religious. While network religious broadcasts enjoyed the greatest attention, a glimpse into the breadth of local religious broadcasts is instructive. In Chicago in 1941, seventy-seven different religious broadcasts were aired every week on commercial stations. Of them, twenty-five were sponsored by fundamentalist churches, three by liberal Protestants, and the rest were Roman Catholic, Jewish, Christian Science, and unclassified Protestant.[89]

Because few mainline Protestant churches owned and operated radio stations, the Federal Council of Churches of Christ encouraged its local councils of churches to forge cooperative radio ministries and to seek access to local stations for broadcasting opportunities. One such cooperative effort in the New York area began in 1923 and featured noted Brooklyn preacher S. Parkes Cadman. His popularity led NBC to make this a weekly network broadcast, named *National Radio Pulpit*, when the network was formed three years later. The *Pulpit* became the first religious broadcast to originate from a studio rather than from a remote, church location, when NBC asked Cadman to broadcast from its network facilities in 1928. From the beginning, NBC offered religious groups "sustaining" (free) airtime, soon adding Catholic and Jewish offerings to the initial Protestant programming. Fulton Sheen's *Catholic Hour* program would become one of the most popular such NBC broadcasts.

When CBS formed in 1927, it initially sold airtime to preachers seeking a network audience, primarily as a means to generate much-needed revenue.

---

[89]Quentin J. Schultze, "Evangelical Radio and the Rise of The Electronic Church, 1921–1948," *Journal of Broadcasting & Electronic Media* 32, no. 3 (Summer 1988): 289-306. According to one estimate, three-fourths of all religious programs were broadcast on a sustaining-time basis in the early 1930s. While commercial stations offered less free airtime for such broadcasts by the end of the 1930s, many stations continued to offer sustaining time for religion. See Voskuil, "Power of the Air," 75.

The politically charged rhetoric of one such preacher, Father Charles Coughlin, caused the network's executives to rethink this policy and cease selling airtime for religious programming in 1931. At that time, CBS adopted a similar policy to NBC and offered sustaining time to mainline, nonsectarian preachers. From its founding in 1934, the MBS provided *only* purchased time to religious broadcasters. Though it would eventually scale back some religious programming, one-fourth of Mutual's revenues came from religious broadcasts in the early 1940s. The two most visible such programs were Walter Maier's *The Lutheran Hour* and Charles Fuller's *Old-Fashioned Revival Hour.* When NBC spun off its Blue network resulting in the formation of ABC, management of this new network also adopted a policy of offering sustaining time primarily to mainline Protestant groups—a policy it maintained until the late 1940s, when it began selling airtime for religious programs to offset declining network radio revenue as television began to rise.[90]

Whether over local stations or via national networks, outreach-minded clergy took their messages beyond the walls of their churches' sanctuaries from the earliest days of the radio medium. For those effective preachers who obtained access to network microphones, either by sustaining time or through purchased access, loyal listener bases developed and grew, stretching from coast to coast, and in several cases, lasting for decades.

In the development of mass culture in the United States, the advent of broadcast radio was a watershed event. In light of the bewildering speed with which society has since embraced newer forms of technology and allowed itself to be reshaped, it is easy to overlook the cultural impact of radio itself, relegating its quaint wooden cabinets to our literal and mental attics. Only in recent years have historians begun to plumb the depths of its impact on the culture of the 1920s, 1930s, and 1940s, and the way its influence has

---

[90]Voskuil, "Reaching Out," 81-86; Lowell Saunders, "The National Religious Broadcasters and the Availability of Commercial Radio Time" (PhD diss., University of Illinois, 1968), 211-12; William F. Fore, "A Short History of Religious Broadcasting," unpublished manuscript dated August 10, 1967, Eugene Bertermann Collection, box 8, folder 12, Wheaton College Billy Graham Center Archives. (William Fore was the executive director of the Broadcasting and Film Commission of the National Council of Churches.)

endured—albeit in evolved states.[91] Radio, especially network radio, provided shared communal experiences that brought together a nation in unprecedented ways, during the most trying of years. It opened the way to an informational global village, however unevenly this village was covered in its early days. Yet radio also produced a sense of intimacy, personal empowerment, and individual autonomy that was powerful in the context of the times, if not intuitively obvious to today's casual observer. These factors, along with others such as consistent, eloquent delivery, broadcasting professionalism, and projected expertise, caused listeners to vest radio speakers with considerable authority. Radio's perceived threats to individual minds were perhaps overestimated, but highlighted the need for critical judgment and thoughtful receptiveness.

From the beginning, religion made up a consistent and important component of radio programming lineups, and religious programming shared in all the major features of the new medium. While many religious programs appeared on local radio stations, national networks devoted weekly air time to religious broadcasts, on a coast-to-coast basis. Embracing radio's intimate relationships with listeners, tapping into the medium's sense of community, and leveraging the authority radio spokesmen enjoyed from their listeners, network preachers delivered substantive religious messages that addressed the national and individual uncertainties of the times. Listeners tuned in week after week, often in numbers rivaling those associated with more consciously entertaining programs, for admonition, comfort, and hope. Right at the top of the most adept and influential network radio preachers were Walter Maier and Fulton Sheen.

---

[91]For an excellent overview of the historical treatment of radio broadcasting, see Michele Hilmes, "Rethinking Radio," in Hilmes and Loviglio, *Radio Reader*, 1-15.

Chapter Three

PURPOSEFUL PREPARATION

MAIER'S AND SHEEN'S FORMATIVE YEARS

For even as it is better to enlighten than merely to shine, so is it better to give to others the fruits of one's contemplation than merely to contemplate.

ST. THOMAS AQUINAS

O, when it comes to faith, what a living, creative, active, powerful thing it is.

MARTIN LUTHER

AT THE BEGINNING OF THE CHRISTIAN SEASON of Advent in 1949, Walter Maier delivered a rather bleak sermon on the religious trajectory of America and her citizens, on his popular *The Lutheran Hour* radio program. However, as he had done since his seminary training, Maier concluded his message with a hopeful proclamation of the gospel, assuring his listeners that the "all-enduring Savior" will ultimately triumph over "all His foes . . . and take His own home to Him in heaven."[1] Though he could not have known it,

---

[1] "World Is Not Getting Better, Says Minister," *Zanesville Times Recorder*, December 5, 1949. The editorial staff of this Ohio newspaper apparently considered Maier's jeremiad against a "Pollyanna picture of a world . . . growing better," potential global "bloody strife," increasing "crime of

this eschatological vision held more immediacy for the preacher than for most of his "congregants." Just three weeks later, Maier delivered a joyous Christmas day sermon, "Heaven's Love Lies in the Manger," which he closed by inviting his listeners to "receive" the "Christ Child's . . . love [that] will warm your soul with its divine glow."[2] It would be the last invitation he issued, the last radio sermon he would ever preach. In the early morning hours of December 29, Maier suffered the first of a series of heart attacks that would culminate in the death of the seemingly indefatigable fifty-six-year-old radio preacher on January 11, 1950. Millions of radio listeners around the world were shocked, since at his demise Walter Maier had preached the Christian message to more people than anyone in history.[3] In his relatively short lifespan, Maier had built a true multimedia presence on the American religious scene—as editor and columnist for a noteworthy Christian periodical, as author of numerous popular Christian books, as preacher/cheerleader at *The Lutheran Hour* rallies across the country, and preeminently as the voice of TLH. Though it had never been his objective, this American cleric with a German surname departed this life in firm possession of a household name.

As the voice of Maier went silent, that of fellow radio preacher, Fulton Sheen, continued to project from radio cabinets in countless living rooms on the *Catholic Hour*. On New Year's Day of 1950, Sheen began a series of radio addresses he would publish later that year under the title *The Rock Plunged into Eternity*. These sermons focused on the endurance of the "one, holy catholic and apostolic Church," over a period spanning countless generations, due to the "rock solid" foundational faith of St. Peter, and the ongoing providential protection of God Almighty. As with Maier, Sheen's radio popularity also enhanced his success as a popular writer (and vice versa, no doubt); his book, *Peace of Soul*, began 1950 near the top of the *New York Times* Best Seller list. It shared the list with other spiritual books by the Catholic monk Thomas Merton and Protestant preacher Norman Vincent

---

'every form,'" the "Red atheist rebellion against the Almighty," and "churches and denominations [that] hurry away from Christ and His truth," worthy of attention, as they ran a thorough summary, including extensive quotations.

[2] Walter A. Maier, "Heaven's Love Lies in the Manger," *The Walter A. Maier Memorial Booklet* (St. Louis: The Lutheran Laymen's League, 1950), 7-19.

[3] See Mark Ward Sr., *Air of Salvation: The Story of Christian Broadcasting* (Grand Rapids, MI: Baker Books, 1994), 75.

Peale. More interestingly, Sheen's bestseller outpaced sales of Paul Blan-shard's frontal assault on Roman Catholicism, *American Freedom and Catholic Power*.[4] Like Maier, Sheen had broadened his pastoral reach to ranges unimaginable just a generation earlier, through the skillful embrace of a radio studio microphone. Millions of listeners would continue tuning in to Monsignor (soon to be bishop) Sheen's radio services, until he rede-ployed his clerical oratory in the ascending medium of television, with the launch of *Life Is Worth Living*, over the DuMont network in 1952.

FORMATIVE YEARS—MAIER

Home life and education. On October 4, 1893, German immigrants Anna and Emil Maier welcomed the birth of their third child, Walter Arthur Maier, in their Boston home. The Maiers had come to America seeking economic opportunity in 1880, and after living for short periods in New York and New Haven, had settled in Boston. Emil made a living as an organ builder/tuner—a craft he had honed in the sanctuaries of German and Swiss churches. In their early years in Boston, Anna ran a grocery/sundries store beneath their living quarters, until Emil had established himself in his trade. In addition to homemaking, Anna became active in church and community circles, and served as the spiritual anchor of her family. Though never an outright un-believer, Emil would become a committed Christian only once he was well into his adulthood. Nonetheless, later in his own life, Walter stated, "My earliest clear recollection is that of my father on his knees in the bedroom, praying." He credited "the prayers, support, and outstanding example of my parents," as the "most influential factor" in his life.[5] The unwavering words of faith of his mother, in particular, were a source of reassurance as Maier and his brother endured dire warnings, from neighborhood playmates that were predominantly Roman Catholic, of the eternal torment awaiting them should they fail to spurn their Protestant heresies.[6]

From the days of his youth, Maier was a dynamo whose keen mind was clearly evident. He completed his elementary education at the Cotton

---

[4]"The New York Times Best Seller List," 1950, www.hawes.com/1950/1950-01-08.pdf.
[5]Paul L. Maier, *A Man Spoke, A World Listened: The Story of Walter A. Maier* (New York: McGraw-Hill, 1963), 10.
[6]Elmer A. Kettner, *Grossie: "The Woman Everyone Loved"* (Grand Rapids, MI: Eerdmans, 1949), 59.

Mather Public School, where he finished first in his class. Maier was no less engaged in his religious development. His pastor would later recall that unlike his classmates, Maier did not just recite memorized catechism passages when called on, but would quiz the pastor on a wide range of topics.[7] While attending a mission festival in Boston at the age of twelve, Maier heard Henry Stein, a professor from Concordia Collegiate Institute in suburban New York, appeal for "more men to spread the saving gospel of Christ." The lad's course was set.

Maier would go on to spend six years in what was effectively a combined high school and junior college program at Concordia Collegiate Institute in Bronxville, New York.[8] In addition to working part-time in the campus kitchen, he held various class offices, served as business manager of the yearbook, engaged in literary and debating activities, and played center field on the baseball team. Academics, however, came first, and in 1912 Maier once again graduated at the top of his class. He excelled in languages, including Latin, Greek, German, and Hebrew. As a foretaste of his later career, he demonstrated his ascending public speaking skills when called on to deliver the valedictory address—an address he concluded by advocating the establishment of a true Lutheran university in the New York area. The ed-

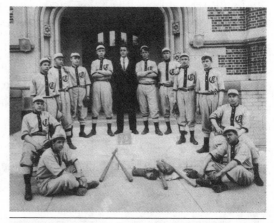

Figure 3.1. Walter Maier (fourth from right) on Concordia Bronxville's baseball team, 1912

itors of Concordia's yearbook, *The Echo*, provided this jocular summary of their classmate: "The Hub of the Universe became too small to hold this young prodigy, so he left the bean-pots of Boston for Concordia's classic soup-bowls. Since his arrival, 'Beaner' has accumulated a vast store of

---

[7]Maier, *A Man Spoke*, 9-10.

[8]Concordia Collegiate Institute was converted to a separate prep school and junior college in the 1930s, and into a four-year, liberal arts college in the 1970s.

knowledge by 'grinding.' . . . He is as shrewd as the proverbial Yank, always occupied in doing something—or somebody."[9]

Upon graduating from Concordia, Maier was accepted into Boston University's undergraduate program, where he earned a bachelor's degree in just one year of study by taking a double course load. On graduation, Maier began formal training for Lutheran ministry at Concordia Seminary in St. Louis, completing such studies in 1916. That fall he was granted a fellowship by Harvard Divinity School and began doctoral studies in Old Testament. Maier continued studies in Cambridge for the next two academic years, during which time he gained a reputation for academic, teaching, and oratorical excellence.[10]

Maier was ordained at the oldest Lutheran church in New England, Zion Lutheran Church of Boston, and accepted their call to become assistant pastor in 1917. This church had originally been organized by German Lutheran immigrants on February 18, 1839, as the German Lutheran Society of Boston. By coincidence, the following day, February 19, 1839, marked the arrival of the first group of Saxon immigrants in St. Louis, who would go on to form what became known as the Lutheran Church–Missouri Synod (LCMS) in 1847. Zion of Boston would become the first New England congregation of the LCMS, when it joined this denominational body in 1863.[11]

As a harbinger of Maier's future proclamatory accomplishments, local Boston-area newspapers took note of this young preacher and scholar. In August 1917, the *Clinton Daily Item* reported on a Maier mission address, noting that he considered announcement of the gospel message "throughout the globe" to be the primary goal of Christianity. "One's highest privilege . . .

---

[9]Maier, *A Man Spoke*, 18.

[10]The biographical information in this section is gleaned primarily from Maier, *A Man Spoke*, especially chapters 2–6, and Kettner, *Grossie*, especially chapters 1–4. The former is a fine biography and is the most complete single source of information on Walter Maier's life; however, it does bear the understandable reflection of the author's admiration of his late father. The latter is a biography of Maier's mother, Anna Maier, written by her long-time Lutheran pastor. See also Tona Hangen, "Man of the Hour: Walter A. Maier and Religion by Radio on the Lutheran Hour," *Radio Reader: Essays in the Cultural History of Radio*, ed. Michele Hilmes and Jason Loviglio (New York: Routledge, 2002), 113-34.

[11]Today, Zion Lutheran Church operates as "the First Lutheran Church of Boston." See Tom Beineke, *Built on a Rock: A History of Missouri Synod Lutherans in New England* (Springfield, MA: New England District of the Lutheran Church–Missouri Synod, 1997), 9-10; see also "Parish History," First Lutheran Church of Boston, flc-boston.org/parish-history.

would be to aid that aim," declared an enthusiastic Maier. When he was invited back to Clinton two months later to give an address commemorating the four hundredth anniversary of Luther's posting of the Ninety-Five Theses, the *Daily Item* encouraged its readers to take in "a special treat," as the quadricentennial orator "is possessed of rare eloquence and is a forceful speaker." After another celebration in North Plymouth in 1918, the *Old Colony Memorial* of Plymouth reported that the twenty-four-year-old "Rev. W. A. Maier of Harvard University had the attention of his hearers riveted from beginning to end." Other papers referred to him as "the best Lutheran pulpit orator of Boston and vicinity."[12]

While the press devoted considerably more attention to preachers, religious services, and general ecclesiastical activities during this period than it has in more recent years, it is significant that the young cleric gained any attention at all in the Boston area, given the relative paucity of Lutherans in New England. As the nineteenth century drew to a close, Lutheranism ranked below the top six denominational affiliations in Massachusetts, part of a subset of the 4.2 percent "other" church body affiliations. During this same period, the only New England state where Lutheranism did rank in the top six denominations was Connecticut, where it claimed an anemic 1.9 percent of denominational adherents.[13] The relative weak presence of Lutheranism in Boston, and in New England as a whole, did not change significantly as the twentieth century proceeded. Though Walter Maier would move from these New England surroundings to locales in which Lutherans were more prominent (relatively speaking, at least), he had acquired an understanding of what it was like to be in a denominational minority that he would retain. Such experiences no doubt heightened his attentiveness to how religious vocabulary and phraseology could be "heard" by different members of an audience.

POW ministry. America's entry into World War I in April of 1917 provided Maier an opportunity to hone his pastoral skills among "parishioners" less congenial than those of a typical Boston congregation. In the weeks leading up to the US declaration of war, several German ships had anchored

---

[12]Maier, *A Man Spoke*, 27.
[13]See Edwin Scott Gaustad and Philip L. Barlow, *New Historical Atlas of Religion in America* (New York: Oxford University Press, 2000), figures C.17, C.18.

in Boston Harbor to avoid attack by British warships on the Atlantic. With the Kaiser now formally an enemy, the US government seized these German ships and interned the collective crews of over three hundred men as enemy aliens on the harbor's Gallup's Island. Upon realizing that these prisoners had no chaplain, Maier petitioned the Commissioner of Immigration to minister to their spiritual needs. The commissioner granted his request and governmental officials introduced Maier to the prisoners.[14]

Initially, Maier's outreach was met with skepticism by the captive Germans; however, his ability to preach and converse in their native tongue overcame their resistance. His ability to engage in conversational German is a testament to Maier's linguistic aptitude. While his parents were native German speakers, little German had been spoken in their home when Walter was growing up, due to his mother's insistence that they converse as Americans—in English. However, Maier had grasped conversational proficiency while studying German in college, and now put it to good use.[15] Additionally, Maier enlisted his mother to organize a group of Back Bay families to supply the prisoners with items of food and clothing, and persuaded his brother to help provide social activities, such as motion picture screenings. The detainees soon warmed to the energetic young pastor.

According to Maier's biographer, his "welfare" work on Gallup's Island was soon "support[ed]" by the YMCA, who appointed him "a secretary of the organization."[16] Though it is not clear how this arrangement came about, Maier himself may have initiated the relationship during the summer of 1917. In a letter to Maier from one of his former seminary professors, reference is made to a request for a recommendation (presumably from the YMCA) that had been sent to Francis Pieper, president of Concordia Seminary. While Pieper apparently had reservations about Maier's affiliation with the pandenominational YMCA, he "agreed . . . to give [Maier] a good recommendation without saying anything of our opinion of Y.M.C.A. work as such."[17] The

---

[14]For summary narratives of Maier's (and his mother's) work with German prisoners during and immediately after World War I, see Maier, *A Man Spoke*, 28-34, and Kettner, *Grossie*, 82-84.

[15]Maier, *A Man Spoke*, 28-29.

[16]Maier, *A Man Spoke*, 29.

[17]Professor L. Fuerbringer to Pastor Walter Maier, August 4, 1917, Walter A. Maier Collection (hereafter, WAM Collection), box 2, folder 72, Concordia Historical Institute, St. Louis (hereafter, CHI). In this letter, Fuerbringer expresses enthusiasm for Maier's effort to minister to POWs, promising to procure "papers for distribution" and (presumably German language) hymnals.

following year, the Boston Commissioner of the US Department of Labor stated that Maier had been "in charge of the Y.M.C.A. work at the German encampment" on Gallup's Island, and that he had "performed" satisfactorily.[18] Once again, he displayed a characteristic willingness to cooperate with those outside of his denomination that would mark his later radio career.

In October 1917, the Gallup's Island detainees were transferred to Hot Springs, North Carolina. Maier attempted to maintain active contact with this group, but his efforts produced little success. More importantly, his paternalistic efforts with these Germans, even after they had become part of a much larger Hot Springs prisoner population, produced friction between Maier and both the YMCA and the US military. As Christmas 1917 approached, Maier appears to have been overly persistent in demanding access to the former Gallup's Island prisoners, who were now a subset of roughly 1,600 prisoners in Hot Springs. Additionally, he repeatedly insisted that he be allowed to bring Christmas gifts to the former Gallup's Island men, but not for the rest of the prisoners. YMCA Associate Secretary A. A. Ebersole scolded Maier for failing to recognize the strife that such inequitable treatment could cause within the detention camp, and for his insensitivity to the potential "embarrassment" his actions could bring on YMCA administration. Ebersole further reprimanded Maier for presuming to refer to the former Gallup's Island detainees as "[his] former seamen." Maier was given the choice of providing funding for Christmas presents for all prisoners in the camp, or none at all.[19]

It is unclear what Maier chose to do, but whatever action he ultimately took did not smooth over the matter. In the following year, when Maier was seeking a military chaplaincy, he sent a letter to the YMCA requesting assurance that he was not viewed as "disloyal" (presumably to the United

---

Pieper's and Fuerbringer's support for Maier's work with the YMCA is significant, given LCMS resistance to collaborating with other Christian groups, lest they be construed as engaging in "unionism." (See chapter 8.) Pieper's and Fuerbringer's cooperative attitude likely reflects respect that Maier had earned as a recent seminarian under their tutelage, recognition of the political and ecclesiastical complexity of being a denomination largely comprising German-Americans at a time when America was at war with Germany, and genuine pastoral concern for the spiritual needs of the POWs.

[18]US Department of Labor, Office of the Commissioner to "To Whom it may Concern," December 6, 1918, WAM Collection, box 2, Folder 72, CHI.

[19]A. A. Ebersole to Walter Maier, December 13, 1917, WAM Collection, box 2, folder 72, CHI.

States) by that organization. Ebersole assured him that he had not been judged guilty of "any disloyalty," but again mentioned Maier's "indiscretions" regarding former Gallup's Island detainees, including his proclivity to refer to them as "[his] men." Ebersole claimed that Maier's failure to "exercise good judgment" had been deemed "serious" enough "by the authorities at Hot Springs" that it "came very near endangering the continuance of our work there." According to Ebersole's letter, Maier himself had acknowledged that he had been indiscreet.[20] After the war, reports of the Hot Springs quarrel resulted in the commandant of Fort Oglethorpe Prison Barracks forbidding Maier to visit prisoners being held there. (Even though the armistice had been signed, prisoners remained on US soil, while arrangements for their release and repatriation were made.) In a rather sharply worded letter, Col. C. W. Penrose reminded Maier that the YMCA had "repudiated" his actions, and had "requested" his resignation from the organization, in the wake of his actions regarding the transferred prisoners.[21]

Notwithstanding the rocky conclusion of Maier's Gallup's Island/Hot Springs prisoner pastorate, Maier did secure a US Army chaplaincy in the early summer of 1918. He was briefly stationed at Camp Gordon, Georgia. Lest there be any question as to his American loyalty, Maier told the *Boston Globe* that "he knew of no better way to register his disapproval of the Prussian military clique than to enter active service in the United States forces."[22] When the war concluded in November, Maier returned to Boston to continue studies at Harvard, and carry on the work of a parish pastor. His work with German POWs, however, was not finished. Maier obtained a chaplaincy at the Army's Camp Devens, outside Boston. One hundred German POWs, captured from the German raider *Kronprinz Wilhelm* and submarine U-58, remained incarcerated near Camp Devens at United States War Prison Camp No. 1, at Still River. The Secretary of War granted permission for Maier to minister to these prisoners as part of his Camp Devens assignment.[23]

While the prisoners on Gallup's Island had been skeptical, the Still River POWs were openly hostile. Maier's introductory greeting generated the

---

[20]A. A. Ebersole to Walter Maier, August 27, 1918, WAM Collection, box 2, folder 72, CHI.
[21]C. W. Penrose to W. A. Maier, May 9, 1919, WAM Collection, box 2, folder 72, CHI.
[22]"Rev. W. A. Maier Goes to Camp Gordon as Chaplain," *Boston Globe*, June 19, 1918.
[23]Maier, *A Man Spoke*, 31.

following response from one of the German fighting men, "We don't want to have anything to do with the preachers. The preachers did as much to agitate for war as anyone else!"[24] Maier assured them, "But I have not come to speak of war, but of peace—the peace of God."[25] Notwithstanding the Reverend Maier's sincerity, the prisoners kept their distance during the coming weeks. Maier devised a new strategy. He asked his mother to knit one hundred pairs of socks for the prisoners by Christmas. With rapid deployment of her nimble fingers, and those of her friends, Mrs. Anna Maier produced the socks on time. They presented the socks, small presents, and a homemade Christmas dinner to the surprised POWs on December 25, 1918. Toward the close of the day's celebration, Maier led a Christmas service, which the cookie-softened captives all attended. Maier went on to establish close relationships with many of the prisoners as he tended to both spiritual and social needs, until they were sent home.[26]

Though the war was over and POWs held in the United States were returning to Germany, Maier continued to concern himself with pastoral care of prisoners until they all had repatriated. The same assertiveness and persistence that he had demonstrated with regard to Gallup's Island prisoners surfaced with regard to postwar prisoners. At the time, the LCMS directed its military chaplaincy activities via the Lutheran Church Board for Army and Navy, USA (LCBAN). The purpose of LCBAN was to meet the spiritual needs of US soldiers, especially Lutheran soldiers. Maier repeatedly pressed the LCBAN to expand their endeavors to include ministering to "Germans

---

[24]Kettner, *Grossie*, 83. It should be noted that in Maier's son's telling of this encounter, the German prisoner specifically accused "American preachers" of "agitat[ing] for war." See Maier, *A Man Spoke*, 31. In 1936 and 1940 radio sermons, Walter Maier himself recounted that these prisoners produced a scrapbook containing clippings of anti-German comments by American clergy. See Walter A. Maier, *Fourth Lutheran Hour: Winged Words for Christ* (St. Louis: CPH, 1937), 139-40, and Maier, *Peace Through Christ: Radio Messages Broadcast in the Seventh Lutheran Hour* (St. Louis: CPH, 1940), 191. However, the harboring of a *general* disdain for preachers by German prisoners, as per Kettner's account, seems probable. While they may have indeed developed a distaste for American clerical commentary on their nationality, via whatever limited access they would have had to it during this period, subsequent scholarship has demonstrated that the relevance and validity of Christian truth claims, and the importance of clergy themselves, came under harsh scrutiny by German citizens after the disastrous Great War. Such was precisely due, at least in large part, to the vocal support German preachers had provided for a nationalist agenda during the war. See J. S. Conway, *The Nazi Persecution of the Churches, 1933–1945* (1968; repr., Vancouver: Regent College Publishing, 2001), especially chapter 1.

[25]Maier, *A Man Spoke*, 31.

[26]Maier, *A Man Spoke*, 31-34; Kettner, *Grossie*, 82-84.

interned at various places" in the United States. In December 1918, the
LCBAN secretary sent a letter to Maier explaining that after "careful consideration," the organization had decided that it "cannot take up this work."[27]

Maier's youthful cheekiness soon became an annoyance, as he appears to
have implied that the LCBAN leaders were derelict in their ecclesiastical
responsibilities. In a letter sent the following month, in reply to correspondence from Maier on January 15, the LCBAN secretary wrote, "We are
indeed sorry that you believe we are neglecting our duty in not giving proper
attention to the spiritual needs of the German wa[r] prisoners." Secretary
Streufert went on to explain that the sole purpose for the establishment of
the LCBAN had been "only to minister to the spiritual needs of *our* boys
with the colors." He explained that the board had "a heart for German war
prisoners," and that consideration had been given to some sort of ministry
to POWs, but that LCBAN leaders feared that such efforts could "mean
many obstacles" with US military authorities. Streufert flatly claimed that
"our former chairman, just because he showed great interest in the German
war prisoners, was more or less under surveillance." The conclusion of the
letter makes it clear that the LCBAN did not wish to discuss the issue further.[28] A couple of weeks later, the LCBAN board again discussed the possibility of ministering to German prisoners, apparently at the urging of
Maier. They again rejected the idea and informed Maier, suggesting that he
take up the matter with the Atlantic District Mission Board of the LCMS.[29]

It does not appear that Maier pursued the matter with the Atlantic District Mission Board, perhaps because repatriation of prisoners was quickly
reducing the need for ministry. Maier's pastoral care of German POWs did
generate positive press coverage in the Boston area during this period. He
was applauded for his effort to "heal the fractures of war."[30] A ten-plus
column-inch article in the *Boston Globe* highlighted Maier's attempts to
"teach American principles" to the prisoners, while engaging in "social work,"

---

[27]Rev. F. C. Streufert to Rev. Walter A. Maier, December 11, 1918, WAM Collection, box 2, folder 72,
CHI.

[28]Rev. F. C. Streufert to Rev. Walter A. Maier, January 20, 1919, WAM Collection, box 2, folder 72,
CHI.

[29]Rev. George F. Schmidt to Rev. Walter A. Maier, February 6, 1919, WAM Collection, box 2,
folder 72, CHI.

[30]Maier, *A Man Spoke*, 35.

leading religious services, and arranging for entertainment (e.g., movies). Interestingly, the article concluded with Maier stating, "I was not connected with any organization in this work, but had permission of the Government to help the men and considered I was doing my duty to the Government by my work." The article referred to Maier as "a young minister of Dorchester," but failed to mention the name of his parish, or that he was Lutheran.[31]

Maier's outreach to German WWI prisoners occurred over roughly a two-year period. His biographer justifiably summarizes this brief ministry in very positive ways, but primarily as a demonstration of Maier's boundless dedication to sharing the gospel, wherever possible, and as an example of his early success as a young, energetic pastor. While agreeing that those are important components of

Figure 3.2. Maier as World War I American military chaplain

the story, one can argue that the significance of these events is much greater. This episode demonstrated the tenacity, and the impatience, with which Maier would respond whenever obstacles to more general Christian outreach arose. This personality trait would drive his success in the arena of religious broadcasting, commencing less than ten years after the last POWs sailed eastward from American shores. More importantly, his WWI experiences provided him with valuable lessons, from which he no doubt drew as he launched a radio station, entered network airwaves, and spread his message around the globe.

First, this was Maier's initial opportunity to minister cross-culturally. True, he was only one generation removed from the German lands the POWs called home. Nonetheless, the perceptions of appropriate governmental models, economic forces, ecclesiastical structures, and expressions of popular culture would have differed rather significantly between the captive German "parishioners" and their Yankee "pastor," notwithstanding his Teutonic surname. Of course, there was also the matter of their respective nations being in a state of war with each other, which in and of itself raised

---

[31]"Boston Man Chaplain to Hun Prisoners," *Boston Globe*, March 23, 1919.

barriers to Maier's gospel message. Yet Maier soon learned the value of common language, of a respectful tone, and of the need to tend to both eternal and temporal needs of those whom he aspired to reach. Second, Maier gained firsthand experience, and established personal contacts within the US military. Years later these would bear abundant fruit, especially when expanding TLH internationally, and in distributing TLH programs during World War II.

Third, he learned important lessons about working in ministry with organizations (e.g., YMCA) beyond the boundaries of the LCMS and Lutheranism in general—lessons not typically pursued by parochial-minded Missouri Synod Lutherans. Though Maier had stepped on some YMCA toes through tactlessness and an overly possessive attitude toward "his" German POWs, he had ultimately conducted successful work under the auspices of this large, nondenominational Christian organization. In that he acknowledged to his YMCA superiors that he had not handled matters with appropriate discretion, he appears to have gained insight into organizational behavior, consensus building, and proper communications. Additionally, he would have benefited from exposure to the sensitivities, vocabulary, and modes of thinking of non-Lutheran, but equally committed, Christians. And fourth, Maier had his first taste of denominational bureaucracy. Though it seems that the LCBAN had sound reasons for rejecting the inclusion of POW ministry in their work—reasons that Maier did not fully appreciate at the time—this affair demonstrated that denominational structure and polity were not well-suited for urgent ministerial opportunities and rapidly changing circumstances. Memories of this experience likely account, at least in part, for Maier's later-acuminated knack for minimizing LCMS interference with his radio enterprise. He may have gained a few pointers on communicating with diplomatic restraint on those occasions when denominational involvement could not be avoided, as well.

Walther League and academia. In 1920, the LCMS granted official recognition to the Walther League, a national organization for older Lutheran youth and young adults, which had been organized in 1893. In anticipation of the responsibilities likely to come with such an endorsement, and in light of opportunities for growth in membership and ministry, Walther League leaders determined that their organization required the installation of a full-time, national executive secretary (director).[32] Although he had not pre-viously been drawn to youth ministry, Maier responded positively when offered this position, and moved from New England to the organization's headquarters in Milwaukee.[33]

He was particularly pleased that the executive secretary bore responsi-bility for editorship of the organization's monthly magazine, *The Walther League Messenger* (*The Messenger*). Maier was no passive editor, as he used this publication to opine on current events, expound on the responsibilities of Christian living (in particular, related to young people), and to highlight the challenges of, and the necessity for, evangelistic outreach. In a rapidly changing, modern world, making the truth claims of an ancient faith rel-evant and engaged would be Walter Maier's task. Revealing the unconven-tional ways Maier contemplated going about this task, in 1923 he editorialized to *The Messenger's* readers,

> Things aren't the same as in [nineteenth century American Lutheran Leader] Walther's day. . . . For this new age, with its changed conditions and sur-roundings, we need a church that fully realizes its changed responsibilities and its high and holy purpose in a new world. We do not need a new faith . . . but a new, more determined and more universal statement of faith. . . . What our Lu-theran Church needs today is the inspiration of the hour and a God-strengthened determination to follow the new vision which the Lord has revealed to us.[34]

With such a mindset, the energetic executive secretary revitalized the Walther League in rapid fashion, with membership and the number of af-filiated societies doubling—to 50,000 and 886, respectively—within two years of his taking the helm. Existing ministries were strengthened and new programs were implemented.[35] It appeared that the Walther League had its leader for the foreseeable future.

---

[32]Organized as the "General Organization of Lutheran Young Peoples Societies," the Walther League had been established to foster Christian knowledge, worship, and service. It was named in honor of the Rev. C. F. W. Walther, one of the founding fathers of the LCMS. See Jon Pahl, *Hopes and Dreams of All: The International Walther League and Lutheran Youth in American Culture, 1893–1993* (Eugene, OR: Wipf & Stock, 1993), 1-23, 107-8. See also Maier, *A Man Spoke*, 37.

[33]Walther League headquarters would be relocated to Chicago shortly after Maier's tenure began. See Maier, *A Man Spoke*, 53.

[34]As quoted in Pahl, *Hopes and Dreams of All*, 109.

[35]Maier, *A Man Spoke*, 56.

At this two-year mark with the Walther League, however, Concordia Seminary in St. Louis surprised Maier by extending him a call to become a

full professor of Old Testament Interpretation and History, even though he had yet to achieve his PhD degree from Harvard. At the time, Concordia Seminary was the LCMS's flagship institution for preparing pastors, and had recently become the largest Christian seminary in the United States.[36] He accepted this position with the stipulation that he be allowed to continue serving as editor of *The Messenger*—a position he retained for twenty-five years.[37] While teaching at Concordia, Maier eventually finished the necessary research and completed required examina-

Figure 3.3. Maier after receiving his PhD from Harvard University in 1929

tions to earn a PhD from Harvard in 1929. He had shifted his area of concentration to Semitics, which required the acquisition of a working knowledge of ten languages. Prior to granting Maier his doctorate, Harvard had bestowed PhDs in Semitics on only nineteen other scholars in its history.[38]

---

[36]In 1920, Concordia Seminary's enrollment was at 383 students, followed by Southern Baptist—360 students, Princeton—150 students, Drew—150 students, Union (NYC)—146 students, and McCormick—146 students. See Peter Wallace and Mark Noll, "The Students of Princeton Seminary, 1812–1929: A Research Note," *American Presbyterians* 72, no. 3 (Fall 1994): 205.

[37]When Maier began editing *The Messenger*, it was a "modest little sheet" with "limited circulation." By the time Maier reluctantly gave up its editorship in 1945 (due to increasingly demanding responsibilities for TLH and with the National Religious Broadcasters), it had become a high quality, monthly magazine with 70,000 regular subscribers, and an estimated readership of "at least triple that." Whatever the exact numbers, *The Messenger* was one of the largest evangelical-type publications in America at that time. See E. R. Bertermann, "Walter A. Maier, Editor of the Walther League Messenger, 1920–1945: An Appreciation," *The Walther League Messenger* 54, no. 2 (October 1945). See also Ward, *Air of Salvation*, 43.

[38]Maier, *A Man Spoke*, 87-88.

Maier's mastery of Semitics clearly required an uncommon set of intellectual tools—tools that one would not automatically associate with popular mass communication. After all, the audience for radio programming in Hittite was rather petite. It is not difficult to speculate, however, that Maier's nuanced understanding of languages and the subtle power of word choices became a potent aid in reaching broad audiences via radio in years to come. His careful sermon preparation, which will be discussed in chapter 5, reflected such sensitivities. Not only did Maier possess the ability to turn a phrase for maximum impact, but his appreciation of local language and cultural contextualization led to rapid, effective global expansion of TLH, especially during the 1940s.[39]

Rising recognition pre-radio. It is important to understand that during the latter 1920s, Maier's reputation as a pulpit preacher, his visibility as the editor of *The Walther League Messenger*, and his full professorship at one of the country's leading seminaries, generated significant demand for him as a public speaker. What is more, Maier's Christian commentary wrapped in oratorical flourishes drew significant attention in the press, often on a national scale, which in turn led to more speaking opportunities. Maier would go on to attain celebrity status as a radio preacher, and would be quoted frequently in the press until his death. (The breadth and impact of Maier's stature *during* his TLH years will be discussed in greater detail in chapter 8.) But even prior to gaining attention over network airwaves, Maier's visibility as a spokesman for traditional Christianity was on the rise.

Already in 1922, organizers of the St. Louis American Theater Lenten Noonday Services invited Maier to serve as preacher for their series of brief worship services targeting downtown businessmen and professionals. At the conclusion of the Lenten season, they observed that Maier spoke of original Holy Week events "as if he had witnessed them himself," and asked him back on an annual basis for a number of years. Maier's adeptness at relating scriptural texts to the "whole political-social-intellectual milieu

---

[39]For a summary of the international expansion of TLH and Maier's leadership role related thereto, see Kirk Farney, "Bringing Christ to the Nations: Walter A. Maier, *The Lutheran Hour*, and Global Christian Broadcasting," part 1, *Concordia Historical Institute Quarterly* 86, no. 2 (Summer 2013): 48-61, and Farney, "Bringing Christ to the Nations: Walter A. Maier, *The Lutheran Hour*, and Global Christian Broadcasting," part 2, *Concordia Historical Institute Quarterly* 86, no. 3 (Fall 2013): 6-30.

of his era" soon gave rise to speaking engagements around the country. In 1925, he addressed his first mass meeting, as he stood before ten thousand attendees of the Luther Day Festival at Ocean Grove, New Jersey. The enthusiastic reception of the audience resulted in frequent invitations to return to the famed Christian camp. An even larger audience turned out to hear Maier as the featured speaker at the celebration of the quadricentennial publication of Luther's Catechism in June of 1929. Approximately seventy thousand packed Chicago's Soldier Field for this remarkable event. Maier addressed similar Lutheran celebrations in numerous locales.[40] Recapping another of his Ocean Grove addresses, *Time* reported, "With the enthusiasm of a dozen Martin Luthers pelting a dozen devils with inkpots, Rev. Dr. Walter A. Maier of Concordia Theological Seminary . . . flayed 'this cynical, scoffing self-willed generation that bows down before the idol of profit and production, that knows not God and prides itself in this ignorance.'"[41]

In a speaking style and substance increasingly labeled "Luther-like," Maier warned of the evils he saw as increasingly prevalent in the Roaring Twenties. He attacked lax moral standards as evidenced by debased popular entertainment, rising divorce rates, declining personal values, rising alcoholism, abject idleness, unsettling crime rates, and the like. He warned of threats to genuine Christianity posed by modernism, agnosticism, atheism, and legalism.[42] America's downward spiral, especially as evidenced by its decline in active church life, revealed that "we are not as far from Russia as we think we are."[43] Maier saw the problems as not only societal, but also ecclesiastical, as he assailed "pulpit infidels" who obliterated "Christ's truth" and the "ideals of spiritual honesty" in "a manner that would make Judas blush."[44]

Yet he also stressed that "Christianity is not a joy killer," emphasizing that its primary message was about the freedom and peace provided by the

---

[40]Maier, *A Man Spoke*, 75-80, 93.

[41]"Seven Follies," *Time*, July 27, 1931, 28.

[42]"Seven Follies," 76-80.

[43]"25,000 Churches Empty, Lutheran Assembly Told: Ocean Grove Celebrants Hear Atheism Is Progressing," *New York Herald Tribune*, August 6, 1930, 8.

[44]"Denounces the Rise of 'Pulpit Infidels': Professor Maier Tells Walther League We Greet and Fete Apostles of Free Love," *New York Times*, June 22, 1931, 17.

gospel. He advocated a full embrace of life's pleasures, within proper Christian boundaries. Maier surprised many by suggesting that the "flapperism" of the period was sometimes exaggerated as evidence of societal decline. In contrast to other conservative Christian commentators, he went so far as to suggest that "the moderate use" of cosmetics by women was no grave threat to society. Almost as if anticipating the coming Great Depression, Maier also noted the great prosperity of the era, and warned against the idol he feared it had become. He lambasted the "great national sin, the worship of Mammon and the craze for gold." Avarice had become "the cancer eating into the very vitals of our national life."[45]

Maier advocated a rejuvenation of Spirit-led, Christian family life, with appropriate attention to biblical teaching. Using a metaphor that caught the attention of *New York Times* editors, Maier told the 1929 Walther League convention, "The home of yesterday used to be a sanctuary and a veritable haven of spiritual refuge, but today it is hardly more than a human filling station." He continued, "The question used to be 'What shall we do tonight?' and the answer was found in the radiant companionship that encircled the family hearth, but the question today is, 'Where shall we go tonight?' and the answer is found in a series of suggestions which lead very definitely away from the home." What was the solution to the situation Maier described as "a pathetic caricature of true home life" in "uncounted multitudes of American homes"? He suggested a central role for the teachings of Luther's Catechism as a guide for a sound home life.[46]

One of Maier's more noteworthy speeches at this time came at the Institute of Public Affairs at the University of Virginia, on August 9, 1930. (Note that the invitation to speak at this event, and the event itself, occurred prior to the launch of TLH or his ever speaking over a national radio network.) This "was an annual forum in which national leaders in a range of fields met to discuss political, economic and religious problems of the nation." The planners for the event asked Maier to address "church-state relationships." His address, which he titled "The Jeffersonian Ideals of Religious Liberty," would demonstrate Maier's mindset regarding preachers

---

[45]Maier, *A Man Spoke*, 76-80.

[46]"Calls Modern Home Mere 'Filling Station': Walther League Editor Urges Luther's Catechism as Guide to Happy Establishments," *New York Times*, July 17, 1929, 14.

expressing political opinions in their roles as spiritual leaders—a mindset that would be reflected in his radio preaching. The speech caused a bit of a stir.[47]

Maier opened by retracing the history of First Amendment guaranties of religious freedom. He proceeded to praise the church-state wisdom of UVA's founder, Thomas Jefferson, and to draw parallels between the nation's third president and the sixteenth-century German Reformers at Augsburg. While admitting that Jefferson possessed "religious convictions" different from his own, he even made a modest attempt to buff up Jefferson's reputation toward such matters by asserting that he was a more devout man than typically depicted. However, Maier's negative comments about modern clergy spending more time addressing political issues than spiritual matters caught the most attention. Armed with Lutheran "two kingdom" doctrine—though not explicitly referred to as such—and a biting wit, he tore into fellow clerics who brazenly asserted "godly" positions on public policy issues such as minimum wages, foreign affairs, and "regulation of . . . dance-halls." Making no attempt to mince words, Maier flatly stated, "Too many crusading pastors are political imposters; too many Scriptural texts are mere partisan pretexts; too many militant clergymen are really virulent policemen."[48]

Even more controversially, Maier brought up perhaps the hottest policy issue of the day: prohibition. Without claiming that Jefferson would have endorsed its content, Maier argued that Jefferson would have considered the Volstead Act appropriately belonging in the realm of civil legislation. Therefore, speaking on behalf of Jefferson and himself, Maier concluded that the Eighteenth Amendment should not be "assailed or championed . . . by any Church or denominational group." This did not mean, however, that church leaders should be silent regarding the use of alcohol. Maier again claimed common ground with the founding father, stating that Jefferson would have considered it the legitimate "duty of churches to emphasize . . . the virtue of temperance and the vice of drunkenness, yet such indoctrination under no circumstances is to assume a definite political coloring."[49]

---

[47]For the complete text of this speech, see Walter A. Maier, *The Jeffersonian Ideals of Religious Liberty: Address Delivered at the University of Virginia at Charlottesville, Va., August 9, 1930* (St. Louis: Concordia, 1930).

[48]Maier, *Jeffersonian Ideals*, 17-18.

[49]Maier, *Jeffersonian Ideals*, 20-21.

Many of the forum attendees were amazed by Maier's words, including members of the clergy who resented his chastisement.[50] Newspaper reporters scrambled to submit their stories about the speech, to which editors attached such attention-grabbing headlines as "Dr. Maier Attacks Church in Politics: Calls Their Dry Attitudes Unjeffersonian," and "Jefferson Seen as Foe to Church Dry Bickering: Too Many Crusading Pastors, Editor Says."[51] Although the content of his speech was much broader and more erudite, Maier's "preaching" against preachers in politics was summarized as a political commentary of his own, regardless of his intent. The young professor's opinions were gaining weight.

Marriage. One more important development occurred during this key period in Maier's life. Early in his role as director of the Walther League, Maier met Hulda Eickhoff, a school teacher in Indianapolis. Eickhoff drew Maier's attention as she became actively involved in the Walther League in Indiana. Maier asked her to join the national staff, where they worked closely together on League activities, and soon developed a romantic relationship. After Maier assumed his responsibilities as a Concordia professor, he proposed to his charming Lutheran colleague, who shared his passion for the church, and they were married in 1924. From the start, Hulda proved to be an avid and active supporter of Maier's work as a professor and church leader, and later as a radio preacher. Their successful marriage would serve as a source of material (of a general, rather than personal nature) for articles and sermons, and would inspire Maier to publish a bestselling book on marriage, *For Better Not for Worse: A Manual of Christian Matrimony*, in 1935.

In reviewing Maier's formative years and early career, it becomes clear that many of the patterns and skills he employed so successfully in his radio

---

[50]"Churchmen Resent Dr. Maier's Attack: Controversy Develops at Virginia Institute over St. Louisan's Denunciation of Lobbies," *New York Times*, August 11, 1930, 12.

[51]See "Dr. Maier Attacks Church In Politics: Calls Their Dry Attitudes Unjeffersonian," *Daily Boston Globe*, August 10, 1930, A17; "Speaker Attacks Church Dry Lobby: Institute of Public Affairs Hears Editor Speculate on Jefferson's Views," *Washington Post*, August 10, 1930, 3; "Virginia Forum Hears Plea for Jeffersonian Ideals: Told Third President Would Oppose Church's Championship of Prohibition," *New York Herald Tribune*, August 10, 1930, 18; "Jefferson Seen as Foe to Church Dry Bickering: Too Many Crusading Pastors, Editor Says," *Chicago Daily Tribune*, August 10, 1930, 5; "Public Career Training Urged At Virginia: Political Lobbying by Churches Deplored by Dr. Walter A. Maier," *Christian Science Monitor*, August 12, 1930, 3; "Speaker Assails Church Attitude on Prohibition: Politics Declared Not a Church Affair," *Atlanta Constitution*, August 10, 1930, 5C.

ministry were already visible in his pre-radio career. His evangelistic fervor and his determined mindset drove him to find new means of sharing the gospel, unhindered by denominational boundaries and previous methods. The early phases of Fulton Sheen's life were equally formative, in equally traceable ways.

FORMATIVE YEARS—SHEEN

Home life, education, and academia. Fulton Sheen was born in the small, north-central Illinois town of El Paso, on May 8, 1895, the first of four sons of Newton (Newt) and Delia Sheen. While Newt's mother was from Indiana, and believed to be of English extraction, his father and both of Delia's parents were first-generation Irish immigrants who apparently came to the United States in hopes of a better economic life. The infant Sheen was actually christened Peter John Sheen, named after both of his grandfathers. Though there is some confusion as to when he adopted his maternal grandfather's surname, Fulton, as his first name, according to Sheen's autobiography the change occurred when his grandfather replied "Fulton" when asked the child's name during initial enrollment at St. Mary's school in 1900. When confirmed at the age of twelve, Sheen took the name John, thereby finalizing the moniker that would be recognized one day throughout the country and around the globe—Fulton J. Sheen.[52]

As had Walter Maier, Fulton Sheen spent a brief portion of his early childhood living above a family-owned retail store. Newt and his brother were the local hardware purveyors, operating their store in El Paso's modest business district. Newt, Delia, and their young family made a home in the floor above the store, until the store and surrounding businesses burned to the ground when an errand boy carelessly discarded a lighted cigarette. Rather than rebuild the home and business, the family moved to an inherited tract of land near Peoria, where Newt resumed his previous

---

[52]The biographical information in this section is primarily from Sheen's autobiography: Fulton J. Sheen, *Treasure in Clay* (New York: Doubleday, 2008), especially chapters 1–4; and from Thomas C. Reeves, *America's Bishop: The Life and Times of Fulton J. Sheen* (San Francisco: Encounter Books, 2001), especially chapters 1 and 2. See also Kathleen L. Riley, *Fulton J. Sheen: An American Catholic Response to the Twentieth Century* (Staten Island, NY: Society of St. Paul, 2004), especially chapter 1. For a more concise biography of Sheen, which draws heavily from *Treasure in Clay* and *America's Bishop*, see Janel Rodriguez, *Meet Fulton Sheen: Beloved Preacher and Teacher of the Word* (Cincinnati: Servant Books, 2006).

occupation of farming. Not long thereafter, when Fulton was old enough to attend school, the family relocated to Peoria so that he could enroll in St. Mary's school and begin a Catholic education. Newt made a living by managing multiple farming operations from this locale.

From early on, young Sheen demonstrated more interest in religion and learning than in his bucolic surroundings. This was due, at least in part, to the devoutly Catholic environment of the Sheen home. Though not a religious man prior to marrying, Newton had adopted Delia's dedicated faith life, and their children were taught to attend mass regularly, say grace before meals, associate with clergy, read the Bible, and say the rosary nightly. Sheen would later recall, "Our family life was simple and the atmosphere of our home Christian."[53] Just as Anna Maier served as the spiritual anchor for her Lutheran home, Delia Sheen played a similar role in her Catholic home. (In addition, both of these strong but gentle women provided their homes with order and constancy that their respective sons recognized.) Nonetheless, Newt was respected as the head of the house and taught Fulton and his brothers the importance of hard work, especially when they served as hired hands for their father's tenant farmer. The future priest's lack of agricultural enthusiasm did not go unnoticed, as a well-meaning neighbor commented, "Newt, that oldest boy of yours, Fulton, will never be worth a damn. He's always got his nose in a book."[54] Sheen would recall that there was never a time when he did not want to become a priest. While "watching young corn come up under [his] eyes," he would "say the rosary begging for a vocation."[55] By the time he was twelve, Sheen had "a very conscious vocation" to the priesthood, paralleling Walter Maier's own clerical aspirations at the same age.

During Sheen's youth, Roman Catholicism held a substantive position in central Illinois, but was still perceived as an immigrant religious body and effectively subordinate to the Protestant majority. Reflective of small

---

[53]Reeves, *America's Bishop*, 12-13. Newt's embrace of Delia and her Catholicism was not without cost. He had been married previously to a Protestant woman who bore him a daughter. This young wife and mother died soon thereafter, and when Newt decided to marry Delia, his first wife's parents successfully used the courts to gain custody, so as to protect the child from the perils of "popery." It appears that Newt and his other children had minimal contact with the girl after her maternal grandparents adopted her.

[54]Sheen, *Treasure in Clay*, 20.

[55]Quoted in Rodriguez, *Meet Fulton Sheen*, 3.

American towns in general, El Paso had one Catholic church and six Protestant churches when the Sheens resided there.[56] There had been a Catholic presence in the Peoria area (and elsewhere in Illinois and neighboring states) since Father Jacques Marquette and explorer Louis Jolliet stopped at this spot on the Illinois River in 1673, and the good Jesuit missionary baptized a dying Indian infant.[57] Yet the Catholic population in the area remained modest and scattered until the influx of European immigrants, the largest components of which were Irish laborers (followed by Germans), increased in the mid-nineteenth century and continued into the twentieth century.[58]

To enable the church to respond more effectively to ministerial needs, in 1875 Pope Pius IX established the diocese of Peoria, which ran from the Mississippi River to the Indiana border. Two years later, John Lancaster Spalding was consecrated as bishop, a post he would hold until retiring in 1908.[59] Spalding held an impressive academic record, having studied theology, philosophy, and canon law in Louvain and Rome. Notwithstanding that his only bishopric would be this relatively rural region in Illinois, Spalding would prove to be an energetic and influential cleric on the American Catholic scene. His broad vision for Catholicism's potential would influence, and be personified by, the life of Fulton Sheen.

Spalding's was a leading voice in adapting the Roman Catholicism disembarking from European ships, especially from the ports of Ireland, to its new American environs. Having witnessed the economic exploitation of Irish immigrants in New York, Spalding became a strong advocate and facilitator of efforts to colonize immigrant Irish from their Atlantic coast urban squalor and hopelessness, to financial opportunities offered by relatively inexpensive farmland in the Midwest and beyond. The bishop served as president of the Irish Catholic Colonization Association of the United States, from its inception in 1879, to the conclusion of its work in 1892. This organization, whose success was at least partially restrained due to modest

[56]Christopher Owen Lynch, *Selling Catholicism: Bishop Sheen and the Power of Television* (Lexington: University Press of Kentucky, 1998), 17.

[57]See website for the Catholic Diocese of Peoria: cdop.org/. For a more complete history of the Peoria Diocese, see Alice O'Rourke, OP, *The Good Work Begun: Centennial History of Peoria Diocese* (Chicago: Lakeside, 1977).

[58]O'Rourke, *Good Work Begun*, 22–26.

[59]O'Rourke, *Good Work Begun*, 35, 56.

capital resources, relocated Irish immigrant families to agriculturally engaged settlements, primarily in Minnesota, Nebraska, and Arkansas.[60] It should be understood, however, that in Bishop Spalding's eyes, colonization was much more than an enterprise in economic advancement for Americans of Irish extraction.

The "general truth" for which Spalding argued was "that the Irish Catholics are the most important element in the Church of this country, and that their present surroundings and occupations are, for the most part, a hindrance to the fulfillment of the mission which God has given them."[61] The problematic "surroundings" and "occupations" that he had in mind were urban "tenement-houses" and "factory towns," in which duped Catholic workers mistakenly thought they would eventually move up the American ladder of success.[62] Spalding contended that such an environment had become a pernicious "vortex" that weakened Catholic spiritual life and hindered Catholic influence on wayward Protestants.[63] Thus, "all honest attempts to bring about a redistribution of our Catholic population are commendable."[64] Spalding's agenda—and God's, according to the bishop—encompassed tasks beyond agronomy and animal husbandry for "redistributed" Irish Catholics on the prairie. Through virtuous labor on the land, the establishment of stable families, and the nurture of strong faith communities, Spalding envisioned Irish immigrants overcoming "the increasing feebleness of Protestant sectarianism" to usher in the "rebirth of Catholicism amongst the English-speaking peoples."[65] After all, divine providence had provided a precedent in the Middle Ages, when "the monks who converted the barbarians and preserved the writings of the Greeks and Romans were the pioneer farmers of Christendom."[66]

Independent-minded Irish Catholics, as well as those who availed themselves of earlier colonization efforts, had already formed a significant

[60]Sister Mary Evangela Henthorne, BVM, *The Irish Catholic Colonization Association of the United States* (Champaign, IL: Twin City Printing Company, 1932), 7, 11, 100-101.

[61]J. L. Spalding, DD, *The Religious Mission of the Irish People and Catholic Colonization*, 3rd ed. (New York: Catholic Publication Society, 1880), 13.

[62]Spalding, *Religious Mission*, 115, 131-32.

[63]Spalding, *Religious Mission*, 83, 115.

[64]Spalding, *Religious Mission*, 14.

[65]Spalding, *Religious Mission*, 61-62.

[66]Spalding, *Religious Mission*, 71.

presence in Illinois, prior to Spalding's arrival. Fulton Sheen's family was part of this group. At the time of Spalding's installation, Catholics in the Peoria Diocese totaled forty-five thousand, and were served by fifty-one priests.[67] With limited resources, Spalding presided over a period of significant Catholic growth, as diocesan parishes multiplied across the region, largely driven by immigration. When the diocese gained jurisdiction for five additional counties (from the archdiocese of Chicago) in 1880, ninety thousand Catholics resided under Peoria's authority, which equated to 10.8 percent of the population in the area comprising the diocese.[68] This level was only slightly below the 12 percent Catholic makeup of the US population as a whole at that time.[69] When Spalding resigned in 1908, his bishopric was home to 123,500 Catholics. The bishop's emphasis on education was demonstrated by an increase in Catholic schools in the diocese under his leadership, from eighteen in 1878 to seventy in 1908.[70] In the latter nineteenth and early twentieth centuries, anti-Catholicism would occasionally emerge within the Peoria Diocese, but by and large, the Catholic population in the region enjoyed an unmolested existence.[71]

Even while attending to his abundant responsibilities, Bishop Spalding could not help noticing the bright, devout Sheen, while the boy was still in grade school and serving as an altar boy at St. Mary's Cathedral. On a day when the eight-year-old Sheen dropped a wine cruet on the marble floor during mass, the forgiving bishop predicted his future academic and ecclesiastical successes, explaining to the lad that he too would eventually study in Leuven, and "someday you will be just as I am."[72] In 1909, Sheen entered the all-male Spalding Institute, a high school established ten years earlier near St. Mary's Cathedral, in downtown Peoria. (The school was named after one of Spalding's clerical relatives.) Bishop Spalding's dedication to academic advancement would have a significant impact on Sheen's scholarly

[67]John Tracy Ellis, *John Lancaster Spalding: First Bishop of Peoria, American Educator* (Milwaukee: Bruce, 1961), 29.
[68]O'Rourke, *Good Work Begun*, 24, 38.
[69]Reeves, *America's Bishop*, 33.
[70]Ellis, *John Lancaster Spalding*, 29.
[71]O'Rourke, *Good Work Begun*, 52, 74–76.
[72]Sheen, *Treasure in Clay*, 14.

life beyond the halls of the Spalding Institute, as the bishop had earlier been a driving force in the establishment of the Catholic University of America (CUA), an institution at which Sheen would both study and teach in years to come.

Spalding resigned from diocesan leadership in 1908 due to health reasons, and would not live long enough to witness Sheen's ecclesiastical accomplishments. Yet one can speculate that as the aging bishop looked at the young Sheen peering up at him from under his surplice, he saw affirmation of his ministerial visions and priorities. Here was the son of Irish immigrants who had settled on Midwestern lands and established a stable, devout Catholic home. His parents and a robust Catholic school system were training the lad's mind, and strengthening his faith. He would advance through Catholic institutions of higher learning—both domestically and abroad—ultimately taking a leadership position in the Church in the eastern, urban settings from whence many Irish Catholic immigrants had come. From there, he would be able to build up Catholicism on American soil, edifying those in the faith and drawing in those outside the faith, thus fulfilling God's providential role for Irish Catholic immigrants.

On June 16, 1913, Fulton Sheen graduated from the Spalding Institute. As valedictorian of his high school class of seven, Sheen had the honor of delivering one of the commencement speeches. After the class salutatorian, Ralph Buchele spoke on "The Catholic Young Man in Social and Political Life," and classmate James Phalen delivered an oration titled "The Catholic Young Man in Business and Professional Life," Sheen followed with a valedictory address on a topic on which he had contemplated more than most boys his age: "The Catholic Young Man's Duties to his Church."[73] Forty years later Buchele recalled, "I thought I gave a pretty good speech. But when Fulton got up, I felt like taking a back seat. . . . I certainly remember his valedictory speech. It was a real humdinger and the people at the graduation loved it."[74] Interestingly, the Spalding Institute's motto held an unintended prophetic meaning for its alumnus and future *radio* preacher: "*Esse Quam Videre*"—"Be, Rather Than Be Seen."

---

[73]"Spalding Institute Commencement Program," 1913, Fulton J. Sheen Archives (hereafter, Sheen Archives), diocese of Rochester, Rochester, NY, "Memorabilia 1907–1934" file, "1913" folder.
[74]Ken Crotty, "'Spike' Nickname For Bishop Sheen," *Boston Post*, May 11, 1953.

As fall approached, Sheen's path to the priesthood led him to St. Viator College in Bourbonnais, Illinois. He excelled under the Viatorian Fathers.[75] The author of the senior class biography wrote of Sheen, "His favorite pastime is the devouring of endless treatises on philosophy, art, and a hundred other kindred topics with which we ordinary mortals have hardly more than a passing acquaintance." Reflecting Sheen's future visibility more fully than he could have anticipated, the author explained that the Peorian possessed "the fire and enthusiastic optimism of a ray of light," which empowered his "eminently successful course as a star of the first magnitude."[76]

Having studied English, Latin, and German in high school, Sheen continued to expand his linguistic knowledge at St. Viator by completing additional classes in English and Latin, as well as coursework in Greek and French. Wishing to broaden his educational experience, Sheen joined the

Figure 3.4. Dan Sullivan, Charles Hart, and Fulton Sheen on St. Viator College Debate Team, 1914–1915

---

[75]The Viatorian Fathers, also known as Clerics of St. Viator (CSV), is a Catholic order founded in Lyons, in 1835. Their original purpose was to counter the decline of Christian literacy in post-Revolutionary France. After the 1903 suppression of religious schools in France, many Viatorians immigrated to Canada, from which they established educational missions in Illinois and elsewhere. See *The HarperCollins Encyclopedia of Catholicism* (New York: HarperCollins, 1995), s.v. "Viatorian Fathers."

[76]"Fulton J. Sheen, A.B.," *The Viatorian* 34, no. 5 (June 1917).

debating team as a freshman. The debate coach's initial critique of Sheen's oratorical skills did not portend his future mastery. After his coach bluntly informed him that "you're the worst speaker I ever heard," Sheen worked to hone a more "natural" style that would serve him throughout his career. (While Sheen may have developed a natural style, it would be "naturally" rather dramatic.) Such stylistic efforts, along with his innate intellect, developed into an oratorical force with which to be reckoned. Providing a more secular foreshadowing of later comparisons to St. Chrysostom, his academically gifted classmate and fellow debater, Charles A. Hart, referred to Sheen as a "golden-tongued . . . young Demosthenes" who displayed "quick wit, versatility and power of mind," while "flood[ing] you with his striking personality." One of the top two scholars in his class, Sheen was one of the speakers during the graduation day celebrations of 1917.[77]

Upon Sheen's graduation from St. Viator, the diocese of Peoria sent him to St. Paul Seminary in St. Paul, Minnesota. While studying at St. Paul, Sheen came to understand that a priest needed to care about temporal, social concerns as well as the eternal destiny of souls. He also embraced the neo-Thomism championed by Rome, which would influence his thinking from that point on. Once again, Sheen excelled academically, distinguishing himself in biblical studies, church history, apologetics, and moral theology.[78]

Figure 3.5. Sheen and fellow student at St. Paul Seminary

After two years of study at St. Paul, Sheen transferred to CUA en route to doctoral studies in philosophy. Prior to moving to Washington, Sheen had

---

[77]"Fulton J. Sheen, A.B.," *The Viatorian*; Reeves, *America's Bishop*, 22-24.
[78]Reeves, *America's Bishop*, 27-33.

a busy summer. He completed additional academic work at St. Viator so as to attain a master of arts degree. Then, in September, he was ordained a priest by Bishop Edmund Dunne at St. Mary's Cathedral in Peoria.[79] Sheen proceeded from there to spend three years in residence at CUA, serving as chaplain for St. Vincent's Orphan Asylum. He also made himself available to Washington-area parishes, gaining experience in preaching and evangelizing. It was during this period that he gained his first convert—a gravely ill woman with a hostile disposition toward Catholics. This first conversion had a humbling effect on Sheen, who later recalled that the event "illustrates how much Divine Light in the soul, rather than the efforts of the evangelist, produce the harvest."[80] Sheen would devote considerable effort to bringing about conversions over the years that followed, and indeed produced a number of high-profile converts (e.g., Clare Booth Luce, Henry Ford II).

In 1920, Sheen graduated from CUA with two degrees: the bachelor of canon law (JCB) and the bachelor of sacred theology (STB). He proceeded to the leading European center for Thomistic studies—the University of Louvain in Belgium. Sheen's courses covered metaphysics, experimental and rational psychology, cosmology, and modern space and time. Additionally, he was "drenched" in Aristotle, Plato, and the ancients, and "immersed" in Thomas Aquinas.[81] After completing exams and defending his dissertation, "The Spirit of Contemporary Philosophy and the Finite God," Sheen received his PhD in 1923. In light of his academic excellence, the faculty invited him to pursue a highly selective postdoctoral degree—the *Agrégé en Philosophie*—which he attained with "Very Highest Distinction" in 1925.[82] Sheen's dissertation for this degree was published as a book in both England and the United States, under the title *God and Intelligence in Modern Philosophy*. The University of Louvain awarded him the Cardinal Mercier International Philosophy Award, granted once every ten years for the best dissertation in Thomistic philosophy. This was the first time that this award was given to an American.[83]

---

[79]Reeves, *America's Bishop*, 37; Sheen, *Treasure in Clay*, 23.

[80]Reeves, *America's Bishop*, 42.

[81]Reeves, *America's Bishop*, 42, 46.

[82]See Sheen, *Treasure in Clay*, 29-30. The *Agrégé en Philosophie* is referred to as a "super Ph.D." and "a kind of 'super doctorate,'" by two of Sheen's biographers. See Rev. D. Noonan, *Missionary with a Mike* (New York: Pageant, 1968), 6, and Rev. Charles Connor, *The Spiritual Legacy of Archbishop Fulton J. Sheen* (New York: Society of St. Paul/Alba House, 2010), xi.

[83]Riley, *Fulton J. Sheen*, 8-10; Reeves, *America's Bishop*, 53-54.

G. K. Chesterton authored the introduction to Sheen's book, in which he enthusiastically endorsed the content's suitability for marshaling Thomistic thought against the baleful alternatives proffered by modern secularism. Chesterton had initially resisted writing the introduction to Sheen's book because he claimed to "know nothing about philosophy." After Sheen explained to Chesterton that many of the Brit's own writings contained "excellent philosophy," whether or not he thought of his literary output as such, Chesterton agreed to provide an introduction. "After all," Chesterton commented, "we both belong to that great Mystical Body, the Catholic Church, in which we can stand responsible for one another's opinions."[84]

"In this book," his introduction assured, "the Catholic Church comes forward as the one and only real Champion of Reason." In Hogarthian tones, Chesterton railed against those "running after every raving fad of mysticism and credulity," often "seiz[ing] on the sentiment without the reason for it."[85] Sheen had met Chesterton while teaching dogmatic theology at St. Edmund's College and preparing for the *agrégé* in England during the 1924–1925 academic year.[86] On their initial meeting, the formidable British writer no doubt sized up Sheen's mental "horsepower" and came away impressed. When Sheen published *God and Intelligence in Modern Philosophy*, Chesterton clearly appreciated its intellectual and philosophical heft. Yet interestingly, without abandoning his academic endeavors, Sheen would go on to publish much more literature targeted at popular audiences than at scholarly colleagues, much as Chesterton had. While there were apologetic components to Sheen's academic writings, he would tailor such apologetics for a more pedestrian reader, for broader impact, as had Chesterton. In his autobiography, Sheen credits Chesterton as his greatest influence in writing, since the elder Catholic critic "never used a useless word . . . saw the value of a paradox and avoided what was trite."[87] Such influence appears also to

---

[84]"G. K. Chesterton with His American Counterpart," *The Universe*, July 22, 1932.

[85]According to Chesterton, "This sentiment is a sediment; it is the dregs of our dogma about a divine origin." See "Introduction" of Fulton J. Sheen, *God and Intelligence in Modern Philosophy* (New York: IVE, 2009), 9-11. (Original publication by Longmans, Green, 1925.)

[86]Reeves, *America's Bishop*, 52.

[87]Sheen, *Treasure in Clay*, 83. By the early 1930s, Sheen found himself referred to as "the American Chesterton." See "G. K. Chesterton with His American Counterpart." When Chesterton died at the age of sixty-two in 1936, Sheen traveled to England to attend his funeral. See "Funeral Scenes at Beaconsfield," *The Catholic Times* (London), June 19, 1936.

Figure 3.6. 1932 sketch of friends G. K. Chesterton and Sheen by British artist Fred A. Farrell. A similar sketch by Farrell appeared in the London Catholic newspaper *The Universe* in July 1932, referring to Sheen as "the American Chesterton."

have been present when Sheen eventually honed Christian messages for network radio airwaves.

Though Sheen had prepared vigorously for the *agrégé* after completing his PhD, he did not ignore other opportunities to polish his skills for ecclesiastical duty. While studying in Rome during the 1923–1924 academic year, he took voice lessons. Sheen recalled in a 1963 interview that this was the "only training [in public speaking] I ever had"—not counting his experiences on the St. Viator debating team and the ineffective "training for an hour or two from an elocutionist in Washington." Sheen credited these tutoring sessions, which stressed deep breathing and speaking with a full diaphragm, with providing him with the invaluable "key to resonance." The voice teacher "gave me this example, which I never, never forgot. . . . He gave me the example of a rubber ball on a fountain—a water fountain. The rubber ball will bounce on the top of that fountain of water, and the voice will bounce on top of lungs full of air," Sheen explained.[88]

---

[88] William J. Hanford, "A Rhetorical Study of the Radio and Television Speaking of Bishop Fulton John Sheen" (PhD diss., Wayne State University, 1965), 110-11.

Additionally, he gained crosscultural preaching experience during this period, addressing the faithful in such venues as Westminster Cathedral in London and St. Patrick's Church in Soho, all the while earning a reputation for outstanding pulpit oratory.[89] Sheen would end up spending the summers of "six or seven years" living and serving at the latter location, where his knack for winning converts to Catholicism was put to effective use.[90] Finally, the scholarly priest moved to the front of the lecture hall, as he took on teaching assignments—at the aforementioned St. Edmund's College, Ware, which was the seminary of the archdiocese of Westminster, and at the University of Cambridge Summer School.[91]

It was at the conclusion of a lecture on a complex theological theme, while teaching at St. Edmund's, that Sheen learned a valuable lesson on the conveyance of knowledge and ideas. Years later he recalled,

> On the way out of the classroom, I heard one deacon say to another: "Oh, Dr. Sheen is a most extraordinary lecturer, most extraordinary." I said to him: "What did I say?" And in the best British accent he clipped: "I don't quite know." And I answered: "Neither do I." That day I learned that sometimes when you are confusing, you are mistaken for being learned.[92]

This lesson would bear no small amount of fruit in Sheen's classrooms thereafter, and even more when he later addressed the common men and women who tuned into his radio and television programs.

Oxford University and Columbia University immediately offered Sheen teaching positions. As he contemplated such attractive opportunities, Sheen was stunned to be recalled to his home diocese. Bishop Edmund Dunne placed him in parish ministry in the "lower end" of Peoria, at St. Patrick's Church. Though less than thrilled, Sheen poured his energies into pastoral care, and continued to demonstrate an uncanny knack for making converts out of hostile sinners.[93] Decades later, his pastoral supervisor at St. Patrick's,

---

[89] Reeves, *America's Bishop*, 51, 52; Riley, *Fulton J. Sheen*, 6. St. Patrick's-Soho remains proud of having served as Sheen's occasional parish home, noting that he often referred to himself as the "un-appointed curate of the Parish." See www.stpatricksoho.org/about-us/history.

[90] See Sheen, *Treasure in Clay*, 276. Sheen tells of reclaiming a twenty-year-old troubled actress for the church, culminating in her joining a London convent.

[91] Reeves, *America's Bishop*, 51; Riley, *Fulton J. Sheen*, 6.

[92] Sheen, *Treasure in Clay*, 52.

[93] Sheen, *Treasure in Clay*, 59.

Monsignor Patrick Culletin, recalled, "He was a wonderful curate." The aging monsignor remembered Sheen's "terrific energy," and his ability to immediately build a positive rapport with parishioners. Additionally, his series of sermons during Advent and Lent drew capacity crowds in the church's sanctuary. In a matter of months, Sheen grew to love St. Patrick's—so much so that he would return to its pulpit to say his first pontifical mass after being consecrated a bishop in 1951. Over the years, Sheen also preferred to stay in St. Patrick's rectory whenever he returned to Peoria.[94]

Nine months after deploying the intellectual curate to parish ministry, Bishop Dunne summoned the rookie cleric to his office. He told Sheen, "I promised you to Catholic University over a year ago. They told me that with all your traipsing around Europe, you'd be so high-hat you couldn't take orders. But Father Culleton says you've been a good boy at St. Patrick's. So run along to Washington."[95] Dunne had put Sheen through an exercise to test his obedience and instill humility in the wake of his academic success in Europe, and Sheen passed with flying priestly colors. To the nation's capital he went, at which time Sheen was named professor of theology and philosophy at CUA. CUA would be his academic home for the next twenty-five years.

As had been the case with Maier, Sheen's experiences growing up and in his early career laid the groundwork for his successful radio ministry in the years ahead. He learned to navigate and be comfortable in the ecclesiastical environment of the Roman Catholic Church, while also learning to function in the broader community where Catholics were a minority. His keen mind honed through rigorous education, his aptitude for languages, and his oratorical skills sharpened by practice and training, all combined to make him a highly effective communicator. Finally, his sense of calling instilled in him a sense of urgency with which to engage in his evangelistic efforts. Opportunities were on the horizon.

---

[94]Ken Crotty, "Bishop Sheen Quick with Quip Always," *Boston Post*, May 18, 1953.
[95]Crotty, "Bishop Sheen Quick."

Chapter Four

CATCHING THE [AIR]WAVES

SHEEN AND MAIER MOVE TO RADIO

But you shall receive the power of the Holy Ghost coming upon
you, and you shall be witnesses unto me in Jerusalem, and in all
Judea, and Samaria, and even to the uttermost part of the earth.

ACTS 1:8 (DOUAY-RHEIMS VERSION)

RELIGIOUS PROGRAMMING was a significant component of radio broadcasting from the beginning of commercial radio itself. Purveyors of "old-time" religion were quick to grasp "new-fashioned" microphones to spread their message. During the 1920s, numerous religious organizations obtained broadcast licenses and began operating their own stations. Additionally, program directors at both local commercial stations and emerging networks allotted time for religious content to be aired. As more and more households acquired radio sets and tuned in, Christian broadcasters contributed to, as well as benefited from, the growing momentum of this cultural force.

Fulton Sheen and Walter Maier both took to the airwaves in the 1920s, via a variety of local broadcast opportunities. They both transferred their homiletic voices to network hookups in 1930. Soon they built up and retained national (and international) listening audiences in the millions.

They maintained their respective leadership positions as radio preachers until the beginning of the 1950s. Notwithstanding these and other parallels, both clerics would also face their own unique challenges, as they carried on radio ministries.

NETWORK ACCESS

Network radio had come into existence in 1926, when RCA launched NBC, thereby creating a truly national audience. As a public service, NBC soon developed a policy of donating "sustaining" time to broadcasts of the three leading faith groups in the United States—Roman Catholic, Protestant, and Jewish.[1] NBC insisted that radio messages be "nonsectarian and nondenominational," "interpret[ing] religion at its highest and best so that as an educational factor it will bring the individual listener to realize his responsibility to the organized church and to society"—a kind of civil religion to edify the populace. Because NBC's policy stated that the "national religious messages . . . be broadcast by the recognized outstanding leaders of the several faiths as determined by the best counsel and advice available," it looked to what its executives considered representative organizations to choose who met such standards and should go on the air.[2]

NBC allowed the Greater New York Council of Churches to decide which preachers would be featured representing Protestantism. (In 1934, this task would move to the Federal Council of Churches of Christ in America—later the National Council of Churches.) Given the liberal leanings of the leaders of these mainline Protestant bodies, access to NBC's microphones was limited to prominent "progressives," such as Harry Emerson Fosdick, S. Parkes Cadman, and Ralph W. Sockman.[3] As for the

---

[1] As a reminder, "sustaining" time was airtime provided free of charge.

[2] Spencer Miller Jr., "Radio and Religion," *Annals of the American Academy of Political and Social Science* 177 (January 1935): 135-40.

[3] Tona J. Hangen, *Redeeming the Dial: Radio, Religion, & Popular Culture in America* (Chapel Hill: University of North Carolina Press, 2002), 21-25; Mark Ward Sr., *Air of Salvation: The Story of Christian Broadcasting* (Grand Rapids, MI: Baker Books, 1994), 41-49. All three of these clerics served in New York pastorates. Fosdick (1878–1969), the most prominent of the three, filled Baptist, Presbyterian, and nondenominational pulpits, while also serving as a professor of practical theology at New York's Union Theological Seminary. Cadman (1864–1936) was an English-born Methodist pastor who moved to the United States after ordination. He eventually accepted a Congregational pastorate and became a key voice within American Congregationalism. Cadman also wrote a nationally syndicated religious newspaper column. Sockman

Catholic sustaining time slots, NBC handed responsibility to the National Council of Catholic Men (NCCM)—a federation of US lay societies whose purpose was to foster a positive image of Catholicism to non-Catholics.[4] NBC worked with a number of groups regarding sustaining-time Jewish programming, but primarily relied on the oversight of the United Jewish Laymen's Committee.[5]

While NBC had established network religious broadcasting, and had included such programming from its first year of existence, CBS was founded in 1927 and soon offered religion via its own broadcasts. Unlike NBC, CBS was willing to sell broadcasting time to religious programs in its initial years; however, it would soon follow NBC's path and ban paid religious broadcasts. In the early 1930s, CBS did shift to a policy of offering access to a revolving restricted group of "leading representatives of thirteen communions," on a sustaining time basis, under the condition that their messages possessed "a constructive character."[6] Yet a third network appeared in 1934, when a group of broadcasters formed the cooperative Mutual Broadcasting System (MBS). MBS, the self-promoted "Network for All America," modified its policies regarding religious programming over time, but would consistently accommodate paid religious broadcasts.

THE CATHOLIC HOUR—BEGINNINGS, CONTROL, CHALLENGES, SUSTENANCE

NBC approached American Catholic Church officials in 1928, with an offer of airtime and studio space in New York for a regular Catholic radio broadcast. Apparently, NBC expressed a preference for dealing with a "lay-run" Catholic organization. Additionally, such an organization was to be "thoroughly representative of the Catholics of the country and . . . authorized

---

(1889–1970) was a leading Methodist pastor, who also served as a professor of practical theology at Union Theological Seminary.

[4]"N.C.C.M. Inaugurates Weekly 'Catholic Hour,'" *N.C.W.C. Review* 12, no. 3 (March 1930): 15; Charles A. McMahon, "The First Year of the Catholic Hour," *N.C.W.C. Review* 13, no. 3 (March 1931): 9–11.

[5]See David S. Siegel and Susan Siegel, *Radio and the Jews: The Untold Story of How Radio Influenced America's Image of Jews, 1920s–1950s* (Yorktown Heights, NY: Book Hunter, 2007), 157–66; *The Word of God: Fifteen Years of Religious Broadcasts; The National Broadcasting Company, 1926–1941* (this commemorative/promotional booklet bears no copyright, but appears to have been produced by NBC, presumably in New York, in 1941 or 1942), 10.

[6]Miller, "Radio and Religion," 137.

by the church."[7] Thus, the NCCM was the natural organization to fill the role of establishing and producing the *Catholic Hour*.[8]

Given its mission, the NCCM was eager to respond, especially in the midst of the pronounced anti-Catholic bigotry of the late 1920s. Such had been exhibited only too well in the virulent anti-Catholicism directed toward Democratic candidate Al Smith, the Catholic governor of New York, during the 1928 presidential campaign. In their November 1928 convention, disconcerted NCCM delegates voted to step up their efforts to "fill in the valleys of ignorance and level off the mountains of prejudice about the Catholic Church and its relation to the American scene."[9] Surely if anti-Catholic Americans only understood their genuflecting co-citizens better, their negative opinions would dissipate. And so to put a positive face on its faithful, the NCCM entered into a contract with NBC, and the CH went on the air in early 1930. The CH would continue under the auspices of the NCCM throughout and beyond Fulton Sheen's tenure on the program.

Though NBC was offering airtime to the CH gratis, the NCCM still needed to cover the production cost of the program, plus "money . . . for an administrative, stenographic, and clerical staff, for music, for travelling expenses and at least a gesture toward an honorarium for the speakers, for postage, telephone, and telegraph."[10] During the first year, these expenses came to roughly eight hundred dollars per week. The NCCM raised the necessary funds via "voluntary subscriptions," an effort jump-started by the Knights of Columbus, which pledged "the magnificent sum" of five thousand dollars for the first year of broadcasts, prior to the CH going on the air. In confirming his organization's commitment, Supreme Knight Martin H. Carmody wrote, "I feel no hesitancy in giving assurance of the whole-hearted

---

[7] Alexander Pavuk, "Constructing a Catholic Church Out of Thin Air: *Catholic Hour's* Early Years on NBC Radio," *American Catholic Studies* 118, no. 4 (2007): 39-40.

[8] The NCCM was a subgroup of the National Catholic Welfare Council (NCWC), which was indeed lay run, but had been sanctioned by the American Catholic bishops in 1919. See Pavuk, "Constructing a Catholic Church," 40; "Brief History of the N.C.C.M.," *National Council of Catholic Men Monthly Bulletin* 1, no. 3 (June 1933): 1-2.

[9] See Pavuk, "Constructing a Catholic Church," 42; Edward J. Heffron, "Ten Years of the Catholic Hour," *The Ecclesiastical Review* 102 (January–June, 1940): 238; "20th Anniversary Program of the Catholic Hour," *The Catholic Hour, 1930–1950* (New York: The National Broadcasting Company, 1950). (This is a commemorative/promotional booklet published by NBC to celebrate the success of the CH, but to also call attention to the network's commitment to religious programming.)

[10] Heffron, "Ten Years of the Catholic Hour," 239.

support of the K. of C. body to the splendid work contemplated."[11] Remaining first-year funding was provided by "about seventy-five men who . . . donated sums ranging from $100 to $1,000," and "approximately two hundred and fifty individuals" who gave "smaller sums which together aggregate about $3,000." Combined subscriptions came to thirty-two thousand dollars during the CH's first year, which covered actual expenses.[12] Annual production and related costs increased only modestly over the next ten years, falling within the thirty-five- to forty-thousand-dollar range in 1940.[13]

Raising necessary funds for the CH was no small task, especially in the midst of the Great Depression. Yet because NBC provided the CH sustaining time, the financial resources required to keep the program on the air were a fraction of those required to maintain airwave access for programs such as TLH, which had to pay commercial rates for airtime. What is more, because the NCCM was able to solicit the relatively modest funding needs of CH production, CH's speakers, including its most popular speaker, Fulton Sheen, were shielded from primary fundraising tasks. The more demanding realities of TLH's financial situation would require Walter Maier to shoulder much of the responsibility for ongoing fundraising, as will be described in subsequent sections.[14]

As they prepared to take the CH to the airwaves, NCCM leaders sought "priests noted for their scholarship and eloquence" to launch the program. The inaugural network broadcast occurred on March 2, 1930, as Patrick Cardinal Hayes, archbishop of New York, dedicated the CH to the "glory of God 'for the American people.'" NBC propelled the archbishop's voice over an initial chain of twenty-two stations. What is often overlooked is that NBC had

---

[11]"N.C.C.M. Inaugurates Weekly 'Catholic Hour,'" 15.

[12]McMahon, "First Year of the Catholic Hour," 10.

[13]Heffron, "Ten Years of the Catholic Hour," 245.

[14]Although Sheen did not have to work actively to raise funds for network access, he was, in fact, quite active as a fundraiser for Catholic causes. Sheen was a captivating dinner and pulpit speaker, who generated financial responses from audiences and congregations in countless local venues. (See "Memorabilia" files, Sheen Archives, Rochester.) His periodic appeals to radio and television listeners to "send in a dime for the poor" generated tremendous responses. As the national director for the Society for the Propagation of the Faith, a position to which he was appointed in 1950, Sheen is credited with raising "more money for the poor than any other American Catholic, an effort that was augmented by the donation of more than $10 million of his personal earnings." See Thomas C. Reeves, *America's Bishop: The Life and Times of Fulton J. Sheen* (San Francisco: Encounter Books, 2001), 4; Fulton J. Sheen, *Treasure in Clay* (New York: Doubleday, 2008), 67-69.

offered the first program to seventy-three stations, but only 30 percent chose to carry it—either because of latent anti-Catholicism, or out of concern that listenership for such a program would be too low to warrant giving up the airtime.[15] Setting the tone for future messages, Hayes declared, "The purpose of the Catholic Hour is not to triumph or to boast; not to attack or blame; but to serve . . . with good will, with kindness and with Christ-like sympathy for all."[16] In the first year of CH broadcasts, numerous bishops, academics, and pastors served in the capacity of CH speaker. As a prominent professor at a leading Catholic university, Fulton Sheen was included on this roster.[17]

Rising recognition—pre-radio. Sheen had already built a reputation as an outstanding public speaker, preaching series of sermons from a number of visible pulpits in eastern US cities, including at St. Patrick's Cathedral in New York. His St. Patrick's sermons were often quoted extensively in the pages of New York newspapers. Each excellent oration seemed to lead to new invitations. It is important to understand that prior to attaining celebrity via radio, Sheen was in high demand as a speaker at numerous communion breakfasts, Catholic women's conferences, Knights of Columbus celebrations, Catholic teacher conventions, college commencement exercises, lecture halls, and Holy Name Society banquets across the country. More importantly, the attention generated by Sheen's speaking appearances had led to his first radio appearance over New York's WLWL, in 1927. This series of Lenten sermons was sponsored by the Paulist order of New York, which sought a cleric who could carry out their "mission of teaching the truth about Catholic faith and exerting a greater influence on American society."[18]

As a public orator, Sheen's messages were often distinctly Catholic, but he spoke on a wide range of topics, whether from a podium or a pulpit. He was intent on engaging ancient truths with contemporary thought and life, and his skill in delivery was unmatched. Whether speaking on Christian doctrine, philosophy, science, education, history, or any of a number of

---

[15] *A Nationwide Audience for God* (Washington, D.C: NCCM, 1940). This promotional booklet can be found in the "Catholic Hour I" file, "History" folder, Sheen Archives, Rochester, NY.

[16] As quoted in *The Catholic Hour, 1930–1950*.

[17] McMahon, "First Year of the Catholic Hour," 11.

[18] Kathleen Riley Fields, "Bishop Fulton Sheen: An American Catholic Response to the Twentieth Century" (PhD diss., University of Notre Dame, 1988), 95, 128; Sheen, *Treasure in Clay*, 66. Several sources, seemingly based on Sheen's own autobiography, date his first radio sermon in 1928; however, Fields discovered correspondence indicating a 1927 radio debut.

other subjects, Sheen emphasized God's eternal "Truth," humanity's obligation to pursue it, and the Christian's commission to share it. He elaborated on these themes in an interview for the Catholic periodical, *The Queen's Work*, in 1931. He warned against the increasingly prevalent "idea of temporalism," whereby "supposedly great thinkers are guided by the principle that the latest is the truest."

Sheen claimed that the outgrowth of such misguided assumptions was an increasingly common drift from orthodox profundity to unorthodox novelty. He lamented, "No man can gain a hearing by saying that two plus two equals four; but there is no limit to the size of his audience when he says that two plus two equals six." "Novelty has its charms," he conceded. Thus, convincing others of Christian truths was becoming more difficult "for want of a common denominator." "No common denominator" existed in the twentieth century, according to Sheen, "except science and our psychological needs and aspirations." A new strategy for truth sharing was called for and Sheen had one, which he had already adapted to congregations and audiences. He explained, "The first way is to establish a common denominator . . . by discussing things that [the listeners] are primarily interested in." "Secondly, we must try to present the eternal truths in a new and modern way: retain the content but vary the expression. . . . Then, thirdly, we must not hurl syllogisms at the modern world. . . . The world today is convinced not by formal arguments, but by showing that one truth which it does not accept fits into another truth which it does accept," Sheen concluded.[19] Such thinking was now going to be used to craft Sheen's radio sermons.

On the day that he gave his very first CH address, the *Boston Globe* referred to Sheen as "one of the foremost scholars in the Catholic church in this country and known as an eloquent speaker both here and in Europe."[20] His fame was about to soar to greater heights, thanks to America's newfound love for voices entering their living rooms through electronic audio devices. In the words of Sheen biographer Kathleen L. Riley, the eloquent priest and scholar proved to be the "right man in the right place at the right time."[21]

---

[19]Margaret Mary Gannon, "Dr. Fulton Sheen, Philosopher and Catholic-Hour Celebrity," *The Queen's Work* (St. Louis), April 1, 1931, 1-2, 9.

[20]"Rev. Dr. Sheen in Catholic Hour," *Daily Boston Globe*, March 9, 1930, A57.

[21]Kathleen L. Riley, *Fulton J. Sheen: An American Catholic Response to the Twentieth Century* (Staten Island, NY: Society of St. Paul, 2004), 58.

The **Catholic Hour** *debut.* NBC gave CH a primetime Sunday evening slot that led into the popular the *Fred Allen Show*. Sheen premiered on March 9, 1930, choosing as a theme "a popular presentation of the Christian doctrine on the existence of God, the divinity of Christ, the Church and the spiritual life."[22] In this sermon titled "Man's Quest for God," Sheen reflected his Thomistic mindset and presented questions that he would explore with his audience in the years to come:

> The quest for God is essentially the search for the full account and meaning of life. If we but had the power to take our soul from our body, put it in a crucible, and distil out the meaning of that quest, what would we find it to be? If we could but make the inmost heart of all humanity speak out its inmost yearnings, what would we discover them to be? Would we not find that every heart and mind and soul in creation desires fundamentally three realities and only three realities—Life, Truth, and Love? In fact, so deep are these realities, Being, Truth, and Love, that we can say the whole universe overflows with them.[23]

Even before the CH went on the air, the Catholic press highlighted its denomination's entry into the network radio world. Once the CH actually commenced, such press coverage only intensified. Perhaps more importantly, the secular press called attention to Sheen and the CH. For instance, the *New York Times* ran a daily listing of all radio programming in the New York area. At the top center of each day's broadcast page, the editors would highlight ten to fifteen programs under the heading, "Outstanding Events on the Air Today." Shortly after Sheen's first broadcast, the *Times* began listing his broadcasts among such events. This was not inconsequential, as his name now appeared on the same list as more established Protestant radio preachers, such as S. Parkes Cadman and Harry Emerson Fosdick, who had been so recognized for some time.[24] It should also be noted that the large majority of the featured programs were not religious in nature, but were entertainment or informational in content. Numerous newspapers across the country began listing the eloquent Sheen and the CH with their

---

[22]Fields, "Bishop Fulton Sheen," 101; Sheen, *Treasure in Clay*, 66-67.

[23]Fulton J. Sheen, *The Divine Romance* (New York: Century, 1930), 3.

[24]For examples, see "Outstanding Events on the Air Today," *New York Times*, March 9, 1930, 157; "Outstanding Events on the Air Today," *New York Times*, March 23, 1930, XX13; "Outstanding Events on the Air Today," *New York Times*, April 6, 1930, 153.

selections of other noteworthy programming.[25] Over time, the same newspaper editors developed a habit of quoting Sheen's radio sermons rather frequently in their pages.

The CH began as an hour-long program, but was shortened to a half-hour format in late 1931, along with a general shift toward shorter broadcasts.[26] After his initial appearances on the CH, Sheen became the most popular speaker, and soon became the principal CH sermonizer.[27] He would typically deliver a series of addresses that ran from Christmas or the first of the year through the Lenten season.[28] During each radio season, the NCCM would employ six to nine speakers to deliver CH radio talks. Yet only Sheen and James M. Gillis were annual participants in the lineup—the former until 1952, the latter until 1942. In fact, the majority of CH speakers served for a single talk or series of talks. More specifically, in the period from the CH's initial broadcast through 1940, sixty-four priests served as CH speakers. Of those, aside from Sheen and Gillis, only one speaker served as many as three times, nine served twice, and the remainder served only once.[29]

While Paulist priest and the *Catholic World* editor Gillis enjoyed a significant following for an extended period, Sheen was clearly the CH "star"— both in relation to radio competition generally, and when compared to other CH speakers.[30] As *Pageant* magazine reported, "To nobody's astonishment,

---

[25]For examples, see "This Week's Radio Entertainment," *Washington Post*, April 13, 1930, A5; "This Week's Radio Entertainment," *Washington Post*, April 20, 1930, A5; "Features on Air Tonight," *Berkeley Daily Gazette*, March 29, 1930, 2; "Youth Hour on Air Today," *Oakland Tribune*, April 6, 1930; "Sermons About Palm Sunday to Be on Air Today," *Sioux City Sunday Journal*, 1.

[26]Pavuk, "Constructing a Catholic Church," 46-47; "Catholic Hour Now Broadcast Each Sunday from 6 to 6:30 P.M., Eastern Standard Time," *N.C.W.C. Review* 13, no. 12 December, 1931.

[27]Reeves, *America's Bishop*, 79.

[28]Riley, *Fulton J. Sheen*, 63-64.

[29]See "List of Clergymen Officiating on Programs," *The Word of God: Fifteen Years of Religious Broadcasts*.

[30]As editor of the *Catholic World* and as a visible public speaker, James Gillis was not bashful about expressing strong political views. While Gillis generally abided "by the rules" against politicizing his CH broadcasts, NCCM leadership apparently concluded that he was too controversial to be associated with their religious program. By the end of 1942, their invitations for him to appear on the CH had ceased. The Paulist departed the CH somewhat embittered. For greater detail of Gillis's involvement in, and dismissal from, the CH, see Richard Gribble, CSC, *Guardian of America: The Life of James Martin Gillis, C.S.P.* (Mahwah, NJ: Paulist Press, 1998), 118-22, 163-77. For a description of Gillis's political views and their expression, and some similarities in these views to those of radio priest Charles Coughlin, see Richard Gribble, CSC, "The Other Radio Priest: James Gillis's Opposition to Franklin Delano Roosevelt's Foreign Policy," *Journal of Church and State* 44 (2003) 501-19.

the [*Catholic Hour's*] rating, which is the trade term for the size of its listening audience, reaches 4.6 as compared with the average of 3.1 which prevails when [Sheen] is not on hand."[31] His speeches and radio sermons were quoted extensively in the Catholic and secular presses. In addition to selling his radio sermons in book form after each season, Sheen "at the urgent behest of his listeners," mailed out over three million copies of his broadcasts between 1930 and 1950.[32] His speaking and preaching engagements, which had been plentiful even before the CH built his popularity, became more frequent and geographically dispersed—averaging 150 speeches and sermons per year.[33] Moreover, his photographic images were just short of ubiquitous, displayed in newspapers, magazines, promotional mailings, posters, and brochures.[34]

When NBC opened its new broadcasting studios in Radio City, New York, in 1933, its producers invited the on-air blessing of the CH's most popular priest. In a nationwide broadcast, Sheen turned the tables on the provider of CH's sustaining time, assigning to the network a higher calling than perhaps it sought. Rather than speak of radio as a mouthpiece for religion, he declared, "This is what religion can do for radio. . . . It can be radio's spokesman, praise God for it, thank God for it, love God for it, and in a word, like the three youths in the fiery furnace, sing a living *Benedicite* to God the Creator." He noted how fitting it was that with the opening of Radio City, "one of the first messages sent out on the air should be light's thanks to the Creator of Light, and radio's thanks to the Radiant God." Drawing hyperbolic parallels between Radio City and the heavenly city, Sheen noted that there exists "a heavenly City of Light, from whence God is sending out His message of life and peace and grace," and "just as we cannot receive the comforts of Radio City without being attuned to its waves, so neither can we receive the blessings of God without being attuned to His Laws." He concluded by exhorting his listeners to be "tuned in to the sweet inspirations of the Infinite God."[35]

---

[31]George Frazier, "Fulton J. Sheen: Unprofitable Servant," *Pageant* 5, no. 12 (June 1950): 40.

[32]Frazier, "Fulton J. Sheen," 41. Most of the proceeds of Sheen's book sales were donated to Catholic charitable causes, especially the Society for the Propagation of the Faith, over the course of his career.

[33]Dickson Terry, "His Voice Is Known to Millions," *St. Louis Post-Dispatch*, March 31, 1947.

[34]For extensive examples, see "Press Clippings" and "Memorabilia" files, Sheen Archives, Rochester.

[35]See NCWC News Service press release, "Religious Service to Radio Is Cited by Dr. Fulton J. Sheen," dated Nov. 20, 1933, found in "Memorabilia 1907–1934" file, "1933" folder, Sheen

From early on in his radio ministry, even Vatican observers took note of Sheen's impact as a spokesman for truths catholic and Catholic. On June 5, 1934, Sheen was named by Pope Pius XI as a papal chamberlain, with the title of "Very Reverend Monsignor," which garnered no small amount of additional press in the United States.[36] The editors of the *Catholic University Bulletin* noted of their faculty member, "Although young in years, Monsignor Sheen's name has become a household word in the Catholic homes of the nation. A rare combination of felicitous expression and power of oratory has made him one of America's most popular radio preachers." Exhibiting tones of admiration and perhaps envy, they concluded, "His legion of friends wish that among the many other blessings with which he is endowed he may continue to enjoy the physical vigor necessary for a man who undertakes such an ambitious program of priestly service."[37] The following month, the pope granted Sheen an audience at the Vatican, during which he "commended Msgr. Sheen for his apostolic work on the Catholic Hour . . . and extended his Apostolic Blessing to him and his thousands of radio listeners." While the bishop of Rome also commended Sheen on his latest book and his broader scholarly contributions, his work on the CH drew the greatest admiration.[38]

Shortly thereafter, New York's Patrick Cardinal Hayes sent Sheen a letter telling him "how elated" he was "to learn of the distinguished recognition you have received from the Holy Father." He expressed appreciation for

---

Archives, Rochester. Sheen's Protestant and Jewish counterparts at Radio City's on-air opening offered their own rhetorical linkages between the divine purposes and those of NBC. Dr. John W. Langdale, radio chairman of the Federal Council of Churches, confidently asserted, "We recognize that the Providence of God, the genius of man and the generosity of the National Broadcasting Company are providing for religion the farthest reaching opportunity it ever had." Rabbi David de Sola Pool drew parallels between Talmudic references to "radio" (historically meaning "the spirit of rainfall"), and radio of the twentieth century network variety. Excitedly mixing metaphors, he promised, "The inauguration of the studios of [NBC] means the opening of a new storehouse of potential blessing for mankind. We are this day consecrating a mighty workshop of the most powerful agency." See "Interfaith Dedication Ceremonies at Radio City," *The Word of God: Fifteen Years of Religious Broadcasts.*

[36] See "Dr. F. J. Sheen Made Monsignor by the Holy Father," *New World* (Chicago), June 29, 1934; "University Teacher and Orator Made Monsignor," *The Catholic University Bulletin* 2, no. 6 (September 1934): 3. Many additional examples of press coverage of this papal recognition can be found in the "Press Clippings" files, "1934" folder, in the Sheen Archives, Rochester.

[37] "University Teacher and Orator," 3.

[38] Msgr. Enrico Pucci, "'Catholic Hour' Lectures by Monsignor Fulton Sheen Praised by Holy Father," *Catholic Messenger* (Davenport), August 9, 1934.

Sheen's "exceptional service" in teaching and preaching, and specifically
noted his work on radio, all rendering "such recognition inevitable." Hayes
concluded, "May the Lord bless you that you may continue your own unique
mission of glorifying God and sanctifying souls."[39]

Sheen's contract with the NCCM required that "the speaker expresses the
views of all of us as Catholics." Additionally, "doctrine should be presented in
a positive rather than a negative manner," and "phrases which imply antagonism or which irritate" were to be avoided. Yet, so long as Sheen did not
violate Catholic dogmatic boundaries, the contract explicitly granted "the
widest liberty possible" to cover topics and express opinions that were his own.
While the contract demanded submission of each radio address in advance of
the broadcast, and the NCCM's Director of Speakers' Program had complete
license to "delete or amend" as he saw fit to bring addresses "into conformity,"
it does not appear that the NCCM served as a meddlesome editor. In short,
scholarly cleric Sheen and the devoted lay leaders of the NCCM forged a
positive, mutually beneficial relationship from the start of the CH—a relationship based on common theology, reciprocal trust, and shared objectives.

While a key NCCM goal was to combat anti-Catholic bigotry and gain
for Catholicism a more comfortable seat at the table of American Christianity, and while it often stated that the CH was not designed to be a proselytizing vehicle, one is struck by the distinctly Christian, missional nature of
their enterprise. They were not trying to espouse some "lowest common
denominator" religiosity. Though they may have been pleased to contribute
to American civil religion, they had no intention of limiting their efforts to
something that bland. At the beginning of the contract's terms, the parties
thereto agree: "The purpose of this broadcast being a clear and capable explanation to the American public of the Catholic faith and of life guided by
the faith, the charity of Christ and of His Church that seeks to save souls
shall dominate and control all the radio talks."[40] The stakes were high, in
both temporal and eternal terms, and no one bought into that more than
the Reverend Doctor Sheen.

---

[39]Letter from Cardinal Hayes to Very Rev. Monsignor Fulton J. Sheen, DD, "Correspondence A-F"
    file, "P. Cardinal Hayes, 1933–1935" folder, Sheen Archives, Rochester.
[40]See "Contract between the National Council of Catholic Men and Rev. Dr. Fulton J. Sheen,"
    "Memorabilia File 1907–1934," "1933" folder, Sheen Archives, Rochester.

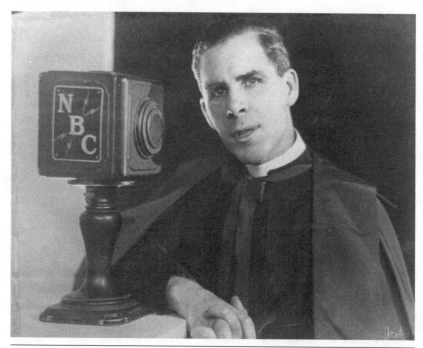

Figure 4.1. Promotional photograph of Monsignor Fulton Sheen at the NBC radio microphone

Sheen marveled at the evangelistic power radio gave him: "Radio has made it possible to address more souls in the space of thirty minutes than St. Paul did in all his missionary journeys. . . . Broadcasting . . . [produces] the distant echoes of the Gospel."[41] NBC would continue to expand, along with network members who chose to broadcast the CH, giving Sheen access to fifty-four stations by 1933.[42] By the end of the decade, NBC offered the program to one hundred stations, 95 percent of which chose to carry the CH.[43] Correspondence from listeners indicated that Sheen had a profound effect on those tuning in. Roughly three thousand listeners per month were writing to him by 1933. By 1940, that number would sometimes be reached on a daily basis.[44] Additionally, listeners all over the world tuned into Sheen's messages via shortwave radio. Within ten years of first speaking into an NBC microphone, Sheen had built an audience estimated by the NCCM at

---

[41] As quoted in Fields, "Bishop Fulton J. Sheen," 94.
[42] Reeves, *America's Bishop*, 81.
[43] See promotional booklet *A Nationwide Audience for God* (Washington, DC: NCCM, 1940).
[44] Reeves, *America's Bishop*, 81, 110.

17.5 million.[45] Sheen would remain the chief voice of the CH until 1952, when he would redeploy his energies to television.[46] At that time, the CH was broadcast via 127 domestic radio stations, located in forty-two states, the District of Columbia, and Hawaii.[47] At the height of his radio popularity, it was estimated that up to one-third of his audience was non-Catholic.[48] It is interesting that Sheen's popularity with non-Catholic audiences became even more pronounced when he moved to television, since his distinctly Catholic identity, if not his message, was then reinforced by visual presentation of his episcopal regalia and other Catholic symbols. Sheen accepted these developments as a natural, perhaps providential, progression, not without precedent, as he observed, "Radio is like the Old Testament, hearing wisdom, without seeing; television is like the New Testament because in it the wisdom becomes flesh and dwells among us."[49]

THE LUTHERAN HOUR—BEGINNINGS, CONTROL, CHALLENGES, SUSTENANCE

While Fulton Sheen responded favorably when presented the opportunity to preach over the airwaves, Walter Maier energetically pursued radio broadcasting as a gospel medium from the early 1920s. Less than a year after KDKA of Pittsburgh had birthed commercial radio in November of 1920, Maier was contemplating the establishment of a Lutheran radio station. In August 1921, while still serving as executive secretary for the Walther League, he traveled to Denver for the dedication of the Wheat Ridge Sanitarium—a tuberculosis treatment facility underwritten by the League. While there, Maier shared a room with Richard Kretzschmar, a St. Louis pastor and chairman of the Board of Control of Concordia Seminary. In what was likely the first serious discussion of the potential erection of a Lutheran radio station, these visionary roommates discussed the possibility of attaching

---

[45]Edward J. Heffron, *Ten Years of the Catholic Hour* (Washington, DC: NCCM, 1940), 5. (This booklet is a "slightly revised" version of Heffron's previously cited article of the same name that appeared in *The Ecclesiastical Review* in March 1940.)

[46]Heffron, *Ten Years of the Catholic Hour*, 238. See Michael E. Starr, "Prime Time Jesus," *Cultural Correspondence*, no. 4 (Spring 1977): 21.

[47]Fulton J. Sheen, *The Life of Christ* (Washington, DC: NCCM, 1952), 110.

[48]Janel Rodriguez, *Meet Fulton Sheen: Beloved Preacher and Teacher of the Word* (Cincinnati: Servant Books, 2006), 17.

[49]See Starr, "Prime Time Jesus," 21.

such a project to the LCMS's Concordia Publishing House or to Concordia Seminary.[50] This budding friendship was to bear fruit in the very near future.

Maier first stepped in front of a radio microphone in mid-1922, when he addressed the annual convention of the Walther League in Louisville. As he experienced firsthand the technological reality of projecting his gospel message beyond the walls confining young Lutherans in their Kentucky meeting hall, to varied listeners in varied locales donning headphones attached to crystal sets, Maier's enthusiasm for the medium only grew. Around the same time of this Walther League address, after moving from his position as executive secretary of the League to professorial duties at the Concordia Seminary, Maier struck up a friendship with a St. Louis engineering student and neighbor, Herman Gihring. Gihring helped him understand the technical possibilities and challenges of establishing a radio station, while also serving as a sounding board for Maier's preliminary thoughts on Christian broadcasting.[51]

In March of the following year, Maier penned an editorial for *The Messenger*, titled, "Why Not a Lutheran Broadcasting Station?" Maier began by stating that he had been listening to broadcasts over his own crystal set, and was not pleased with what he heard. Scientific lectures "made our ears tingle" as they "insult[ed] . . . Biblical Christianity." He warned of the "wishy-washy moral talks, misnamed sermons" that were regularly broadcast. A Lutheran station to "send a one hundred per cent Gospel message from coast to coast," and eventually "even to Europe," could serve as a necessary countermeasure, argued Maier. With uncharacteristic understatement, he declared, "It seems that the radio sermon is destined to play a somewhat important role in American life."

Interestingly, in a rhetorical move meant to both compliment a perceived ecclesiastical competitor and to prime the competitive juices of his fellow

---

[50]Shawn Barnett, "Keep Forward—Upward Onward!," *Historical Footnotes Concordia Historical Institute* 58, no. 3 (Fall 2013): 2.

[51]Maier, *A Man Spoke*, 69-71; Ward, *Air of Salvation*, 43-44. While Maier gathered enough technical knowledge to understand the operational requirements of radio broadcasting, his son points out that Maier was not naturally drawn to new technology or gadgets. He allowed seminary students to set up their ham radio sets in his home; however, his interest was primarily in radio as a communication medium, rather than as a technological achievement. The evangelistically progressive Old Testament professor was content to appreciate what he termed "the miracle of radio," without delving into its scientific intricacies. (Paul L. Maier interview with author, May 16, 2013.)

Lutherans, Maier noted that the Catholic Church had already recognized radio's potential. He directly quoted nearly a full paragraph from a current issue of *Catholic World* that had advocated for a Catholic "wireless transmitting station." Its author had argued that such an ethereal venture would "reach untold millions at the very poles of the world," would issue "a swift reply to every calumny against the church," and plant the "seed of further conversions." Maier's implication was clear: if the Catholics could wield this new tool, why not those who "can bring the message of pure Lutheran Christianity?" Such would "offer a powerful and effective antidote against the many and varied forms of unbelief" that were becoming more prevalent. Maier pointed to the potential to reach souls that the Lutheran Church would not otherwise reach, and to do so in a "least expensive" manner. And, displaying a self-awareness not possessed by many American Lutherans at that time, Maier promised that radio could "assist us in removing the misunderstanding which makes people view our faith as that of a foreign church."[52]

In February 1923, Kretzschmar, backed by Maier, proposed the launch of a radio station to the seminary's Board of Control. The board approved the proposal, but it was a hollow victory since no funds were appropriated for actual implementation.[53] Faculty support for a radio station was mixed. While there were indeed supporters, practical considerations such as financial constraints and the long-term viability of radio itself worried some faculty members.[54] Theodore Graebner, Concordia professor and editor of the LCMS's the *Lutheran Witness* magazine, had written several pieces during the previous year warning about the possible temptations radio could bring into Christian homes. Additionally, many were tepid because of their own uncertainty as to the Lutherans' place in American Christianity. During this period many Lutherans—theologians, pastors, and laymen— wrestled with the trade-offs between neat denominational boundaries and broader evangelistic opportunities on the American field. In other words, even if practical constraints could be overcome, some questioned whether Lutherans, or the LCMS more specifically, *should* step further into the

---

[52]Walter A. Maier, "Why Not a Lutheran Radio Station?," *Walther League Messenger* 31 (March 1923): 314-15.

[53]Alan Graebner, "KFUO's Beginnings," *Concordia Historical Institute Quarterly* 37, no. 3 (October, 1964): 82-83.

[54]Maier, *A Man Spoke*, 71-72.

religious "marketplace" with a new medium "widely employed in the secular, commercial world," or whether such work should be left to more domestically oriented church bodies.[55]

The initial lukewarm response of the faculty was eventually overcome when Maier, with the help of Kretzschmar, John H. C. Fritz, Concordia dean of students, and a few others, raised significant "seed" funding via appeals to Maier's loyal Walther Leaguers and to other Lutheran laymen. Dean Fritz even convinced the seminarians to support the project by hitting up friends and family back home for donations, and by dipping into their student organizational fund. (They contributed $2,500—not bad for financially strapped clerics-in-training in 1923.)[56] More importantly, this generated enthusiasm and "ownership" among Concordia's student body that would prove beneficial to the soon-to-be launched KFUO, and eventually TLH.

In the summer of 1924, contracts were signed for the purchase of a Western Electric five hundred watt transmitter and broadcasting towers were erected on Concordia Seminary's campus. Makeshift studios were installed in the attic of one of the seminary buildings. In honor of the Walther League's foundational aid, and to affirm linkage of the station to the seminary, Maier and his colleagues requested that the Federal Radio Commission grant the new station the call letters *WLCS*, standing for *Walther League—Concordia Seminary*. However, the federal regulators had already adopted the policy that stations west of the Mississippi River would receive call letters beginning with *K*. The commission assigned the letters *KFUO* to the Lutheran station. Recognizing the appeal of giving these letters a higher meaning than just an ethereal identifier, Maier declared that they would henceforth mean "*Keep Forward Upward Onward.*"[57]

KFUO's aforementioned entry into radio airwaves occurred on October 26, 1924, as the festivities around the cornerstone laying of Concordia Seminary's new campus were broadcast, via an improvised hookup. The *official* dedication of KFUO's studio occurred as the station went on the air at 9:15 p.m. on Sunday, December 14 of the same year. In the earliest days,

---

[55]Graebner, "KFUO's Beginnings," 82-90.

[56]Herman H. Hohenstein, "The History of KFUO," *Walther League Messenger* 35, June 1927, 636; Maier, *A Man Spoke*, 72.

[57]Graebner, "KFUO's Beginnings," 84-85; Maier, *A Man Spoke*, 72.

KFUO broadcast only on Sunday and Wednesday evenings.[58] Program offerings were quickly added, with Maier taking responsibility for two weekly
programs, including a Sunday vespers service, and a current events commentary feature called "Views on the News." In the fall of 1926, he began a
series of lectures on contemporary religious issues as well. It should be noted
that although Maier was an Old Testament scholar, his primary focus was
on engaging biblical truths with the times in which he lived. Very early on,
he grasped that radio was a superb vehicle for accomplishing that goal.

Maier would not only continue to carry "on air" duties for the young radio
station, but would work with its first full-time station manager, Herman H.
Hohenstein, to solidify KFUO's viability. Hohenstein was a young St. Louis
pastor who took the newly created position in early 1925 as a ministerial
"call." When Hohenstein accepted these new responsibilities, the progressive
Christian Century magazine—no bedfellow with a denomination it considered isolated and uninfluential—could not help but take note. Under the
heading, "He Leads the Way," its editors noted that a pastoral appointment
as a radio station manager "is said to be the first appointment of its kind in
Protestant history." They concluded, "Mr. Hohenstein seems to be in line for
remembrance as a pioneer in a new type of Christian ministry."[59] Part of
such pioneering included expansion of KFUO's programming. While interacting with Maier, Hohenstein pointed out that "religious addresses and
wholesome musical entertainment are not the only possibilities" for their
young station. Maier agreed and they moved forward with more substantive
educational offerings.[60] While KFUO was unmistakably a Lutheran endeavor, as the breadth of programs and speakers expanded, Maier and his

---

[58]Graebner, "KFUO Beginnings," 85-86.

[59]Graebner, "KFUO Beginnings," 86. While the *Christian Century* may have found the creation of
a "called" clerical position as a radio station manager innovative, it did not change its general
opinion of the LCMS or its leading seminary. In July of the following year, the magazine referred
to Concordia Seminary–St. Louis as a "kind of corporate pope" that exercised "rigid discipline"
on the denomination by enforcing "conformity to a theology which may be described as an
ossified seventeenth century orthodoxy." The LCMS, the editorial asserted, "has isolated itself
from other churches with an effectiveness . . . not surpassed by any other body," thereby rendering its "social influence upon American life . . . very slight." See "What Is Disturbing the Lutherans?," *The Christian Century* 43 (July 22, 1926): 909.

[60]See correspondence: Herman H. Hohenstein to Prof. Walter A. Maier, September 28, 1927 and
Walter A. Maier to the Rev. Herman H. Hohenstein, October 1, 1927, WAM Collection, box 1,
folder 93, CHI.

colleagues maintained a strict policy that he would effectively take with him to TLH in the years to come: "We do not use the radio for direct attacks on sectarian or Catholic Churches."[61]

Given the novelty of radio at that time, KFUO's early broadcasts were broadly publicized by St. Louis newspapers, which augmented the size of early audiences.[62] Additionally, with less competitive activity on the airwaves in these early days of radio, KFUO's signal could produce clear reception over a vast geographic area. During the month of January 1926 alone, listener mail came in from forty-five states, Canada, Mexico, and Cuba.[63] And yet, Maier repeatedly promised, "This is only the beginning!"[64] While Maier was not the only person who led the efforts to launch a Lutheran radio station, he was at the center. His strong Walther League ties and the numerous, abiding connections they provided, his enthusiastic entry into the Concordia Seminary faculty and rapid establishment of key allies for the radio project, his expanding relationship with the LLL, and his natural talent as a communicator all served as vital assets in the establishment of KFUO as an effective venture. Lutheran historian Alan Graebner noted that no individual had dominated KFUO programming in its early day; however, "by the close of the Twenties the auditioning time was over." By "a combination of talent and drive," Walter Maier "emerged" to become the personification of "Lutheran radio."[65] More importantly, within a denomination not known for nimbleness and innovation, Maier had placed Lutheranism on the forefront of Christian radio during its infancy.

In June 1927, the *Walther League Messenger* celebrated the history of KFUO since its conception a few short years earlier. One of the articles' authors provided a verbal tour of KFUO facilities, employing hyperbole of which Maier, as the periodical's editor, must have at least tacitly approved:

> Turning our eyes toward the slowly setting sun, we see . . . two higher towers . . . lifting their heads two hundred feet into the air. . . . How slender, yet how stately and inspiring! Seemingly so frail, apparently at the mercy of the

---

[61]See "Suggestions for Speakers over KFUO," WAM Collection, box 1, folder 93, CHI.
[62]See Maier, *A Man Spoke*, 69-73, 110; Ward, *Air of Salvation*, 43-44; Graebner, "KFUO's Beginnings," 86.
[63]Graebner, "KFUO's Beginnings," 90.
[64]Maier, *A Man Spoke*, 73.
[65]Graebner, "KFUO's Beginnings," 93-94.

elements, yet well-built of strong and lasting material, firmly anchored in a
solid mass of concrete, fully able to withstand wind and weather. And withal,
how significant! Fit emblems of the Church of Christ, which they serve! Just
so the Church, seemingly so weak and helpless, yet is insuperably strong,
grounded on and anchored in, the foundation of the apostles and prophets,
Jesus Christ Himself being the chief cornerstone, rearing its head high into
the air to proclaim the Gospel of peace; a source of inspiration, yea, salvation,
to the millions of men, drawing earth-born, sin-cursed mortals heavenward
to the realms of eternal glory on high.[66]

Make no mistake—the enterprise to which Maier, the Walther League, and
the Lutheran Laymen's League (LLL) were increasingly devoting themselves
involved "towering" stakes. In this regard, it would appear that they had
something in common with Fulton Sheen and the NCCM.

While Maier's visionary role and energetic leadership in KFUO's founding,
and eventually in network broadcasting, should be recognized for what they
were, he likely benefited from the fact that LCMS denominational leaders
were paying minimal attention to the evangelistic possibilities offered by a
fledgling radio industry. Thus, one can surmise that Maier's new ventures
were effectively "below the radar," perceived as a relatively small matter, allowing him to avoid getting bogged down in the synod's often-ponderous
administrative and theological bureaucracy. As TLH eventually grew to
global stature, this precedential asset would prove invaluable to Maier.

To the networks. As Maier sought a larger stage, he approached NBC
about the possibility of adding Lutheran programming to their sustaining
time religious menu. NBC reaffirmed that their Protestant time slot would
remain under the gate keeping of the Greater New York Council of Churches/
Federal Council of Churches. Given the theologically progressive leanings
of these mainline churches, and in light of NBC's policy against selling
airtime for religious broadcasts, Maier knew he would need an alternate
route to network airwaves. As a matter of fact, liberal church leaders such as
Harry Emerson Fosdick, one of the leading preachers on NBC's Protestant
sustaining time broadcasts, were influential in convincing NBC (and soon
CBS) to reject all paid religious programming. Fosdick (and likeminded
mainline Protestant leaders) feared that "belated forms of denominational

---

[66]Theo. Laetsch, "A Trip to the Gospel Voice," *Walther League Messenger* 35 (June 1927): 638.

organization"—his term for more conservative, doctrinally rigid church bodies—would glean an undeserved respectability for their brand of traditional Christianity, should they gain a share in network microphones.[67] The Federal Council of Churches went so far as to push contractual obligations on local radio stations to only air religious broadcasts that they controlled.[68]

At the conclusion of Maier's meeting at NBC, one of the network representatives struck a nerve by inadvertently highlighting the peripheral nature of American Lutheranism, thereby increasing Maier's resolve to break out of traditional Lutheran confines. The NBC employee inquired, "Do you really think a Lutheran sermon is suited for the broad American public?" Before Maier could reply, the man added, "Isn't Lutheranism primarily for Germans?" Maier assured the NBC executives that there would be nothing so parochial about his proposed radio messages, even though the founder of Lutheranism had been a German. He must have been at least somewhat persuasive, as the NBC personnel left open the possibility of his periodic participation in their Protestant sustaining time programming; however, this only convinced Maier further that a *regular* program was needed to spread his gospel proclamations.[69]

In turn, Maier gained an audience with executives of the smaller, newer CBS network. Unlike NBC, CBS had accepted paid religious programming

---

[67]Fosdick's "take no prisoners" approach to the religious broadcasting battleground was evident in a speech he made at a 1938 banquet at the Waldorf-Astoria, celebrating fifteen years of national religious broadcasting under the auspices of the Federal Council of Churches. In the presence of Radio Corporation of America's President David Sarnoff, NBC President Lenox Lohr, and likeminded NBC radio preachers, Fosdick proclaimed, "Whatever may be the future uncertainties, it is sure that we have an opportunity in religion-on-the-air to make an incalculable contribution that will outflank, overpass, undercut sectarianism in religion." He inferred that sectarian truth claims were childish distortions of the "cosmic" nature of religion. Fosdick declared that "you can't talk that way over the air." Quote taken from a "stenographic report" of the Waldorf-Astoria banquet, published to preserve "the proceedings . . . in a permanent form." See "The Church of the Sky" (New York: Federal Council of the Churches of Christ in America, 1938), 31-35. See also Joel A. Carpenter, *Revive Us Again: The Reawakening of American Fundamentalism* (New York: Oxford University Press, 1997), 131; Robert Moats Miller, *Harry Emerson Fosdick: Preacher, Pastor, Prophet* (New York: Oxford University Press, 1985), 214, 379-80; Ernest Gordon, *Ecclesiastical Octopus: A Factual Report on the Federal Council of Churches of Christ in America* (Boston: Fellowship Press, 1948), 87-89.

[68]James DeForest Murch, *Co-operation Without Compromise: A History of the National Association of Evangelicals* (Grand Rapids, MI: Eerdmans, 1956), 73-74; see also Lowell S. Saunders, "The National Religious Broadcasters and the Availability of Commercial Radio Time" (PhD diss., University of Illinois, 1968), especially chapter 8.

[69]Maier, *A Man Spoke*, 112.

from its inception. The pioneering Philadelphia Presbyterian Donald Grey Barnhouse had become the first preacher to purchase network airtime, when he entered into a contract with CBS in 1928.[70] Yet by the time Maier met with CBS personnel in 1930, the network was in the process of adopting a policy of eliminating paid religious programming. This shift was partially in response to the aforementioned pressure from progressive Protestants (e.g., those composing the Federal Council of Churches), and partially in response to the politically charged radio preaching of Father Charles Coughlin, which the network had been broadcasting.[71] Nonetheless, until such policy was solidified, CBS executives were willing to consider selling Maier network access.

Specifically, they agreed to sell him airtime at standard commercial rates—the then-staggering sum of $4,500 per weekly, half-hour timeslot, which would exceed $200,000 over an entire year of broadcasts.[72] (Given such realities, Maier concluded that "our Lutheran Radio Hour has now become the Lutheran Half-Hour." Indeed, TLH was a thirty-minute program from its inception, notwithstanding its name.)[73] To place such amounts in perspective, CBS's proposed weekly remuneration demands were roughly three times the average weekly funding required for Professor Maier's employer, Concordia Seminary, to maintain its entire operation during the same year.[74]

Maier immediately approached the LLL, an LCMS organization formed in 1917 by twelve successful Lutheran laymen, who had met to discuss the burden of their denomination's one hundred thousand dollars of indebtedness. In the cigar-hazed Milwaukee parlor of one of these men, the concerned group not only devised what would be a successful debt elimination plan, but formed a lay society with a broader purpose: "To Aid Synod [the LCMS] with Word and Deed in Business and Financial Matters."[75] Now,

---

[70]Hal Erickson, *Religious Radio and Television in the United States, 1921–1991* (Jefferson, NC: McFarland & Company, 1992), 36.

[71]Erickson, *Religious Radio and Television*, 61-62; Ward, *Air of Salvation*, 42.

[72]Hangen, *Redeeming the Dial*, 21-24; Maier, *A Man Spoke*, 110-115; Ward, *Air of Salvation*, 41-49.

[73]Maier, *A Man Spoke*, 111.

[74]Concordia Seminary incurred expenses, including faculty and staff salaries, of $79,448 for the year 1930. Thus, the average weekly expense for that calendar year totaled $1,528. See *Statistical Yearbook of the Evangelical Lutheran Synod of Missouri, Ohio, and Other States for the Year 1930* (St. Louis: CPH, 1931), 178.

[75]Gordon Meyers, *There Is a God; Let the Nations Be Glad!* (St. Louis: The International Lutheran Laymen's League, 1980), 7; Maier, *A Man Spoke*, 113; Fred Pankow and Edith Pankow, *75 Years*

thirteen years later, Maier determined that his purpose and the LLL's were meant for each other. He requested funding to commence a weekly network broadcast of a program on CBS to be known as *The Lutheran Hour*, for an initial half-year commitment.

Radio was not a topic on which the LLL needed to be sold. In 1925, it had funded the hiring of the first full-time director of radio station KFUO. The following year, LLL members voted in convention to fully sponsor KFUO, which included taking responsibility for building a new facility on the newly relocated seminary site, and for upgrading its equipment in response to evolving governmental regulations. The League's resulting commitment totaled fifty thousand dollars for the initial capital expenditures, and an additional twenty to twenty-five thousand dollars per year for operating costs.[76] The convention resolution stated that the LLL "recognizes the fact that the radio provides the greatest single means of doing missionary work."

As enthusiastic as the LLL was about KFUO's gospel-broadcasting venture, its leadership was not content to offer the blessings of Lutheranism over just a single station. In its membership periodical, LLL editors touted the "greater opportunities . . . beckon[ing]" from "the chain systems of broadcasting"— opportunities that "national advertisers" already "realiz[ed]." In a clear reference to NBC's Protestant sustaining time slot, they warned that "the Federal Council of Churches, which is under Modernist control," already sponsored "speakers of great charm and profound learning" who "are engaged for the purpose of bringing the Modernist view of Christianity into hundreds of thousands of American homes." They mentioned approvingly Presbyterian Barnhouse's willingness to counter the "modernistic message" by purchasing network airtime. They concluded that Lutherans should fill the critical void for "a spiritually hungry multitude crying out for better food than is now being offered to them."[77]

In case the specter of modernism did not sufficiently rattle Lutheran laymen, a few months later LLL writers highlighted another threat in the

---

and *The Best Is Yet to Come: The International Lutheran Laymen's League* (St. Louis: International Lutheran Laymen's League, 1992), 18.

[76]Alan Graebner, *Uncertain Saints: The Laity in the Lutheran Church–Missouri Synod, 1900–1970* (Westport, CT: Greenwood, 1975), 50; Pankow and Pankow, *Best Is Yet to Come*, 30-31.

[77]"The Greater Possibilities of Radio," *Lutheran Laymen's League Bulletin* 1 (November 15, 1929): 28-29.

competitive field for human souls. The "Russellite sect" (known today as Jehovah's Witnesses) was broadcasting the "Watch Tower" program from New York over a network of thirty stations. So that the "soul-destroying" magnitude of this endeavor could not be missed, they explained that the "propagandists of a false prophet are reaching more people by radio than all the Lutheran churches in the United States taken together and then multiplied by three." The editors concluded with a question only partially rhetorical: "Must we really learn from them before we set free the funds for a nation-wide radio broadcasting service?"[78]

So, when Walter Maier presented the opportunity to purchase network airtime, LLL was ready to respond. LLL leadership held Maier in high regard, and its board of directors included several of his personal friends. On May 31, 1930, the national convention of the League, meeting at Chicago's Palmer House, adopted a resolution "to sponsor a national Lutheran Radio Hour over the Columbia Broadcasting System beginning in the fall."[79] Sounding similarly zealous as the aforementioned Knights of Columbus leader toward the sponsorship of the *Catholic Hour,* an LLL spokesman referred to their new venture as "the boldest undertaking ever conceived by a body of American Lutherans." When the Associated Press reported on the LLL undertaking, response via mail from across the country confirmed broad Lutheran support. "There seems to be no dissent voiced," observed the *Lutheran Laymen's League Bulletin.* LLL members and friends raised forty-four thousand dollars by late summer, and Maier's appeal to his Walther League colleagues produced a commitment of fifty thousand dollars. With collected and anticipated funding near the one hundred thousand dollars needed for the upcoming partial radio season, LLL's executive committee approved the final plans for TLH on August 13, including the formal naming of Maier as "the first speaker." Shortly thereafter, a contract with CBS was inked. LLL leader and Walther Leaguer Albert Fitz later recalled, "This development was a highlight in our lives."[80]

As the country staggered from the 1929 stock market crash and its aftermath, Maier was convinced that the time was right for straightforward

---

[78]"A Lutheran Hour on the National Network—When?," *Lutheran Laymen's League Bulletin* 1 (April 15, 1930): 85.

[79]Maier, *A Man Spoke,* 114.

[80]Maier, *A Man Spoke,* 112-15; Pankow and Pankow, *Best Is Yet to Come,* 40-41. From this point to the present, TLH has operated under the auspices of the LLL.

preaching of the Christian message. Out of concern that religious broadcasts could conflict with, or serve as a substitute for, Sunday worship services, a Thursday evening time slot was selected. On October 2, 1930, in the
10 p.m. (Eastern) time slot immediately following CBS's popular *The Shadow*,
Maier took to the airwaves from CBS affiliate WHK in Cleveland, transmitted to thirty-six network stations, coast to coast. (The Cleveland location
was used so as to feature the Cleveland Bach Chorus in the inaugural program's music selections.)[81]

With his message, "There Is a God!" Maier urged his listeners to "cultivate
faith built on the sure promises of the Bible, not on hoarded wealth and gilt-
edged investments."[82] He concluded his first sermon with the following
words, which reflect the urgency with which he would proclaim his message
to the nation:

> Men can live without money, without fame, without erudition; they can eke
> out an existence without friends, without health, or without personal liberty
> and the possibility of the pursuit of happiness; but they cannot live in the
> fullness of a life that lives beyond the grave without God. Let them repeat their
> age-old challenge of blasphemy by standing up before large audiences to deny
> the existence of God and condescend to grant Him five minutes to strike
> them down dead! But in the crises of life and the pivotal hours of existence,
> only the Christian—having God and with Him the assurance that no one can
> successfully prevail against him—is able to carry the pressing burdens of
> sickness, death, financial reverses, family troubles, misfortunes of almost in-
> numerable kinds and degrees, and yet to bear all this with the undaunted
> optimistic faith and Christian confidence that alone make life worth living
> and death worth dying.[83]

Notwithstanding their last-minute concerns that Maier's preaching
would fall flat in the wake of more popular, secular programming, CBS executives soon concluded that TLH was a "winner." After the initial broadcasts, listeners had sent in over fifteen thousand letters, many to CBS's New

---

[81]Maier, *A Man Spoke*, 115.

[82]As quoted in George H. Hill, *Airwaves to the Soul: The Influence and Growth of Religious Broadcasting in America* (Saratoga, CA: R & E, 1983), 12.

[83]As quoted in Maier, *A Man Spoke*, 118-19; for the published version of this sermon, which has
slight variations, see Walter A. Maier, *The Lutheran Hour: Winged Words to Modern America,
Broadcast in the Coast-to-Coast Radio Crusade for Christ* (St. Louis: CPH, 1931), 45-53.

York headquarters. In just eight weeks, more mail would be sent to TLH than to any other religious program, including those sponsored by the Federal Council of Churches such as the four-year-old *National Radio Pulpit*, featuring the aforementioned Protestant progressives Fosdick, Cadman, and Sockman.[84] Even more striking, more mail was generated by Maier than by such popular "secular shows" as the top rated *Amos 'n' Andy*.[85]

Over eight hundred newspapers gave coverage to TLH during its first few weeks, with the *New York Herald Tribune*, the *New York Post*, and the *New York Times* frequently recommending the program.[86] For instance, the *Times* highlighted Maier and TLH in their "Outstanding Events on the Air Today" listings after TLH's October debut, as they had Sheen and the CH when they went on the air earlier that same year.[87] Similarly, the *Herald Tribune* featured a complete "Today's Radio Programs" page in its daily publication. Like the *Times*, its editors deemed approximately fifteen programs worthy of special note under the listing, "Bright Spots for Today." Maier and TLH soon received top billing in this column, as well.[88]

Financial crisis. Despite the successful debut of TLH, as demonstrated by a number of such indicators, finances remained the most worrisome constraint as Maier tried to maintain his grip on a network microphone. As Americans began to realize that the economic downturn that had begun on Wall Street in New York toward the end of the previous year was making its way to the Main Streets in their hometowns, they began holding their wallets more tightly. Financial support for TLH broadcasts during the 1930–1931 winter season averaged $2,000 a week—well short of the weekly charge from CBS of over $4,500. What is more, as was the case with the CH, TLH was

---

[84]Ward, *Air of Salvation*, 48-49.

[85]Maier, *A Man Spoke*, 119-21; Ward, *Air of Salvation*, 48-49.

[86]Maier, *A Man Spoke*, 119-20. For examples of press coverage, see "Lutheran Radio Program," *The Daily Herald* (Biloxi), October 2, 1930, 6; "On The Air Tonight," *Appleton Post-Gazette*, November 28, 1930, 10; "Lutherans Inaugurate Radio Hour," *Oak Parker* (Oak Park, IL), October 3, 1930, 29; "Aces of the Air," *Hammond Lake County Times*, October 23, 1930, 8; "Christmas Greetings," *Washington Post*, December 25, 1930, 8. Several newspapers noted that TLH was the first effort by a denomination to spread its message via paid network programming.

[87]For examples, see "Outstanding Events on the Air Today," *New York Times*, November 6, 1930, 22; "Outstanding Events on the Air Today," *New York Times*, December 4, 1930, 31.

[88]For examples, see "Bright Spots for Today," *New York Herald Tribune*, November 13, 1930, 15; "Bright Spots for Today," *New York Herald Tribune*, December 11, 1930, 24; "Bright Spots for Today," *New York Herald Tribune*, December 18, 1930, 22.

racking up administrative expenses at its headquarters. TLH was nearly out of cash by February, and CBS executives traveled to St. Louis, threatening to pull the plug on the remainder of the broadcast season.

Maier sent an urgent message to his good friend, New York manufacturer and contractor Henry A. Dahlen. A committed Lutheran, Dahlen had worked his way up from an orphaned childhood in Minnesota spent under the auspices of Lutheran social service agencies, to the presidency and majority ownership of Deslaurier Column Mould Company. Maier's relationship with Dahlen went back to the early 1920s, when the former had begun serving as a principal speaker at annual one-day Lutheran rallies at the well-known Ocean Grove Camp in New Jersey. By the mid-1920s, Dahlen had concluded that one-day excursions to the Jersey Shore were inadequate for edifying the faithful, and became the driving force to acquire land on which a more remote Lutheran resort, designed for longer visitor stays, could be established. While many Lutherans from the greater New York area embraced this idea, Dahlen and his financial resources were key to bringing into existence a five hundred acre resort dedicated as "Lutherland" in 1926. Conveniently located in the Poconos, approximately one hundred miles from Philadelphia and New York, Lutherland's mission was to create for urbanites an atmosphere in which to "make their faith a living, active force."[89]

Maier's and Dahlen's friendship grew closer and in 1929 Maier began what would be an eleven-year stint as the "Dean of Summer Conference" at Lutherland, which required him to preach and lecture to vacationers at the resort, but also afforded him time to study each summer in a relaxed, scenic setting with his family.[90] Now, with TLH in dire financial straits and CBS becoming increasingly impatient, Dahlen would have the opportunity to repay any favors Maier may have accrued at Lutherland. Dahlen answered Maier's summons and immediately traveled to St. Louis for a meeting with LLL leaders and the CBS representative. When Dahlen suggested the enlistment of a handful of donors who could immediately underwrite up to ten thousand dollars each, starting with himself, the others in the room

---

[89]See Ted Suttmeier, *Lutherland: A Dream Fulfilled and Memories . . . History of Lutherland/Pocono Crest, 1926–1982* (Pocono Pines, PA: Printing Craftsmen, 2007), 8-18, 42-44. Henry Dahlen served as the key administrator for Lutherland from its founding until 1942; Maier, *A Man Spoke*, 97-99, 123.

[90]Suttmeier, *Lutherland*, 42-44.

considered that unrealistic. With only thirty hours until airtime for the next TLH program, and CBS balking at allowing TLH to proceed without manifest financial means, Dahlen signed a note for fifty thousand dollars to keep TLH on the air. Enough donations eventually came in to cover Dahlen's gutsy backing of TLH in its infancy. This was not the last time that Maier's ability to co-opt businessmen in his vision for radio ministry would prove crucial to his success.

Notwithstanding the need for Dahlen's "white knight" heroics, the first season of TLH was a remarkable success. In nine brief months, through thirty-six broadcasts, a Missouri Synod Lutheran scholar had become a popular preacher to listeners across the land, and the object of attention from a range of influential observers. Nonetheless, the darkening realities of the Great Depression could not be ignored. In the spring of 1931, listener contributions declined precipitously, to well under one thousand dollars per week. Even loyal LLL and Walther League members could not fill the financial gap between fundraising reality and the $250,000 that CBS demanded for the coming, full broadcast season. Additionally, if TLH was to continue, the network intended to move it to a Sunday evening timeslot—a development about which LLL leaders and membership had substantial reservations. As the time to renew the CBS contract drew near, the LLL board of governors concluded that "the circumstances did not warrant a continuance" of TLH.[91]

TLH's June 11, 1931 broadcast began with the announcer solemnly stating, "This will be the concluding broadcast of the Lutheran Hour." Less than thirty minutes later, Maier reluctantly withdrew from national airwaves. He

---

[91]"Why the Lutheran Hour Was Suspended," *Lutheran Laymen's League Bulletin* 2, no. 11 (June 22, 1931): 157-58. Aside from financial issues, LLL attendees at the 1931 convention were generally supportive of continuing TLH, even if CBS forced a move to a Sunday timeslot. However, the board of governors of the LLL considered a Sunday program, which could conflict with actual church attendance, at least in perception, such a sensitive issue that they chose to "determine by a referendum the attitude of our audience on this subject." Shortly thereafter, during a regular broadcast, the TLH announcer asked "listeners-in" to write in their feelings about a Sunday broadcast. Of "924 replies . . . from 40 of the 48 States of the Union," only "41 favored a Sunday broadcast in preference to Thursday." The board concluded that "overwhelming sentiment against the change forced upon the League by the broadcast system" was yet another reason to suspend national broadcasts. Of course, while Maier and LLL leaders were genuinely concerned about the ramifications of moving to a Sunday program assignment, had adequate funding for a second season seemed likely, it is entirely possible that they would have rationalized a Sunday timeslot as preferable to no time slot at all.

and the LLL were far from throwing in the towel, however. LLL leadership informed their members that as "sponsor of these programs," they "look[ed] upon this suspension of the endeavor as an interruption and not as an abandonment of the project."[92] Shortly thereafter Maier wrote, "It seems to us that an effort so signally directed to the fulfillment of the Savior's last commission to His Church, 'Preach the Gospel to every creature,' must continue."[93] Though he did not know when such would occur, Maier was confident that TLH would eventually return. As it turned out, the wait would be three and a half years.

The great Dane. In the interim, Maier accepted multiple invitations to preach on local broadcasts sponsored by the Detroit Lutheran Pastoral Conference. Maier, the LLL, and the Detroit pastors continued to explore ways to relaunch TLH. Lutheran historian Alan Graebner described this period with imagery to which Maier and his colleagues would have subscribed: "Having once reconnoitered the philistinian territory of network broadcasting, [they] looked forward to radio as the promised land."[94] One of the leading pastors in the Detroit Lutheran community, E. T. Bernthal, took Maier to seek the aid of one of the "pillars" of his congregation—William S. Knudsen, president of the Chevrolet Division of General Motors.[95] The Danish-born manufacturing guru was a dedicated Lutheran layman who had a genuine interest in the spreading of the gospel. He had also expressed interest in the potential of religious radio for his denomination.

Knudsen had demonstrated an uncommon appreciation for the need to take the Christian message to "where people are," just a few years prior to this. In 1928, when his pastor asked him for a donation toward a new church edifice, Knudsen insisted that the planned building was too large. When the

---

[92]"Why the Lutheran Hour Was Suspended," 157-58.

[93]Walter A. Maier, foreword to *The Lutheran Hour*, vi.

[94]Graebner, *Uncertain Saints*, 141.

[95]Maier, *A Man Spoke*, 164-68. Knudsen, Henry Ford's leading production executive prior to heading up Chevrolet, would become president of General Motors in 1937. In 1940, President Roosevelt called on Knudsen to become one of his leading "dollar-a-year" men, charging him with overseeing America's rearmament. As such, he initially led the Office of Production Management, and then served as lieutenant general (three-star) in charge of industrial production for the US military. He is the only civilian to receive a military commission of this rank in American history. For an account of Knudsen's contribution to the Allied war effort, see Arthur Herman, *Freedom's Forge: How American Business Produced Victory in World War II* (New York: Random House, 2012).

minister explained that the building was designed to accommodate anticipated increased attendance from residents driving from Detroit's west side,
the Dane had a better idea. "What you should do is build two churches, one
here and one over on the west side so your people there will not have to
come all the way across the city to attend services. Do that, and I will build
both churches for you," he promised. Knudsen not only made good on his
pledge, but in his characteristic fashion pushed the contractor to have the
first building ready for Christmas services only five months away. Thrusting
a scriptural motivator toward both the cleric and the contractor "of little
faith" as to his timetable, he pointed out, "The Lord made the Universe in
six days, and I don't see why we can't build one small church in nearly five
months." Knudsen personally unlocked the doors on the new sanctuary for
worship services on the morning of December 25.[96]

Although Knudsen had few qualms about being directive to his pastor,
he apparently had great respect for men of the cloth. His biographer tells of
his attendance at the annual New York auto show, while he was president
of Chevrolet. Hans Kleist, the Lutheran clergyman who had married
Knudsen and his bride several years earlier in Buffalo, stopped by the exhibition to reintroduce himself to his now-prominent former parishioner.
Knudsen was so delighted to see Kleist that he called over a company representative and instructed him to show Reverend and Mrs. Kleist around
the exhibit. Whichever Chevrolet they liked best was to be delivered to a
location of their choosing, as a gift from Knudsen. He explained to the
stunned pastor that he felt he had cheated the man by having paid him only
twenty dollars for his nuptial services so many years earlier. According to
Knudsen, a shiny new Chevy represented "interest" accrued since his 1911
wedding day.[97]

Needless to say, the successful enlistment of Knudsen in any effort to
relaunch a national TLH broadcast would be a significant step in the right
direction. Although Walter Maier had spoken at the dedication service of
Knudsen's Epiphany Lutheran Church building in Detroit, they had not had
an opportunity to become acquainted. However, when Bernthal introduced
Maier to Knudsen at the latter's home in 1934, they hit it off well. In an

---

[96]Norman Beasley, *Knudsen: A Biography* (New York: Whittlesey House, 1947), 137-38.
[97]Beasley, *Knudsen*, 46, 201.

"animated conversation which ranged from automobiles' bodies to men's souls," Knudsen and the man he would thereafter address as "the little doctor" found considerable common ground. The auto executive lamented the effect of the Great Depression on the American people, and saw Christianity as a beacon of hope. By the end of the evening, he had "cheerfully volunteered" to underwrite an entire new season of TLH, which would run from February 10 to May 5, 1935. Walking them to the door, Knudsen bade Maier and Bernthal farewell, and issued the following instruction to Maier: "Now you teach the people to look up to God—they've been looking down too much nowadays." As it turned out, enough donations were gathered, especially from individuals responding to the radio messages, so that Knudsen did not have to make good on his financial guarantee.[98] Yet, without Knudsen's assumption of the role of bankable benefactor, TLH's second season would have remained solely in the hopeful minds of Walter Maier and a handful of fellow Lutherans.[99] (While Knudsen did not have to reach into his pockets to pay any broadcasting obligations pursuant to his guarantee, he did make a $2,500 "seed" gift toward the relaunch of TLH, prior to the start of the early 1935 broadcasts. This covered roughly one-third of the expense of the abbreviated Second Lutheran Hour Season, on a new, less expensive network.)[100]

One might marvel that a single meeting between Maier and Knudsen could produce such a watershed moment, leading to TLH's second inauguration and subsequent sustainability. Yet while Maier's personal charm and sense of urgency, and Knudsen's penchant for decisiveness and action, should not be downplayed, the seeds for this personal partnership appear to have been planted a few years earlier. While in the midst of the first year of TLH, Maier had sent a lengthy letter to Knudsen (perhaps at the suggestion of Bernthal, who was copied on the correspondence), acknowledging his

---

[98] Maier, *A Man Spoke*, 164-68; Pankow and Pankow, *Best Is Yet to Come*, 51-53.

[99] As an indication of just how "bankable" Knudsen's support was, in 1935 the GM executive's salary and bonus totaled $325,869. This placed the Danish immigrant's pay in the very top tier of American compensation levels, and according to *Time* magazine, Knudsen "had become the seventh highest-paid person in the US by merit, starting from scratch." See "National Affairs: Labor" and "Business and Finance: Salaries," *Time*, January 18, 1937, 19; 59-60.

[100] See "Minutes of the Meeting of the Board of Governors of the L.L.L. Held on Friday, January 31, 1935," Lutheran Hour Archives, St. Louis. The minutes do not explicitly name Knudsen as the $2,500 donor, but it is clear that he was the benefactor to whom the minutes refer.

generosity to Lutheran causes, and requesting that he consider supporting future network broadcasts.

Though the usually meticulous Maier misspelled the Chevrolet chief's last name, the letter is impressive otherwise. Dated November 28, 1930, it immediately speaks of the "crisis in the coast-to-coast chain broadcasting of our Lutheran Church." While verifying broad financial support for TLH, Maier acknowledged the toll the "industrial depression of the country" was having on charitable causes, and the need for a few substantial donors to solidify the future. He touted the "constructive power of the Christian religion" to inspire its followers to meet the temporal needs of feeding and clothing the "unemployed and suffering." He emphasized the "Christian duty of translating Thanksgiving into Thanksliving," during such dire times. Then Maier turned to the eternal perspective, arguing that the "message that goes to men's souls and shows them the Christ of hope and pardon" was needed to counterbalance competing modernist broadcasts that "really deny Christ." He added that he had received positive encouragement in letters from "clergy of every denomination" and from listeners "from every section of our country and from neighboring nations." Maier stressed the "responsibility toward God" that men like he and Knudsen had to keep pure Christianity on the air. Last, he appealed to Knudsen's business sense by stating that radio broadcasts were "one of the cheapest ways that we have of spreading the Gospel." He concluded by confidently asserting that "we have the Divine assurance that this effort will not be in vain."[101]

For whatever reason, Knudsen did not respond to Maier's initial 1930 appeal. However, Maier was speaking his kind of language, albeit without the Scandinavian accent. Maier's mention of cost-effective evangelism no doubt resonated with the production efficiency genius of Knudsen. Knudsen would have welcomed the "little doctor's" directness, given the Dane's lack of patience with vague requests. (During his World War II service, the first question Knudsen would ask generals responsible for procurement of military hardware was, "What do you want?" He insisted that they clearly state "how many pieces" of what specific "equipment you need for these men."[102])

---

[101]Walter A. Maier to W. S. Knutson (William Knudsen), November 28, 1930, WAM Collection, box 1, folder 114.
[102]Herman, *Freedom's Forge*, 78.

Maier's assertion of "responsibility" to God and humanity would have struck a chord with Knudsen's oft-expressed mindset: "All of us in time have a duty to perform in the world."[103]

Most importantly, Maier tapped into Knudsen's genuine Christian commitment and mindfulness of his potential legacy. True, Knudsen had summed up his commercial endeavors by flatly declaring in 1940, "My business is to make things."[104] What is more, he was known for his efforts to elevate appreciation for the manufacturing process. For example, Knudsen had been the driving force behind a massive General Motors exhibit at the 1933 Chicago World's Fair, that included an actual assembly line on which Chevrolets were produced right before fair goers' eyes. The floor plan of the exhibit was meant to "glorify" the assembly line, after attendees had passed through an entrance hall that had "the beauty and dignity of a medieval cathedral."[105] Yet, even with such affinity for production processes, the Dane wanted his life to mean something more than rusting chassis and obsolete equipment, however well-made they may have been. He observed, "No one is ever remembered for the commercial things he did. They are forgotten very soon because, after they are gone, they are represented by figures. Men are remembered for the human things they do. They remain in the minds of people for years, for centuries, for an eternity, if you please."[106] For Knudsen, such "human things" included those done for God. Walter Maier helped connect him with such an opportunity. As he would demonstrate over and over, Maier knew how to forge meaningful, productive relationships by casting a compelling vision and situating it within a set of mutually held, personal beliefs and commitments.

TLH returns for good. On Sunday, February 10, 1935, at one o'clock in the afternoon (EST), TLH returned to the airwaves over a portion of the new MBS. Whatever qualms that had previously existed regarding a Sunday broadcast had fallen by the wayside with the emergence of opportunity to access an MBS timeslot. At that time, MBS covered 75 percent of the nation and boasted the world's strongest station—WLW in Cincinnati—as an

---

[103]Beasley, *Knudsen*, 389.
[104]Herman, *Freedom's Forge*, 14.
[105]Cheryl R. Ganz, *The 1933 Chicago World's Fair: A Century of Progress* (Urbana: University of Illinois Press, 2008), 80-81.
[106]Beasley, *Knudsen*, 388.

affiliate. WLW's signal strength was no modest advantage. In 1935, the WLW transmitter generated five hundred thousand watts, which was ten times the maximum transmission allowable today.[107] TLH was on the air for fourteen programs via eleven stations for the remainder of that partial radio season, and would benefit from the enthusiastic publicity in church bulletins and local newspapers, from pastors and local congregations happy to have TLH back. TLH would return for the full following season and all subsequent seasons.[108]

While William Knudsen may not have been an adherent of the adage "He who pays the piper calls the tune," he apparently believed that "he who pays for the preacher, picks the pulpit." As a condition to his financial support, Knudsen had stipulated that the new season's broadcasts originate from his home church, Epiphany Lutheran of Detroit.[109] The benefit of this arrangement was that Epiphany Church's proximity to MBS's Detroit affiliate, WXYZ, resulted in several thousands of dollars in savings on wire and station charges. Additionally, Brace Beemer, radio's "Lone Ranger," lived in the Detroit area and lent his well-known voice to TLH broadcasts, serving as the announcer for the series. (The popular *Lone Ranger* program originated from the studios of WXYZ.) The drawback of the Detroit location was that it required Maier to travel by train from St. Louis to Detroit each Saturday, and to depart Detroit each Sunday evening, arriving just in time to lecture at Concordia Seminary at 7:30 a.m. Monday mornings.[110]

Despite the grueling schedule, later that year Maier reflected, "After the first program it was evident that the blessings of the Lord were to rest upon the entire project to an astonishing degree . . . the broadcasts were greeted with a response that few endeavors of comparable size in broadcast history have ever received."[111] Gratifying though it was to have regained a network microphone, Maier could not completely hide his resentment toward NBC, CBS, and the Protestant-elite recipients of their sustaining time. In the

---

[107]See TLH's 50th anniversary commemorative booklet, *There Is a God*, 12.

[108]Walter A. Maier, *Christ for Every Crisis: The Radio Messages Broadcast in the Second Lutheran Hour* (St. Louis: CPH, 1935), 150-51; Maier, *A Man Spoke*, 165-67; Pankow and Pankow, *Best Is Yet to Come*, 51-52.

[109]See "Minutes of the Meeting of the Board of Governors of the L.L.L. Held on Friday, January 31, 1935," Lutheran Hour Archives, St. Louis.

[110]Maier, *Christ for Every Crisis*, 152; Maier, *A Man Spoke*, 166-67.

[111]Maier, *Christ for Every Crisis*, 151.

publication of his 1935 TLH sermons, Maier commented, "What a tragedy that the facilities of the nation's greatest broadcasting systems, which are granted free of all charge to leaders in the modernist denial of Christ, are arbitrarily denied to those of us who would exalt Christ and who would pay for the privilege!"[112]

In the fall, practical reasoning prevailed and Maier originated TLH broadcasts from the KFUO studio in St. Louis. For the remainder of the 1930s, TLH gained true coast-to-coast penetration as MBS continued to add affiliates, and as TLH served as a pioneer in the use of transcription disks for nonnetwork stations that could not carry the program live.[113] Even with the lingering hardships of the Great Depression, listener donations and LLL supporters covered the production and broadcasting costs. As a measure of listener engagement with the program, TLH saw mail received climb from 16,000 pieces during the partial 1935 season to 177,000 pieces during the 1939–1940 season. By 1939, TLH was carried by 171 stations (twelve of which were outside US borders), including seventy-two by transcription.[114] Maier would remain the driving force as well as the distinct voice of TLH until his premature death in January 1950. By that time, his global audience was estimated at twenty million.[115] TLH was broadcast in thirty-six languages, from fifty-five countries, over twelve hundred stations.[116] Incoming mail indicated listeners were tuning into TLH in 120 countries around the world, when the man whose urgent voice stirred their souls was laid to rest.[117]

---

[112]Maier, *Christ for Every Crisis*, 4.

[113]Gerald Pershbacher, archivist of TLH, interview by author, March 10, 2009. Perschbacher explained that two complete TLH broadcasts would be recorded on two transcription discs in a single production run, then sent to nonnetwork stations, which their "disc jockeys" would play on the air.

[114]Tona Hangen, "Man of the Hour: Walter A. Maier and Religion by Radio on the Lutheran Hour," *Radio Reader: Essays in the Cultural History of Radio*, ed. Michele Hilmes and Jason Loviglio (New York: Routledge, 2002), 118-20; Maier, *A Man Spoke*, 164-76; Pankow and Pankow, *Best Is Yet to Come*, 51-56. Within another ten years, TLH mail would reach 13,000 to 25,000 letters per week, requiring a staff of one hundred people to handle. See Judy Maguire, "The Lutheran Hour," *Radio and Television Life* 18 (October 31, 1948): 34; and William F. McDermott, "Old-Time Religion Goes Global," *Collier's*, May 6, 1944, 50; and Ben Gross, "The World's Largest Congregation," *Pageant*, February 1945, 120.

[115]See William F. McDermott, "Twenty Million Hear Him Preach," *Christian Herald* 70 (March 1947): 43; and Hartzell Spence, "The Man of the Lutheran Hour," *The Saturday Evening Post*, June 19, 1948, 17, 88.

[116]Pankow and Pankow, *Best Is Yet to Come*, 77.

[117]Maier, *A Man Spoke*, 393-94.

Shortly after Maier's death, the Reverend Doctor John W. Behnken, president of the LCMS, took to the airwaves to comfort Maier's grieving au-

dience. He reflected on Maier's urgency in assailing sin and declaring the gospel. Behnken assured the listeners that "all things," even the death of the indefatigable Maier, "work together for good to them that love God." He concluded by reassuring the faithful: "This great mission of the air with its precious soul-saving message must continue, yes,

Figure 4.2. Promotional photograph of Rev. Walter Maier at the Mutual radio microphone

shall continue to the glory of God and the salvation of precious, blood-bought souls."[118]

Indeed, because of Maier's extraordinary foundational work and gospel-spreading prowess, other voices would extend his legacy for generations to come. Nine Lutheran clergymen have served as regular TLH speakers since Maier's death, the longest-serving and most well-known of whom was the late Oswald C. J. Hoffmann, who was speaker from 1955 to 1988. As of the beginning of 2021, over 1,800 radio stations continued to carry TLH's weekly broadcasts. The program can also be heard over the internet and by US military personnel via the American Forces Network. Since Maier's day, the LLL has leveraged the perpetual success of TLH into a broad array of global ministries, both within broadcasting and beyond. But alas, notwithstanding the achievement of TLH continuing as the longest-running Christian radio program in history, times have changed. TLH's current weekly audience of one million is a modest fraction of the number of "parishioners" who sat in Walter Maier's ethereal pews during radio's Golden Era.[119]

---

[118]See John W. Behnken, "Christ, Your Matchless Advocate," *The Walter A. Maier Memorial Booklet* (St. Louis: Lutheran Laymen's League, 1950), 52-59.

[119]"About Us," Lutheran Hour Ministries, www.lhm.org/about/default.asp.

In sum, two middle class boys, Walter Maier and Fulton Sheen, grew up in families only one or two generations removed from the European home-lands of their origin. In their boyhood homes the religious heritage of their respective ancestries was devoutly lived under the spiritual leadership of their mothers. Both young men would feel called to a life of pastoral ministry early in their youth, with their firm courses set by their twelfth year. Each possessed a boundless drive to achieve much for the kingdom of God. Both were endowed with keen intellects and both would go on to earn impeccable academic credentials, achieve ordination in their respective denominations, and attain professorial positions within ecclesiastical academies associated therewith. Each fervently espoused Christian commitment at a personal, individual level, but neither spent significant time in parish ministry. Each would practice their priestly vocations within denominations that, at the time, were marginalized within the American religious landscape—due to immigrant composition, language barriers, theological issues (both real and imagined), and self-imposed ecclesiological isolationism. Their work would change that.

Both men gained significant renown as orators through personal lec-turing, preaching, and speaking appearances, and were much in demand around the country, even prior to their network radio stardom. They were both especially open to, and adept at, applying the ancient truths in which they firmly believed to the context of the times in which they lived, and rendering such truths relevant for their auditors. With remarkable success, they transported their learning and eloquence from their classrooms, pulpits, and podiums to the pedestrian airwaves of radio, and the impact was profound—for themselves, for their individual listeners, for mass media in general, and for their respective denominations. They carried out such radio ministries under the auspices of lay-led organizations affiliated with, but not formally part of, the ecclesiological structures of the Catholic Church and the LCMS. While this did not free them from ecclesiastical oversight or politics, it did enhance their freedom and maneuverability in a rapidly changing medium. It also provided a dedicated, proactive support base of laymen who were bothered more by their respective denominations sitting on the sidelines of the American religious scene than perhaps were their leaders wearing clerical collars.

Yet despite many parallels between the lives and ministries of Fulton Sheen and Walter Maier, there were differences. Sheen eagerly took to radio when presented the opportunity, while Maier was involved in building a radio presence, both at the station level and the network level, from the ground up. Sheen enjoyed network-provided sustaining time for the CH, while Maier was forced to purchase network airtime for TLH—no small task during the Depression. Though Sheen was not bashful about asking for donations to Catholic causes, he did not have to worry about raising funds to stay on the air. This was due to his being the beneficiary of free airtime and of the NCCM's ability to generate adequate funding for the modest administrative costs associated with the CH. Maier, on the other hand, carried heavy responsibility for fundraising so as to keep TLH on the air. While the Walther League, and especially the LLL, provided significant financial support for the radio ministry, Maier was instrumental in prompting listeners to send in donations. He also led large "Lutheran Hour Rallies" across the country to generate increased enthusiasm for the radio program and to harvest donations to fund it.

Chapter Five

FILLING THE HOURS

PROGRAM FORMAT, PREPARATION, DELIVERY

A mighty Fortress is our God, A trusty Shield and Weapon;
He helps us free from ev'ry need That hath us now o'ertaken.
The old evil Foe Now means deadly woe;
Deep guile and great might Are his dread arms in fight;
On earth is not his equal.

MARTIN LUTHER, "A MIGHTY FORTRESS IS OUR GOD"

Holy Spirit, come and guide us,
For Thy Light I daily pine;
All around is dark and gloomy,
Let Thy Rays upon us shine;
Let Thy Rays upon us shine.

W. TREACY, "HOLY SPIRIT, COME AND GUIDE US"

DURING THIS GOLDEN ERA of radio, broadcasters' menus and audience audio appetites covered a remarkable range. Programming stretched from slapstick comedies to intense dramatic serials, from variety shows to symphonic productions, from farm reports to international news, and from educational presentations to religious services. Within this competitive and dynamic mix, Walter Maier and Fulton Sheen carved out audiences comprising millions of loyal listeners. While their program formats were not identical to other broadcasts, they admittedly were not particularly novel. The unique components of the Catholic Hour (CH) and The Lutheran Hour (TLH), the sources of their appeal, were their speakers and the carefully crafted messages they delivered.

Program Formats

The CH, as noted previously, began as an hour-long broadcast in 1930, but NBC converted the show to a thirty-minute program in late 1931, in keeping with a general trend toward shorter programming formats.[1] NCCM leaders initially worried that this change would damage CH's popularity, but their fears were quelled as listeners responded favorably. Mail volume increased immediately, seemingly indicating that the network's less generous allocation of minutes, whether intended or not, actually boosted the audience size.[2] TLH was a thirty-minute program from the beginning, partially due to funding constraints, but also in keeping with broadcasting trends. By the mid-1930s, in addition to TLH and the CH, most other national religious broadcasts were of the half-hour variety, including *National Radio Pulpit*, *National Vespers*, the *CBS Church of the Air*, and *Message of Israel*.[3] (Two notable exceptions to the thirty-minute norm were Charles Fuller's *Old-Fashioned Revival Hour* and Charles Coughlin's *Golden Hour of the Shrine of the Little Flower*. These programs, which could not have been more dissimilar, both achieved significant success in sixty-minute formats.)

On the tenth anniversary of the CH launch, Edward J. Heffron, executive secretary of the NCCM, boasted that their program had met its competition "without compromise, without sensationalism, without 'jazzing up' its

---

[1]"Catholic Hour Now Broadcast Each Sunday from 6 to 6:30 p.m., Eastern Standard Time," *N.C.W.C. Review*, December, 1931; Alexander Pavuk, "Constructing a Catholic Church Out of Thin Air: *Catholic Hour's* Early Years on NBC Radio," *American Catholic Studies* 118, no. 4 (2007): 46-47.

[2]"Catholic Hour Effective on New Schedule," *Catholic Action*, February, 1932, 22.

[3]OTRRpedia: Database of Old Time Radio Programs and People, www.otrrpedia.net.

program in the slightest." Rather, a "high level of dignity" was "maintained exceptionally throughout—a dignity without pomposity or ostentation."[4]

The CH was broadcast from NBC Studios in New York, at which Sheen was contractually obligated to arrive at least fifteen minutes prior to airtime.[5] The program was produced in the presence of a studio audience, participants of which had received free tickets courtesy of NBC, by requesting them from the NCCM.[6] Sheen interacted with members of his studio "congregation" after the program's conclusion, paying special attention to the "regulars." As was his habit, Sheen wore "impeccable attire," notwithstanding the inability of radio listeners to appreciate this aspect of his fastidiousness.[7] Maintaining the perpetual priestly personage for which he would be

Figure 5.1. Fulton Sheen with program announcer, Paulist Chorister director Father William Finn, and choir on the *Catholic Hour* set at NBC

[4]Edward J. Heffron, "Ten Years of the Catholic Hour," *The Ecclesiastical Review* 102 (January–June, 1940): 242.

[5]See "Contract Between the National Council of Catholic Men and Rev. Dr. Fulton J. Sheen," file "Memorabilia 1907–1934," folder "1933," Fulton J. Sheen Archives, Rochester, New York (hereafter "Sheen Archives").

[6]"The Catholic Hour," *Monthly Bulletin, N.C.C.M.*, April, 1933, 3.

[7]Thomas C. Reeves, *America's Bishop: The Life and Times of Fulton J. Sheen* (San Francisco: Encounter Books, 2001), 80.

recognized throughout his career, Sheen stood before the microphone at Radio City donning a cassock, surplice, and Roman collar.[8]

Each program began with a sacred musical selection of roughly three to five minutes.[9] As it began, the announcer identified the program and introduced the musical piece, while the music momentarily faded to the background. The announcer then introduced Sheen and his topic for the day. While all of his sermons had their own titles and specific topics, each was typically part of a multiweek series centered on a main theme, which Sheen chose prior to each season. Sheen usually kept his sermons to roughly twenty minutes or slightly less, even in the early days when CH broadcasts were sixty minutes long.[10] The sermon was followed by a Sheen prayer of one to one and a half minutes, and another musical selection of three to five minutes, though the musical number sometimes occurred before the prayer. The announcer concluded by inviting listeners to write the NCCM or their local NBC station for a copy of that day's sermon, and informing the audience of the following week's topic.[11] In the early years of the CH, programs frequently included a "Question and Answer" segment. This feature, which worked better in the initial, hour-long format, was eventually phased out.[12]

Throughout the first ten years of the CH, the Paulist Choristers, under the direction of their founder, Father William J. Finn, provided most of the music for the program. The Choristers, made up of boys and men, were "known chiefly for the tonal quality of the boy soprano voices," adept at

---

[8]See Aileen Soares, "The Catholic Hour," *Radio Varieties* 3, no. 1 (January 1940): 3; see also fig. 5.1, an undated 1930s photograph of Sheen, the Paulist Choristers, and other *Catholic Hour* participants at NBC studios. "Photograph" files, Sheen Archives, Rochester.

[9]"Holy Spirit, Come and Guide Me," the opening and closing hymn of CH during World War II, was adapted from a hymn by W. Treacy, which can be found in the Marist Brothers, *American Catholic Hymnal: An Extensive Collection of Hymns, Latin Chants and Sacred Songs for Church, School and Home* (New York: J. Kenedy and Sons, 1913), hymn 42.

[10]Reeves, *America's Bishop*, 79; Timothy H. Sherwood, *The Preaching of Archbishop Fulton J. Sheen: The Gospel Meets the Cold War* (Lanham, MD: Lexington Books, 2010), 12. For an example of the CH's sixty-minute program format, see "Catholic Hour Radio Program for March 30," *The Catholic News* (New York), March 29, 1930.

[11]See numerous original recordings of the CH, available from Old Time Radio Catalog, www .otrcat.com/p/catholic-hour.

[12]See "Catholic Hour Radio Program For March 30," *The Catholic News* (New York), March 29, 1930; Joseph M. Tally, "The Catholic Hour—Outstanding Work of the N.C.C.M.," *Catholic Action*, May 1933, 28; Edward J. Heffron, "Measuring the Influence of the 'Catholic Hour,'" *Catholic Action*, January, 1937.

producing "extraordinary flexibility . . . in ensemble interpretation."[13] Finn also formed a second choral group of adult women and men, which he named "The Medievalists," to provide an alternate sound for CH broadcasts. The interesting challenge for Finn and NBC's "engineers and acousticians" was to learn what types of music and musical selections could be transmitted well over radio. Finn, who with his Paulist Choristers enjoyed a substantial reputation prior to his work on the CH, stated that he "came to dislike broadcasting, realizing that our characteristic style of singing might or might not be reproduced" on air. Well-known vocalists such as Irish tenor John McCormack and soprano Jessica Dragonette also periodically performed solos or joined Finn's ensembles. Weekly selections ranged from liturgical and classical selections, to more modern hymns—some more distinctly Catholic than others—though Finn had a preference for the former.[14]

Finn's direction of CH music, which consistently generated praise in the press and from the radio audience, added to his reputation. The preaching of Fulton Sheen and the angelic choirs of Finn attracted listeners of Catholic and non-Catholic stripes. Yet, the sensitive Finn resented the fact that he could not please everyone's musical tastes in "radioland." For a professional musician accustomed to the more homogeneous audiences of church sanctuaries and concert halls, the unsolicited opinions of unseen listeners were not entirely welcomed. Some complained about too little liturgical music, while others requested more contemporary hymnody. Other letter writers "found that [Finn] offered too much Gregorian chant and polyphony." Always the perfectionist, Finn also disliked the Depression-related financial realities imposed by the NCCM that forced minimal instrumental accompaniment, restricted funding for adult talent, and abbreviated rehearsal opportunities—on the rare occasions when orchestral support or guest vocalists were available.[15]

After his retirement in 1940, Finn praised the "initiative and boldness" of the CH enterprise, but lamented that "most of the time, for ten long years, the Catholic Hour was a dreary task and an undertaking full of hazards for

---

[13]"Elevating Music," *A Nationwide Audience for God* (Washington, DC: NCCM, 1940).
[14]William J. Finn, *Sharps and Flats in Five Decades: An Autobiography* (New York: Harper & Brothers, 1947), 269, 280-81; "Month by Month with the N.C.W.C.," *Catholic Action*, March, 1938, 13; "The Catholic Radio Bureau," *Catholic Action*, February 1940, 19.
[15]Finn, *Sharps and Flats in Five Decades*, 279-82.

an organization as well known as the Choristers."[16] Nonetheless, in a period in which broadcasters and listeners were sorting out "what worked," Finn's gifted leadership contributed to the popularity of the CH, complementing the theological oratory of Sheen (and other CH speakers) with more melodious depictions of divine themes.

After Finn's departure, music remained an integral component of the CH, but its producers no longer relied on a single group or director to serve as its primary provider of program music. While music selections continued to include liturgical chants, classical pieces, and worshipful hymns, a roster of "outstanding choirs, guest soloists, and distinguished organists" was presented by the NCCM to maximize the impact on "the auditory sense."[17] Choirs performed both at NBC Studios and at remote locations, the latter of which would be heard live via a wire hookup to the studio provided by NBC technicians.

The description just provided relates to the standard CH broadcasts over the NBC network—the primary vehicle by which Fulton Sheen spoke to a CH audience of millions. In late 1940, however, the NCCM began producing transcription discs of Sheen radio addresses, to be made available to non-network stations, through the local efforts of NCCM-affiliated lay organizations (e.g., Knights of Columbus Councils, Holy Name Societies). At that time, the CH nearly blanketed the country, as it was carried by 106 NBC Red Network stations, located in forty-one states, the District of Columbia, and Hawaii. Nonetheless, the NCCM wanted to make Sheen's sermons available in remote areas, and over local stations at alternative times.[18] Transcription broadcasts were allowed "over any station in any community except those where the 'live' Catholic Hour is offered." Additionally, the NCCM made it known that even in markets where the CH was available over an NBC station, transcriptions could be used "if the manager of the local Catholic Hour station [i.e. an NBC affiliate] has no

---

[16]Finn, *Sharps and Flats in Five Decades*, 280.

[17]"Some Notes On Catholic Radio Programs," *Catholic Action*, November, 1944, 18. For examples of choirs appearing on the CH, see "Radio Schedule January, 1947," 19; "Purposes of the Catholic Hour Restated on 11th Anniversary," *Catholic Action*, March, 1941, 27.

[18]"Msgr. Sheen's Popular Radio Broadcasts Are Being Recorded," *Catholic Action*, November, 1940, 30; "Complimentary Response Received by Sponsors of New Radio Program," *Catholic Action*, January, 1941, 23.

objection."[19] (It is not clear just how many such NBC station managers were that generous.)

The NCCM made each transcribed program available for a three dollar "rental fee," helpfully pointing out in its publicity that "twenty-five cents a week from twelve men will take care of this." These addresses were abbreviated versions of Sheen's CH talks, each limited to ten minutes. This provided local sponsors with the flexibility to seek fifteen or thirty minute slots from local stations. The former would require an opening and closing announcement, with only background music, while the latter would allow for more musical selections and announcements. The NCCM's broader flexibility for transcription broadcasts was rather remarkable. Potential local sponsors were told, "It will be *your* [emphasis original] program in every respect—the name of the National Council of Catholic Men is not mentioned on the transcriptions and need not be used at all." Instead, the local sponsor could use their name solely in the broadcasts. The NCCM went so far as to provide "instructions, sample continuities, sample newspaper handouts, newspaper mats of Monsignor Sheen, and a full biographical sketch of Monsignor Sheen . . . without additional cost." Shortly after launching its transcription project, the NCCM reported that "thirty-five societies inaugurated their first [transcription] programs during Christmas week" of 1940. Yet due to inconsistent transcription production by the NCCM, and to the benefits of the CH receiving sustaining time on the vast NBC network, transcription broadcasts were never a major part of Sheen's or the NCCM's ministries.[20] Transcriptions would serve a more substantial role for Walter Maier and TLH.

As for *The Lutheran Hour*, after broadcasting from Detroit during its second season, the program permanently originated from KFUO's studios in St. Louis. Maier took to the airwaves in front of his own studio audience in Studio C of station KFUO—an audience consisting of his two young sons, Walt Jr. and Paul, who watched their animated father with pride. The program announcer and the station engineers were the only other personnel

---

[19]"Program Featuring Msgr. Sheen Available to N.C.C.M. Affiliates," *Catholic Action*, September, 1941, 27.

[20]"Program Featuring Msgr. Sheen Available," 27; "Msgr. Sheen Recordings Offered Affiliates for Own Radio Programs," *Catholic Action*, December, 1940, 24; "Complimentary Response Received by Sponsors of New Radio Program," *Catholic Action*, January, 1941, 23.

on hand in the cramped facilities.[21] Musical offerings were interwoven in the program, usually provided by director Norman Gienapp and the Lutheran Hour Chorus. The choir, composed of seminary students, was assembled two blocks away at the Concordia Seminary chapel, with its musical contributions wired into the studio at the appropriate times.[22]

Whereas Fulton Sheen spoke to his studio and radio audiences fastidiously attired in clerical garb, Maier's rather private studio setup allowed him to take a more comfortable approach. He preached in his t-shirt. As the *Saturday Evening Post* reported in a lengthy feature article on Maier in 1948, "He drives home [his] words with extravagant gestures, even in the sanctuary of a radio studio in which he permits no audience. To command complete freedom of physical action, he strips down for his broadcast as though he were entering the prize ring—removes his coat, vest, shirt and tie, and even his belt, and appears at the microphone in an undershirt." The reporter marveled at his physical preparation, as well: "Just before he goes on the air, he loosens up his arm and shoulder muscles by calisthenics in the manner of a shadow boxer."[23] Interestingly, Maier allowed the *Post* to include a photograph of him in his t-shirt speaking and gesturing into the KFUO microphone. Once the article was published, more than a few traditionalist Missouri Synod Lutherans, including Concordia Seminary's President Louis J. Sieck, were aghast that the most visible member of their denomination would so crassly represent the Office of the Keys.[24] Editor of the *Lutheran Witness* and fellow Concordia Seminary faculty member Theodore Graebner summed up such assessments by complaining that the *Post* coverage constituted "offences against good taste."[25] In this one regard,

---

[21]Email exchange between Paul L. Maier and the author, April 24, 2014.

[22]Paul L. Maier, *A Man Spoke, a World Listened: The Story of Walter A. Maier* (New York: McGraw-Hill, 1963), 163-64, 198. When seminarians were away from campus, the St. Louis Lutheran Hour Chorus, comprising area laymen, provided music. Additionally, the St. Louis A Cappella Choir, a mixed chorus under St. Louis Bach Society founder Dr. William B. Heyne, periodically appeared on TLH. Finally, when the program occasionally originated from the location of Lutheran Hour Rallies across the country, local choirs assembled for the event, sometimes providing up to two thousand harmonic voices for the uplift of rally participants and the broader radio audience.

[23]Hartzell Spence, "The Man of the Lutheran Hour," *Saturday Evening Post*, June 19, 1948, 88.

[24]Email exchange between Paul L. Maier and the author, June 8, 2014.

[25]Letter from Theodore Graebner to Dr. Eugene R. Bertermann (Lutheran Hour Office), dated September 30, 1948. See box 1, folder 128, WAM Collection, Concordia Historical Institute, St. Louis.

at least, they would have preferred Maier adopting a more Sheen-like, priestly decorum.

The Lutheran Hour program, which varied little over Maier's career, centered on his Christian message, while "surrounding it with the best in church music."[26] During the 1930s, each broadcast opened with the announcer intoning, "The Lutheran Hour . . . Bringing Christ to the Nation . . . from Coast to Coast!"[27] After TLH expanded to become an international broadcast through the use of transcription discs in Canada (1939) and via station HCJB in Quito, Ecuador (1940), the opening announcement was altered, with the words "from

Figure 5.2. Walter Maier delivering a *Lutheran Hour* sermon in the radio studio wearing a T-shirt. A similar picture appeared in the June 19, 1948, edition of *The Saturday Evening Post* in a lengthy feature on Maier.

Coast to Coast" eliminated, and "Bringing Christ to the Nation" changed to "Bringing Christ to the Nations."[28] Following this announcement came the first verse of Martin Luther's well-known hymn, "A Mighty Fortress Is Our God."[29] The announcer then provided a brief setup for Maier's topic of the

---

[26] Maier, *A Man Spoke*, 171.

[27] "Continuities" from 1935–1940 broadcasts of *The Lutheran Hour*, Lutheran Hour Archives, St. Louis. ("Continuities" were the pretyped scripts for each week's program, to be read by the TLH announcer.)

[28] "Report of the Executive Secretary, Board of Governors Meeting, Lutheran Laymen's League, February 24, 1940," Lutheran Hour Archives, St. Louis; "Continuities" from 1941 broadcasts of *The Lutheran Hour*, Lutheran Hour Archives, St. Louis. Note: Maier's son Paul takes responsibility for the more expansive opening announcement, explaining that his father initiated the change after the young boy spoke up at the dinner table and said, "What's this 'nation' stuff, Dad? It's nation*s*!" Paul L. Maier interview with author, April 23, 2009.

[29] This was an English translation of Martin Luther's hymn, "Ein feste Burg ist unser Gott." It can be found in *The Lutheran Hymnal* (St. Louis: CPH, 1941), hymn 262. Maier's Protestant listeners would have been familiar with this hymn, as it was included in most American Protestant hymnals of the time. Non-Lutheran Protestants would have noticed, however, that the translation was slightly different from the one with which they were familiar. The choir on *The Lutheran Hour* sang a composite translation originally published in the Pennsylvania Lutheran *Church Book* of 1868. An alternate translation, which appeared in numerous non-Lutheran hymnals and was most familiar to American Protestants, was by Frederic H. Hedge. Additionally, while the broader Protestant audience would have recognized Luther's melody for "A Mighty Fortress," many would have noticed a subtle difference in the way it sounded

day, followed by a hymn selection, from either Lutheran or non-Lutheran sources. Maier followed with a thirty- to sixty-second prayer, requesting God's blessing on his radio sermon. After a fifteen-second "Amen" by the choir, Maier launched into his message of roughly nineteen minutes. The address was followed by another hymn selection, after which the announcer encouraged listeners to write in.

In addition to offering copies of Maier's sermons to TLH correspondents, the TLH announcer usually offered inexpensive gifts, such as decorative crosses of various sizes and finish, printed images of Christ, a "bedtime prayer reminder," lapel pins, and inspirational booklets. While such printed sermons and gifts were indeed free for the asking, the announcer invited supportive listeners, in low-key fashion, to consider supporting the program financially. (The solicitation of funding ceased in the fall of 1944, when the MBS adopted a policy prohibiting religious programs from even indirectly seeking financial contributions over the air—including on programs like TLH that paid full commercial rates for airtime.)[30]

Finally, listeners were invited to write to "Dr. Maier" if they had "spiritual" or "religious" problems, or a "personal difficulty," so that he could provide "personal counsel." This offer was made with one stipulation, however: it was meant for those "with no church connection" or those who had "no one to counsel" them. Maier had no desire to encroach on the territory of local pastors in their care of souls, or even give the impression that this was his intent. The program then closed with the singing of one or two verses of its "signature" theme, "Beautiful Savior," after which the choir continued humming the melody as the announcer completed the final TLH and network announcements. The only variation on this closing was the occasional use of "God Bless Our Native Land" to complement or replace "Beautiful Savior," in the months following America's entrance into World War II.[31]

---

on *The Lutheran Hour*. Maier's radio choir sang the hymn in what Lutherans considered the authentic "rhythmic" fashion, while most non-Lutheran hymnals employed a smoother "isorhythmic" version. In sum, Maier opened his weekly broadcasts with a hymn that communicated a connection with Protestants of various stripes, while also reinforcing a core connection to his fellow Lutherans.

[30]See "Mutual Broadcasting System: Program Standards," WAM Collection, box 7, folder 454, CHI, St. Louis; see also Maier, *A Man Spoke*, 277-79.

[31]See "Continuities" from Lutheran Hour Broadcasts, Lutheran Hour Archives, St. Louis.

DELIVERY

The broad content of radio programming during this era required different speakers to employ different styles and methods of saying things on the air, depending on the message being conveyed and the response desired. Tone, pace, and timing were critical elements in whether speakers were successful or not with their audiences. In their on-air preaching, Sheen and Maier sounded quite different from each other, yet both of their styles proved effective. Sheen was an elegant and eloquent orator, reflecting both his learned mind and a common touch. John Tracy Ellis, by no means an uncritical observer of Sheen, recalled the compelling nature of Sheen's "extraordinary preaching": "I often followed his spoken discourses with rapt attention."[32] John J. Myers, archbishop of Newark and former bishop of Peoria, found Sheen's "sparkling wit and dramatic flair" when preaching to be "very attractive" and inviting qualities.[33] In 1940, the *Denver Catholic Register*, perhaps with some bias, stated that Sheen was "one of the country's best-known and best loved orators."[34]

While listeners responded with steady, strong demand for printed copies of Sheen's radio sermons, as individual reprints and in book form, some observers felt that such sermons were not all that impressive as religious literature. It was Sheen's delivery that vivified the words, stimulated the intellect, stirred the emotions, and moved the soul. As one student of Sheen's radio preaching observed, "The real essence of Monsignor Sheen's *radio oratory* . . . that is to say the power of Monsignor Sheen's *orating*," could only be grasped via "*oral* study" (emphasis original).[35]

When asked about his style, Sheen commented, "I don't concentrate on style. My worry is in getting the idea across. That is the style."[36] The explanatory factor in his success as a speaker was, "in one word—sincerity,"

[32]John Tracy Ellis, *Catholic Bishops: A Memoir* (Wilmington, DE: Michael Glazier, 1984), 83.
[33]Gregory Joseph Ladd, *Archbishop Fulton J. Sheen: A Man for All Media* (San Francisco: Ignatius Press, 2001), 13.
[34]Kathleen Riley Fields, "Bishop Fulton J. Sheen: An American Catholic Response to the Twentieth Century" (PhD diss., University of Notre Dame, 1988), 108.
[35]See Henry Everett Malone, "The Radio-Preaching Art of Monsignor Sheen," (MA diss., Catholic University of America, 1949), 2-4. See also Ellis, *Catholic Bishops*, 81-83. Ellis judged the "written messages" of "the nation's stellar Catholic pulpit orator" to be "less satisfying." With gracious humility, however, Ellis was willing to assume that the fault may have been his own rather than Sheen's.
[36]Malone, "Radio-Preaching Art," 55.

according to Sheen. "I speak with conviction," he explained, insisting that he would not speak on anything that he did not personally believe.[37] Responsibility for the content and presentation of his messages was his alone. He explained to a reporter, "To be an orator, you have to use your own words and be on fire with them. To be a talker—somebody else can write your words and you can read them."[38] At a time when listeners desired a feeling of intimacy with those who spoke to them through their radio sets, Sheen was a master at convincing individuals that he was interested in them on a personal level. He began each broadcast with a warm "Friends," followed by a short pause. He closed every talk with his signature, "God love you." In between, as priest Henry Everett Malone observed, "He makes you feel that he is talking to you alone, and that you are the only one that matters. The result is that you want to do what he tells you; you want to believe what he believes. . . . He personalizes the truth so well that we love it and want to embrace it."[39] As Sheen explained to his audience at the beginning of his 1949 series, "The most beautiful gifts are invisible, such as air for our lungs, grace for our souls and devoted friends of the radio. To further the intimate bond between us, may these broadcasts flower and blossom in the Eternal Triangle: You and me, in and through God. That is what I mean by 'Friends.'"[40]

When Sheen began a new CH series in December of 1940, the *Seattle Times* encouraged its readers to tune in to the Right Reverend Monsignor, and its writer particularly focused on his inviting style. The article opened,

> Today there will return to the airlanes a voice with a certain prayerful quality. It will carry more personality, even sifted through a microphone and a loud speaker, than many a voice from a person with whom you may be speaking face to face. It will be a warm voice—warm, intimate, vital and most of all, convincing. The words cradled in the voice, the voice itself, the personality, the vigor of an energetic man and a tremendous radio following all are centered in one priest.[41]

---

[37]Sherwood, *Preaching of Archbishop Fulton J. Sheen*, 26.

[38]Chester Morrison, "Religion Reaches Out: By Radio, TV and Movies, the Churches Speak to Vast New Congregations," *Look*, December 14, 1954, 44.

[39]Malone, "Radio-Preaching Art," 8, 10, 81.

[40]Fulton J. Sheen, *The Love That Waits for You* (Washington, DC: NCCM, 1958), 7.

[41]Robert Heilman, "Monsignor Sheen Returns to Catholic Hour: Beloved Voice Will Be Heard in New Series," *Seattle Times*, December 15, 1940, 5.

It was not just one characteristic, but a combination of qualities reflecting the "naturalness" that his college debating coach had urged. In 1947, *Look* magazine published an article covering Sheen's successes at gaining converts through his preaching and instruction. Sheen characteristically gave God the credit for conversions, adding that priests were little more than "gardeners, hoeing the earth a bit and watering the roots" in providential fields. *Look*'s reporter gushed, "Monsignor Sheen has many gifts for such celestial gardening: he commands a supple, rhythmic English, so that his instructions are very nearly poetry. . . . His speaking voice is magnificent."[42] Speech scholar William Hanford described his voice as "richly timbred and controlled," exhibiting a "deep and pleasant quality of tone which, in itself, contributes so much to the credibility of the speaker." Hanford also noted the emotional impact of Sheen's ability to "whisper" and "thunder" with "richness."[43] Sheen believed that physical exercise was a vital supplement to public speaking, as it enhanced his breath control. He attributed this to his regular tennis playing, and his habit of going "up stairs two at a time," resulting in a lower "register of my voice [by] one or two notes."[44] On the tenth anniversary of the CH's launch, *Time* said, "Monsignor Sheen is a persuasive, lucid speaker, with a well-cultivated voice, who can make religion sensible and attractive to great masses of people."[45] After the twentieth anniversary of the CH's commencement, *Pageant* referred to the "quality of Monsignor Sheen's declamation" to be nothing short of "spell-binding."[46]

A few years later, after Sheen had gained success on television, *Time* made him the cover story. It quoted TV columnist Harriet Van Horne as saying that Sheen was "the finest Catholic orator since [preacher of the First Crusade] Peter the Hermit." (It would appear that Ms. Van Horne had been auditing Catholic homilists for quite some time.) The article's author marveled that Sheen's "voice (with a wisp of a brogue) ranges from tremulous whispers to Old Testament rage. . . . His serious passages are carefully balanced with

---

[42]Gretta Palmer, "Why All These Converts? The Story of Monsignor Fulton Sheen," *Look*, June 24, 1947, 38.

[43]William J. Hanford, "A Rhetorical Study of the Radio and Television Speaking of Bishop Fulton John Sheen" (PhD diss., Wayne State University, 1965), 144.

[44]Hanford, "Rhetorical Study," 112.

[45]"Monsignor's Tenth," *Time*, March 11, 1940, 60-61.

[46]George Frazier, "Fulton J. Sheen: Unprofitable Servant," *Pageant* 5, no. 12 (June 1950): 40.

anecdotes or jocular footnotes, some well-worn."[47] Sheen's biographer, Thomas Reeves, summarizes, "Radio was the perfect outlet for [his] talents. . . . His ability to think clearly, his desire always to reach beyond clichés and say something meaningful, his flair for persuasive speaking . . . his charm and wit, and his extraordinary voice made his popularity inevitable."[48]

On reviewing a sampling of Sheen's recorded radio addresses, the author generally concurs with the contemporary assessments cited—sans any comparisons to Peter the Hermit, which he is not qualified to make. Seldom explicitly mentioned, but likely embedded in many of the positive critiques Sheen received, was his impeccable enunciation. In an era when radio voices were often intertwined with static and interference, this attentiveness to phonetic clarity, along with the tonal qualities of his voice, would have made his messages more effective and inviting. He varied his cadence for effect, but created a sense of what can be described as a "comfortable urgency." Sheen paused at just the right moments to let specific points "sink in," yet avoided a pace that might imply leisureliness. At other moments, he steadily built to a crescendo so as to drive home a point and stoke emotion, after which he often softened his tone as if to verbally place his arm around the shoulder of the listener.

In the course of twenty minutes, Sheen could convincingly convey moral indignation and hopeful joy, bare matter-of-factness and eager wonderment, abhorrence of sin and love of the sinner, gravitas and self-deprecating humor, authority and congeniality, and any number of related emotions. Unlike many of his fellow radio preachers, Sheen was not reluctant to weave humor into his discourses. On occasion, he was criticized for sinking to "corniness."[49] While this accusation may have been accurate, one gets the sense that such jocularity was seldom overdone. More importantly, the listeners rolling their eyes were no doubt far outnumbered by those who perceived the highly educated priest to be closer to their own level precisely because he was willing to be "corny."

Walter Maier's academic depth and dexterity were on par with Sheen's and his own eloquence attracted millions of listeners. Especially in comparison

---

[47]"Microphone Missionary," *Time*, April 14, 1952, 72, 78.
[48]Reeves, *America's Bishop*, 80; to hear a Sheen CH sermon, see Old Time Radio Catalog, www .otrcat.com/p/catholic-hour.
[49]See Hanford, "Rhetorical Study," 145.

to Sheen's, however, his delivery was breathlessly energetic and relentless. Like Sheen, Maier insisted that God's gracious intervention, not his delivery, was what caused souls to convert and hearts to change. (While neither Sheen nor Maier lacked for ego, both were consistent in attributing conversions to the work of the Holy Spirit.) Nonetheless, his style proved powerful and generated no small amount of commentary. The notoriety as an orator that Maier knew from his college days onward only grew as he acquired a national audience. As early as 1933, *Time* referred to Maier as "the most eminent speaker."[50] "A hard-hitting preacher of the old-time gospel of repentance and faith, Maier pulls no punches on national or individual sins," said the evangelical *Sunday* magazine.[51] An executive of the MBS described Maier's radio speaking technique as "the soapbox delivery of a Harvard script."[52] "The air sizzles and crackles when this 53-year-old, high-strung, athletic-formed and youth-vigored Maier lets go his flaming message . . . every Sunday," wrote William McDermott of *Christian Herald* in 1947. "The words pour out of his mouth—and soul—in a perfect torrent."[53] "The radio preacher bangs away at the microphone like a Fourth of July orator of the old school," added the *Saturday Evening Post.*[54]

While Maier's ability to convey "old-time religion" content with clarity and applicability was fully acknowledged by the press and his loyal listeners, his rapid tempo and elevated decibel level generated constant attention. In the same article in which *Time* magazine declared him as a modern-day "Chrysostom," its editors noted that he "literally shouts into the microphone at a machine-gun pace."[55] He had done so from the beginning. During the brief period in 1935 when Maier broadcast TLH from Detroit, Brace Beemer, the professionally trained actor who played the original Lone Ranger on network radio, served as the program's announcer. Beemer repeatedly coached Maier to modulate his voice: "No, No, Dr. Maier! You're too fast and loud here. Tone it down, but give it depth . . . dramatic pathos . . . engulf

---

[50]"Religion: Back to Luther," *Time*, September 4, 1933.

[51]Donald E. Hoke, "He Throws Inkwells on the Air," *Sunday*, April 1945, 14.

[52]As quoted in Hartzell Spence, "The Man of the Lutheran Hour," *Saturday Evening Post*, June 19, 1948, 88.

[53]William F. McDermott, "Twenty Million Hear Him Preach," *Christian Herald*, March 1947, 43.

[54]Spence, "Man of the Lutheran Hour," 88.

[55]"Lutherans," *Time*, October 18, 1943, 46, 49.

your hearers in the mood!" Maier followed Beemer's advice up to the moment he actually went on the air, and then reverted to his usual vigorous style.[56] Years later, when radio engineers finally persuaded him to soften his tone, listeners "wrote to ask if he was sick and fan mail dropped off 1,000 letters a day."[57] Needless to say, Maier resumed his shouting, earning another nickname: "Billy Sunday of the Air."[58] In an admiring, two-part article on Maier titled "He Throws Inkwells on the Air," evangelical writer Donald Hoke summarized, "Though he violates all modern approved techniques of radio speech by virtually shouting into the mike, his hard but pleasant voice has a gripping appeal that commands and holds attention, and his audience loves it."[59] Several years after his death, *Coronet* magazine attributed TLH's enduring success to the contributions of Maier in the program's earlier days, characterizing him as "a flamboyant man of God who apparently never really believed that he could be heard on the air unless he shouted at the top of his lungs."[60]

Maier's voice was not the only thing that he exercised during a radio sermon. Comparisons to Billy Sunday, the former Major League Baseball player turned preacher, also invited descriptions of Maier's athleticism. The primary reason Maier preached in his radio studio with his upper body stripped to his undershirt was because his animated delivery generated so much perspiration.[61] "He lambastes Beelzebub with the drive of a Joe Louis moving in for the knockout," proclaimed *Pageant* magazine. Also drawing on the fisticuffs analogy, another friendly critic asserted, "He sounds as if he is pronouncing the benediction with boxing gloves."[62] "When the humble professor faces the microphone . . . he undergoes a metamorphosis. Gone

---

[56]Maier, *A Man Spoke*, 166-67.

[57]"Lutherans," *Time*, October 18, 1943, 46, 49.

[58]William F. McDermott, "Old-Time Religion Goes Global," *Collier's*, May 6, 1944, 50. Maier would have taken this moniker as a compliment. Though most Lutherans would have recoiled from Billy Sunday's bombastic, revivalist methods, Maier admired him. When Sunday died, Maier wrote in *The Walther League Messenger*, "The nation lost one of the best preachers. . . . Few men in the pulpit have been more systematically and perhaps more unjustly criticized than he." As quoted in Richard J. Shuta, "Walter A. Maier as Evangelical Preacher," *Concordia Theological Quarterly* 74, nos. 1–2 (January/April 2010): 21.

[59]Hoke, "He Throws Inkwells on the Air," *Sunday*, May 1945, 24.

[60]Graham Mark, "The Word in 56 Languages," *Coronet* 39 (February, 1956): 142.

[61]"Lutherans," *Time*, October 18, 1943, 49; see also Spence, "Man of the Lutheran Hour," 17, 88-94.

[62]E. Clifford Nelson, *Lutheranism in North America: 1914-1970* (Minneapolis: Augsburg, 1972), 67.

are his normally soft voice and gentle approach. He shouts [and] gesticulates emphatically," said another.[63] One writer observed, "As he races on with his fervent plea . . . he gestures violently, often coming to a climax with his whole body poised as a lion for a spring."[64]

Without downplaying Maier's primary approach of a *preacher*, at times his urgent cadence and verbal punch mirrored that of popular network news commentators of the day. Just as those sober men delivered serious information about current events as if they were short of time, this sober pastor hurriedly delivered serious information about matters contemporary and matters eternal as if time were short. One of Maier's admirers, Billy Graham, noted that when he began his own radio ministry shortly after Maier's death, he rejected a "folksy and informal" format suggested by some. Instead, he patterned his delivery after "the styles of those who had the highest ratings at the time—newsmen such as Walter Winchell, Drew Pearson, and Gabriel Heatter, as well as the late Dr. Maier." "All four were fast and intense speakers," Graham added.[65]

It should be understood that Maier's fast-paced, high-decibel approach delivered something much more substantive than the ranting of your average pulpit-pounding fire-breather. *Collier's* observed, "Most ministers today would be afraid to 'burn 'em up' as Doctor Maier does, scolding and exhorting sinners to repentance, but his public seems to like it."[66] The fact is that Maier's urgent message was conveyed with an eloquence reflecting his erudition and mastery of language. One student of Maier's rhetoric noted, "[He] was a brilliant linguist, capable of doing detailed etymological studies of words before selecting that word he would use to create the symbol he desired."[67] Another scholar credited Maier with an inviting

---

[63]Ben Gross, "The World's Largest Congregation," *Pageant*, February 1945, 120.

[64]William F. McDermott, "Twenty Million Hear Him Preach," *Christian Herald*, March 1947, 43.

[65]Billy Graham, *Just as I Am: The Autobiography of Billy Graham* (San Francisco: HarperCollins, 1997), 180. Just as Maier's observers credited him with a "machine-gun pace," early observers of Graham referred to him as "God's machine-gun." See Grant Wacker, *America's Pastor: Billy Graham and the Shaping of a Nation* (Cambridge, MA: Belknap, 2014), 61.

[66]McDermott, "Old-Time Religion Goes Global," 50. Not quite all of his public liked his speaking style. One California listener wrote to Maier, "4 Christ's Sake, Change Your Voice. It Sounds Like Hell!" Maier was amused and wanted to frame that card, but his wife would not allow it. See Maier, *A Man Spoke*, 186.

[67]David T. Volz, "The Rhetoric of Walter A. Maier" (MA thesis, Florida Atlantic University, 1994), 27.

"ornateness" that he created through "word choices" and "stylistic devices,"
in particular "alliteration and imagery."[68] Like Fulton Sheen, he communicated by engaging a scholarly mind, but did so without being off-putting.
His successor on TLH, Oswald Hoffmann, noted, "In the cultivated accents
of Harvard, he spoke of Christ to the common man. Whatever he touched
leaped into life."[69]

In a 1937 article on how to carry out a radio ministry, Maier instructed,
"Plain, direct, crisp, expressive language must be used. Drab, prosy English,
stilted phraseology, obscure theological references, must be avoided. . . .
Meticulous attention must be offered the correct pronunciation of words
and the consistent use of correct English." Additionally, so as to assure "clear
enunciation" the "radio speaker must talk slowly, but not too slowly; distinctly, but not too distinctly." Demonstrating his attention to every detail of
communicating, Maier even warned that "soft paper rather than crisp bond"
be used for manuscripts, so as to avoid the sound of "rustling" on the air.
Like Sheen, he also expressed the opinion that radio broadcasts were not to
proselytize, but were to evangelize.[70] The speakers of both the CH and TLH
were eager to serve as spiritual shepherds, but had no desire to be seen as
stealing sheep of another ecclesiastical pasture.

On a weekly basis, the urgency with which Maier approached his ministry came through as his delivery over the airwaves conveyed gospel energy
to his massive congregation.[71] Though his staccato delivery and tendency to
raise his voice could have produced negative reactions, they were more than
offset by the perception that Maier was deeply sincere. One theological
scholar stated that such sincerity made him remarkably persuasive: "He
sympathized with the hurt of the listener. He displayed genuine interest in
the salvation of the lost. He became personally involved in the quest for
peace amidst a troubled world."[72] Many felt that his style came across as

---

[68]Kenneth H. Sulston, "A Rhetorical Criticism of the Radio Preaching of Walter Arthur Maier"
(PhD diss., Northwestern University, 1958), 323.

[69]Oswald C. J. Hoffmann, *What More Is There To Say but Amen* (St. Louis: CPH, 1996), 14.

[70]Walter A. Maier, "The Radio for Christ," *The Concordia Pulpit for 1938* (St. Louis: CPH, 1937), 485.

[71]To hear a recording of a Maier radio sermon see Lutheran Hour Ministries, "History of the
Lutheran Hour," www.lutheranhour.org/history.asp#maier.

[72]James L. Anderson, "An Evaluation of the Communicative Factors in the Radio Preaching of
Walter A. Maier on the Tenth Lutheran Hour Series in 1942–1943" (ThD diss., Southwestern
Baptist Theological Seminary, 1976), 200.

more sincere precisely because his fervent pleading implied that he cared so deeply for his listeners. It was noted that Maier "preached as never to be able to preach again, as a dying man to dying men."[73]

Upon review of audio recordings of Walter Maier's TLH sermons, I would add the following observations. First, and most importantly, while Maier spoke rapidly and elevated his voice, descriptions of him "hollering" or "shouting at the top of his lungs" are simply exaggerated. There were indeed times when he may have benefited from slowing down or softening his voice, but David Volz's description seems fitting: "He had a powerful voice that would grab the attention of nearly everyone, even a sleepy and disinterested listener."[74] His voice and delivery were firm, sometimes stern, yet not unpleasant. Maier always sounded confident and sincere, but he often conveyed an upbeat excitement about what it was he was telling the listener.

While sermon content is discussed more fully in the next chapters, Maier's Lutheran presentation of "law" and "gospel" comes through in the way he delivers his message. When speaking of sin, of both the national and individual varieties, Maier's warnings were unwavering and accusatory. Illustrations and alliterations helped him build to a crescendo, making the loathsomeness of sin and the reality of its perils all too real. What prevented this from being off-putting was Maier's frequent placement of himself among the sinners he was accusing, and the inviting tone to which he shifted when moving into the "gospel" portion of his message. Maier frequently made it clear that he needed forgiveness from a gracious Savior just as his listeners did, by inserting phrases such as "my friends and fellow-redeemed" or "my fellow sinners and fellow redeemed." When offering the free forgiveness by faith in Christ that such properly indicted transgressors needed, Maier adopted a tone filled with emotional assurance and the promise of "perfect peace for you and I." Maier once said, "In our entire radio-preaching, as indeed in our pulpit-preaching, the injunction of the Old Testament evangelist 'Comfort ye, comfort ye, My people,' must be the uppermost thought in the speaker's message."[75] A fair hearing of his TLH recordings only confirms the sincerity of Maier's comforting mission.

---

[73]Anderson, "Evaluation of the Communicative Factors," 88.
[74]Volz, "Rhetoric of Walter A. Maier," 128.
[75]Maier, "Radio for Christ," 487.

Fulton Sheen's radio sermons were often characterized as "lectures"—a fitting description in many cases. At other times, Sheen could adopt a conversational tone. None of Maier's radio sermons were likely to be mistaken for a lecture, even though he was an experienced seminary lecturer. Nor did he come across as conversational in most instances, even though he was known as a great conversationalist. When Maier stepped up to the radio microphone, he was *preaching*—pure and simple. Maier began each broadcast sermon with a prayer and he concluded each one with a firm "Amen." In between, he was preaching to save the lost and to edify the found, and doing so in not-so-subtle a fashion.

Nearly fifteen years after Maier's death, Illinois State Senator (and future United States Senator and Democratic presidential candidate) Paul Simon wrote a letter to Hulda Maier—Walter's widow. Simon, himself the son of a Lutheran minister, recalled Maier's rhetorical gifts: "Your husband was by all odds the most powerful and dynamic speaker that I have ever heard in my life and the most dynamic I ever expect to hear." He noted that in his legislative experiences he had heard "most of the men on the national scene who are supposed to be the great orators, yet none can compare with your husband."[76] Walter Maier's distinctive style left a lasting impression on the bow-tied senator from the Land of Lincoln, as it did on millions of others across the country and around the globe.

THE SERMONS

While Sheen and Maier may have been blessed with the oratorical skills that generated comparisons with great, historical preachers—ancient and modern—mellifluous and nimble exhorting alone would not have kept listeners tuning in for over twenty years (and much longer on television, in the case of Sheen). Their sermon content was thoughtful, substantive, topical, and well-suited for the American public. True, their universal message of salvation proved efficacious with foreign audiences as well, but domestic broadcasts were clearly crafted with American hearers in mind. Both men

---

[76]Letter from Paul Simon to Mrs. Walter A. Maier, dated August 25, 1964, WAM Collection, box 2, folder 105, CHI. Many years later, Simon recalled, as a high school student, hearing initial reports of the Japanese attack on December 7, 1941, from the "eloquent national radio preacher, Dr. Walter A. Maier, who totally changed his Sunday [TLH] sermon because of Pearl Harbor." See Paul Simon, *P.S.: The Autobiography of Paul Simon* (Chicago: Bonus Books, 1999), 16.

combined a traditional theological conservatism with an equally traditional American idealism.[77] While carrying out their primary task of proclaiming the gospel of Christ in a national forum, Sheen and Maier contributed to an American civil religiosity as well.

Length. The twenty-minute (give or take) time periods available to Maier and Sheen for their respective broadcasts' sermons differed from the norms of the time for Lutheran and Catholic parish preachers' sermons, but in different ways. While Sheen had been recognized as a gifted homilist from his initial, postordination days at St. Patrick's in Peoria, sermons were not a dominant component of pre–Vatican II American Catholic masses. In a 1941 article in *Catholic World*, Congregationalist minister turned Catholic priest W. E. Orchard acknowledged that the lack of emphasis on the sermon in a Catholic service "may occasion some surprise and sense of loss in the convert" from Protestantism, such as himself. In this article, which was sometimes humorous, perhaps without the author's intent, Orchard lamented the lack of seriousness with which Catholic clerics and parishioners took the act and art of preaching.

He noted that in "the Catholic Church . . . the sermon may dwindle to a few minutes, or may be abandoned for various reasons." When priests actually did give homilies, they were "not often of a very striking nature or particularly informative character; sometimes consisting of a few disconnected remarks which it is obvious have not had much thought or care spent in their preparation." To make matters worse, "this will make no difference to the congregation," since "they have an obligation to be present anyhow," but clearly "don't want sermons . . . don't like them . . . and don't give much attention to them anyhow." Overworked and underprepared priests, combined with the demand by the laity for Masses to proceed with "swift succession," were "crowding out" substantive sermons—to the point that "a sermon of more than five minutes would disorganize everything and produce chaos if not a riot."[78]

---

[77]While both Sheen and Maier were strongly patriotic, neither was blindly so, especially when they perceived moral issues at stake. See Reeves, *America's Bishop*, 161-62; Richard Joseph Shuta, "The Militant Evangelicalist of Missouri: Walter Arthur Maier and His Theological Orientation" (PhD diss., Drew University, 1990), 309-15.

[78]W. E. Orchard, "The Place of Preaching in the Catholic Church," *Catholic World* 153, issue 913 (1941): 46-50. For a narrative of Orchard's journey from Presbyterian, to Congregational, to

In such an environment, Sheen's twenty-minute radio homilies were generally longer than those of his priestly counterparts in Catholic sanctuaries.
Yet unlike Catholics in weekly mass, Sheen's congregants did *not* "have an
obligation to be present." Nonetheless, they were "present" every week,
seated in parlors rather than pews. The medium of radio allowed Sheen to
unfetter his listeners, at least the Catholic ones, from their ingrained low or
indifferent expectations relating to priestly preaching. He consistently demonstrated that twenty minutes of relevant, well-crafted oratory was not only
bearable, but downright stimulating.

The same twenty-minute window that gave Sheen greater sermonizing
freedom than that normally available to his fellow priests was actually con-
straining on Walter Maier, in relation to time available for his fellow Lutheran pastors to preach from their pulpits. While Lutherans placed more
emphasis on the sacraments than most of their Protestant brethren, they
placed more emphasis on the preached Word than did their Catholic counterparts. Thus, like other Protestants, Lutherans devoted more of their
regular Sunday worship services to preaching. Demonstrating the emphasis
placed on preaching at the time, especially in Lutheran circles, the year
before Maier launched TLH, Concordia Publishing House began producing
an annual book of sample sermon texts and detailed outlines, crafted with
the coming liturgical year in mind. This series, titled *The Concordia Pulpit*,
noted that worthy preachers must repeatedly "arise in public" to "deliver . . .
the truth of spirit and life, which penetrates, arouses, feeds, sustains, satisfies,
and produces response"—obviously, a weighty charge.[79]

At the time of Maier's foray onto network radio, the standard Lutheran
textbook on preaching, used by seminarians and ministers, was Michael
Reu's *Homiletics*.[80] Noting that "a true sermon cannot be limited as a brief,
impassioned harangue can," Reu cautioned, "the warning today must be
against unduly short rather than against unduly long sermons." He

Roman Catholic pulpits, see W. E. Orchard, *From Faith to Faith: An Autobiography of Religious
Development* (New York and London: Harper & Brothers, 1933).

[79]Martin S. Sommer, ed., *The Concordia Pulpit for 1930* (St. Louis: CPH, 1929), iii. In subsequent
years, Walter Maier was one of many contributors to *The Concordia Pulpit*. Established in 1869,
Concordia Publishing House is the publishing entity of the LCMS.

[80]Carl C. Fickenscher II, homiletics professor, Concordia Theological Seminary, Fort Wayne,
Indiana, interview with author, April 14, 2014, and email exchange, June 2, 2014.

estimated that "thirty minutes . . . may be given as a fair average for the length of the sermon in the main service." Reu suggested that only "on occasion" should preachers deliver sermons shorter than thirty minutes, and pointed out with evident approval that famed Baptist preacher, Charles Spurgeon, "considered . . . forty minutes to be an adequate period in which to acquit himself of his task as preacher."[81] Lutheran homiletics scholar Carl C. Fickenscher II confirms Reu's suggested sermon lengths: "The sermons I've studied from [this period] suggest that thirty minutes was a standard," though that was "sometimes slightly conservative . . . for Sunday morning LCMS preaching."[82]

In sum, Maier had to adapt his sermons to a time limit that was shorter than he and other Lutheran preachers usually preached. Yet such time constraints likely added to Maier's effectiveness as a communicator, given the differences between the dynamics of radio and the church sanctuary. The required relative brevity of TLH preaching enhanced his audible sense of urgency, demanded a cogent establishment of relevance, forced a clear, crisp progression of thought in each message, and avoided the overtaxation of listeners' attention spans.

Preparation. Maximizing the impact of twenty minutes required extensive preparation of a considerable multiple of that amount of time, by both Maier and Sheen. With regard to Sheen's CH addresses, the Catholic newspaper *Our Sunday Visitor* commented, "Father Sheen . . . forges brilliant thoughts on the anvil of his mind."[83] Sheen meticulously prepared his weekly radio sermons, estimating that he devoted forty to sixty hours to each one.[84] In an interview in the late 1940s, he went so far as to report that he practiced his radio sermons for "thirty or forty hours," matching "the same amount of time thinking out the subject."[85] On the assumption that Sheen's days were twenty-four hour periods like everyone else's, these claims have to be overstated, or the exception rather than the rule. Whatever the actual time committed was, however, it is safe to assume that it was

---

[81]M. Reu, *Homiletics: A Manual of the Theory and Practice of Preaching* (Minneapolis: Augsburg, 1924), 506-7.

[82]Interview by author of Fickenscher, June 2, 2014.

[83]"Enthroned In His Crib He Rules Over All Men," *Our Sunday Visitor*, December 24, 1933, 1.

[84]"Mgr. Sheen, the Radiant Voice of Catholicism," *Boston Sunday Post*, May 3, 1936.

[85]Malone, "Radio-Preaching Art," 97.

significant. More importantly, Sheen emphasized, "The real secret of my work is that all my sermons are prepared in the Presence of the Blessed Sacrament."[86] In his autobiography, he observed, "As recreation is most pleasant and profitable in the sun, so homiletic creativity is best nourished before the Eucharist."[87]

Sheen was "convinced that preaching and lecturing are impossible without much studying and reading." He lamented that "one of the weaknesses of the modern pulpit and lecture platform" was "the neglect of continuing education." Ongoing replenishment was vital: "When the intellectual larder is empty, it is difficult to prepare a homiletic meal." "My reading embraces literature, science, philosophy of politics—in a word . . . everything that would be useful for a priest in instructing or discoursing with others, or in supplying material for communication."[88] Comparing a good library to a "smorgasbord," Sheen boasted that his personal library contained ten to twelve thousand volumes. "I try to keep up to date on all subjects," he added, but admitted that this required him to just "skim through" certain books, "enough to know" what was in them should he "ever have to talk on this subject."[89] By incorporating such broad knowledge into his sermons, Sheen drew in listeners with different life experiences and different interests, establishing both a personal connection and credibility. Central to his reading was Scripture, which he studied with the aid of numerous commentaries. Interestingly, he preferred Protestant commentaries because "Protestants have spent more time on Scripture than most of us."[90] Notwithstanding his insistence that priests read broadly, Sheen warned of the dangers of abandoning "spiritual reading," especially the Bible. The cleric who "substitutes the 'Book of the Month' for the Book of Revelation" could not prepare sound sermons—or, for that matter, appropriately execute his vocation.[91]

Sheen's "forging" of a sermon required an iterative, honing process. "When the general plan of the sermon has been formulated, I will then talk my thoughts to Our Lord, or at least meditate on it, almost whispering the

[86]Malone, "Radio-Preaching Art," 8.
[87]Sheen, *Treasure in Clay*, 79.
[88]Sheen, *Treasure in Clay*, 80, 82.
[89]Hanford, "Rhetorical Study," 114-15.
[90]Sheen, *Treasure in Clay*, 83.
[91]Sheen, *The Priest Is Not His Own* (San Francisco: Ignatius Press, 2004), 179.

Figure 5.3. Sheen working at his desk in his Washington, DC, residence

ideas," explained Sheen. "After the material is gathered and the points formulated, I follow with either meditation or a quiet vocalization without ever
referring to notes." The actual verbalization was critical, as the "material of
the sermon is not wholly that which comes from the paper to the brain, but
which proceeds from a creative mind to the lips."[92] Sheen never wrote out
the texts of his sermons (or any other talks), even avoiding detailed outlines.
He explained, "I just diagram them, generally in terms of, perhaps, three big
ideas." Then he would tear up even these skeletal notes. In his opinion, "The
writing out of sermons or talks discourages fresh thinking." "Why should a
living mind become a slave to a piece of paper? What is so perfect about
something that you put down in script that the mind has to become subser-
vient to it? If the mind is living, let it think it out and think it out." While
Sheen practiced verbalizing his sermon ideas, he claimed never to formulate
or memorize sermons or speeches word-for-word.[93] Although Sheen lacked
neither intellect nor self-confidence, it is truly remarkable that week after

---

[92]Sheen, *Treasure in Clay*, 79-80.
[93]Hanford, "Rhetorical Study," 115-17.

week he stepped before NBC microphones, and later DuMont television cameras, without a written text or outline.

Sheen often stated that his sermons were never designed to be proselytizing instruments—a point he reiterated in his autobiography.[94] Nonetheless, from the beginning of his work on the CH, he was mindful of "the problem of creating" the right "spirit." Sheen "thought long" about two questions: "What is the purpose of this hour and what will the non-Catholic think of a purely sectarian radio program?" As to the first question, he answered, "I will preach Christ and Him crucified." To the second, he decided to overcome preconceived ideas outsiders might have about Catholicism by presenting it in a winsome fashion, reflecting "refinement and intelligence."[95]

In fact, when Sheen claimed that he did not "proselytize" on the air, he apparently meant only that he did not harangue his listeners or attack other non-Catholic groups. He did, however, prepare his sermons with strong evangelistic goals. In an interview near the end of his radio ministry, Sheen outlined his approach. First, in an obvious overstatement, Sheen claimed that when on the air he was concerned with non-Catholics "alone." Said another way, he was extremely mindful of how his words, and the way he spoke them, would sound to those outside of his denomination. Second, his "whole purpose was to bring souls to God." Third, when approaching these souls, "the positive approach is better than the negative and critical." Fourth, he needed to always identify "something in common" with the audience, and prepare a sermon "from that common viewpoint." And fifth, he constantly reminded himself "that great charity is needed at all times."[96]

It was much the same with Walter Maier. In a two-part 1945 article placing the *Lutheran Hour* speaker in impressive company, *Sunday* magazine writer Hoke pointed out, "Luther may have thrown inkwells at the devil from his monastery cell, but his modern counterpart, Walter Maier, makes his thrusts over the entire world." Hoke highlighted Maier's careful preparation, marveling that before he threw his inkwells on the air each week, he spent "20 hours at least" crafting his sermons, which was "two or three times the

---

[94]Sheen, *Treasure in Clay*, 77.
[95]"Mgr. Sheen, the Radiant Voice of Catholicism," *Boston Sunday Post*, May 3, 1936.
[96]Malone, "Radio-Preaching Art," 17.

national average for preachers." His "aim" was "to quote at least one scripture per minute of the 20 he . . . preaches."[97] In *Time* magazine, Maier justified his biblically saturated sermons, contrasting them with empty "sawdust" sermons, for which "he has no use." He wanted it understood that his audience clamored for not just his quantity of scriptural content, but also for the manner in which it was employed. Taking a not-so-subtle swipe at more modernist fellow Protestants, he added, "I don't quote Scripture with my fingers crossed."[98] Though Maier, like Sheen, demonstrated a well-read awareness of contemporary literature and affairs, in a striking parallel to his Catholic counterpart, he insisted that "Book-of-the-Month discussions must not crowd the Book of Eternity from the pulpit."[99]

As for nonscriptural reading, the *Sunday* article noted that "every evening and in spare moments, Maier reads voraciously." Since "explanations, illustrations, amplifications . . . all must be fresh, timely, accurate," the TLH preacher kept "voluminous files . . . crammed full to overflowing with gathered facts . . . and information on every subject under the sun."[100] A review of Maier's information files, many of which are held at the Concordia Historical Institute, demonstrates that Hoke's descriptions are understated, rather than overstated. In addition to files on expected topics such as hermeneutics, religious movements and leaders, and evolution, there are hundreds of files covering quite specific topics within the fields of politics, education, science and medicine, literature, agriculture, economics, fashion, music, the arts, popular entertainment, social problems and remedies, athletics, and so on. While Maier's inquisitiveness is impressive in both its breadth and its systemization, one is left wondering what sermonic content he contemplated gleaning from his files on such things as *banana production*, or *credit unions*, or *rheumatism*.[101] Expressing a similar commitment to Sheen's, Maier explained his voracious reading habits, "I must keep pulse on human affairs."[102] Be that as it may, it is obvious that Maier put considerable, consistent effort in making sure that his foundational biblical texts were made

---

[97]Hoke, "He Throws Inkwells," April, 1945, 13-16, 52, and May, 1945, 20-24, 62, 64-65.
[98]"Lutherans," *Time*, 48-49.
[99]Judy Maguire, "The Lutheran Hour," *Radio and Television Life* 18 (October 31, 1948): 34, 39.
[100]Hoke, "He Throws Inkwells," May, 1945, 23.
[101]See WAM Collection, CHI, St. Louis.
[102]Hoke, "He Throws Inkwells," May, 1945, 23.

relevant to his listeners by interweaving them with wide-ranging topical subjects and illustrations.

Maier's weekly preparatory routine went as follows. Early in the week he would pick his sermon topic and scriptural passages for the coming Sunday. Unlike Sheen, who usually expounded on a general theme as part of a series of sermons, Maier was more flexible in his approach.[103] According to his son,

Figure 5.4. Maier habitually strung paper clips together as he prepared his sermons each week. His wife, Hulda, is shown taking notes.

[103]This is not meant to be an evaluative statement. In that Sheen served as CH speaker for only a portion of the year, he chose to expound upon an overarching theme over the course of each of his annual series. Since Maier was the sole TLH speaker for each entire radio season, he had more opportunity to cover a broader range of topics.

the subject could depend on a variety of factors, such as the liturgical season, a doctrinal topic, concerns expressed in letters from listeners, or current events worthy of religious commentary. After teaching his last class on Fridays, he asked his secretary for whatever informational files related to his planned topic, while he studied his chosen biblical text in the original language. Then, in a habit strikingly similar to Sheen's jotting of *JMJ* (for Jesus, Mary, and Joseph) on the top of his handwritten pages, Maier marked *INJ* (for the Latin *in nomine Jesu*—"in the name of Jesus") at the top of his page, and began sketching out a sermon.[104]

"When the sermon is well in form, Maier dictates it to his secretary the first time, praying over every page," reported *Sunday* magazine.[105] His wife recalled that he would pace back and forth as he dictated, completely engrossed in the creative, communicative task at hand. Sometimes he would begin connecting paperclips end-to-end as he thought about his words and phraseology, until he had inadvertently created a long chain during the dictating session.[106] Maier meticulously dictated punctuation in each sentence. Revisions and edits occurred on Saturday, after which fellow Concordia Seminary professor William Arndt reviewed the manuscript and offered suggestions. Maier orally rehearsed the sermon on Saturday evening and Sunday morning, making sure it read smoothly and conformed to time constraints.[107] After this intense Friday to Sunday scramble, "when the time comes to broadcast, the message is a part of [Maier], and he reads it so well that few realize every word is before him."[108] Interestingly, while both Sheen and Maier had the intellect to think on their feet, Sheen preached on radio without a written text, but Maier preferred to do his "thinking on his feet" prior to airtime.

As radio rapidly rose in popularity, in the early days of the Great Depression, the riddle for the radio industry was this: What will appeal to the common man and woman? As traditionalist churches fretted over the erosion of

[104]Maier, *A Man Spoke*, 200-201.
[105]Hoke, "He Throws Inkwells," May, 1945, 23.
[106]Anderson, "Evaluation of the Communicative Factors," 41.
[107]Maier, *A Man Spoke*, 202-3.
[108]Hoke, "He Throws Inkwells," May, 1945, 23.

orthodox Christian belief in these same anxious days, the riddle for the doctrinally solid cleric was the same. In no small way, the CH and TLH, and their star preachers, answered the question with surprising clarity. Without any particular programming novelty, TLH and the CH took thirty minutes of music, messages, and prayer, centered on traditional Christian theological themes, into the living rooms of eager listeners every week. From the beginning, program content was consistent and high in quality, as it would remain for decades to come.

While the featured musical performances contributed to this quality on both broadcasts, the eloquent, impassioned sermons by Walter Maier and Fulton Sheen were the primary components of each program's perceived worthiness. Although their respective preaching styles were rather different, they both polished their sermonic approaches into attention-grabbing, thought-provoking, personally inspiring deliveries of divine truths. Neither one attempted to hold an audience with mere stylistic artistry, however. Their sermon content, which was produced through hours of study and preparation each week, offered the substance that brought listeners back to the CH and TLH time and time again. Sheen and Maier skillfully wove together scriptural content, systematic theological thought, historical facts, current events, and scientific discoveries in ways that enhanced the authority with which they spoke. This, combined with their masterful balancing of urgency and admonition, sincerity and warmth, rendered the ancient truth claims of Christianity they espoused relevant for twentieth-century radio devotees.

In the following chapters, this study will provide a more in-depth analysis of the homiletic content of Maier's and Sheen's radio addresses, with special attention paid to broad theological themes on which they frequently expounded. It is important to remember that this content became effective because of *how* it was delivered, as well as for what it said.

Chapter Six

HOMILETIC HEFT

PREACHING FOUNDATIONAL THEOLOGY

*The preacher's mission is the grandest on earth: he holds in his
hands a power the proudest monarch might envy. . . . He has the
sublimest and most soul-stirring truths that can be conceived. . . .
He may speak if he will, with the power of Truth itself, with the
strength of the prayers of the saints, the sympathies of all good
men and angels, and with the omnipotence of God on his Side.*

ORESTES A. BROWNSON

*To some few who have the gift to treat the Holy Scriptures and
to explicate them, a particular public office is given that is carried out
for the common benefit. . . . The . . . [period] that [preachers] spend in
the pulpit is most valuable time. It may help determine the present and
eternal salvation of thousands of people. Woe to the preacher who does not
redeem that time by offering his listeners the very best he is able to give.*

C. F. W. WALTHER

WALTER MAIER AND FULTON SHEEN prepared their radio sermons diligently. Their programs' format, style, and musical elements provided high quality, popular enhancements to each broadcast. Whether on par with John Chrysostom, Peter the Hermit, or Billy Sunday, Sheen and Maier delivered their proclamations with appealing style, eloquence, and urgency. Yet it must be acknowledged that even the most arresting of elocutionists will eventually lose their audiences if they fail to deliver substantive information and stimulating ideas, deemed relevant by their auditors. This Maier and Sheen did, week after week, for two decades. To be clear, the most important factor in understanding the popularity and the impact of their radio ministries is to grasp the homiletic content of their spoken words. Therefore, a few prefatory comments are in order. The following survey is designed to allow Sheen and Maier to speak for themselves, by providing representative quotations from their sermons. Because it may be hard for us to imagine today that so many people were eager to listen to these two preachers speak at length on such seemingly esoteric or uninviting topics as scriptural authority, the atonement, sanctification, and the consequences of sin, I have quoted them extensively. My purpose is not only to demonstrate Maier's and Sheen's consistency and fervor around such themes, but to present the rhetorical breadth and creativity they employed to keep such heavy topics riveting. This chapter examines the foundational theology they presented, and the following chapter will look at what they made of that theology by way of practical application.

A thorough review of Sheen's and Maier's radio sermons reveals a remarkable richness of content. Due to the popularity of their preaching, both preachers' sermons were published annually, in book form, at the conclusion of their respective radio seasons. Maier's radio sermon content is more extensive than Sheen's, as the former was the sole speaker on TLH for each radio season, while the latter was one of several annual speakers on the CH.[1]

---

[1] Until the fall of 1942, TLH broadcasts generally ran from October through April, with Maier serving as the *sole* preacher. Beginning with the 1942–1943 radio season TLH became a year-round program. From that point, Maier typically preached on the air from October through May or June, with various other Lutheran leaders filling in during the remainder of each summer. See Paul L. Maier, *A Man Spoke, A World Listened: The Story of Walter A. Maier* (New York: McGraw-Hill, 1963), 271. Sheen's annual series on the CH usually ran for less than twenty weeks, from Christmas to Easter. Because of the greater volume of sermon texts produced by Maier, my treatment of his content, at least with regard to certain topics, will require more extensive

Perhaps because Sheen expounded on a multiweek theme in each of his series, and as a reflection of his role as an academic in the field of philosophy, his radio sermons sometimes exhibited a lecture-like quality.[2] Maier was an experienced lecturer as well; however, he carried out his professorial duties at a seminary, training future preachers. While his sermons reflected his intellect and learning, no one would have characterized them as lectures.[3] Nonetheless, both Sheen and Maier crafted the content of their radio addresses as *sermons*—first and foremost.

The Jesus Christ for whom Fulton Sheen and Walter Maier labored on the air once said to his followers, "If you abide in My word, you are My disciples indeed. And you shall know the truth, and the truth shall make you free" (Jn 8:31-32 NKJV). Sheen and Maier were dedicated to the spreading of such truth—truth that was unchanging, truth that was reliable, truth that was sufficient and sustaining, truth that was salvific for time and eternity. Their missions of truth, however, faced a problem as they went on the air in 1930. Enduring truth was falling out of fashion. Sheen wrote that modern thinkers, both religious and secular, had become "so obsessed with" the "mood of temporalism," drinking so deeply its "intoxicating draughts," that

---

treatment than Sheen's content requires. This occasional disparity in written analysis is due only to my desire to fully represent the breadth of Sheen's and Maier's content.

[2]From time to time, NBC executives and radio listeners complained that CH addresses, including those by Sheen, were "too academic and high-toned." Historian Alexander Pavuk observes that while "Sheen was not immune from making abstruse allusions," his rhetoric became much more "lowbrow" and "general" over time. (See Alexander Pavuk, "Constructing a Catholic Church Out of Thin Air: *Catholic Hour's* Early Years on NBC Radio," *American Catholic Studies* 118, no. 4 [2007]: 48-49.) Though I have yet to run across a Sheen utterance that would be described as "lowbrow," the general conclusion that Sheen became increasingly attuned to more pedestrian ears appears accurate. The NCCM was sensitive to complaints that the content of the CH was occasionally "over listeners' heads," but concluded that audience response, from "the unlettered as well as the learned," confirmed that their speakers were fulfilling the proper objective of conveying a "high level of dignity . . . without pomposity or ostentation." See Edward J. Heffron, "Eight Years of the Catholic Hour," *Catholic Action*, February 1938, 9.

[3]Maier occasionally threw out a reference that likely left a few listeners scratching their heads, such as when he mentioned "the oldest epic poem known to men, written thousands of years ago, in cuneiform characters pressed into Mesopotamian clay" (see Walter A. Maier, *The Lutheran Hour: Winged Words to Modern America: Broadcast in the Coast-to-Coast Radio Crusade for Christ* [St. Louis, CPH, 1931], 71-72). However, he usually went out of his way to assure that he did not speak over the average listener's head. Kenneth H. Sulston argued that the only exception to this was Maier's use of terms containing specific Christian meaning, such as *grace*, or *triune God*, or *God's children*, without always providing definitions. See Kenneth H. Sulston, "The Rhetorical Criticism of the Radio Preaching of Walter Arthur Maier" (PhD diss., Northwestern University, 1958), 322, 372.

they taught "with unbuttoned pride that there is no such thing as Truth with a capital 'T,' for Truth is ambulatory: we make it as we go; it depends on the Time in which we live."[4] Somehow, people had forgotten that "Truth is not our making, but God's." The "indifference to the oneness of truth is at the root of all assumptions so current in present-day thinking that religion is an open question, like the tariff, whereas science is a closed question, like the multiplication table." As Sheen saw it, the modernists who resisted certainty in religious opinion, but exalted human reason and empirical observation, in fact, subverted the very reason on which they claimed to rely: "The kind of broadmindedness which sacrifices principles to whims, dissolves entities into environment, and reduces truth to opinion, is an unmistakable sign of the decay of the logical faculty."[5]

Maier shared Sheen's concern. He noted in an early TLH sermon that when the present "restless, disillusioned world echoes [Pontius Pilate's query of Jesus], 'What is truth,' people often ask the question with a calculated seriousness that is born of distrust and suspicion."[6] A few months later, Maier lamented, "There is a haze of doubt and uncertainty that rises from the unbelief so rampant in our day; there is the smoke-screen of modernist delusion by which the verities of our faith disappear in the black barrage of human speculation."[7] "Our modern, grasping, skeptical age," he observed, had come to rely solely on "human reason"—the "cold, calculating" and highly flawed reason it had unwisely "enthroned." The outrageous outcome of this reliance was that reason so ensconced "tells us that the only religious verities are those which can be tested and proved by the results of modern scientific investigation."[8] While Maier indicted the many secular contributors to the lubricious state of truth, he particularly regretted that at a time when the church should have been reemphasizing the immutable nature of its truth claims, its modernist wing only added to the confusion. He complained that the "devices of the weather-vane pulpit are as froth that is blown

---

[4]Fulton J. Sheen, *Moods and Truths: How to Solve the Problems of Modern Living* (New York: Popular Library, 1956), 121-22. (Originally published in 1932 by The Century Co.)
[5]Sheen, *Moods and Truths*, 90-91.
[6]Maier, *Lutheran Hour*, 28.
[7]Maier, *Lutheran Hour*, 163. For a complete listing of the specific dates of Maier's radio sermons, see Sulston, "Rhetorical Criticism," 556-88.
[8]Maier, *Lutheran Hour*, 28.

away with every change of the wind: and these chameleon-like preachers, who can change their color to match every shade of popular flavor, only lead men more deeply into sloughs of despair."[9]

Sheen and Maier believed in capital-T Truth. Sheen and Maier were certain that they knew and understood capital-T Truth, and were confident of its transformative power. The presentation and explanation of capital-T Truth were the main ingredients of their radio sermons, week after week.

Maier and Sheen considered the Bible to be the fount out of which their sermon content flowed. They took St. Paul at his word when he instructed, "All scripture is inspired by God and profitable for teaching, for reproof, for correction, and for training in righteousness, that the man of God may be complete" (2 Tim 3:16-17 RSV). Scriptural references indeed permeated their messages, but in slightly different ways. Maier was more inclined to craft an expository sermon around a specific biblical text, which he stated at the beginning of his talk. He quoted Scripture directly and frequently, usually from the King James text, but not always with "chapter and verse" specificity. Sometimes Maier seemed to assume that the listener would know when Scripture was being quoted, without his saying so directly—perhaps a reasonable assumption in a more biblically literate era.

While Sheen often focused a sermon on a single biblical teaching, or event, or person, he was less inclined to begin with a specific scriptural text and then expound on it. Instead, he often centered on a topic or idea and then brought in biblical texts or stories or concepts relating to his primary points. Sheen did quote Scripture verbatim, but more often summarized what the Bible taught about his present topic. When he did quote the Bible, Sheen usually drew from the Doauy-Rheims-Challoner version; however, Sheen became fond of Monsignor Ronald Knox's New Testament translation (the Knox Bible), often quoting from it after its publication in 1945.[10] Though Sheen occasionally used phrases like "as we know from Genesis," or "the Old Testament story of," or "our Lord taught," he stated specific biblical sources

---

[9]Walter A. Maier, *Christ for Every Crisis: The Radio Messages Broadcast in the Second Lutheran Hour* (St. Louis: CPH, 1935), 66-67.

[10]Both the Doauy-Rheims and the Knox translations used the Latin Vulgate as their primary source. Knox's translation of the Old Testament was published in 1950.

(i.e., chapters and verses) less than Maier. More generally, Sheen also seemed to believe that his audience knew when he was drawing from Scripture.

THE FOUNDATION FOR SHEEN: BIBLICAL/
DOCTRINAL AUTHORITY

Maier and Sheen wanted their listeners to know that objective, eternal truth was indeed apprehensible, and that its source was the revealed Word of God. The need to preserve and promote historical, orthodox Christian doctrine, which they both considered a direct outgrowth of biblical texts, was their critical task. Concern over these foundational matters was particularly acute as Sheen and Maier launched their radio ministries, since modernist inter-preters of the faith were gaining ground within Christianity, and scoffers and skeptics were expressing greater voice in academic, ecclesiastical, and social settings. Thus, with firmness and conviction Sheen and Maier emphasized, from their very first broadcasts, the *authority* and *reliability* of the scriptural texts and the related theological dogmatics of which they spoke, and this never waned in the decades on the air that followed.

While Maier constantly hammered on the validity of the Bible and "Holy Writ," Sheen made frequent appeals to scriptural authority with both explicit references (e.g., "Sacred Scripture"), and more subtle appeals with words such as *light of revelation, words of heavenly wisdom,* and *immutable truth.* Sheen gave human reason its due, but noted that "this knowledge of God which came from reason working on visible things of the world gives a very incomplete concept of [God]."[11] Only the Word of God could provide vital, salvific knowledge. Sheen acknowledged that some things in Scripture were difficult to understand; however, that did not mean that they were untrue. In his first year on the Catholic Hour (CH), while speaking of the workings of the Trinity, Sheen admitted, "How all this is done, I know not, but on the testimony of God revealing, I know."[12] He was quite comfortable bearing a faith seeking understanding, and encouraged his listeners to feel com-fortable with the same. Sheen pointed out that Scripture's reliability and completeness actually put the twentieth-century student of Christ at an ad-vantage over even Jesus's apostles: "The Truth the theologian seeks as he uses

---

[11]Fulton J. Sheen, *The Divine Romance* (1930; repr., Garden City, NY: Garden City, 1950), 21.
[12]Sheen, *Divine Romance*, 32-33.

Revelation to ravel the secrets of God which far surpass those that John heard as he leaned his head upon the breast of the Master."[13]

But such inquiry was not to be limited to "theologians." In a 1934 sermon titled "Divine Intimacies," Sheen stated that God showed his love to humankind "by speaking to us." "The speech of God is Revelation. Open Sacred Scripture at any page and you will find written down the voice of God speaking to us."[14] Being the dutiful son of Rome, it was not uncommon for Sheen to reinforce the authority of the Roman Catholic Church in mediating doctrinal truths, including those derived from Scripture. For instance, in the first sermon of his 1937 series "Our Wounded World," he laments that "religious individualism emphasized the private interpretation of scripture," which produced "as many different religions as there are heads."[15] Nonetheless, it is clear that he desired his listeners to know the content of the Bible for themselves. This was no doubt due to his general belief that Christians benefit from reading the Bible; however, it is easy to speculate that he was also mindful of the emphasis placed on Scripture among many American Protestants, and wanted to demonstrate that Catholics could meet them on the same field.

Sheen recognized symbolism in the Bible, which he interpreted for his audience when it enhanced his homiletic message. But Sheen reminded his audience that Scripture was not just a collection of symbolic or parabolic texts. The events of the Bible occurred in history and the characters were actual beings. The incarnation of God himself really occurred when "the Creator of the human race," the "Perfect God took on a visible human likeness in the Person of . . . Jesus Christ."[16] "We know not Christ," if we do not study and understand all of the "phases" of Jesus' earthly life.[17] And of paramount importance in these actual events described, Christians were to accept that "the Resurrection was a fact," if their faith was to have meaning.[18]

In order to reinforce the historical reality of the biblical narrative, as well as to enhance the impact of such accounts, Sheen sometimes embellished

---

[13]Fulton J. Sheen, *Manifestations of Christ* (Washington: NCCM, 1932), 114.
[14]Fulton J. Sheen, *The Eternal Galilean* (1934; repr., Garden City, NY: Garden City, 1950), 146.
[15]Fulton J. Sheen, *Our Wounded World* (Washington: NCCM, 1937), 5.
[16]Sheen, *Eternal Galilean*, 10.
[17]Sheen, *The Fullness of Christ* (North Haledon, NJ: Keep the Faith, 1935), 18.
[18]Sheen, *Eternal Galilean*, 269.

his retelling of stories with greater detail than was in the text. He was particularly adept at this when recounting events in the life of Christ. For example, when describing the wise men journeying to pay homage to the Christ child, Sheen not only brought the story to life in striking fashion, but in the process threw in a subtle point about intelligent, educated persons trusting in, and subordinating themselves to, divine realities:

> These first scientists of the Christian age saw a star and envisaged a God. . . .
> And so they followed the light of the star, but instead of leading them over the
> mountains beyond the sun and the shining chandeliers of the Pleiades to the
> hid battlements of heaven, it rather led them along the sandy courses of earth
> to the end of the trail of the golden star, where the Wise Men bent on the
> voyage of discovery made the Discovery of God. The wise, learned, mighty
> men, kneeling in pontifical robes upon a bed of straw, before a Babe who
> could neither ask or answer questions.[19]

In describing Jesus on trial before the Sanhedrin, Sheen set the scene as if he were a court reporter:

> The presiding official in that court was Caiphas, a low type in a high place, the
> type that finds in religion not a conviction, but a career. At the central point
> of the inner circumference of a semi-circle he sat—president of the court; at
> right and left were seated his colleagues. At each end was a clerk, the one to
> record votes for his acquittal, the other to record votes for his conviction.
> Some of the members that night were sure to have been only half awake, but
> Caiphas was thoroughly alert.[20]

A few weeks later in this 1932 sermon series, Sheen moved on to the subsequent events in Pontius Pilate's courtyard: "That Friday, at dawn, Pontius Pilate, wrapped in toga, still sleepy and yawning, was waiting for a mob in Herod's palace, very ill disposed towards the trouble-makers who forced him to rise at such an early hour." Sheen then painted a "word picture" that both brought the historical event into clearer view, and framed the moral absurdity of the moment: "before Pilate's judgment seat, on the paved stones of Lithostratos, was painted a long white line, marking the boundaries beyond which no Jew could pass without becoming defiled. . . .

---

[19]Sheen, *Eternal Galilean*, 25-26.
[20]Sheen, *Manifestations of Christ*, 73.

So Caiphas, Annas and the other accusers stopped at the line. The hypocrites! They were not afraid of innocent blood, but they were afraid of a white line."[21]

Sheen's description of the last moments of Jesus's life is gripping and evocative:

> Christ's eyes now look downward as the last few drops of blood reluctantly wed themselves to the rocks, splitting them open like hungry mouths. There is always a strange power in the eyes of the dying, which enables them to follow the ones they love, even when other senses are mute and dead. His eyes are now resting on the same object He rested on when he was born—His sweet and beloved Mother. She felt His eyes fixed on her.[22]

As these examples demonstrate, Sheen was willing to enhance biblical narratives with extrabiblical details. Yet he did this not because of a deficiency he found in scriptural content, but precisely because he wanted such content to have the impact on his listeners that it had on him personally. The historical and theological truths of Scripture needed to penetrate the hearts and minds of modern listeners who were more prone to tune into radios than turn the pages of their Bibles. While it is possible that the wise men actually did not wear "pontifical robes" when they met the Christ child, and it is possible that Pilate did not yawn when Jesus appeared before him, such embellishments only made the scriptural stories more vivid and their lessons more powerful, without altering their substance.

While understanding the person and work of Christ was the most important literal truth to be taken from Scripture, the perils of dismissing certain other facts were particularly grave. When recounting the story of Jesus being tempted in the desert, Sheen exclaimed, "Oh! Do not mock the Gospels and say there is no Satan. Do not say the idea of Satan is dead and gone. Satan never gains so many cohorts, as when, in his shrewdness, he spreads the rumor that he is long since dead."[23] In tones paralleling those of C. S. Lewis, Sheen criticized his more "sophisticated" contemporaries who either dismissed the existence of "the devil" as myth, or caricaturized him as "a buffoon who is dressed" in "red tights," "vomit[ing] sulfur," and

---

[21]Sheen, *Manifestations of Christ*, 82-83.
[22]Sheen, *Fullness of Christ*, 158.
[23]Sheen, *Eternal Galilean*, 56-57.

"carry[ing] a trident."[24] What is more, since Satan himself was real, so was the reality of his eternal residence. While hell was not a frequent topic for Sheen, he was quite willing to lambaste modern interpreters of the Bible who denied its existence in an effort to render the faith less judgmental sounding. In his 1943 series named "The Crisis in Christendom," Sheen warned, "This sugary, pale ersatz of Christianity has set at naught the very words of the Christ Whom they preach—the Christ Who on more than a dozen occasions said there was a hell." In an interesting turn of the tables on the revisionists who wanted to break the shackles of traditional Christian constraints, he added, "Hell is the eternal guarantee of human freedom."[25]

In his enterprise to stem the erosion of belief in scriptural truths—whether historical, prophetic, or doctrinal—Sheen took on both unbelievers and those who claimed to be Christians, but diluted biblical teaching. He frequently targeted the supposedly enlightened "modernists" and "liberals," who seemed bent on undermining the objective truth claims of scriptural Christianity with a deceptive, elastic version of the faith combined with a faux intellectual superiority. Following his first year on the CH, Sheen published a book titled *Old Errors and New Labels*, in which he framed the problem, as he saw it:

> America, it is said, is suffering from intolerance. It is not. It is suffering from tolerance: tolerance of right and wrong, truth and error, virtue and evil, Christ and chaos. . . . The man who can make up his mind in an orderly way, as a man might make up his bed, is called a bigot; but a man who cannot make up his mind, any more than he can make up for lost time, is called tolerant and broad-minded. A bigoted man is one who refuses to accept a reason for anything; a broad-minded man is one who will accept anything for a reason— providing it is not a good reason.[26]

Sheen put his cards on the table: "It is the burden of this broadcast to suggest that broadmindedness sometimes could be just plain ordinary flat-headedness, and what is sometimes called an 'open mind' could be in reality

---

[24]Fulton J. Sheen, *Light Your Lamps* (Washington: NCCM, 1947), 13.
[25]Fulton J. Sheen, *The Crisis in Christendom* (Washington: NCCM, 1943), 83.
[26]Fulton J. Sheen, *Old Errors and New Labels* (1931; repr., Staten Island, NY: St. Paul's/Alba House, 2007), 59.

only a vacancy."[27] In a 1932 sermon titled "The Curse of Broadmindedness," which the NCCM published in pamphlet form after its on-air delivery, Sheen observed that the label of "intolerant" had been placed on the Catholic Church by modernists so as to frighten people away like a "yellow fever sign." Yet he pointed out that while Jesus was "tolerant about the shortcomings in His fish-smelling Apostles," and of those "who nailed Him to the Cross," just as the church should be, "[Christ] was absolutely intolerant about His statement that those who believe not in Him shall be condemned."[28] On the other hand, Satan, whom "Our Lord tells us" will "deceive even the elect," will be "so broadminded as to identify tolerance with indifference to right and wrong," all the while promoting "slogans and propaganda," rather than "immutable principles from the lofty heights of a Church."[29] As far as Sheen was concerned, the modernists were serving as Satan's spokespersons.

By "freeing" twentieth-century minds from historical dogmas, modernists and liberals had created false "progress" when they "confused a step forward with a step in the right direction." Sheen suspected that for many the discovery of genuine truth was no longer even the goal. Sheen observed, "Such false freedom created minds more interested in the search for truth than in truth itself. . . . They knocked not to have the door of truth opened, but to listen to the sound of their knuckles." He concluded, "They loved to talk about the glorious quest for truth, but were very careful to avoid discovering it."[30] In short, the trouble with "modern prophets" was that they "would rather be up-to-date than right, rather be wrong than behind the times."[31]

Truth needed to be understood as an "organic" whole. "Religion is not a sum of beliefs that we would like, but the sum of beliefs God has given"— given in Scripture. Modernists who accepted the counsel of God in modular fashion, believing certain teachings, yet rejecting portions that did not fit with their approval, were compared to the two women who claimed to be the mother of the same child in "the courtroom of Solomon." "The real

---

[27] Fulton J. Sheen, *Peace* (Washington: NCCM, 1942), 51.
[28] See pamphlet titled "The Curse of Broadmindedness," "Catholic Hour" Files, Sheen Archives, Rochester.
[29] Sheen, *Light Your Lamps*, 14.
[30] Fulton J. Sheen, *Freedom and Peace* (Huntington, IN: Our Sunday Visitor Press, 1941), 12.
[31] Sheen, *Eternal Galilean*, 104.

mother of the babe would accept no compromise," explained Sheen. "She was intolerant about her claim," insisting on "the whole babe, or nothing"; however, "the false mother was tolerant. . . . She was willing to divide the babe,—and the babe would have died of broadmindedness!"[32]

Though Sheen seldom mentioned problematic "modern prophets" by name, especially when they were fellow clergy, early in his radio ministry he specifically identified one such cleric who was quite prominent. In a 1930 editorial titled "The New Paganism," published under the auspices of the NCWC (National Catholic Welfare Conference), Sheen devoted over fifty column-inches to refuting liberal Protestant minister Harry Emerson Fosdick. What had raised Sheen's hackles was an article Fosdick published in *Harper's* magazine, in which he dismissed the "supernaturalism" of historical Christianity as "an obsolete word" that "stands for an obsolete idea." Sheen allowed that Fosdick was a "well-informed and distinguished preacher," and complimented his "eloquent refutation of the New Humanism"; however, he described him as "grossly misinformed" about the reality of the supernatural. Sheen equated the churchman Fosdick's writing against the historical teachings of the church to the inconceivable thought of the great American military commander General John J. Pershing publishing an article titled, "The Unreasonableness of Defending America." Sheen concluded, "When I hear men with loyalties to Christ decry the supernatural, I feel as if they are trying to sap the blood of the King of Kings from our veins."[33]

Throughout his radio career and its aftermath, Sheen would remain a vocal opponent of modernist churchmen and the destructiveness that he attributed to their ideas. Though visible, popular ecclesiastical modernists were a thorn in Sheen's flesh, specific attacks such as this one on Fosdick were rare. Given Sheen's inherent graciousness, he likely considered criticism of individuals to be unseemly, not to mention off-putting to his audience. Furthermore, given the wariness even nominal Protestants still may have harbored toward Catholics, any attack on a prominent Protestant spokesman

---

[32]Sheen, *Manifestations of Christ*, 71-72.

[33]Fulton J. Sheen, "The New Paganism: Rev. Mr. Fosdick Aims at a Dragon, Imperils God in Readers' Minds—Newtonian Fog-The Supernatural," NCWC, 1930, Sheen Archives, Rochester, "Press Clippings 1930-1935" file, "1930" folder.

could have produced a negative response, regardless of the soundness of Sheen's arguments. Additionally, in the case of Fosdick, specific attacks by Sheen on a fellow recipient of NBC's sustaining time allotments would not likely to have gone over well with a number of constituents, not least of which would have been network executives. As will be demonstrated, Walter Maier felt no such restraints regarding the Reverend Doctor Fosdick.

More broadly, when a raging World War led to calls for greater unity "among men of good will," Sheen agreed that religious people should unite "on the basis of certain moral principles necessary to guide the political, economic, and social life of our times." He cautioned, however, against the dismissal of scriptural and doctrinal disagreements in a push for a "Union of Churches on the basis of the least common denominator." Such movements "do violence to truth," and do "violence to history"—truth and history revealed in Scripture and vouchsafed to the true church. Once again anticipating the accusation of "intolerance," Sheen noted that "modern tolerance has a bad history." "Tolerance" had become "indifference to truth," as its proponents defaulted to "the favorite slogan . . . 'There are two sides to every question.'" The problem was that they were "forgetful that religion, truth, and justice, if they have two sides, have the same two sides as fly paper, that is, the right side and the wrong side." The perils of war were manifest; however, indifference to truth in the name of unity, even in the midst of war, was more perilous than the war itself, from where the Monsignor sat.[34]

While Fulton Sheen had plenty to say about modernists, liberals, and unbelievers, in general, he was particularly wary of so-called intellectuals, especially those within the academic world, in matters of faith. While far from being anti-intellectual or anti-educational, Sheen disliked what he saw as haughtiness exhibited by many members of the academy, especially in their hostility toward the church and its teachings. Moreover, he worried about the denigrating effect of such voices on Christian belief, particularly on the minds of their students. The "modern world" was "stealing away their faith" through "false education."[35]

Sheen was confident that the truth claims of Christianity could stand up to scrutiny, but he feared that modern teachers stifled genuine inquiry. He

---

[34]Fulton J. Sheen, *One Lord: One World* (Washington: NCCM, 1944), 9-13.
[35]Fulton J. Sheen, *The Prodigal World* (Washington: NCCM, 1936), 130.

contrasted the humble quest of the wise men seeking the Christ child in the New Testament to the modern "self-wise inquirer, with a sophomoric mind stuffed with the pride of his little learning . . . so convinced of his knowledge that he will not dig because he thinks nothing can be deeper than himself."[36] Such shallowness was teaching the world that "happiness . . . is to be found in the pursuit of three things: Humanism, Sex, and Science."[37] Sheen lamented, "Modern education is very skillful in telling students the purposes of electricity, dynamos, and Diesel engines, but it ignores entirely the real purpose of education, namely, to give the purpose of living." By casting aside eternal truths, academics no longer sought answers to the big questions such as, "Why do I exist?" In turn, the so-called educated person "would not have a ten cent gadget in their homes for five minutes without knowing its purpose, but they go through life without knowing why they are living."[38]

Sheen was not pleased with where intellectuals—academic or otherwise— had taken moral standards and concepts of absolute truth. In a 1941 broadcast, Sheen noted that "we are witnessing in our national life what might be called the Betrayal of the Intellectuals, or the Treason of the Educated." He then provided definitions to his listeners. "By intelligentsia, I mean the intellectuals who have been educated beyond their intelligence; those who deny absolute standards of right and wrong . . . and completely ignore the will and its discipline in the training of youth." Sheen cited H. G. Wells, George Bernard Shaw, and John Dewey as misguided "specimens of the intelligentsia."[39] A few years later, Sheen began a sermon by noting that "every age has its intelligentsia," which he again defined as persons "educated beyond their intelligence." In this case, he added imagery: "A sponge can hold so much water; a person can hold so much education. When the point of saturation is reached in either, the sponge becomes a drip, and the person a bore."[40]

While Sheen devoted considerable attention to individual moral issues, he fretted that the path intellectuals had led their disciples down had

---

[36]Sheen, *Eternal Galilean*, 22.

[37]Sheen, *Eternal Galilean*, 112.

[38]Sheen, *Freedom and Peace*, 22-23.

[39]Fulton J. Sheen, *War and Guilt* (Washington: NCCM, 1941), 123. While Sheen seldom mentioned by name clergy or theologians with whom he disagreed, he had no reluctance to name secularists whom he opposed.

[40]Sheen, *One Lord: One World*, 67.

eroded America's moral authority as war loomed on the horizon. In a March 1941 CH sermon titled "Anti-Christ," Sheen noted that modern "college and university education," in conflict with scriptural teaching, was arguing that evil and guilt were obsolete terms, depending "entirely upon one's point of view." Now, the "products" of this "a-moral education" point their fingers at Hitler and Mussolini, calling them "evil," when such fascists had only taken such "a-moral" teaching to its logical culmination. Sheen drew this analogy:

> Like a man who, when his wife awakens him saying she hears a burglar down-stairs, insists violently that it is only her imagination, and yet goes downstairs trembling like a leaf fearful of bumping head on with the marauder, so modern man, who says evil is only a survival of the imagination of Medieval Theologians, now shakes in fear from the evil he denied but which he knows in his heart to be only too real.[41]

In rhetoric that no doubt appealed to much of his radio audience, Sheen commented, "If I wanted a good moral judgment about the war, I should a thousand times prefer to get it from a garage man, a filling station attendant, a WPA worker, a grocer's clerk, or a delivery boy, than from twenty-three Ph.D. professors I know about in just one American University. . . . The educated know how to rationalize evil; the masses do not."[42]

During the same broadcast season, Sheen accused intellectuals of making themselves gods, but proving that they were not particularly good at it, offering little more than "the husks of humanism and behaviorism." Said another way, modern intellectuals had placed themselves in judgment of Scripture and the church, rather than the other way around. In tones similar to those of his Protestant contemporary, H. Richard Niebuhr, Sheen concluded, "As a sop to sentimentalism, [modern man] made a religion without Hell, a Christ without Justice, a Kingdom of God without God, salvation without a Crucifix, and a Church where a pulpit and an organ replaced the altar of sacrifice."[43]

---

[41]Sheen, *War and Guilt*, 105-22.

[42]Sheen, *War and Guilt*, 125.

[43]Sheen, *War and Guilt*, 153. In his 1938 book *The Kingdom of God in America*, Niebuhr had cautioned that contemporary renderings of Christianity had reduced the faith to a bland version of the real thing: "A God without wrath, brought men without sin into a Kingdom without judgment through the ministrations of a Christ without a Cross."

Many colleges and universities spewed forth "crazy quilt information" that would appall "Our Divine Lord," complained Professor Sheen. Referring to foundational Christian truths, he added, "If we may paraphrase [Jesus'] words, He said, 'Oh Heavenly Father, I thank thee that Thou hast hidden these things from the university professors and the experts.'"[44] Sheen was particularly grieved by the erosion in the faith commitments of academicians at historically Christian institutions. In 1940, he rhetorically asked his radio audience, "How many universities in our land founded as religious institutions for the propagation of a particular Christian creed, today adhere to the creeds they were founded to propagate?"[45] Ten years later, near the end of his radio ministry, Sheen continued to inveigh against "intelligentsia" in the halls of the academy: "Education believes that religion is dead, as students are taught that man is not God's image but only a physiological bag filled with psychological libido."[46] From Fulton Sheen's vantage point, the intellectual purveyors of "false philosophy in education, and so-called Liberal Christianity," were "saboteurs . . . knock[ing] away the supports" of the church and society.[47]

Since in Sheen's view so-called intellectuals were clearly willing to place their faith in broad-ranging academic theories, many of which lacked empirical proof, he thought it incongruous that they were so unwilling to even consider the possibility that Scripture and church teachings were worthy of faith. For Sheen, Scripture was important because it explained reality, with dogma then emerging from Scripture, as mediated by the church, to provide a construct for grasping such realities. Though Sheen presented church dogma as authoritative, he stressed that such teachings were not meant to hinder the enterprise of intellectual inquiry. "The Church does not dam up the river of thought," explained Sheen to his listeners in 1935, "She builds levees to prevent it from overflowing and ruining the countryside."[48] The sturdy dogmatics of the church, reflecting truth revealed by God, actually enhanced freedom of thought and discovery of complementary truth, rather than hindered it, he argued.

---

[44]Sheen, *Peace*, 114.
[45]Sheen, *Freedom and Peace*, 74.
[46]Fulton J. Sheen, *The Rock Plunged into Eternity* (Staten Island, NY: St. Paul's/Alba House, 2004), 143-44.
[47]Sheen, *Crisis in Christendom*, 82.
[48]Sheen, *Fullness of Christ*, 70.

Doctrine was vital and reliable because God's providential supervision had formulated and preserved it through the centuries. With emphasis perhaps aimed at the United States' dominant Protestant population, Sheen confidently asserted that from apostolic days, God's vehicle through which true doctrine was codified and preserved was the "one, holy catholic and apostolic Church." In a 1932 sermon on genuine authority, Sheen explained, "If one small blunder concerning the doctrine of original sin were made in [the church's] twenty centuries of charting the course of men to God, huge blunders would have been made in human happiness. A mistranslation of a single word one thousand years ago might have smashed all the statues of Europe." He concluded the broadcast by describing the ongoing doctrinal navigation as follows: "But the Church has avoided all these pitfalls and all these errors, and as the bark of Peter, with sails flying high, cuts the waters of the sea, she looks before and aft. . . . Heresies . . . mental fashions," and threatening "sentimentalism" can be seen in her wake, but she will weather the "storms and tempests of the world" and eventually arrive at her eternal harbor "because as Peter stood at the helm of his bark, there rested on his hands the invisible, eternal hands of Christ."[49]

In a poignantly crafted sermon titled, "Religion Without Dogmas," which took on intellectuals represented by both liberal churchmen and self-sufficient academics, Sheen commented that "modern man wants a religion without dogmas." To the former he noted, however, that "to say that one must have a religion without dogmas is to assert a dogma . . . a dogma that needs tremendously more justification than any dogma of the Church." To the latter, he asserted, "The only difference between the dogmas of religion and the dogmas of science is that the latter are grounded upon the authority of fallible men, while the dogmas of the Church are grounded upon the authority of God revealing." Sheen concluded with the following observation to hubristic intellectuals: "Cabbages have heads, but they have no dogmas."[50]

While Sheen's radio addresses were designed to explain, systematize, and commend sound doctrine to his listener, Sheen guarded against a cold, purely knowledge-based or "abstract" orthodoxy. Lest his listeners lose track

---

[49]Sheen, *Manifestations of Christ*, 44-45.
[50]Sheen, *Manifestations of Christ*, 73-80.

of the essence of their faith, he reminded them, "Our Faith is, first and foremost, in Christ living in His Mystical Body and then, only secondly, in explicit beliefs. If He did not reveal them, we would not believe them. . . . There is no doctrine, no moral, no dogma, no liturgy, no belief apart from [Christ]. *He* is the object of our Faith, and not a dogma."[51]

A Similar Foundation for Maier

In light of the well-known antagonism between Protestants and Catholics since the sixteenth century, it is remarkable that the Protestant Maier came very close to repeating what the Catholic Sheen asserted about the foundations for faith and life. That both, with such parallel teachings, remained so popular for so long also indicates something about the radio audiences that tuned in. Whether taking comfort in the reinforcement of already-held beliefs, or looking for something in which to place their trust for the first time, listeners sought a firm foundation at a time when so many aspects of everyday life seemed wobbly. The firmer the foundation, the greater the appeal. And whatever Maier and Sheen may have lacked in their preaching, firmness was not it.

Like his Catholic radio counterpart, Walter Maier exhorted his TLH listeners to accept scriptural content and accept the dogmas that flowed therefrom. Maier considered himself a son of the Protestant Reformation, and the sixteenth-century mantra of *sola scriptura* was bedrock. Frequently referring to the Bible, he declared, "It is the one eternal Book. . . . Why? Because it comes from God! . . . What personal and powerful comfort every one of you can find in this marvelous assurance that in your Bible through faith in your Redeemer you have everlasting, immovable, unchangeable heavenly assurance!"[52] Maier promised his hearers that the providential hand of God would protect biblical truths in modern times, as it had in biblical times and subsequent periods. Comparing modernist revisionists and scoffers to "brash, head-strong, know-it-all" Old Testament King Jehoiakim, who unsuccessfully attempted to destroy the words of the prophet Jeremiah, Maier claimed that Scripture was "under divine protection." Quoting the words of Christ that appear in all three Synoptic Gospels, Maier

---

[51]Sheen, *Rock Plunged into Eternity*, 100-101.
[52]Walter A. Maier, *Christ, Set the World Aright!* (St. Louis: CPH, 1945), 114.

adds that the Bible is "blessed by the promise, 'Heaven and earth shall pass away, but My words shall not pass away!'"[53]

At the beginning of each radio season, Maier often assured his audience that they could count on his unwavering commitment to the Bible and its orthodox interpretation. For instance, adding institutional commitment to his own, he commenced the 1935–1936 season by noting that he was broadcasting "from the campus of a divinity school that for almost a century has dedicated its resources to the Christ of the Bible." "With my hand on the Bible," he continued, "I dedicate this radio mission." "I offer you in the name of the Triune God not the Christ of present-day compromise and concession, not the Christ of twentieth-century indifference and indecision, not the Christ of modern doubt and denial . . . but (above all the evasion and distortion, the rank unbelief of our day) the Christ of the Cross."[54]

At the beginning of the 1937–1938 season, Maier explained that Scripture would serve as the basis for his radio preaching: "To us the Bible is more than a book which *contains* the Word of God; we teach and declare that it *is* the Word of God, the divinely and literally inspired record of our heavenly Father for the guidance of His children and the proper appraisal of their immortal souls." He then provided a catalog of orthodoxy that he considered nonnegotiable:

> We insist on these Scripturally founded doctrines: the Trinity of God; the Creation of Man in the Image of God; the Fall of Man and His Total Depravity; the Deity of Our Lord and Savior Jesus Christ; His Virgin Birth; His Vicarious Atonement; His Resurrection; His Second Coming to Judge the Quick and the Dead; the Necessity of Regeneration by the Holy Spirit; the Operation of the Holy Spirit by the Means of Grace, the Word and the Sacraments, Baptism and the Lord's Supper; the Church Universal; the Reality of Heaven and Hell; and the Promise of Life Everlasting.[55]

Though he would have begged to differ on the number and mechanics of the sacraments, Monsignor Sheen would have generally approved.

---

[53]Maier, *Christ, Set the World Aright!*, 105-14. This quote of Jesus can be found in Mt 24:35; Mk 13:31; Lk 21:33.

[54]Walter A. Maier, *Christ for the Nation* (St. Louis: CPH, 1936), 13. Recall that the broadcasts originated at Concordia Seminary, St. Louis.

[55]Walter A. Maier, *The Cross from Coast to Coast* (St. Louis: CPH, 1938), 10-11.

Also like Sheen, though arguably with greater fervor, Maier urged his listeners to read the Bible for themselves, on a regular basis. While Maier often employed his scholarly knowledge to offer detailed explanations of scriptural passages in his sermons, he had few qualms about the laity's ability to comprehend the prophetic, redeeming, and sanctifying messages contained in the Bible. Maier stressed that the Word of God was self-authenticating, if read with an open mind and heart, by its divine power and the assistance of the Holy Spirit. He explained, "This Biblical picture of God, as revealed in His Word and by His Son, is preached into our hearts by the divine power of the Holy Spirit."[56] In one of the earliest sermons in TLH's first season titled "Evident Truth from Heaven," he opened with the question, "Can an enlightened, modern American mind still believe the Bible?" He proceeded to answer unequivocally: "The power of the Word is operative whenever it is read and heard and believed. Let the host of modern infidels reject the Bible by rehashing the threadbare arguments advanced by unbelief since the Savior's day, we have evidence of its truth." Such truth would be clear by "examination of its contents." Maier concluded, "So I ask you to-night to take this truth, to read it, to study it now, and you will find between the covers of your Bible the divine cure-all for the ills and woes, the problems and anxieties, that may crowd themselves into your life. . . . Here, in this ageless, priceless, deathless volume, you have the answer to every question."[57]

In a 1936 sermon, "The Word—Forever Unbroken," Maier exhorted, "Take your Bible, read it, study it, and you will experience that the Savior's promise of soul-strength, unlike the vain and empty soothsaying of men, is the high truth of Heaven itself." He concluded with a further appeal: "I plead with you: Believe God's book; make it yours; immerse yourself in its promises; cherish it; defend it; support it; and I promise you God's unbroken love, His unchanging power, His undiminished blessing."[58] For those less likely to follow his directive, Maier reached out: "Some of you, however, are prejudiced against Scriptures . . . without taking time to investigate Holy Writ." With a tone implying confidence in the judgment of such listeners, if they were properly informed, he invited reconsideration: "Why not be fair and at

---

[56]Maier, *The Lutheran Hour*, 52.
[57]Maier, *The Lutheran Hour*, 14-17.
[58]Walter A. Maier, *Fourth Lutheran Hour: Winged Words for Christ* (St. Louis: CPH, 1937), 20-21.

least give the Bible a chance to prove its heavenly origin and its divine power by a careful, personal, unbiased study of its record?"[59] Near the end of Maier's radio ministry, he lamented, "Even in our own country millions do not know the Bible nor find the time to read it . . . do not daily delve into the sacred treasury of guidance and comfort. . . . The cry that must re-echo throughout the land is not only, 'America, Back to the Bible!' but 'American Christian Families Back to the Bible!' 'American Believers, Back to the Bible!'"[60]

As members of his ethereal congregation read their Bibles, Maier held a similar desire to that of his contemporary on the CH—he wanted them to understand that Christianity was a religion based on historical events. He too recognized the symbolic, allegorical, and parabolic elements of Scripture, but the characters and actions described in chapters and verses involved real people, acting in real space and time, with an omnipotent God as the director of the drama, quite willing to act in human affairs. Thus, as did Sheen in defense of supernaturalism, Maier argued for the reality of the miraculous in the biblical narrative. He compared modern dismissal of historical events that lack scientific explanation to Pontius Pilate's cynical question to Jesus: "What is truth?"[61] "In an age when men glibly and confidently prate about the twilight of Christianity, as they compose their obituaries on the Biblical truth," Maier pointed to the incarnation as the most important "truth." He asked his listeners to embrace "The Miracle" and "mystery of God's becoming man," yet refused to allow such complex incarnational concepts to become too abstract by also asking the audience to follow the footsteps of "the lowly shepherds to that glorious Child in Mary's arms."[62]

Of course, Maier frequently noted that the miracle of the incarnation was ultimately made significant by the miracle of the resurrection. During the first year of TLH, Maier noted, "The fact of Christ's resurrection, the very keystone in the arch of our Christian faith, is one of the most definite, most repeated assurances of divine revelation." Its occurrence in first-century Palestine was of paramount significance: "If the Easter-story is not actual history, there is no history."[63]

---

[59]Walter A. Maier, *Victory Through Christ* (St. Louis: CPH, 1943), 114.

[60]Walter A. Maier, *Go Quickly and Tell* (St. Louis: CPH, 1950), 221-22.

[61]Maier, *Lutheran Hour*, 28.

[62]Maier, *Lutheran Hour*, 132-33.

[63]Maier, *Lutheran Hour*, 150.

When Maier spoke of other narrative accounts from both Old and New Testament sources, he often made their historicity come alive by describing the events with contextual detail. Though he did not always exhibit the rhetorical panache of Fulton Sheen in embellishing biblical stories, Maier was skilled at bringing history alive. An interesting comparative example is their treatment of the visit of the magi. In a 1944 Epiphany sermon, Maier enlivened the story by pointing out the incongruities experienced by these visitors from the East. "They had anticipated a palace, but they were directed to a humble dwelling. They had looked for a royal court in attendance on the newborn Ruler, but they beheld only a young mother. Despite all these surprises they expressed not a word of hesitancy, doubt, or disbelief."[64] When aligned with Sheen's 1933 radio narration, which included flourishes about "the shining chandeliers of the Pleiades" and of "mighty men kneeling in pontifical robes," Maier's description contains less grandeur. Yet they both drew their listeners into a more dramatic story than the plain text conveys. More importantly, in what was presumably coincidence, Maier and Sheen ended up at the same sermonic point, making the story relevant to twentieth-century thinkers. Sheen had lauded the wise men as the "first scientists" who had humbled their "learned, mighty" selves before an infant God. Maier observed, "The virgin birth and the truth that the cradled infant was a King contradicted their reason: yet these men, not ignorant, misinformed, superstitious illiterates, but scholars, distinctly called 'wise men,' found no conflict between reason and religion. They bowed humbly, unconditionally, reverently, before the Lord Jesus."[65]

Maier made both Old and New Testament stories seem less distant by adding descriptive rhetoric. For example, in a sermon on the exodus, Maier created a scene with much more vividness than does the Hebrew text: "The children of Israel, marching on through the waterless waste, finally came to Marah; and it is hard to overestimate their joy when they there beheld inviting wells. Yet, can you imagine their despair and utter misery when, as they frantically drew up the water and pressed their swollen lips to the drinking bags, they could not swallow it, thirsty as they were? It was bitter

---

[64]Maier, *Christ, Set the World Aright!*, 9-10.
[65]Maier, *Christ, Set the World Aright!*, 9-10.

beyond endurance."[66] In another representative instance, Maier described Christ's followers in a way that interwove divine and human drama: "Several weeks after the Savior's Easter triumph we find the disciples back in Galilee. . . . When the news came that Jesus was risen from the dead, these men again began to cherish dreams of worldly greatness. The living Christ, so they thought, would soon establish a mighty kingdom on earth. The risen Redeemer had other plans, however."[67]

Like Sheen, Maier saved his most powerful descriptive efforts for the trial and crucifixion of Jesus. Maier, too, described the Sanhedrin and its leaders with detailed disdain:

> You may recall that it was about two o'clock on Friday morning when the Jewish Council was hastily convened at Caiaphas' palace, where the Savior was to be reexamined, after the private hearing before the ex-high priest, Annas. Who constituted the court which was to pronounce the verdict that finally meant life or death for Jesus? If you picture this Council as a group of godless men, sworn enemies of religion, a "kangaroo court" impaneled by politicians and from city gangs, revise your opinion! This was a blue-ribbon jury, an assembly of Jerusalem's noteworthy citizens. . . . Every one of the seventy who voted in that Sanhedrin was a respected community leader; and the seventy-first ballot was cast by the pinnacle of Jewish society, the high priest himself![68]

Maier would not allow his listeners to contemplate Christ's suffering lightly. Asking the audience to "join the jury" trying Jesus, he exclaimed, "Sitting in the high priest's headquarters, you want to close your eyes to the hideous brutality that follows. But don't turn your head away!"[69] In a Lenten sermon titled "Suffered Under Pontius Pilate," Maier pulls back the curtain on the biblical scene:

> Under the roof of that Old Testament church-leader, the Savior was subjected to the agony of indescribable torture. During these after-midnight hours the enmity and jealousy pent up during the three years of the Lord's ministry were

---

[66]Walter A. Maier, *Rebuilding with Christ: Radio Messages of the Second Part of the Twelfth Lutheran Hour* (St. Louis: CPH, 1946), 5.

[67]Walter A. Maier, *America, Turn to Christ!* (St. Louis: CPH, 1944), 53.

[68]Walter A. Maier, *Peace Through Christ: Radio Messages Broadcast in the Seventh Lutheran Hour* (St. Louis: CPH, 1940), 236.

[69]Walter A. Maier, *Global Broadcasts of His Grace* (St. Louis: CPH, 1949), 144.

let loose against Him. The high priest's servants . . . began to spit on the Savior. With heavy rods they rained blow after blow on His defenseless body. While His hands were tied, they amused themselves in hellish glee by striking Jesus with clenched fists or slapping His face with their open hands. They blindfolded Him, and one servant after another brutally beat Him. . . . We would wonder . . . why the heavens did not collapse on these fiendish torturers and the earth swallow them.[70]

As for the execution itself, Maier noted that the "great artists of the ages have vied with each other to produce worthy, gripping studies of the crucifixion . . . yet the real, flesh-and-blood crucifixion was so horrifying with its agony, pain, and thirst, its fever, tension, and exposure, its lacerated arteries, loss of blood, and, sometimes, gangrene, that the sun itself would no longer behold the arch-sufferings."[71] The great artists may have come up short in conveying Christ's demise on canvas, but Maier would repeatedly try to do so verbally, with considerable effect. He described not only the physical tortures, but Christ's emotional anguish. "Added to these agonies was the heartless ridicule of the wretches beneath the cross . . . the moaning of the malefactors crucified on each side; the half-stifled sobs of His mother, His disciple, and the friends who had ventured to come to Calvary," all producing "that convulsing terror of agony . . . that made him cry" out.[72]

In similar fashion to Fulton Sheen, Maier reinforced biblical events with his enhanced narrative descriptions, not only to make the stories more compelling, but to bolster biblical authority by demonstrating that Scripture was composed of more than a collection of mythical tales. His accounts of Christ's torture and death were designed to stimulate comprehension of the brutality involved and prompt reconsideration of their significance by the skeptic, the unbeliever, and the lukewarm Christian. Calling sinners to saving faith in the atoning work of Jesus on the cross was, after all, Maier's primary vocation. It would seem that Maier also wanted to jar any subconscious docetism from the minds of the faithful, lest they take the genuine, human suffering Jesus endured *for them* too lightly. Whatever his

---

[70]Maier, *Peace Through Christ*, 250-51.

[71]Maier, *Cross from Coast to Coast*, 374.

[72]Walter A. Maier, *The Radio for Christ: Radio Messages Broadcast in the Sixth Lutheran Hour* (St. Louis: CPH, 1939), 374.

theological intention, the directness of his sometimes pungent style proved ideal for radio.

One other characteristic marked Maier's treatment of Scripture, which enhanced its authority and impact by demonstrating applicability to twentieth-century life. Maier's sermons were always tied to specific biblical texts, but rather than risk losing listener attentiveness by narrating a biblical passage prior to homiletic application, Maier often drew parallels and application during such narration itself. For instance, in 1939, as the Depression maintained its ruthless grip, he began a sermon exhorting Americans to pray by referring to his Old Testament text and then drawing a parallel to the present:

> Nehemiah's age shows remarkable similarity to ours. It was a time of recon-struction, a new era for Israel. A few who had returned from the Babylonian Exile were rich and oppressive; the masses were poor, and loudly did they complain of debts and heavy mortgages. Many were hungry and unem-ployed; particularly unhappy was the lot of young people, often sold into slavery because business and commerce were paralyzed. From without, en-emies threatened to overrun the country; but the danger from within was even greater.[73]

In another example, taken from the 1945 exodus-based sermon cited above, Maier contemporizes the story in an unmistakable way:

> When Moses heard the sullen, resentful murmuring of the masses against him, he did not wash his hands of the whole Exodus program for liberating his people and in deep-rooted disgust resign as national leader. Neither did he give a snarling, sarcastic reply of rebuke, nor did he institute a WFA, a Water Funding Authority. He did what every national leader should do in a crisis, *"he cried unto the Lord."*[74]

It is true that most preachers, at least the effective ones, apply biblical texts to present-day life from their pulpits. Indeed, many sermonizers of Maier's day were skilled at doing this, especially his fellow radio pastor,

---

[73]Maier, *Peace Through Christ*, 54-55.

[74]Maier, *Rebuilding with Christ*, 6. In that Maier was careful to avoid political commentary, on persons or policies, this passage should be understood as a plea for leaders to trust in God more (especially through prayer), and their own judgments less, particularly in light of the war-torn globe of the times.

Fulton Sheen. Yet one cannot read or listen to a Maier sermon without noting how adept he was at interweaving biblical narrative with the narrative of the times, from the beginning of the sermon to the end, in ways that reinforced the validity of Scripture for his listeners.

In his constant efforts to commend and validate Scripture and its divinely imbedded authority, Maier considered himself in a battle with temporal and eternal consequences. Satan, whom he believed to be as real as Sheen did, was the primary enemy. Maier warned of Satan's diabolical designs for those whom he could deceive into rejecting the Word of God. The Lutheran further clarified that indifference toward, or failure to consciously accept, the validity of Scripture and its message was an equally damnable form of rejecting God's Word. As Sheen did, Maier warned of the reality of hell. Maier spoke of it more frequently, but often with a tone of sadness, in light of the free grace that could save anyone from such destiny if the promises of God were only believed.

Though Maier did not definitively claim that the world was nearing its end and final judgment, he did suggest that such possibility should be considered—especially as the world waged war, morality declined, and unbelief became more prevalent. In December 1942, he rebuked the "masses of Americans" who failed to discern the "score of . . . signs" pointing to pending judgment. "I beseech you: Believe that Jesus is coming soon! Prepare yourself for His advent! It will be too late if you postpone accepting His grace until He comes."[75] On other occasions, Maier more specifically aligned biblical signs of latter times with a catalog of their current manifestations. For instance, in a 1944 broadcast, he repeated St. Paul's New Testament description of latter times, and then cited eighteen examples, ranging from World War II events, to divorce rates, to communist agitators, to moral ills, to shallow religion. How could "any unbiased mind" fail to see the "predicted signs"? Said another way, scriptural authority was being affirmed in each morning's newspapers, which Maier used to increase the urgency of his messages. Regardless of the ultimate date, Maier promised that "the Redeemer's return will be proof of His power to fulfill His predictions, His threats, and His promises."[76]

---

[75]Maier, *Victory Through Christ*, 137.
[76]Walter A. Maier, *Jesus Christ Our Hope* (St. Louis: CPH, 1946), 141-45.

While Satan may have been the archvillain, Maier directed much more of his on-air breath to those he considered that foe's co-conspirators of perdition—the modernists, the liberals, and the outright atheists. Their attacks on the truths of Scripture imperiled souls, and someone had to stand up to them. Like Sheen, Maier confronted those dismantling Scripture, whether from within the church or from the outside. Also like Sheen, he paid special attention to unbelief in educational institutions and among the so-called intelligentsia.

While Maier targeted unbelief in all these forms, when he used the term *modernist* he typically was referring to those holding positions of ecclesiastical authority or influence. From the beginning to the end of his radio ministry, he relentlessly criticized modernist preachers. In his first year on network radio, he explained that what made "modern infidelity all the more repulsive and damnable," when compared to unbelief during Christ's time on earth, was that "today the persecutors of our Savior are zealous in their appropriation of the Christian name and profuse in their exultation of the man Jesus; today the opposition to Christ is disguised as the modern message of the Christian Church . . . mock loyalty to Christ is the traitorous spirit beneath the Judas kiss."[77] In his second radio season, Maier promised to "grant no quarter to that unholy and destructive denial of God's Word and that despicable betrayal of our Lord and Savior which has laid its curse on too many of America's churches." Instead, he pledged to "offer the whole counsel of God."[78]

In less harsh tones, he sometimes scolded his listeners for allowing modernists to retain their pulpits. "Hold fast to the one blessed foundation of our faith!" he warned the laity. "Protest against every change, every question-mark, every addition, or every deletion!"[79] He framed the issue with a practical approach, noting that "today . . . it is popular to be broad, wide, and liberal, in religion . . . [but] people hardly appreciate broadness, wideness and liberality" in professions other than preachers. One would not, for instance, appreciate a physician offering an array of medicines without regard to a patient's malady just because they "are all good for something."[80]

---

[77]Maier, *Lutheran Hour*, 108-9.
[78]Maier, *Christ for Every Crisis*, 11.
[79]Maier, *Fourth Lutheran Hour*, 40.
[80]Maier, *Christ, Set the World Aright!*, 296-97.

Occasionally Maier broadened his complaints to include the leaders of whole denominations who embraced "the menace of Modernism": "Within the memory of thousands in this audience entire denominations, once loyal to Scriptural truth and Christ's atonement, have disavowed these two pillar doctrines."[81] Modernism had become an internal "dry rot."[82] As Sheen had observed, reflecting modernity had become more important than espousing truth. "The . . . sin of contemporaneous churches is the craving for an up-to-the-minute creed, the passion for creating a new Christianity," Maier warned.[83] Denominational indictments were rare, however, and never specific. More importantly, Maier was always careful to avoid painting denominations, or members of specific church bodies or congregations, with too broad a critical brush, lest he unsettle the souls of the truly faithful within those bodies. The life-giving faith of the Bible was dispensed by a gracious God, not by ecclesiastical structures or artful preachers. After reiterating the need for individual repentance from sin, and faith in the atoning work of Jesus Christ, Maier often reassured his listeners with words such as these: "If you have this faith, you are a Christian. You may be Catholic or Protestant, Lutheran or Reformed; but first of all you are a Christian."[84]

"It is much to be regretted that the Scripture slashers operate . . . in churches . . . the brazen, outspoken pulpit pirates, who cast every truth concerning Christ . . . overboard," observed Maier in 1945.[85] The chief clerical embodiment of such mischief, as gleaned from Maier's radio addresses, was fellow radio preacher Harry Emerson Fosdick. As mentioned, Sheen would have felt constrained to openly criticize Fosdick, a fellow recipient of NBC sustaining time. Maier enjoyed no such free airtime, and therefore, was at liberty to target the popular modernist. The ardent Lutheran referenced Fosdick in multiple sermons, but not by name. Such mentions were sometimes more subtle than others, but Maier's strategy appears to have been to speak of Fosdick in a way that would make it clear to whom he was referring for those who paid attention to Fosdick's preaching or popular writing, but

---

[81]Maier, *Peace Through Christ*, 209.
[82]Maier, *Radio for Christ*, 315.
[83]Maier, *Christ for Every Crisis*, 94.
[84]Maier, *Fourth Lutheran Hour*, 40. On other occasions Maier mentioned other denominations in similar fashion (e.g., Methodists, Nazarenes, "Greek Catholics," Presbyterians).
[85]Maier, *Christ, Set the World Aright!*, 112.

did not provide publicity for Fosdick to those who may have been unaware of his liberal interpretations of Christian truths.

For instance, in a 1935 broadcast aimed in part at Fosdick, Maier took a swipe at discriminatory networks who placed themselves "at the disposal of leaders in American unbelief," while withholding "the same privileges" from Bible-believing preachers such as himself.[86] A year later, Maier eliminated such vagueness, as he referred to Fosdick, his patron John D. Rockefeller Jr., and his New York pastorate, Riverside Church, without specifically naming them, and by rhetorically making them part of a broader group: "The high priests of thinly veneered unbelief, enthroned in Gold Coast cathedrals, the pampered favorites of American plutocrats, preaching a silk-hat, kid-glove religion that leaves the soul problems of the masses untouched."[87]

When Fosdick published his *A Guide to Understanding the Bible* in 1938,[88] Maier took to the airwaves to warn the unsuspecting. In a sermon titled "The Book That Blesses," Maier celebrated the four hundredth anniversary of William Tyndale's translation of the New Testament into English. He then noted the "unbelievably appalling contradiction" of "a leading Modernist" writing "a large volume that masquerades as a guide to the Scriptures." Again without actually naming Fosdick, Maier notes that "the author, regarded as a spokesman for Protestantism," who is "mimicked and imitated by an irresponsible fringe of the clergy that is unwilling or unable to think or act for itself," denies in his commentary that "the Bible is the inspired Word of God."[89] Maier did not think too highly of the house of worship on which Fosdick and Rockefeller had collaborated either. With their Riverside Church in his sights, Maier voiced his disgust:

> When a church decorates its entrance, as a pretentious, highly publicized millionaire's church in New York adorns its portals, with figures of Confucius and Buddha alongside our Savior and places in competition with Christ some fifty-nine scientists, philosophers, religious leaders, and kings [who in various ways denied Biblical truths] . . . if churches thus drag Christ from His exalted preeminence as the Son of God to the bawdy levels of pagan debauch, this

---

[86] Maier, *Christ for Every Crisis*, 12.
[87] Maier, *Fourth Lutheran Hour*, 4.
[88] See Harry Emerson Fosdick, *A Guide to Understanding the Bible: The Development of Ideas Within the Old and New Testaments* (New York: Harper & Row, 1938).
[89] Maier, *Radio for Christ*, 45–46.

liberal, modernist Christianity can never offer satisfactory answers to the eternal questions of the race.[90]

In addition to doing battle with open modernists in the church, Maier cautioned against preachers who may not have been modernists themselves, but had lost their will to stand up for traditional orthodoxy in the face of modernists. Enough of the "listless, phlegmatic religion" of such ministers: "Some preachers are pussyfooting when they ought to stand fast, preaching Pollyanna sermons instead of Law and Gospel sermons; with all this dabbling in side-issues instead of concentrating on the supreme privilege of bringing Christ to sin-sick and world-weary souls, the appeal of the hour is unmistakably for the declaration of war against the milk-and-water indifference that masquerades under the name of Christ's holy faith."[91] As many pastors tried hard to be popular and current, they failed in their primary task—the care of souls. "The devices of men amend and nullify the eternal counsels of God," and, thus, imperiled trusting congregants.[92] To reinforce the obvious nature of this problem, Maier even invoked the name of a man who had "never supported divine truth," newspaper columnist and outspoken satirist of religion H. L. Mencken. Mencken had chided preachers for being "too silent on Bible prophecy" during the "dangerous days" of contemporary times—this reticent "phenomenon" he labeled as "curious" and "incredible." Maier quoted Mencken's observation in his sermon: "All I desire to point out is that the New Testament offers precise and elaborate specifications of the events preceding the inevitable end of the world, and that a fair reading of them must lead any rational man to conclude that these events are now upon us."[93]

While maintaining his barrage on scriptural infidelity within the church, Maier added his voice to that of Sheen in countering attacks on biblical authority from the intelligentsia and the academy. To be sure, Maier did not

---

[90]Maier, *Cross from Coast to Coast*, 49.

[91]Maier, *Fourth Lutheran Hour*, 243-44.

[92]Maier, *Christ for Every Crisis*, 66-67.

[93]Maier, *Go Quickly and Tell*, 290. The quote Maier is using in this 1948 sermon is from a column Mencken published in 1932. See H. L. Mencken, "What's Going On in the World?," *The American Mercury* 25, no. 100 (April 1932): 385-90. In that Maier refers to Mencken's comments as having been made "recently," it is unclear whether he considered a column published sixteen years earlier as "recent," or whether Mencken had reiterated such observations in a more current setting.

see these groups as mutually exclusive, since he often pointed out the inter-woven nature of modernist, liberal thinking among religious and nonreli-gious thinkers. Nonetheless, he confronted directly the skepticism within the scientific and academic communities. In the first season of TLH, Maier observed, "Divine revelation has been rejected by our modern, grasping, skeptical age, and human reason has been enthroned, cold, calculating reason, which tells us that the only religious verities are those which can be tested and proved by the results of scientific investigation." Yet he noted that modern scientific knowledge often contradicted itself, constituting "shifting sands," to which the "Rock of Ages" stood in solid contrast.[94]

Maier disliked the hubris of "pride-bloated scoffers," who placed them-selves in judgment of the Word of God. In a strongly worded 1947 sermon on the reality of the resurrection, Maier noted that the "brilliant" scientist and inventor Thomas Edison had once told an interviewer that he had con-cluded that "there was no such thing as the immortality of the soul, since he could find no evidence of a soul and no proof of immortality." Since Edison had died several years before this sermon, Maier exclaimed, "Well, Edison knows better now!" So as to demonstrate that the "great" mind of Edison was far from "infallible," Maier went on to recall another of Edi-son's pronouncements: "As to the atom, I do not believe that it has any internal energy." "How," Maier asked, "can you scoffers say that he must be right in his opinion on the divine mystery of life beyond the grave," when he was so demonstrably wrong about other realities, in a post-Hiroshima world?[95] Echoing Sheen, Maier accused the "modernists" and "atheists" of his time of "cruelty," in that they were not just wrong, but were guilty of "kicking the crutch from beneath a crippled world."[96]

If Maier generally disliked academics and scientific thinkers who pro-moted antireligious/antibiblical conclusions, he loathed the members of such ranks that spread their heresies to young minds in classrooms. Maier praised the "landmarks" of "American education" established "centuries ago by the founders," that had produced "a higher cultural life that was genu-inely Christian in thought and expression." Regrettably times had changed:

---

[94]Maier, *Lutheran Hour*, 28-29.
[95]Maier, *Global Broadcasts of His Grace*, 240–64. (The reference to Thomas Edison is on 259.)
[96]Maier, *Victory Through Christ*, 217.

"Today campus scoffers are placing academic dynamite under these landmark[s]," and little was being done to stop them.[97] Maier cited examples, provided by listeners, of Bible-believing students leaving home for college, only to return home as "blasphemers" or outright "atheists." "Our education and our culture are steadily becoming more anti-Biblical. Souls are being prepared for hell on some American campuses," he warned.[98] Maier was firm in his assertion that he was "not indicting education in itself," but teachers who "deliberately take every divine influence out of education." It was reprehensible that "impressionable freshman are put through the processes of a four-year course and emerge from the tutelage of the real Public Enemy No. 1, the infidel teacher and scoffer, as sneering sophisticators who have earned their diploma at the cost of their spiritual and moral principles."[99]

On rare occasions, Maier actually mentioned by name colleges and universities that had jettisoned the faith of their charters or their benefactors. For instance, in a 1946 broadcast, he mentioned his alma mater, Harvard, along with Yale, Dartmouth, Amherst, Smith, Bryn Mawr, and Columbia, as institutions that had "nullified" their founding commitments to Christianity. Maier made it clear, however, that he was certain that faculties at such places still included educators holding Christian belief. He begged them to awaken from their "slumbering spirit of Christian testimony," while reciting a quote from nineteenth-century Yale president, Timothy Dwight: "It has always been my experience that the teachers who are religious never mention it in the classroom, whereas those who are antagonistic to religion are always talking about it to the students."[100]

Lest he be perceived as anti-intellectual or hostile to education, Maier expressed appreciation for academic inquiry and sound education. In one of the most striking examples of this, Maier opened a 1936 sermon titled "Back to Bible Truth!" with a celebration "that our age has sworn complete hostility to every form of ignorance." He noted a range of recent research and the resulting benefits to humankind, summarizing: "On all sides we

---

[97]Maier, *Christ for Every Crisis*, 21.
[98]Maier, *America, Turn to Christ!*, 25.
[99]Maier, *Christ for Every Crisis*, 85.
[100]Walter A. Maier, *He Will Abundantly Pardon* (St. Louis: CPH, 1948), 138-42.

behold investigations that daily extend the human horizon and help make this the age of history's greatest enlightenment." Maier affirmed the church's support for such developments, and reiterated its boundaries:

> The Church views all this as a special benediction from God. It does not hide its head in the sand of ignorance while the pageant of science marches on. Wherever the Cross of Christ is raised, ignorance is banished, and the arts and sciences are systematically promoted. The greatest schools of the world were founded by the Church. . . . It is only when human reason rules out God and blasphemously raises unholy hands to pull down the Savior's Cross that the Church voices its uncompromising protest.[101]

As if to counterbalance the influence of the academics speaking against biblical truths from their lecterns, Maier occasionally cited academics and scientists—both living and dead—who were known to subscribe to the Christian faith. For example, in a 1937 sermon titled "Clear-Cut Conviction," Maier cited Louis Pasteur as a "tremendous" scientist who had a prayer closet "near his laboratory." He proceeded to name and describe numerous prominent physicians, scientists, and inventors, including the discoverer of "the thermionic valve" that "helped to make the radio possible," who all held "firm faith" in biblical truths.[102] Later that year, Maier decried faith being pushed from classrooms by some teachers, "when master minds in science have been among the most humble followers of Christ." "The Mount Everest of the Scriptures has not been moved a fraction of an inch by the tiny ants that dig their little tunnels at its feet," he proclaimed. He then listed "an imposing procession" of great scientific minds ranging from an astronomer, a mathematician, a botanist, a pathologist, a geologist, a chemist, and others. These inquirers, some famous, others less so, "together with regiments of other men of science and letters," had "found in Christ their full salvation," which they learned from their Bibles.[103]

On other occasions, Maier mentioned examples of Christian testimony by faculty members "of great American universities." In these instances, he quoted professors without identifying them by name, and stated their college

---

[101] Maier, *Christ for the Nation*, 133-34.

[102] Maier, *Fourth Lutheran Hour*, 196-97. Over the years, Pasteur was one of Maier's favorite examples of a man who possessed a brilliant scientific mind and a faithful Christian commitment.

[103] Maier, *Cross from Coast to Coast*, 48.

or university affiliations.[104] Lest professing professors failed to impress, Maier also mentioned university and college presidents and deans by name, along with the names of their institutions, in other radio sermons.[105] In both of these situations, he made sure to include public (e.g., Ohio State University, University of California, University of Illinois) and private institutions (e.g., Smith College, Princeton University, Johns Hopkins University, Temple University). Over the course of his radio ministry, Maier repeated this pattern of trumping Scripture-denouncing scientists, scholars, and academic leaders with their steady, Bible-believing counterparts in the same fields.

As for liberal, modernist opinion makers beyond academic and research walls, Maier paid as much attention to them as Sheen. He often spoke of prominent "infidels" in general terms, emphatically denouncing their dismissal of scriptural authority. Occasionally, however, Maier took verbal swipes at well-known figures by name, such as H. G. Wells, Bertrand Russell, George Bernard Shaw, and Langston Hughes.[106] While he may have been critical of their work, Maier appears to have actually read their writings prior to offering a critique.

Regardless of the offending party, Maier fought for scriptural authority against all who would degrade it, question it, or be indifferent toward it. Put differently, Maier subscribed to the Reformation doctrinal formulation of *sola gratia, sola fide,* with such eternal, life-giving dogmas derived *sola scriptura.* Thus, notwithstanding the unpopularity of declaring doctrinal rigidity in a world increasingly drawn to a more fluid secular approach, Maier held firm. As a result, the less orthodox heaped the same scorn on Maier that they did on Sheen. Maier acknowledged during his broadcasts that listeners, including clergymen, "wrote to express your disapproval, charging a spirit of self-righteousness and intolerance," especially in response to his sermons on the exclusivity of Christ in matters of salvation. He pleaded with those who

---

[104]For an example, see Maier, *Victory Through Christ,* 24.

[105]For an example, see Maier, *Victory Through Christ,* 153-54.

[106]For examples, see Walter A. Maier, *For Christ and Country* (St. Louis: CPH, 1942), 321; *Global Broadcasts of His Grace,* 92-93; *Victory Through Christ,* 408. Maier found the emergence of Langston Hughes particularly unsettling. He described Hughes's poem "Good-by Christ" as "filth," "savagery," "blasphemy," and "satanic." On one occasion, Maier quoted a brief excerpt from the poem, and warned his listeners, especially the African American members of his audience, against the perils of foregoing biblical promises for such "hideous unbelief." See Maier, *Jesus Christ Our Hope,* 92.

"have completely discarded the doctrine of divine Christ," to be "honest enough to tell the world that they are not Christian," though he knew that this request would cause them "to brand" him "as narrow and bigoted."[107] In addition to echoing the Catholic Sheen, Maier also sounded a lot like the Presbyterian scholar J. Gresham Machen, whose 1923 book *Christianity and Liberalism* sharply criticized the modernists for what Machen considered their misappropriation of the term "Christian."[108]

In a 1945 Christmas sermon, Maier quoted C. S. Lewis "at Magdalen College, Oxford," who insisted that one could not just accept Jesus "as a mighty teacher," but that everyone had to decide whether he "was, and is, the Son of God." Maier concluded the quote with words from Lewis's own radio broadcast, which eventually would be edited and published in the Brit's classic book *Mere Christianity*: "Don't let us come with any patronizing nonsense about His being a great human teacher. He hasn't left that open to us. He didn't intend to."[109] If some thought Maier "one-sided," "restricted," and "intolerant" for his exclusive faith in God's Son, then their issue was with God himself, for his Word declared "that there is 'one Mediator between God and man.' . . . You may defiantly charge your Lord with unfairness . . . when He declares that there is one and only one road to salvation," Maier explained, but understand that "a cricket may chirp against Gibraltar all day, but this will not move the rock."[110]

While "crickets" may have indeed "chirped against Gibraltar," Walter Maier and Fulton Sheen boldly proclaimed its granite permanence. For two

---

[107] Maier, *Radio for Christ*, 327.

[108] Maier corresponded with Machen in 1935, as the Presbyterian continued battling modernists within his denomination. One of the items shared by Machen was a statement he had released on March 18, 1935. With pencil, Maier highlighted a paragraph including the following quotation: "I know nothing of a Christ who possibly did and possibly did not work miracles, but know only a Christ who said to the wind and the waves, with the sovereign voice of the Maker and the Ruler of all nature, 'Peace be still.'" Maier kept a file of articles by and about Machen. See WAM Collection, box 1, folder 129 and box 9, file 10, Concordia Historical Institute, St. Louis.

[109] Walter A. Maier, *Let Us Return unto the Lord* (St. Louis: CPH, 1947), 209. C. S. Lewis did not publish *Mere Christianity* until 1952—two years after Maier's death; however, some of his radio broadcasts from the BBC were published in the United States by Macmillan in 1943. It seems likely that this publication was the source of Maier's quotation.

[110] Maier, *Christ, Set the World Aright!*, 298.

decades they presented biblical truths, and the derivative doctrines the church had codified therefrom, as a foundational rock on which their radio listeners could build their lives for time and eternity. To do this effectively, Sheen and Maier consistently emphasized the reliability of the Bible, in the face of modern thinkers who were hedging their bets—many of whom claimed to be Christians. For millions of auditors in radioland, stable truth claims from a sacred text, as explained by two forceful scholars and clerics, held rock-solid validity.

THE ATONEMENT

An agitated listener once sent Walter Maier a letter that began, "For a long time I have been wanting to ask you a question. Do you use the same sermon on the air every Sunday afternoon? *Always, the blood, the blood.*"[111] As one reads the entire letter, two things become clear about this correspondent. First, even though he claimed that Maier's messages caused him "to turn the dial" to alternative programs, he obviously listened to him regularly. Second, while his accusation that Maier repeated his sermons was completely false, the Lutheran did, indeed, speak of "the blood," Jesus Christ's blood, with regularity. As a matter of fact, in both Maier's and Sheen's assertion of scriptural authority and historical Christian theology, the doctrine of the atonement was front and center. As modernists, in particular, became increasingly embarrassed by historical concepts of substitutionary and propitiatory atonement achieved through Christ's shed blood, suffering, and death, Sheen and Maier argued that they were the very foundation of the faith. They held firm that the redemptive work of Christ was much more than his exemplary moral life; as a consequence, individual salvation required a proper understanding of its meaning.

A 1938 sermon, titled "The Cleansing Christ," provides a noteworthy example of Maier's emphasis on the power of Christ's blood. The Old Testament professor's conveyance of ritual sacrifice and atonement is striking:

---

[111] As quoted in Michael Edgar Pohlman, "Broadcasting the Faith: Protestant Religious Radio and Theology in America, 1920–1950" (PhD diss., Southern Baptist Theological Seminary, 2011), 125. Maier mentioned this letter on the air, noting that it had arrived unsigned. While he noted, "Ordinarily we pay no attention to unsigned letters; for the man who hides behind anonymity has a rodent mind. Like the rat he works in the dark and flees the light," Maier chose "to answer these charges." See Maier, *Cross from Coast to Coast*, 251.

When we study the love of Christ against this black background of our sin, how His grace dazzles us with the promise of forgiveness through Christ's blood! Not the blood of lambs and calves slain on all the sacrificial altars of the aging centuries; not the rivers of patriots' blood that flow through history; not the blood of Christian saints and martyrs! The cleansing, purifying blood is the royal blood of God's own Son; the blood that dripped from His body, when in Gethsemane He began that soul-sorrowing, heart-breaking substitution for all sinners; the blood coursed down His back under the lash when we were healed by His stripes; the blood that stained His wounded head and whitened face under the cruel diadem which assures us our crown of life; the blood that dripped from nail wounds in His holy hands and feet, that streamed from His side when the thrust of a Roman spear established His sin-atoning, substitutionary death,—that holy blood, and that alone, "*cleanseth us from sin.*"[112]

Note that divine and human aspects of Jesus's person are evident in this description. Christ bled because he was human, but he was no mere adopted "son of God" chosen from humanity. The magnitude and power of Christ's sacrifice exceeds that of Old Testament sacrifices, and the sacrifices of subsequent, virtuous fighters and churchmen. Said another way, the crucifixion was something much greater than the exemplary moral act to which many contemporary Christians were reducing it. While Maier did not always include this graphic or lengthy a description of the bloody crucifixion, this emphasis on the harsh realities of this historical event and its derivative outcome, for all who saw them through faith, was his consistent theme.

Lewis E. Jones's 1899 revival hymn "There Is Power in the Blood" could well have been Maier's theme song. While liberals "blasphemously attacked" Christ's atonement, and "tell us that the Gospel of blood is too old-fashioned to fit into our racy, stream-lined age,"[113] Maier countered that "a single drop of His blood can cleanse the whole world of its sin."[114] In a 1944 sermon, Maier noted that, regrettably, modern blood transfusions were not always successful in saving the lives of patients. Yet Christ's shed blood "rescued us from ruin, and unfailingly delivered us from eternal death." Thus, "we ought

---

[112]Maier, *Cross from Coast to Coast*, 241-42.
[113]Maier, *Cross from Coast to Coast*, 246.
[114]Maier, *Global Broadcasts of His Grace*, 36.

to thank the Almighty that on Good Friday Jesus" became "the greatest [blood] donor of all history."[115]

Even for those who fully accepted the atonement doctrine, Maier reminded them that this salvation-producing blood required an awful ordeal for Jesus—agonizing in divine and human ways. He encouraged listeners to "envision the rough-hewn cross upon Calvary, where Jesus Christ, hated as no man has ever been hated, suffered as only God could suffer, paid with His blood the appalling price of all human sin."[116] "My beloved," Maier implored, "count the cost of your redemption . . . the cost to Christ—His bodily anguish . . . bleeding . . . excruciating . . . torture . . . into the darkest death that hell itself can ever know."[117] Time and again, Maier reiterated that the God-man Jesus—no divine creature only appearing to suffer, no adopted man only sacrificing as an example—experienced the crucifixion, thereby constructing an avenue for divine-human reconciliation.

Such reconciliation was available to all who repentantly placed their faith in it, regardless of who they were or what they had done or the times in which they lived. In a 1940 Epiphany sermon, with a turbulent world as a backdrop, Maier attempted to bring comfort to anxious parlors across the country:

> What unbounded comfort for every one of us lies in the fact that Christ is the atonement for every sinner. . . . There are no Negroes or white men, no native-born or foreign-born, no pure-blooded or mixed-blooded, no Aryans or Semites; but that all, whoever they are in the hundreds of racial groups, wherever they may live in this world's far-flung stretches, whatever language of the thousand different tongues and dialects they may speak, are on the same common level, the fallen children of God, whom Christ loved with such divine devotion that He was born as every man's Savior, lived and died as every man's substitute, rose again to become every man's Resurrection and Life![118]

Maier often reiterated the universality of the atonement with listings such as these, typically with a reflection of current events. For instance, at the end of World War II, Maier stressed that "the Lamb" had been "slain" for

---

[115]Maier, *Christ, Set the World Aright!*, 223.
[116]Maier, *Christ for the Nation*, 12.
[117]Maier, *He Will Abundantly Pardon*, 51.
[118]Maier, *Peace Through Christ*, 152.

"Americans and Canadians, white and black, Gentile and Jew, plutocrat and pauper, illustrious and illiterate, Nazis and Nipponese."[119]

In addition to emphasizing that the atonement was a doctrine that applied to all, Maier also stressed its sufficiency for salvation. "The saving Gospel is *all-pardoning*," he declared. "No matter how crimson or hellish black your sins . . . no transgression is too shocking, if you only bring it to Him with contrite hearts!"[120] If seldom with the specific phraseology, Maier clearly promoted the historical Lutheran soteriological formulation of justification before God "by Grace alone, through Faith alone," and such faith was in the complete adequacy of Jesus Christ's atoning endeavor. "Do we want a revival of the creed which tells distracted men and women that they must earn heaven by their own personal penance and good works?" he asked. "God forbid!" Such schemes would only revive "the age-old delusion of salvation by character, achievement, payment—not by Christ's blood and righteousness."[121]

Maier contrasted the "unfinished and incomplete" nature of most human endeavors, where "each day dawns with its new demands," with the full accomplishment achieved by Christ's atonement. "How we ought to thank God on our knees . . . that, while incompleteness is the curse of our existence and the hard struggles of life often remain unfinished or unrewarded, the great blessing of heaven and earth combined, the salvation of our souls, had been finished with divine finality, completed forever by the substitutionary suffering of . . . Jesus."

Failure to recognize this fact and apprehend its blessing through faith was a perilous mistake. Maier especially fretted that this mistake was all too common within mainline churches. "That rejection of Christ's divine redemption and atonement has eaten its cancerous way into many large denominations," he warned, begging "American Christians" to "see to it that their pulpits preach the full free, Gospel of grace in the God-man Jesus."[122]

---

[119]Maier, *Jesus Christ Our Hope*, 29-30.

[120]Maier, *Christ, Set the World Aright!*, 295.

[121]Maier, *Peace Through Christ*, 323. It was not uncommon for Maier to warn against trusting in one's good works for winning favor with God. In this specific sermon, he takes an uncharacteristic (though slightly veiled) swipe at Roman Catholicism, cautioning against "pomp and ritual" for salvation, even if it is carried out "in . . . magnificent churches."

[122]Maier, *Rebuilding with Christ*, 65-67.

Countering modernist characterizations of Christ's death, Maier repeatedly stressed that "Jesus Christ was crucified for you, not simply as a Martyr, not merely as an Example of self-sacrifice, not only as a Pattern of non-resistance, but as your divine Redeemer."[123] Broadening his warning, Maier clarified what was at stake:

> Now if you contradict this truth (and I do not care whether you speak from the most fashionable, highly paid pulpit in the land or whether you are one of the uncouth, obscene infidels that write me letters to which they dare not sign their names) . . . then no matter how you may exalt Him as leader, teacher, master, model, or by any other name except "God," you are not a Christian . . . you are not saved for eternity . . . you are not a member of Christ's true Church.[124]

In short, while Jesus Christ may have exhibited a number of exemplary characteristics while on earth, which Maier was fully willing to acknowledge and commend, the crucial act of atoning for the sins of humankind was at the core of everything else he did. Any other selfless acts or sage advice delivered by Jesus, according to Maier, would have mattered little without the propitiation of sin through his shedding of blood and death. What is more, such a monumental task could only have been executed by a person possessing divine and human characteristics. Failure to recognize and place one's faith in these facts rendered one a non-Christian, no matter how much a person admired the earthly endeavors of Jesus of Nazareth.

Remarkably, for an era during which many Protestants and Roman Catholics looked on each other as representing contrasting visions of the Christian faith, Fulton Sheen saw things similarly regarding the centrality of the atonement, and was not bashful about it. In his first season on the CH, Sheen explained that in the great "drama of Salvation there is a relation between man who is lost in sin, and God Who came to save him—not by gold or silver, but by the outpouring of His Precious Blood." While Sheen made it clear that his cleansing blood applied to all of humankind, he personalized the point for his listeners: "And if you were the only person in the

---

[123]Walter A. Maier, *The Airwaves Proclaim Christ* (St. Louis: CPH, 1948), 53.
[124]Maier, *America, Turn to Christ!*, 286.

world who ever lived, He would have come down and suffered and died just for you alone. That is how much God loves you."[125]

Though Maier specifically mentioned Christ's atoning *blood* with greater frequency, Sheen described its inherent importance in emphatic terms. "Under the shelter of the Blood of Christ the worst sinners may take their stand; for there is power in that Blood to turn back tides of vengeance which threaten to drown the world."[126] Speaking of Jesus going to the cross, Sheen explained that on that day, "what He had prefigured and foreshadowed He realized in its completeness, as He was crucified . . . and His Blood drained from His Body for the redemption of the world."[127] Assigning powerful imagery to blood, in a 1930 sermon titled "Dying and Behold We Live," Sheen spoke of the Roman centurion piercing Jesus' side after his death on the cross: "the Divine Master, Who saved up a few drops of His Precious Blood, now pours them out to prove that His love is stronger than death."[128] Demonstrating his trust in its vitality, Sheen always capitalized the word *Blood* when referring to the blood of Jesus in his published radio sermons.

A bleeding Savior demonstrated the humanity of Jesus, but Sheen also highlighted the divine nature of Christ, explaining that a mere man could not provide sufficient sacrifice for sinful humankind. Reflecting Chalcedonian orthodoxy, Sheen explained, "Such is the central affirmation of our faith that Jesus Christ, who was born at Bethlehem and suffered under Pontius Pilate, is true God and true Man: The introduction, from the outside and above into history and into the world of fallen sinful man, of the Power and Wisdom of God." He added, "The Son of God by becoming Man has made Himself Our Healer and our Saviour, by divinizing our weak human nature." In a 1944 New Year's Eve sermon, "Who Can Re-make You?," Sheen explained in succinct terms, "To re-create fallen man in justice and mercy, Redemption must come from without and be accomplished within. Put both conditions together and the Redeemer was both God and man. If He were only man, He too would need Redemption; if He were only God He would have no relation to fallen man who needed Redemption."[129]

---

[125]Sheen, *Divine Romance*, 77.

[126]Sheen, *Prodigal World*, 80.

[127]Sheen, *Prodigal World*, 71.

[128]Sheen, *Divine Romance*, 125.

[129]Fulton J. Sheen, *You* (Staten Island, NY: St. Paul's/Alba House, 2003), 36-37.

While stressing the two natures of Christ, Sheen often reminded his listeners of the majesty and power Jesus laid aside, or at least cloaked, by as-
suming human flesh via the incarnation. In one of the best examples of this,
Sheen reconstructed the nativity scene, elaborating on the divine mystery:

> The tiny hands that were not quite long enough to touch the huge heads of
> cattle, were the hands that were holding the reins that steer the sun, the moon,
> and the stars in their courses. The tiny fingers that could but clutch clumsily
> at the coarse straw of the threshing floor were fingers that will one day point
> in judgment to the good and to the bad. The tiny feet that could not walk were
> weak, not because they were baby feet, but because those baby feet could not
> bear the weight of Divine Omnipotence. There under the tender skin of a
> baby brow was beating an Intelligence compared to which the intelligences
> of Europe and America amount to naught; an intelligence that, if it had
> moved in other days, would have found Plato and Aristotle but poor philoso-
> phers, Dante and Shakespeare but poor poets, and our modern scientists but
> mumbling beginners.[130]

This all amounted to a "Marvel of marvels!" a "Union of unions!" Combining the events of the nativity with those of the Epiphany, Sheen observed
that both the shepherds and the wise men heard the cry of the infant Jesus.
"The Shepherds found their Shepherd, and the Wise Men discovered
Wisdom. And the Shepherd and the Wisdom was a Babe in a crib."[131] And
the babe in the crib had humbled himself to ultimately bring salvation to
sinful people by atoning for their iniquity.

Although Sheen often described the crucifixion and its resulting
atonement as an outpouring of God's unfathomable love, he also wanted his
listeners to remember the grim price, the grueling ordeal, that were required
of God's Son. In one of his earliest network broadcasts, Sheen recalled the
scene at Golgotha: "The God-man is miserable now. No longer can men say,
'God makes me suffer pain while He goes through none,' for the God-man
is now enduring pain to the utmost . . . for now His own Sacred Heart understands what it is to be abandoned by God and man as He suffers . . . rejected by one and abandoned by the other."[132] This was no docetic appearance

---

[130]Sheen, *Divine Romance*, 74-75.
[131]Sheen, *Divine Romance*, 71-73.
[132]Sheen, *Divine Romance*, 116.

of agony. "He who loved men unto death, allowed sin to wreak its vengeance upon Him, in order that they might forever understand its horror as the crucifixion of Him who loved them most. . . . By the way He suffered, He revealed the reality of sin."[133]

In a 1944 sermon on Christ's final words on the cross, Sheen focused on "My God! My God! Why hast thou abandoned me?" He explained that at this moment, the "disruptive power of sin which is permanent in hell, Christ now allows to devastate His inmost soul that He might suffer what we deserved for our sins." This "price He paid to save us" underscores that redemption, the atonement, "forgiveness is no glib thing!"[134]

While Sheen would say plenty about the expectations and obligations that acceptance of Christ's redemptive work placed on individual Christians, he repeatedly stressed the completeness of the atonement, and its universality. In 1932, he provided this summation: "He who reserved the first fruits of His message for the lost sheep of Israel was the same One whose flame of charity embraced the whole world, and whose life was surrendered on the gibbet of the cross for the redemption of all peoples, for all climes and all times." The atonement not only applied to all people, but equalized all people before the ruler of the universe: "There is only one foundation for equality, and that is the Catholic doctrine that men have been redeemed by the precious blood of Jesus Christ, that all men have been called to share His life, and that President, and citizen, poor and rich, the mighty and the lowly, have been thought so much worthwhile that Christ would have died for the least of them."[135]

The central reason that saved humans were equal before God was because God's salvation was complete, and was achieved by Christ alone. Said another way, mortal men and women did not contribute to their justification before a righteous, holy Creator; therefore, no hierarchy of the redeemed existed. On numerous occasions, Sheen sounded nearly identical to his Protestant counterpart. "Man is a sinner," said Sheen, who "could no more restore himself to the favor of God than a man who owes a million can pay it with a cent, or a soldier who is mortally wounded can bind up

---

[133]Sheen, *Prodigal World*, 79-80.
[134]Sheen, *One Lord: One World*, 69.
[135]Sheen, *Manifestations of Christ*, 87-88.

his own wounds."[136] Elsewhere he reiterated, "Human nature has contracted a bigger debt than it can pay. In sinning against God we piled up an infinite debt, and we have not enough . . . merits in our finite bank to meet the burden. . . . You might just as well tell a man suffering from gout that all he needed was to play six sets of tennis."[137] Walter Maier would have nodded his concurrence.

Like Maier, Sheen compared the completeness of Christ's acts of atonement with the general incompleteness of human engagements. He began by recalling God's initial creative acts during which "[he] labored for six days . . . at the end of which came the divine applause of a work *completed.*" Then shifting to the final hours of Jesus' earthly life, Sheen explained, "For thirty-three years God, made man, burned with the desire to be baptized with the blood of Redemption; and now at the end of three hours on the cross God saw once more 'that it was good.' It took only a word to create, but it took a life to redeem." In short, the atonement—redemption—"was finished." By contrast, Sheen noted, "How few of us ever finish the tasks assigned to us. The world is full of souls that are like unfinished symphonies, and half-completed Gothic Cathedrals . . . souls that never have the joy of looking on a perfect work, seeing that it is good, and . . . crying out the song of victory: 'It is finished.'"

Sheen desired that his hearers take heart in the definitive, whole redemption Christ had earned for them. Sheen did, however, suggest that Christ's example of sacrificial commitment, combined with the knowledge of salvation won by such commitment, should encourage his listeners to devote themselves fully to dedicated discipleship.[138]

Paralleling Maier on yet another issue, Sheen frequently warned his listeners against modernist treatment, or lack thereof, of the doctrine of the atonement. In an early CH broadcast, Sheen declared, "The drying of the blood of Christ on an infamous gibbet, then, is something more than some in our day would have us believe, who declare that Christ's death is interesting and valuable because of the subjective effect it has on the mind of the believer. . . . No! He went to death not to impress us subjectively, but to save

---

[136]Sheen, *Eternal Galilean*, 138-39.
[137]Sheen, *You*, 35-36.
[138]Sheen, *Fullness of Christ*, 155-56.

us objectively."[139] Jesus had earned a forensic declaration of "righteous" for unrighteous sinners, before the bar of a holy judge, and Sheen was appalled that this miraculous intervention could be reduced to merely an example of virtue and a commentary on society. To be sure, "the great Redemptive act of Calvary" had relevance on "social order," but only as an outgrowth of Christ's atonement for sinners.[140]

Modernists and their allies, especially those within the broadly defined church, elevated themselves and lowered Christ in their downplaying of the atonement. "Since nothing can disturb the modern man's good opinion of himself, the Cross and its Redemption is meaningless," observed Sheen in a 1941 Holy Week sermon. He continued, "But it is not as irrelevant as he thinks. The purpose of this broadcast is to indicate that by denying the Cross of Christ, modern man did not escape the cross—no one can; he got a cross—the double-cross." The modernists were deluding themselves in a dangerous and hubristic way. The following week, Sheen told his audience, "God cannot save a man who still retains, in the smallest degree, the illusion that man can be his own savior." Only in "new humility he begins to be free," he explained—humility that included repentance for sin and acceptance of the atonement.[141]

Sheen was disgusted by those who claimed allegiance to Jesus because of some of his ethical teachings, but rejected the reality of sin and the need for redemption. In an Easter sermon in the latter years of his radio ministry, Sheen lectured in earnest:

> There are some who would have an unscarred Christ; they would have a Christ on the Mount of Beatitudes because they love beautiful sayings, but not the Christ on the Mount of Calvary because they deny they have ever sinned. They would have the Son of Man, but not the Son of God; the cowardly Christ Who shuns sacrifice; Who would have a victory without a battle, a glory without a struggle, a heaven without a hell; a broad-minded Christ Who is indifferent to virtue and vice, Who knows no good sublime enough to die to espouse; and no evil wicked enough to condemn; the Tolerant Christ Who never made scourges to drive charlatans out of the Temple, Who never bade

---

[139]Sheen, *Divine Romance*, 75-76.
[140]See the January 1939 sermon "The Relevance of God," in Sheen, *Freedom and Peace*, 1-10.
[141]Sheen, *War and Guilt*, 151, 164.

us cut off hands and feet and pluck out eyes rather than sin, Who never mentions hell or the devil or divorce.

Take your tawdry, cheap Christ Whom you call a moral teacher and ethical reformer, a social planner; Whom you put on the same plane as Buddha, Confucius, Laotze and Whom you call a good man. He is *not* just a good man, for good men do not lie. If He is not the Christ, the Son of the Living God, then He is the greatest liar, charlatan and deceiver the world has ever known! If He is not the Christ, the Son of the Living God, then He is the anti-Christ, but He is not just a good man. . . . If your weak, tolerant Christ be right, then wrong must be right; then what matter if we be saints or devils, if Christ on a tree or Judas on a halter must both taste eternal death!

Take your human Christ Who cannot save the Truth He preached, but drowns with Him for Whom He risked His life. Take your soft Christ, you polluters of Divinity, Who make Him just a man. . . . We need the Risen Jesus of the Scars for our times![142]

In sum, "the wages of sin is death," and Jesus Christ accepted such wages on behalf of sinful men and women. This required him to be fully God and fully man. Failure to recognize these facts and apprehend their temporal and eternal blessings through repentance and faith constituted more than some tedious theological disagreement. It placed one beyond the boundaries of Christ's church and his grace.

For Fulton Sheen, as for Walter Maier, those boundaries were fixed. Unlike many of their counterparts who claimed allegiance to Jesus Christ, Sheen and Maier neither tore down the boundaries nor attempted to move them. Instead, they consistently invited their ethereal parishioners to cross to the salvific side of such boundaries, through the only gateway they knew—faith in the atoning work of Jesus Christ.

---

[142]Fulton J. Sheen, *The Love That Waits for You*, 7th ed. (Washington: NCCM, 1958), 109-11. Sermons in this booklet were preached between January and April, 1949. While Sheen is obviously contrasting Christian orthodoxy with modernist conceptions of Christianity in a general way, he may also be engaging in a veiled criticism of Harry Emerson Fosdick and his Riverside Church.

SIN AND GRACE

Sinful humankind required Christ's atonement because sin was a serious matter that caused a breach in God's relationship with his creatures. God's grace healed this breach for those who repented of their sin and placed their faith in Christ's restorative work. In order to avail oneself of this blessing, however, individuals needed to recognize that they were indeed fallen sinners. Maier and Sheen took to the airwaves each week with the objective of driving listeners to God's grace, about which they spoke in inviting terms. In order to demonstrate the need for such grace, they first had to speak of the reality and gravity of sin with unwavering bluntness. They spoke to those who knew they were sinners. They addressed those who did not acknowledge that they were sinners. And they scolded those who refused to recognize sin for what it was.

In a 1944 Christmas sermon, Sheen cautioned those who "make light . . . of the story of the Fall," thinking it little more than an ancient tale. Adam's disobedience was still relevant because "the Fall disorganized our normal human faculties, making us just as we are now, with a bias toward evil, with a will reluctant to do good, with a tendency to rationalize evil."[143] A daily newspaper would have reinforced Sheen's point. It was critical that his listeners not just see the sin in the world, but that they recognize the sin in their individual lives. "Genuine self-knowledge" would reveal personal fallenness. According to Sheen, there were "two rules" to knowing oneself. "There must be a standard outside of self, otherwise we become victims of self-deceit," he explained as the first rule, and "if a man is to know himself he must use as his standard Our Lord Jesus Christ . . . the Standard of Right and Wrong." The second rule was that "self-knowledge must seek to discover what is our *predominant fault*"—a "fault that varies from person to person." He cataloged these faults by listing the so-called seven deadly sins—pride, avarice, lust, anger, gluttony, envy, and sloth. Sheen explained that "sin must have a disguise to be attractive," and then proceeded to expound on how each of the seven could be alternatively labeled and rationalized into desirable allurements.[144] For listeners who initially resisted thinking of themselves as manifest sinners, Sheen's descriptions were meant to cause reassessment.

---

[143]Sheen, *You*, 28-29.
[144]Sheen, *Love That Waits*, 34-37.

Given the need for men and women to recognize that they were sinners, Sheen was particularly perturbed at those both in the church and outside the church who argued against humankind's inherent sinfulness. The various forms of humanism espoused by the modernists, liberals, and non-believers appalled him, because they ignored the reality of sin, which Sheen considered obvious. He further argued against the high estimation humanists placed on humanity's potential and perfectibility. Additionally, he warned that such failure to recognize sin, combined with overoptimism regarding humankind's trajectory, obscured the need for an atoning Savior.

In a 1934 radio address, Sheen laid out humanism as one of the "panaceas" that "the world" says will lead to happiness. He defined humanism as "the sufficiency of man without God," explaining that "on this theory man finds satisfaction in his own mind without the aid of faith, and in his own will without the aid of grace." He continued, "There is no need, according to this philosophy, to seek God outside of man, but only the man inside of himself, with his thoughts and imaginings." The inevitable futility of this pursuit ultimately drives individuals into other equally hollow sins, which frustrate and jeopardize souls. "Humanism is not a success, but a failure," Sheen explained, "for man cannot live by himself, any more than he can lift himself by his own bootstraps or live on his own fat."[145] In sum, humans not only need a Savior to overcome their sinfulness, but they need a sustaining relationship with God because of the way they are created.

In his opening sermon of the 1935–1936 CH, on the need for regeneration of "a world" and of "men," Sheen told his hearers that "the great experiment of Humanism . . . was now like a sick man who could not cure himself." While the recent versions of humanism seemed particularly insidious, Sheen lamented that "since the days of the Renaissance" humankind "has tried to build its civilization on the self-sufficiency of man without God," but "slowly sinks downward." While humanists portrayed biblical texts as obsolete ancient myths, Sheen countered, "The law of necessary progress is a myth."[146] In his 1931 book *Old Errors and New Labels*, Sheen called humanism "the New Pelagianism," aligning it with the late fourth-century and early fifth-century heresy that "den[ied] original sin," and "held that human nature by

---

[145]Sheen, *Eternal Galilean*, 112-14.
[146]Sheen, *Prodigal World*, 8.

its own power is able to save itself without the help of God's grace."[147] He was to reiterate this assessment throughout his radio ministry.

Because humanists held such a high view of the inherent goodness of humans and their ability to progress, they had a tendency to explain away sin as no fault of an individual, but as an outgrowth of some condition or outside influence. "Today nobody is wrong; they are anti-social or have bad tonsils," Sheen preached. "This makes moral regeneration well-nigh impossible; men are blind and no longer want to see, deaf and no longer want to hear."[148] It was assumed that such disorders could eventually be resolved through human effort—especially scientific or political. Sheen would have none of it. In a March 1941 sermon titled "The Reality of Sin," he began by quoting George Bernard Shaw: "Modern man is too busy to think about his sins." Sheen responded, "It perhaps would be truer to say that modern man denies he can sin." He continued, "It is the fashion today to explain away sin biologically, as a 'fall in the evolutionary process,' or physically by attributing moral aberrations to physical environment, lack of playgrounds, Grade A milk, and bad glands: attributing evil not to violations of conscience, but to something external." While such thinking could appear liberating, in fact, "to deny sin is . . . to reduce man to the status of a *thing*." Such had both individual and national consequences because "indifference to evil, sin, and wrong" created a "national paralysis" against wrong. "There is no nation on earth that is so intolerant of germs as the United States; there are few nations which are so tolerant of evil and sin." No sooner did Sheen mention this national concern, however, than he returned to the individual, noting that "the souls which use" the "remedy" of denying sin "are of the same type who run from bill collectors. Someday the collector will catch up with them."[149]

At the end of 1940, with World War II expanding, Sheen noted that "our illusions . . . that man is naturally good and infinitely progressive . . . and . . . that social perfection is attainable in this world" were being "shattered." The "false prophets" had claimed that "goodness increases with years, that evil and error decline; that evolution takes the place of Providence, science

---

[147]Sheen, *Old Errors and New Labels*, 137-38. Pelagianism, named for the ascetic teacher Pelagius (ca. 350-ca. 425), was condemned by the Council of Carthage in 418.
[148]Sheen, *Freedom and Peace*, 82.
[149]Sheen, *War and Guilt*, 115-20.

supplants grace, and psychoanalysis eradicates guilt." "Then came this War," demonstrating that "our Utopianism, born of sophistication emancipated from religion, crashed on our heads like a hurricane from a clear sky. . . . Liberalism's child became a fierce progeny," and "our disillusioned prophets of progress are now as useless as sundials at night."[150]

Psychoanalysis, behaviorism, and psychology were particularly irksome to Sheen, and he was not hesitant about using sweeping characterizations to criticize them. "Psychology first lost its soul, then it lost its mind, finally it lost its consciousness," he railed in 1931.[151] In that Sheen's primary purpose was to call sinners to repentance and draw them to their only means of salvation, he considered psychological reclassifications and rationalizations of harmful human behavior as deeply pernicious. All too often, psychological explanations removed legitimate, conscience-generated guilt, and prevented sinners from repenting and amending their lives. What is more, it blinded them to their need for a Savior, thereby leaving them unreconciled to God, for time and eternity. While preaching to his radio audience in 1936 on the parable of the prodigal son, Sheen explained that "the final condition of the return to the Father's House was a recognition, on the part of the prodigal, of the sense of sin . . . and the need of penance." Sheen continued,

> Our Blessed Lord never once hints in the parable, when the young man re-
> turned . . . that he ever offered any excuse for his sinfulness . . . that he at-
> tempted to excuse himself or to extenuate his prodigality. He offered no theory
> about sin; he did not say it was a fall in the evolutionary process; he did not
> blame his environment or his wicked companions; he did not tell his father
> that he had inherited a queer Freudian complex from him; he did not say that
> moral decline was only a myth and that sin is just an illusion. . . . He did not
> excuse himself . . . having no responsibility for the past. . . . Out of its torn and
> bleeding self came only tear-drippings, a deep recognition of the horror of sin
> and the need of pardon and redemption.[152]

In short, "prodigals" needed contrite hearts and their Father's loving arms, rather than soothing words of a sympathetic therapist. A few years after this sermon, Sheen preached, "The *denial of sin* is at the base of much of the

---

[150]Sheen, *War and Guilt*, 14-15.
[151]Sheen, *Old Errors and New Labels*, 133.
[152]Sheen, *Prodigal World*, 54-55.

nervous disorders in the world today," the reason being that "neuroses to a great extent are due to frustration." And such frustration can only be alleviated by recognizing personal sin and accepting grace.[153]

---

[153]Sheen, *War and Guilt*, 117. While Sheen was critical of psychology and related sciences during his radio broadcasts, his most memorable attack on "psychoanalysis" occurred in 1947. In a Lenten sermon at New York's St. Patrick's Cathedral, Sheen lambasted "Freudianism" as "escapism," based on "four assumptions, materialism, hedonism, infantilism, and eroticism." He justified his criticism because such psychoanalysis "denies sin and would supplant confession." He added that "there are no more disintegrated people in the world than the victims of psychoanalysis." Detailed coverage of this sermon by the *New York Times* produced a sharp response, especially from those within the field of psychology. Catholic psychologists and psychiatrists complained that their work was being distorted by Sheen, and that his perceived moral authority was now causing patients to shun needed treatment for fear of sinning. Catholic and non-Catholic supporters and practitioners of psychological sciences publicly countered Sheen's broad criticisms. Frank Curren, a Catholic psychiatrist, resigned as chief psychiatrist at St. Vincent's Hospital in New York, because the archdiocese of New York declined to repudiate or clarify Sheen's comments. A leading Jewish psychoanalyst, A. A. Brill was particularly harsh: "Msgr. Sheen is entirely governed by the 'omnipotence of thought' which is characteristic of primitive thinking." The Catholic psychiatrist, Leo Bartemeier, complained, "Through his many radio broadcasts and public speeches, [Sheen] has left a widespread and erroneous impression that he is the official spokesman for the Catholic Church." Three months after the sermon, in a letter to the *Times*, Sheen claimed that his words had been distorted in the press. He assured the readers that he was not critical of all forms of psychoanalysis, and that psychiatry was "a perfectly valid science." He added that he had referred several individuals to psychiatrists in recent months. "The point of the discussion is not the Catholic Church and science, nor have I ever presented myself as the spokesman of the church on the subject of psychiatry except to praise it when it remains within the limits of the scientific. . . . I am, however, a spokesman of the Catholic Church when I say that any positive denial of sin on the part of Freudian psychoanalysis renders that science inadequate for the handling of the problems which affect the whole man." Shortly after Sheen's controversial sermon, Brill suggested that this "unreasonable attack on Freud" was a direct response to the popularity of Joshua Liebman's book, *Peace of Mind*, a bestseller. In this book, Liebman (who also held a presence on radio) criticized "irrational guilt—and Christianity's alleged encouragement of it." Liebman boldly advocated, "Atonement, rather than growth, is the aim of the religious confessional, whereas psychotherapy does not require that you feel sorry for your sins so long as you *outgrow* them" (emphasis original). Attempting to bring psychoanalysis and theology into alignment, Liebman advocated a "theology of self-acceptance." Sheen's immediate reaction to Liebman's publication may have been his sermon in New York, but a longer-term response was his own book titled *Peace of Soul*, in 1949. This bestseller opens, "Unless souls are saved, nothing is saved." In the text, Sheen exhibited greater discipline in use of psychology-related terms. He specified his objections to Freudian psychoanalysis, commended proper use of psychiatry, explained the human condition from a Christian perspective, and offered "peace of soul" via the redemptive work of God in Christ. See C. Kevin Gillespie, SJ, *Psychology and American Catholicism: From Confession to Therapy?* (New York: Crossroad, 2001), 16-19; Robert Kugelmann, *Psychology and Catholicism: Contested Boundaries* (New York: Cambridge University Press, 2011), 193-98; Thomas C. Reeves, *America's Bishop: The Life and Times of Fulton J. Sheen* (San Francisco: Encounter Books, 2001), 197-203; Joshua L. Liebman, *Peace of Mind: Insights on Human Nature That Can Change Your Life* (New York: Simon and Schuster, 1946); Fulton J. Sheen, *Peace of Soul* (New York: McGraw-Hill, 1949).

As the war raged on, Sheen continued to describe the folly of humanism. Noting that many humanists claimed affinity for religion, he observed, "Religion, the Humanists insist, must be love! And who speaks more of brotherhood than humanists? But they want Love without a Cross." He then spoke "directly to" his humanist listeners. By denying the need for the cross, "you have humanized God, and thus you have dehumanized man. . . . The tragedy of your Humanism is believing that dirty things are clean, that cruel things are kind, that hence there is no need of the Cross. . . . To you all men are good. There are halos even in hell." At the conclusion of the sermon, he pleaded with humanists to rethink their assumptions in light of the times, "before 'tis too late."[154]

Sin was real, and sin abounded. Sheen wanted his listeners to know that. Yet like his Lutheran counterpart, he wanted them to know something else: "But where sin abounded, grace did much more abound" (Rom 5:20 KJV). Grace was a gift offered freely by a loving God. Sheen and Maier attached distinctly Catholic and Lutheran conceptions of grace to their respective presentations, especially around the topic of how much human initiative was involved in receiving God's grace. Yet they also shared significant common ground.

In a sermon titled "The Need of Grace," Sheen defined "grace," because "few there are who know its meaning." He explained, "Grace is related to the Latin word 'gratis,' which means free. It is a gift of God which illumines our intellect, strengthens our will and enables us to become something we are not, namely, the sons of God and the heirs of the Kingdom of Heaven."[155] What is more, no one is outside the scope of God's abundant grace. In a 1936 Holy Week broadcast, Sheen assured, "From that first Easter Day on let no one believe he is beyond Redemption. There is nothing too far gone for salvation; there are no hopeless cases; there are no lost sheep that cannot be found . . . no prodigals beyond hope of the embrace of the Father."[156] Unlike "creatures," who "run out of love when betrayed and mocked . . . Divine Love refuses to leave the sinner even in his sin."[157]

---

[154]Sheen, One Lord: One World, 49-51.

[155]Sheen, Love That Waits, 46. A major theme of this 1949 CH series was grace.

[156]Sheen, Prodigal World, 128-29.

[157]Sheen, One Lord: One World, 69.

Grace was to be understood as God's gift brought about by God's re-demptive work, made available by God's initiative. Sheen declared, "The work of salvation is finished. . . . *What* is finished? The redemption of man is finished. Love had completed its mission."[158] In his 1949 sermon titled "Actual Grace: God's First Impact of the Soul," Sheen spoke of "first impulses of God's actual grace summoning you away from misery to union with Him." He described a "black grace" that makes "the soul realize its emptiness without [God]," which is followed by a "white grace" that fills this emptiness with "an impetus, a thrust, or a power which comes from God."[159] This grace would "assist" the sinner "to believe as true those things which [God] re-vealed," and would provide sanctifying strength for the heart and mind.[160] Finally, Sheen reinforced that grace was an objective, substantive reality that came from God to the individual, as opposed to something conjured up by the individual from within. "Rid yourselves of prejudices!" he warned, "At-tribute grace not to emotionalism or sentiment—though I admit there is much so-called religion which is just pietistic mush." Instead, he encouraged his listeners, "Taste and see that the Lord is Sweet . . . the experience of God is not an illusion!"[161]

With grace firmly and frequently defined as a gift from God, Sheen shifted his attention to human agency in apprehending this gift. Grace was freely offered to all, but each person was free to accept or reject the offer. "You must cooperate with this Divine Energy before it is effective," exhorted Sheen. In his sermons, he frequently employed synergistic language, such as in his sermon titled "The Need of Grace": "The Physician can cure, but we must *know* we are sick and want to be cured. God calls: we can either pretend we do not hear, or we can accept or reject."[162] Using a radio analogy, Sheen stated, "The good news of redemption may be eternally broadcast from the empty tomb, but we are free not to tune in on its saving grace."[163] He asserted that "grace strikes the soul sometimes with such a terrific impact, as to be

---

[158]Sheen, *Prodigal World*, 112.
[159]Sheen, *Love That Waits*, 53.
[160]Sheen, *You*, 60; *Love That Waits*, 53. Sheen's thoughts on sanctification will be covered more thoroughly in the following chapter.
[161]Sheen, *Love That Waits*, 96.
[162]Sheen, *Love That Waits*, 46, 49.
[163]Sheen, *One Lord: One World*, 88.

catastrophic, demanding a complete break with a sinful past." Yet even then, "Our choice is not to agree or disagree, it is only to embrace or reject."[164] In another sermon, Sheen described God as "a kind of Divine Squatter on the no-man's land of the soul," who "can be evicted at our word."[165] Sheen not only worried about those who consciously rejected grace, but was equally concerned about those who were indifferent to it: "Some eyes are so filled with the dust of the world's traffic that they cannot see the divine grace in their souls."[166]

Repentance and altered living were important themes in Sheen's explanation of human agency toward divine grace. "God's grace like the sunlight, was outside our window and before it could gladden us, we must clean the windows or reform the way we live. This is done by self-knowledge and the purification of the mind." One's soul will then "be flooded with light and inner peace."[167] With reference to genuine repentant responses to grace, Sheen occasionally put forth Catholic concepts of penance. In a 1949 sermon addressing "reparation for sins," he uncharacteristically used words that would have made many Protestants squirm: "We must blot out our own *past* sins by penance." He explained, "What reparation for sins does is to make God's pardon available to us. God's mercy is always present, but it does not become operative until we prove that we *really* want it, and we *prove* that we want it by amendment for sin."[168] In that Sheen's sermons collectively demonstrate his assertion that Christ had fully paid for the sins of all men and women, Sheen appears to be overstating even his own views on human agency in this sermon. What is clear is that Sheen wanted his listeners to understand that overcoming sin and responding to God's grace required their conscious involvement if God was to achieve all he intended in their lives. What is more, for individual sinners, God's grace and their response were to be understood as a series of interactions that would take place over their lifetimes.

---

[164]Sheen, *Love That Waits*, 54-55.
[165]Sheen, *Love That Waits*, 11.
[166]Sheen, *Fullness of Christ*, 104.
[167]Sheen, *Love That Waits*, 32-33.
[168]Sheen, *Love That Waits*, 87-88.

Like the priest on the CH, the minister on TLH believed that humankind was fallen. Throughout his broadcast career, Walter Maier stressed not only the existence of sin, but its complete permeation of individual lives and human affairs. In his very first TLH sermon, Maier explained that Jesus Christ had come into the world to raise up "the downtrodden masses of *sin-sick* humanity."[169] Such descriptions were to be repeated, as he lamented over, and railed against, a "sin-soaked world," a "sin-cursed world," a "sin-choked world," a "sin-saturated world," a "sin-mad world," and so on.[170] "In Christ's creed," explained Maier, "sin is the leprous, cancerous evil that deforms human life, the barrier that dooms men to the blight of a never-ending separation from their God."[171] He remarked, "One of the most noteworthy distinctions of this remarkable age of this remarkable country is the unparalleled development of cleanliness and sanitation." "With all of our abhorrence of dirt," however, "with the nation-wide battle against germs and infection, we might suppose that the proportionate attention be paid to guarding our inner life against the contamination of sin and the filth of immorality."[172] Lest general references to sin be too vague, Maier often included lists of specific sins, cataloging a range of "human iniquity" meant to prick the conscience of every listener and raise their awareness of "incomputable totals of human wretchedness" to which they contributed.[173]

In the midst of World War II, Maier marveled that Americans did not amend their sinful ways, especially in their homes, even as they witnessed the destructive power of man's sinfulness. Paraphrasing Malachi 3:7, Maier asked, "Wherein shall America return to God?" He proceeded, "In our family life, in purity, decency, clean living! At home sin-loving, self-seeking, pleasure-chasing, have dropped to new levels . . . as though there were no fields of battle . . . no war in which . . . streams of American blood are flowing."[174]

It was critical that his listeners understand that they were indeed sinners, not so that they would despair, but so that they would receive the good news

---

[169]Paul L. Maier, *The Best of Walter A. Maier* (St. Louis: CPH, 1980), 92. Emphasis added.

[170]Maier, *Lutheran Hour*, 7; *Fourth Lutheran Hour*, 110; *Radio for Christ*, 157; *Christ, Set the World Aright!*, 245; *Global Broadcasts of His Grace*, 228.

[171]Walter A. Maier, *Lutheran Hour*, 119.

[172]Walter A. Maier, *Lutheran Hour*, 222.

[173]Walter A. Maier, *Cross from Coast to Coast*, 201-2.

[174]Maier, *America, Turn to Christ!*, 140.

of a Savior from their sins. Maier stressed that everyone, himself included, was a sinner before a holy God. "You may never have committed highway robbery, but hundreds of other crimes stain your soul: sins against God, sins against your fellow men, sins against yourselves."[175] At the beginning of his seventh broadcast season, Maier stated, "For no matter how individuals may differ in learning or ignorance, wealth or poverty, respect or dishonor, achievement or failure, in the sight of God all are on one common level— they are sinners, men and women of unclean thoughts, wicked words, and destructive acts." He admitted that "some of you, hearing this broadcast for the first time, are doubtless saying to yourselves, 'What a narrow, outworn, disappointing message he brings!'" Maier then explained that "you cannot realize what that blessed Son of God means to you unless you know that your sin has separated you from your Father." He invited them to "lay their soul bare before God" and to "confess yourselves sinful, helpless, lost."[176]

Should his hearers think that Maier was passing judgment from some self-righteous vantage point, he explained that "*Christ and His Word* have charged you with continued rebellion against the Almighty, with sinful thoughts, sinful words, sinful actions," by which they had "turned against your Savior and your God [emphasis added]." For those who found this pronouncement off-putting, Maier made no apology: "People do not like to be reprimanded for their wrongs and be forced to see themselves as they really are without Jesus."[177] Uncomfortable though this was, if ignored, "the ravages of sin" should be expected to "rise up as horrible, accusing specters," causing the "lashing scourge of . . . conscience" to disturb the unrepentant.[178]

Sounding the same alarm as Sheen, Maier criticized modern thinkers, especially those in seats of ecclesiastical leadership, for decommissioning the term *sin*, and for downplaying or rationalizing its various manifestations. In a world in which sinful humans needed to be called to repentance, he found the contemporary inclination to explain away violations of God's law to be perilous to souls and to society. "You will find that the short, three-letter word *sin* has been deleted from many modern vocabularies and that

---

[175]Maier, *Go Quickly and Tell*, 132-33.
[176]Maier, *Peace Through Christ*, 5.
[177]Maier, *Global Broadcasts of His Grace*, 126.
[178]Maier, *Lutheran Hour*, 13.

short, three-word sentence 'I have sinned' is one of the hardest confessions to wring from proud human lips," preached Maier.[179] In a 1943 sermon during Lent, a Christian season particularly devoted to repentance, he reported with incredulity to his listeners, "The *New York Times* on its church page used about 4,000 words to print excerpts of sermons preached in New York City last Sunday; yet in all these reports the short, ugly, three-letter word 'sin' does not occur once."[180]

Unlike Sheen, Maier seldom used the term *humanist*. Nonetheless, he shared Sheen's disdain for supposed experts who refused to hold humans responsible for ungodly decisions, all the while claiming that humans had great, progressive potential, if only given the right environment, the proper enlightenment, and access to modern science. As would frequently occur on this topic, Maier seemed to share a script with Sheen, stating in his first year on TLH, "Do not think that you can remove the stains of sin by the application of the score of theories through which men have tried to improve human character and minimize sin. They have used reason and argument . . . education and training . . . they have taken recourse to psychology and surgery; they have experimented with environment and changed diet, but all this . . . has proved as inadequate as an attempt to empty the Atlantic with buckets."[181]

Maier was particularly concerned about the trajectory such rationalizations would cause in the lives of the younger generation. "Radical psychologists have long ago ruled God's will and Christian morality out of existence by telling our young men and women, the pillars of tomorrow's morality, that sin is *passé*, that right and wrong are medieval, that purity and impurity are mere complexes," he complained. He added, "Scientific investigators assure us that immorality and crime often come from cranial bumps, diseased adenoids, overstimulated glands, or an unbalanced diet."[182] To those who saw no need for a Savior, Maier scolded, "You speak in the tone of our times, when men have frantically tried to get rid of that brief, black word 'sin' by changing its name (in its latest disguise it is labeled 'social

---

[179]Maier, *Lutheran Hour*, 224.
[180]Maier, *Victory Through Christ*, 385.
[181]Maier, *Lutheran Hour*, 225-26.
[182]Maier, *Christ for Every Crisis*, 73-74.

maladjustment'!), by silencing it out of existence, by employing psychological make-up to disguise its agents as angels of light."[183]

Though Maier shared Sheen's consternation over psychology's use in rationalizing ungodly thoughts, words, and deeds, he too did not dismiss the
legitimate use of psychological inquiry and theory, or any other field of
scientific inquiry. In his first season on network airwaves, Maier bolstered
his theological claims by noting, "Psychological research has shown that
men and women with a religious background are normally among the very
happiest people on earth," the ultimate form of which, he explained, was a
commitment to "live [one's] life in Christ."[184] Maier fully acknowledged that
"emotional disorders" and "mental cases" abounded, as he quoted medical
experts. While he, first and foremost, prescribed Jesus for "our neurotic
decades," Maier appears to have recognized a role for mental health professionals, in cases of genuine mental illness.[185] Nonetheless, he had little patience for clergy who jettisoned their gospel-proclamation duties to assume
this role. "We hear so much of psychology, psychiatry, psychotherapy, psychoanalysis from some pulpits that little time and less energy remain for the
understanding and the healing of the human soul," Maier lamented.[186] As
he reminded pastors and churches of their primary task of calling sinners
to repentance in light of God's grace, Maier again turned his attention to
the nation's younger generation, observing that as sinfulness "grips
American youth . . . a misled Modernist screams, 'Thank God, the Sunday
school is dying!'"[187]

While Maier stressed humanity's inherent sinfulness and unworthiness
before God, in the face of humanistic and scientific elevations of human
stature and potential perfectibility, the nimble Lutheran turned the rhetorical tables on his adversaries. In a 1938 Christmas sermon, Maier asked
his audience to contemplate their current world:

> Pause before this Christmas Day all too quickly hastens to its end and ask
> yourselves whether you have ever realized how insignificant and puny and

---

[183]Maier, Fourth Lutheran Hour, 153-54.
[184]Maier, Lutheran Hour, 127.
[185]Maier, Cross from Coast to Coast, 210-11.
[186]Maier, Cross from Coast to Coast, 22.
[187]Maier, Christ, Set the World Aright!, 256.

worthless you and I are under the appraisal of men today, yet how priceless everyone is in the loving esteem of our blessed Jesus. To the chemist, man is often a remarkable combination of various substances that ultimately decay. . . . To the physicist he is only a mechanism moved by various forces that refused to be controlled but that must finally stop and leave him lifeless. To the biologist we are accidental creatures. . . . To the astronomer we are infinitesimally small beings that cling to a world not much larger than a dot in the universe. . . . To the modern psychologist men and women are helpless things, swayed by emotions and the dictates of an unconscious mind. . . . To the sociologist man is simply the victim of his environment, with a hundred forces mercilessly hammering his life so it fits its surroundings. But to Christ . . . you and I are of such inestimable value and our souls such a priceless heritage of our heavenly Father that Jesus left the indescribable grandeur of eternity to come down to . . . restore us to His Father's love.[188]

In other words, as modern thinkers dismissed talk of sin and the need for a Redeemer, because science and reason had moved humanity above such a subordinate position, they had actually lowered humankind to something unworthy of redemption.

As is clear, just as Sheen gave no quarter to sin, Maier gave no quarter to sin. As was also the case with his Catholic peer, however, Maier *did* give quarter to sinners. He did so by offering them God's free forgiveness and grace—forgiveness and grace won by Jesus Christ. Maier's sermons were constructed with the classic Lutheran "law-gospel" preaching formula always present. After describing the reality of sin and its damning effect on his listeners' souls, Maier provided them with the soothing hope of abundant grace. Notwithstanding the varied definitions of grace his audience had heard, Maier explained,

When you speak of Jesus Christ and His grace, only one all-inclusive meaning remains: the unmerited love of that Savior for us despite our sinful hearts and lives. . . . The grace of Christ is not a friendly interest, a condescending smile, a tolerant overlooking of human faults and frailties; it is the mightiest power in heaven and earth. . . . The grace that promises our souls everything, yet for our salvation demands nothing, that is all Christ's and in no part ours.[189]

---

[188]Maier, *Radio for Christ*, 156-57.
[189]Maier, *Cross from Coast to Coast*, 256.

For Maier, grace was an object of life-changing beauty: "How many glorious blessings attach to this promise of pure grace! As the diamond sparkles whenever a shaft of light strikes its polished facets, so, view the Gospel of Jesus Christ from whatever angle you will, you behold unparalleled blessing."[190] It was "grace" because it was freely given to unworthy recipients. It was an "unparalleled blessing" because of the certainty it provided troubled souls. Maier reassured his audience, "I want to remove from your hearts any doubt that may linger behind the promises of Christ's mercy. . . . God's love is ours for time and for eternity, above all quibble and question, triumphant over our fears and faithlessness. . . . I offer you this—Grace without a Question-Mark."[191]

Maier consoled even his most licentious listeners, "To those who may regard themselves beyond the pale of grace, who may feel that because of particular, repeated, and grievous sins in their own lives the grace and mercy of God does not extend to them. To all such He, the unfailing friend of sinners, has promised the inestimable riches . . . a peace that surpasses all understanding."[192] Even the "monstrous" and "appalling" Judas could have been forgiven, had he humbled himself to repentance: "The magnificent mercy of Christ and His limitless love, which offers grace and pardon for every sin and every sinner, did not exclude the greedy, silver-loving informer."[193] As he pleaded with hardened sinners to not underestimate the depth of God's grace, Maier also exhorted his fellow believers in this regard. "We often timidly ask God for mole-hills of grace, and He places us upon the mountains of His munificence."[194]

Grace, the undeserved gift, was entirely the result of God's loving ini-tiative. Yet the redemptive efficacy of such grace in the lives of individuals only became operative when such individuals placed their trust in such grace. In short, one only needed to believe the gospel, the good news, of Jesus Christ's atoning work to receive the grace freely offered. Thus, in keeping with Reformation teaching, sinners are saved "by Grace alone, through Faith alone," according to the *Lutheran Hour* speaker. Maier

---

[190]Maier, *Fourth Lutheran Hour*, 41.
[191]Maier, *Fourth Lutheran Hour*, 58.
[192]Maier, *Lutheran Hour*, 187.
[193]Maier, *Christ for the Nation*, 213.
[194]Maier, *Cross from Coast to Coast*, 233.

acknowledged that one could not attain such faith without the converting agency of the Holy Spirit. In a clear statement of Lutheran orthodoxy on this point, Maier explained in a 1935 sermon that "the gift of His mercy [is] bestowed freely, without effort or accomplishment, contribution or cooperation, on our part."[195] Though he was a noted apologist, Maier admitted, "Neither I nor anyone else can argue you into Christianity. To acclaim Jesus as your Savior, you need the Holy Spirit's help."[196] Listeners may have thought that it was Maier who was urging their conversion, but he assured them that "the Holy Spirit pleads with you."[197]

While Maier clearly held to the doctrine of the Holy Spirit's agency in converting sinful hearts, the aforementioned description of conversions "without cooperation" was not a frequent theme in his radio preaching. Rather, throughout his years on the radio, he consistently employed synergistic language when calling his listeners to repentance.[198] Sometimes such language was subtle in its implication of personal cooperation, as when Maier closed a 1930 sermon by saying, "May God grant that you heed this invitation of grace."[199] Commonly, however, Maier was more explicit, pressing listeners to personally "accept" Christ, especially at the end of a sermon. "For your soul's sake, I press you for that decision now," he urgently exhorted; "you may never again be able to answer a personal plea."[200] "Particularly should you, the undecided, who until this Sunday have refused to worship your blessed Redeemer, stop rejecting Him and sending your souls to hell," Maier warned. "Now, without delay, say, 'O Jesus, I give my soul and body, mind and heart, to Thee.'"[201] He also appealed to those who found the gospel difficult to comprehend: "Don't object: 'Everything you have said is too mysterious for me! I can't understand it.' Who asks you to understand

---

[195]Maier, *Christ for Every Crisis*, 131.

[196]Maier, *America, Turn to Christ!*, 63.

[197]Maier, *Victory Through Christ*, 201.

[198]In simple terms, the theological term *synergism*, within a Christian context, maintains that humans cooperate with divine grace in the process of their conversions, as opposed to conversions being the sole accomplishment of the Holy Spirit. Maier's synergistic rhetoric caused a conservative subset of clergy and theologians within the Lutheran circles to criticize him for doctrinal laxity. They held that any hint of human agency in God's work of salvation detracted from the doctrine of grace alone.

[199]Maier, *Lutheran Hour*, 180.

[200]Walter A. Maier, *One Thousand Radio Voices for Christ* (St. Louis: CPH, 1950), 288.

[201]Maier, *Let Us Return unto the Lord*, 17.

it? I am pleading that you believe it."[202] Acknowledging his medium, Maier asked those tuning in, "Will you not approach Him now, before your radios? Come, just as you are, convicted of your sins, to your Savior, just as He is."[203]

On occasion, Maier used analogies to describe human agency in salvation. "No forgiveness is complete until it is accepted," he explained. "Even the United States Supreme Court has ruled: if a prisoner refuses to agree to a pardon, he is not released. The blessings of redemption are not yours until you believe in Jesus."[204] On another occasion, he compared those who failed to accept Christ during his fifteen years on TLH to a man who received a million dollar check from Andrew Carnegie, but failed to cash it in a timely manner. Eventually, Carnegie and the recipient of his check both died, and the check "was worthless." The listener's claim on salvation would likewise expire if "a new life decision" were not made.[205] In sum, Maier presented divine initiative and human responsibility in an interwoven fashion, as when he requested of his audience, "Pray with me that the Holy Spirit will remove any obstruction which would prevent you from accepting Christ and clinging to Him in penitent faith."[206]

In the 1930s and 1940s, the American people had a lot on their minds. The economic environment was bleak. External military powers loomed as threats for an extended period, only to turn into deadly foes on global battlefields. Political winds blew in conflicting directions. And society, in general, exhibited a trajectory that many considered to be heading in the wrong direction. During this period, Americans took their minds off such matters, if only for brief periods, by turning on their radios and enjoying an entertaining mix of comedic, musical, and dramatic programming. Yet listeners did not turn to their radios only for pleasant distraction. They also turned to them for serious information. And none was more serious than eternal truths on which angst-laden individuals could anchor their lives. Fulton

---

[202]Maier, *Jesus Christ Our Hope*, 253.
[203]Maier, *He Will Abundantly Pardon*, 288.
[204]Maier, *Victory Through Christ*, 329.
[205]Maier, *One Thousand Radio Voices for Christ*, 283, 287.
[206]Maier, *America, Turn to Christ!*, 32.

Sheen and Walter Maier stepped in front of network microphones on a weekly basis to provide such truths, and millions tuned in to hear them.

The staunchly committed Catholic Sheen and the equally firm Protestant Maier delivered theological pronouncements that were remarkably similar in substance. Both preachers spoke of capital-*T* Truths, which they promised were apprehensible to all and enduring through time and eternity. They did this not by providing simple, cheery religious messages, but by relentlessly expounding on substantive theological concepts, and the doctrines that flowed out of them. They unabashedly informed their listeners that they were sinners at enmity with God, and then told them what to do about it—or, more precisely, what the Almighty had done about it.

Chapter Seven

HOMILETIC ANIMATION

PERSONAL IMPLICATIONS AND TEMPORAL ENGAGEMENTS

*The Christian life in all its internal and external activities is
produced, inevitably and solely, by faith in the reconciliation
achieved by Christ. . . . Scripture constantly and in manifold
ways impresses upon us the necessity of complying with
the command and will of God in all our activity.*

FRANCIS PIEPER, *CHRISTIAN DOGMATICS*

*A man is justified whose conscience is illuminated by God, so that
he habitually realizes that all his thoughts, all the first springs of his
moral life, all his motives and his wishes, are open to Almighty God. . . .
Let us submit ourselves to His guidance and sovereign direction; let us
come to Him that He may . . . change us, guide us, and save us.*

JOHN HENRY NEWMAN

FULTON SHEEN AND WALTER MAIER preached on weighty theological
themes. On the United States' first genuinely mass public medium, the radio,
they boldly presented scriptural texts as the authoritative Word from a holy

God—a God who would judge every human being at the end of time. As Sheen and Maier explained these texts to a national audience, they described a breach between God and man caused by sin, and explained that this breach could only be repaired by the atoning blood of God's Son, Jesus Christ. To avail oneself of this gracious, restorative act, Maier and Sheen expounded, one only had to repent of one's sins and place one's faith in the person of Christ and his redemptive power. The vivid, heart-hitting theological content of such messages proved appealing to a broad listening audience. The appeal went further, however. Maier and Sheen connected their forceful theology of salvation to the spiritual struggles of their individual listeners, and to the broader struggles of the tumultuous times in which their listeners lived.

God saved sinners from the consequences of sin, because sinners could not save themselves, according to the Lutheran and Catholic radio preachers. But they wanted their audiences to know that he not only saved them *from* something, but *for* something—holy living and godly engagement with the world.

GODLY LIVING

Sheen and Maier informed their listeners about the realities of sin and the wonder of grace. Yet notwithstanding what they broadcast about the completed, atoning work of Jesus, they knew that sin remained a noxious blight in the daily lives of men and women, including those tuning in to the *Catholic Hour* (CH) and *The Lutheran Hour* (TLH). The two preachers warned of the toll sin took on lives, at individual, familial, ecclesiastical, and societal levels. They also extolled the virtues and benefits of sanctified lives and an ethical populous. Thus, while Sheen and Maier offered the gospel to guilty sinners, they also exhorted these sinners to reject sin in their own conduct, and live lives worthy of God's adopted sons and daughters, with the help of the Holy Spirit.

In his first year on network radio, in a sermon titled "From Darkness to Light," Walter Maier presented the doctrine of sanctification. He called on the redeemed to "lead humanity upward and onward to a life that is really worth living because it has conquered sin." He explained, "But there is a power which can change men and bring them into the newness of a sanctified life; there is a light which can dispel the darkness of evil and shed its radiance over humanity to show men how to conquer themselves, how to defeat sin, how to attain to the happiness of a noble and constructive existence . . . [with] a new spirit animating his being."

So as not to discourage even his believing listeners, Maier went on, "Now, I do not mean to stand before the microphone this evening and create the impression that a true, living faith in Christ ever leads to moral perfection . . . there will be grave inconsistencies in the conduct of a Christian." Nonetheless, he invited his audience to embrace the "ennobling and uplifting force . . . the light of Jesus Christ."[1]

Years later, on the eve of V-E Day, Maier spoke of the fall of military enemies by God's provision. He then shifted to a more spiritual type of warfare faced by his audience, proclaiming, "Your sins forgiven, you can conquer every surrounding enemy of your soul."[2] Yet Maier never implied that these battles with "surrounding enemies" would be easy ones, even with God's help. "Thousands of you are asking, 'How can I lead a truer, better, cleaner life?'" He then described a reality of temptation to which most listeners could have related: "You have your individual weaknesses, and the Prince of this world directs his insidious and persistent attacks upon these vulnerable points." After providing examples of sinful proclivities, Maier stated, "Now you want to push all this aside. . . . You want to resist evil, choke off sensuous appeals, and stifle suggestions of Satan."

Maier then mentioned a variety of modern, self-help techniques that he assured would ultimately fail. "Instead of all this, in the name and by the command of the Savior, we give the Christ of all grace, 'Jesus only,' as the sustaining power for the sanctified life."[3] "That Christ-bestowed life is the abundant life," Maier promised, "because it abounds in those happy virtues that are so predominant in the Savior's perfect life."[4]

Maier called for constancy and witness as traits of the sanctified Christian. "Don't be satisfied with head worship and lip service!" Maier pleaded

---

[1]Walter A. Maier, *The Lutheran Hour: Winged Words to Modern America, Broadcast in the Coast-to-Coast Radio Crusade for Christ* (St. Louis, CPH, 1931), 230-35.
[2]Walter A. Maier, *Rebuilding with Christ: Radio Messages of the Second Part of the Twelfth Lutheran Hour* (St. Louis: CPH, 1946), 247-57.
[3]Walter A. Maier, *The Cross from Coast to Coast* (St. Louis: CPH, 1938), 216-17.
[4]Maier, *Lutheran Hour*, 127.

repeatedly. "Your faith must not be like a weather vane, which points one way in sunshine but whirls around in the opposite direction when the storm breaks." Recalling the 1944 World Series between the Saint Louis Cardinals and the Saint Louis Browns, Maier commented, "You should have seen the celebrations in Saint Louis when our two baseball teams each won the coveted pennant. . . . Why is it, however, that Christians, to whom has been entrusted not a world series but a world's salvation, can conceal the fact that they are the Lord's?"[5] And the best way to reveal this salvific fact was the manner in which God's people conducted themselves. "I tell you that one of the most convincing testimonies to the power and truth of the religion of Jesus Christ is the living, breathing, walking advertisement of the Cross of Christ that is found in a sanctified life and in a true Christian character," asserted the Lutheran preacher.[6] When Charles M. Sheldon died in 1946, Maier saluted the Congregationalist preacher and author of *In His Steps*— the book in which members of a fictional community consistently ask, "What would Jesus do?" while carrying out their daily lives. "How sure the blessing we could enjoy with America walking *in His steps*! . . . Vast multitudes of precious souls could be saved for time and eternity."[7]

Yet Maier fully acknowledged that witnessing one's faith to others via sanctified living was not without its perils. "Be clear on this: As Christ's redeemed you must be ready to confess Him before His enemies, walk in His light; and it can cost you more than you realize thus to stand up for Jesus." Maier proceeded to catalog a substantial list of costs: strife with unbelieving family members, ridicule for "young folks" and "consecrated college students," "blackballing" and scoffing in business settings, uncomfortable social interactions, and other self-sacrificial experiences. "Are you ready to pay the price?" Maier inquired. He assured his listeners, however, that "Christ's is a faith worth living and dying for! It offers you Heaven's guidance for this life, the Savior's sustaining presence, the Holy Spirit's enlightenment, peace of mind, a calmed conscience, a new, reborn life, divine courage, strength to resist temptation . . . triumph over all tribulation."[8]

---

[5] Walter A. Maier, *Jesus Christ Our Hope* (St. Louis: CPH, 1946), 10-11.
[6] Maier, *Lutheran Hour*, 236.
[7] Walter A. Maier, *He Will Abundantly Pardon* (St. Louis: CPH, 1948), 139-40.
[8] Maier, *He Will Abundantly Pardon*, 52-53.

It should be understood that Maier did not intend his sobering call for sanctified Christians to be taken as a call for lugubrious or stern Christians. "When a man begins to live his life in Christ, he has a divine peace and tranquility that offers a rich and happy fullness to his existence," he promised.[9] In a broadcast in 1936, Maier used the biblical account of Christ's first miracle at Cana to highlight his point. He explained that as Christ was "about to enter His public ministry," he chose to attend a young couple's wedding in Galilee. "And to show that His creed is no drab, dark system of stifling, pleasure-choking rules and precepts, but that the Christian above all others knows the happiness of joy and ringing laughter, Jesus joined the happy throng," Maier enthused. He then described how Christ performing his first miracle, turning water into wine "in a quick and quiet manner," had "gladden[ed] the heart of a village maiden and her youthful husband."[10] On another occasion, after mentioning a wooden cigar store Indian in a sermon illustration, Maier complained, "Too many 'wooden Christians' are holding back their testimony to the risen Lord."[11] Toward the end of his ministry, Maier preached, "Many people have the mistaken idea that Christians must prefer the plain, the monotonous, the severe, the drab, and the ugly; but the entire Bible protests against this." He asked his audience to just look around: "Our Father made the world His marvelous masterpiece, filled with scenes of exquisite loveliness . . . which Heaven wants us to enjoy. . . . The earth's magnificence is for you who love the Lord."[12]

While sanctification was primarily a matter of individuals conforming their lives to godly standards with the help of the Holy Spirit, Maier held up the family as a special jurisdiction in which sanctification should be nurtured and celebrated. "When you can truly say—and may you make this blessed declaration today!—that Christ is in your home because you are in Him," he preached, "do everything you can to dedicate your whole household to Him and to let the world know that yours is a Christ-exalting home!" He then provided a list of helpful, practical suggestions to bring about this reality, such as removal of "lust-laden" publications, elimination of profanity

---

[9]Maier, *Lutheran Hour*, 127.
[10]Walter A. Maier, *Fourth Lutheran Hour: Winged Words for Christ* (St. Louis: CPH, 1937), 207.
[11]Walter A. Maier, *Christ, Set the World Aright!* (St. Louis: CPH, 1945), 249.
[12]Walter A. Maier, *Go Quickly and Tell* (St. Louis: CPH, 1950), 66.

and "unworthy talk," saying grace before meals, reading of Christian literature, inviting pastors into homes, and so on.[13] He advised "young folks" to "give Christ the decisive place in their future home," suggesting that as they approached marriage they should "make [Christ] the Counselor in your wedding plans!"[14] For established families, Maier counseled, "See what Christ can do for you when His blood-bought peace reigns in your home! He gives those united in His love a sense of calm and joy. . . . Then, the Savior's . . . love helps parents and children mutually to forgive and forget each other's missteps."[15]

One final point, as Maier saw it, central to both individual and familial efforts to live sanctified lives was a devout, active prayer life. "To overcome the temptations of life, to rise to the higher discipleship of Christ, to become a voice that can cry out into the desert of many lives . . . I ask you to learn the power and promise of prayer," exhorted the TLH speaker.[16] On a broadcast near the end of his ministry, Maier boldly declared, "Prayer should be a major activity in your life, a central purpose in your existence, one of the supreme reasons for which God permits you still to live." Prayer was anything but a casual activity.[17] In a 1946 sermon titled "Pray, and Don't Stop Praying!," Maier observed that "few of us realize how important this communion with His heavenly Father was to God's Son. . . . Our blessed Lord began and closed each day with fervent prayer." He explained that if prayer was that important to Jesus, how much more important it should be for His followers. Yet Maier noted, "Some of you, robbed of your own peace, live on, restless and disturbed, because you have never fully learned what a sustaining privilege it is to carry everything, your fears and worries, your doubts and distress, to the Lord in personal pleading."[18]

Fulton Sheen was just as definite in his broadcasts as was Maier; he not only presented Jesus Christ as the perfect exemplar of the sanctified life, but

[13]Walter A. Maier, *Victory Through Christ* (St. Louis: CPH, 1943), 108.

[14]Walter A. Maier, *For Christ and Country* (St. Louis: CPH, 1942), 228.

[15]Walter A. Maier, *Let Us Return unto the Lord* (St. Louis: CPH, 1947), 82.

[16]Walter A. Maier, *Christ for the Nation* (St. Louis: CPH, 1936), 121.

[17]Walter A. Maier, *Global Broadcasts of His Grace* (St. Louis: CPH, 1949), 64-66.

[18]Maier, *He Will Abundantly Pardon*, 21-25.

pointed to him as the initiator of sanctification in individual lives. In his 1935 sermon series, "The Fullness of Christ," Sheen explained, "Our Lord intercedes to the Father for us in virtue of His merits . . . the source of our sanctification."[19] Sanctification was a continuation of the salvific work begun by Christ during his earthly life, death, and resurrection. "Our Lord finished Redemption in His Physical Body," Sheen stated, "but we have not finished it in His Mystical Body. He has finished Salvation, we have not yet applied it to our souls."[20] In short, sanctification was a "gift of God."[21] Yet it was a gift that required cooperative openness and earnest engagement by the recipient, if it was to be fully manifested. In a 1949 sermon titled "Sanctifying Grace," Sheen declared, "If man is ever to be elevated to the Divine Order, God must come down to man . . . while man in his turn by a free act of will must surrender his lower sinful nature to be one in Jesus Christ . . . so to have Divine Life we must be *born* of God. . . . This gift of God, or grace . . . enables us to be partakers of the Divine Life"—the sanctified life.[22]

The concept of "Divine Life" was central for Sheen as he spoke of sanctification. While saying much about moral living over the years at the NBC microphone, he made it clear that "Christianity is not a system of ethics; it is a life." He expounded,

> [Christianity] is not good advice, it is Divine adoption. Being a Christian does not consist in being kind to the poor, generous to relief agencies, just to employees, gentle to cripples, though it includes all of these. It is first and foremost a *love relationship*, and as you can never become a member of a family by doing generous deeds, but only by being born to it out of love, so you can never become a Christian by doing good things but only by being born to it through Divine Love. *Doing* good things to a man does not make you his son, but *being* a son does make you do good things.[23]

Lest this rhetoric of love and adoption and divine living sound a bit out of reach to the average fallen creature to whom he spoke, Sheen made it clear that no one was immune to challenges and shortcomings in leading a

---

[19]Fulton J. Sheen, *The Fullness of Christ* (North Haledon, NJ: Keep the Faith, 1935), 110.

[20]Fulton J. Sheen, *The Prodigal World* (Washington: NCCM, 1936), 115.

[21]Fulton J. Sheen, *The Love That Waits for You* (Washington: NCCM, 1949), 59.

[22]Fulton J. Sheen, *Love That Waits*, 59. Emphasis original.

[23]Fulton J. Sheen, *You* (Staten Island, NY: St. Paul's/Alba House, 2003), 56-57. Emphasis original.

sanctified life. He began a sermon in 1949 by announcing, "This broadcast is not for saints or angels but for penitent sinners," adding, "I will give the saints two seconds to shut me off." Sheen went on to explain that at the very time a person tries "being good," he or she can expect new difficulties. "One finds out how strong the current of a river is not by flowing with the current, but by fighting against it," he warned.[24]

Sheen performed a balancing act between challenging his listeners to live virtuous lives, and comforting them with the acknowledgment that even the most exemplary Christians have to struggle so to be. "No saint ever found it was easy to be good," he assured. "This is the great mistake most people make in judging them. . . . The Church never canonizes anyone unless he shows a degree of holiness that is heroic. The virtues of the saints therefore were the opposite of the natural weaknesses they had to overcome," Sheen explained. For those in his audience discouraged by wavering fortitude amidst moral challenges, Sheen concluded, with inspiration, "The temptations of the saints were for them opportunities for self-discovery. They revealed the breaches in the fortresses of their souls which needed to be fortified."[25]

Struggle was the lot of a committed Christian: "From the beginning of time, souls have asked themselves this question, 'How can I *love* sin and *hate* it at the same time?," Sheen noted, "The principal psychological effect of sin is the constant anxiety in the soul of the sinner due to the inner contradictions between loving and hating, between desiring and despising at one and the same time. This inner tension can be overcome only by resisting and taming our errant impulses and egotistic desires, which is done by self-discipline."[26] Yet even for the most sanctified of Christ's followers, Sheen admitted that such discipline produced imperfect results. In a sermon titled "How It Feels to Be a Catholic," he explained, "Someone inside Christ's Mystical Body . . . experiences at one and the same moment a seeming contradiction: an inquietude and a peace." Such inquietude has two sources. The first is the apprehension of the "sublimity of the Ideal," the "realization of our failings in the face of Infinite Love." The second is "the terrific tension between body and soul . . . the inadequacy of the body to follow the soul,"

---

[24]Sheen, *Love That Waits*, 87-89.
[25]Sheen, *Love That Waits*, 68-69.
[26]Sheen, *Love That Waits*, 39-40.

which Sheen described as the desire to be in more intimate communion with God.[27]

When describing the ongoing process of sanctification, Sheen sometimes used the language of "exchange." "There is a wrong impression abroad in the world to the effect that following Our Lord means giving up the world, abandoning friends, surrendering wealth, and losing all that life holds dear. . . . Such is not really the case." "Sanctity," Sheen explained, "is not a question of relinquishing or abandoning or giving up something for Christ: it is a question of exchange."[28] It was a matter of trading a lesser good or a distorted good for a higher one. Sheen lamented that "our egotism and surface loves" cause the "modern soul" to refuse "to postpone satisfaction," thereby passing opportunities for beneficial "exchange." Presenting multilayered imagery of undisciplined living, he declared, "Over-fed, over-upholstered, double-chinned, [the modern soul] refuses to close doors, to open bridges, and thus misses joy in this life and an eternal life beyond."[29]

In 1932, Sheen preached, "Sanctity, then, is . . . a continuation of that sublime transaction of the Incarnation in which Christ said to man: 'You give me your humanity, I will give you my Divinity,'" and attendant with this process were joy and peace.[30] In the aforementioned sermon in which Sheen spoke of the devout Christian's "inquietude" over moral shortcomings, Sheen provided counterbalance: "Alongside of this pain which comes from our unworthiness there is an ineffable peace and an indescribable joy. . . . our inquietude and our serenity are reconciled in love."[31] Endeavoring to live lives shaped by God's "moral law" empowered his children to "obey the purpose . . . for which we were made, namely, the unfolding and development of our personality by eternal happiness with God."[32]

Sheen wanted his audience to understand that God's call for sanctified choices by his people was meant for their benefit, not their restraint. Utilizing an unexpected analogy, Sheen observed,

---

[27]Fulton J. Sheen, *The Rock Plunged into Eternity* (Staten Island, NY: St. Paul's/Alba House, 2004), 69-71.

[28]Fulton J. Sheen, *Manifestations of Christ* (Washington: NCCM, 1932), 50-51.

[29]Sheen, *Love That Waits*, 40-41.

[30]Sheen, *Manifestations of Christ*, 52.

[31]Sheen, *Rock Plunged into Eternity*, 73-78.

[32]Fulton J. Sheen, *Freedom and Peace* (Huntington, IN: Our Sunday Visitor Press, 1941), 24.

When you buy an automobile, the manufacturer will give you a set of instructions. . . . Really, he has nothing against you because he gives you these instructions, as God had nothing against you in giving you His commandments.
The manufacturer wants to be helpful; he is anxious that you get the maximum
utility out of your car. And God is more anxious that you get the maximum
happiness out of life.

He continued in an apparent effort to channel St. Augustine for the age of
Studebaker motorists:

But of course you are free. You can do as you please. You *ought* to use gasoline
in the tank, but you *can* put in Chanel No. 5. Now there is no doubt that it is
nicer for your nostrils if you fill the tank with perfume rather than gasoline.
But the car simply will not run on Smell No. 5. In like manner we were made
to run on the fuel of God's love and commandments, and we simply will not
run on anything else.[33]

As was the case with Maier, Sheen recognized that sanctified Christians
served as witnesses of the faith to those around them. In the midst of the
Great Depression, he preached, "This whole-hearted surrender to Christ is
the only spirit which will conquer the world today, for the world is through
accepting half-baked philosophies of life and milk-and-water religions. . . .
Men want something that makes demands on them, and possesses both
their bodies and their souls." Sheen called for his listeners to lead by virtuous example—to demonstrate that followers of Christ made substantive
commitments. By modeling a "spirit of sacrificial fortitude," the sanctified
would be "transfigured" into "redeemers with a small 'r' as Christ was a
Redeemer with a capital 'R.'"[34] The properly ordered life of a sanctified
Christian thus comprised "horizontal relations . . . in space and time" with
fellow humans, and "vertical relations with God . . . in Whom is his Peace
and his Joy."[35]

Also like Maier, Sheen saw the family as an important unit within which
sanctified living was to be fostered. Reminding his auditors that "the family

---

[33]Sheen, *You*, 25-26. In his enduring *Confessions*, written around the year 397, St. Augustine had
declared to God, "Thou hast made us for thyself, O Lord, and our heart is restless until it finds
its rest in Thee."
[34]Fulton J. Sheen, *Our Wounded World* (Washington: NCCM, 1937), 41, 44.
[35]Fulton J. Sheen, *The Crisis in Christendom* (Washington: NCCM, 1943), 31.

is the divinely organized society of the natural order," Sheen expressed concern that it was in a state of decline in America, especially during the disruption of World War II. "Humanity is the quarry, husband and wife the sculptors, and every child they beget a living stone to be fitted and compacted in to the temple, the cornerstone of which is God," he reminded.[36] In lives of "mutual self-giving," couples were to bear "responsibility toward one another for solving the riddle of life," being "bound [together] . . . not in collective egotism, but because you are symbols of Christ and His Chaste Bride."[37] When they produced children, they were to embrace the "mysteries" of "fathercraft and mothercraft—disciplining and training of young minds and hearts in the ways of God."[38] In a sermon devoted to "The Christian Order and the Family," Sheen exhorted husbands and wives to love and serve each other with a will that "is not subject to the vicissitudes of passion." Additionally, when they became parents, they were to serve as "shepherds for little sheep ushering them in to the Christ who is the door of the sheepfold." "Every child," he added, "is a potential nobleman of the Kingdom of God," but parents needed to nurture such nobility.[39]

As was the position of his Lutheran counterpart, Sheen also considered a fervent prayer life to be an important element of a devout person's routine. The sanctified and sanctifying nature of prayer he encapsulated: "The essence of prayer . . . is a longing at all costs to be caught up in God's purposes." Proper prayer "really is . . . the lifting up of our hearts and minds to God."[40] Sheen encouraged meditative prayer, during which the supplicant surrenders to God and listens for "the Voice of God in our soul." "Prayer is not a monologue, but a dialogue," he admonished. "It is not a one-way street, but a boulevard. The child hears a word before he speaks it. His tongue is trained through the ear. So our soul is trained through the ear of the soul."[41]

In his 1942 sermon, "Prayer in War Time," Sheen drew parallels between sanctified prayer and radio listening for those he hoped would make both a habit:

---

[36]Fulton J. Sheen, *One Lord: One World* (Washington: NCCM, 1944), 33-37.
[37]Fulton J. Sheen, *Love on Pilgrimage* (Washington: NCCM, 1948), 24, 29.
[38]Sheen, *Love on Pilgrimage*, 28.
[39]Sheen, *Crisis in Christendom*, 40-41.
[40]Fulton J. Sheen, *Peace* (Washington: NCCM, 1942), 133-34.
[41]Sheen, *Love That Waits*, 81.

Now prayer is like tuning in on a radio: It is a means of giving God access to our souls. In order to tune in a radio program you must set your dial to the proper wave-length. In like manner, in order to tune in to God you must make your will correspond to His Divine Will. Once this is done, just as you listen to the radio program to which you are attuned, so now you become obedient to the Divine Will to which your soul is attuned. Once the wave-length of your will is adjusted to the wave-length of God's will, you get what you want. Then all prayers are answered; the program is just what you wanted.[42]

Sheen assured his listeners, "There are many favors hanging from the vault of heaven's blue on silken cords and prayer is the sword that cuts them." Yet he cautioned that while "petition *is* a legitimate form of prayer," it was not the "essence of prayer." "We must not pray on the constant assumption that the purpose of prayer is to get something." He explained that even though "God supplies our needs," He would "not always [supply] our wants," especially if they were "amiss." Sheen noted, "Many a man in the United States is living with only one eye or one finger, simply because his parents gave him exactly what he wanted on the Fourth of July." Additionally, he warned that "prayer is not an insurance policy, a bomb-proof shelter, a bullet-proof vest, a germicide." God would not "suspend the operation of His natural laws every time" someone got "into trouble."[43]

Near the end of his radio ministry, Sheen summarized his thoughts on the Christian's call to a life of sanctity in a sermon titled "The Sanctification of the Now-Moment." He pleaded with his listeners to abandon lives of regret about the past and anxiety about the future. Sheen prescribed "the sanctification of the now-moment or the spiritualization of our state of life" as the "remedy for curing the ills of the time"—both individual and societal. He concluded, "The key word for sanctification is 'Thy Will be done'—*this* instant, and as it reveals itself to me under these circumstances."[44]

While Jesus may have indeed paid the price for humankind's sins, these preachers implored their listeners to turn away from sin in their daily lives.

---

[42]Sheen, *Peace*, 133.
[43]Sheen, *Peace*, 129-134.
[44]Sheen, *Love That Waits*, 73-79.

They inventoried common sins and explained their painful toll on the lives of those who committed them, as well as those around them. In similar fashion to each other, Maier and Sheen promised their listeners that God would help them resist sinful temptation, but also called on these listeners to dedicate their own efforts to earnest, sanctified living, at personal and familial levels. Noting that true discipleship was not without risks and challenges, they offered assurance that constancy in the Christian walk not only was pleasing to God, but also served as a compelling witness to an observing world and a source of holy joy for the devout individual.

Prophecy to the Nation/Engagement with the Times

Sheen and Maier shared the top priority of rescuing souls for eternity. Their sermons were crafted, first and foremost, to bring unbelievers to faith and to edify those who had already accepted the gospel message. Their proclamations were not confined to soul saving, however. Demonstrating broad awareness of the times in which they lived, Maier and Sheen offered prophetic voices to a nation experiencing myriad challenges, not the least of which were a lingering, massive economic Depression, a brutal world war, and their anxiety-laden aftermath.[45] Additionally, while avoiding political debates, both preachers spoke ardently against threats to the American way of life, especially atheistic communism.

Sheen and Maier frequently called for Christians to live sanctified lives— for their own good, as a living witness of the faith to others, and to honor Jesus Christ. Their appeal for sanctification did not end there, however. These popular broadcasters consistently exhorted the country as a whole to abandon its sinful ways, at both the individual and national level. They provided prophetic voices of both admonition and hope. Interestingly, Sheen's and Maier's bold proclamations that a sinful populace and a wayward nation had contributed to, and even caused, their own present calamities, only seemed to add to their appeal. While highly patriotic and critical of enemies in time of war, they were not reticent about highlighting the sinful characteristics America shared with its foes.

---

[45]While TLH and CH broadcasts were heard in numerous countries, this section will focus primarily on Maier's and Sheen's roles with their United States audiences.

In his 1935–1936 radio series "The Prodigal World," Sheen indicted all of Western civilization, comparing it to the prodigal son in the parable told by Jesus in Luke 15. In the midst of the Great Depression and rising turmoil around the globe, Sheen opened the series with these words: "We are living in perilous times when the hearts and souls of men are sorely tried. Never before has the future been so utterly unpredictable; we are not so much in a period of transition with belief in progress to push us on, rather we seem to be entering the realm of the unknown, joylessly, disillusioned, and without hope." He then noted that "modern prophets," in "all this confusion and bewilderment," were blaming failure of "our economics" for the global woes. "No!" exclaimed Sheen, "It is not our economics . . . it is man who has failed—man has forgotten God." He concluded that "social reconstruction is conditioned upon spiritual regeneration."

The following week, referring explicitly to the prodigal son parable, Sheen offered an interpretation for the times: "After many long centuries in union with the Father's house, Western civilization finally asked the Spiritual Father for its inheritance. . . . Carried away by the new-found independence from the Father's House, Western civilization began to spend the spiritual capital which the Father's House had given it." Recounting the multicentury slide from orthodoxy to modernist beliefs, Sheen declared, "Truly, indeed, [Western civilization] has wasted its spiritual capital living riotously." Drawing the final parallel, he concluded that his listeners were witnessing "the fate of all sinful nations and all sinful men . . . the poor prodigal was now . . . feeding on husks and he was still in want." Yet Sheen offered hope, a way out of the current predicament. "The sad and tragic dissipation of spiritual capital by the Western World does not necessarily mean the Decline of the West . . . there is no reason for despair." After all, "However much Western Civilization has been disillusioned . . . suffice it to say here that some are coming back again to God," and he was hopeful that many more would follow.[46]

More typically, Sheen directed his commentary at America specifically. During the Depression, he preached, "A day is fast coming when Christians will have to unite in real Christianity to preserve it against the anti-Christian

---

[46]Sheen, *Prodigal World*, 5-21.

forces which would destroy it. . . . What is all important is spiritual regeneration. . . . The world, to be saved, must be put back into the environment
of religion and morality. . . . The best solution lies in the cross."[47] In 1941,
Sheen warned, "The preservation of America is conditioned upon discipline
and self-sacrifice, but since these are inseparable from religion and morality,
the future of America depends on Americans' attitude toward God and the
Cross of His Divine Son."[48] In a 1938 sermon, he offered an uplifting vision
of national character: "The essence of Americanism is . . . the recognition
of the sacredness of human personality and the inherent inalienable rights
which every man possesses independently of the State." He argued that such
rights were from the Almighty, and "if human dignity and liberty come from
God, then it follows that loss of faith in Him means loss of faith in those
liberties which derive from Him."[49]

Though always gracious in tone, Sheen's sermons occasionally bordered
on jeremiads. In a 1940 broadcast, he made a "plea for a return to God," as
a means "to avert war as chastisement" of a nation experiencing the "loss of
God." To his listeners who were "scandalized by the godlessness" of threatening foreign countries, Sheen cautioned, "Before picking up stones to cast
at the adulteresses abroad, we ought to turn on the searchlight into our own
consciences." Otherwise, America would learn the lesson, "What we sow,
that also do we reap," the hard way.[50] As tragic reaping appeared more inevitable a year later, Sheen preached, "We are living in such a period of
history now—the sad hour wherein we are gathering the bitter fruits of our
apostasy from God. Wars from without; class hatreds, bigotry, anti-Semitism,
anti-Catholicism, atheism, and immoralities from within—are the harvest
of our godlessness." The following week he explained, "A body without the
soul is not a living machine; it is a cadaver. A nation without God is not
humanist; it is godless."[51]

In his first sermon after the bombing of Pearl Harbor, Sheen opened, "If
Divine Providence decrees days of trial for us, we shall accept them patiently,

---

[47]As quoted in Kathleen Riley Fields, "Bishop Fulton J. Sheen: An American Catholic Response
to the Twentieth Century," (PhD diss., University of Notre Dame, 1988), 154.
[48]Fulton J. Sheen, *War and Guilt* (Washington: NCCM, 1941), 148.
[49]Fulton J. Sheen, *Justice and Charity* (Huntington, IN: Our Sunday Visitor Press, 1941), 79-81.
[50]Sheen, *Freedom and Peace*, 70-77.
[51]Sheen, *War and Guilt*, 65, 81.

as we received gratefully His bounteous prosperity."[52] In the sermon series that followed, titled "Peace," Sheen stated that the war was "an opportunity for America to come clean" and "become a new nation and a new people by ceasing to pity ourselves because of what we must sacrifice, and beginning to regard as the supreme tragedy the evil which godlessness has unloosed upon a world and which only God's justice can avenge."[53] Toward the end of this series, he mixed reproach and hopefulness: "Perhaps . . . in the present sorrow of this war, we as a nation will go back to the God we have disobeyed and He in His goodness will console us as a Father."[54] America was still a "good ship" of "democracy," but it had picked up "barnacles which impede its free passage through the waters" that war would scrape off.[55]

As World War II progressed, Sheen balanced messages affirming the righteous cause of America and her allies, with cautionary messages warning against self-righteousness. "The more moral the cause we defend . . . the more energy we can put into that cause," he stated in a January 1942 radio sermon. He continued,

> Consciousness of sin makes us weak, but consciousness of being morally right gives us a power which the physically stronger cannot resist. Because the barbarism with which the totalitarian States would infect the world has no moral basis, there is more apt to be decay within those states than in those which oppose them out of justice. That brings us to this point: America, in the prosecution of this war, must always be morally right. . . . Our victory must come not just from the fact that we are stronger, but from the fact that we are right. Then shall those who say that might is right give way to us who say that right is might.[56]

Sheen was not reluctant to label America's foes in battle—"Nazism," "Fascism," and "Nationalism which identifies itself with deity"—as "intrinsically evil." He spoke of "our enemies" as being "charioteers of evil," and warned that "evil has the devil on its side."[57] Sheen referred to the enemies'

---

[52]Sheen, *Peace*, 3.
[53]Sheen, *Peace*, 29-30.
[54]Sheen, *Peace*, 101.
[55]See "Some Barnacles on the Ship of Democracy," and "More Barnacles on the Ship of Democracy," sermons, in Sheen, *Crisis in Christendom*, 23-27.
[56]Sheen, *Peace*, 31-32.
[57]Sheen, *Crisis in Christendom*, 59, 65, 69.

"evil dictators" as "boils on the surface of the world's skin," who espouse "the Totalitarian world view which is anti-Christian, anti-Semitic, and anti-human."[58] He blended the practical and the prayerful by pleading with his listeners to "buy bonds for the defense of your country; but make Holy Hours for the defense of our souls."[59] As the war continued, Sheen called on Protestants and Jews, as well as Catholics, to rise to a new level of unity. Making it clear that he was not urging theological compromise between faith groups, Sheen stated, "I limit myself to one specific point, to giving a reason why men of good will should unite; *because there is a common enemy. . . . The tragedy of our times is that the moral forces are disunited while the anti-moral forces are united.*" He added that civilization itself was in danger.[60] Yet, he assured, "Evil has its *hour*. God has His *day*."[61]

Notwithstanding the righteousness of the cause of America and her allies, and Sheen's confidence in eventual victory, he explained, "God will not destroy [the enemies] for two reasons: First, all evil is not in them, and all goodness is not in us—the cockle was not sown on the right side of the field and the wheat on the left, but together; second the final adjustments of Divine Justice take place not in time, but at its end."[62]

While Sheen spoke boldly of sin and evil and the need for repentance, both at home and abroad, he exhibited and urged strong patriotism for his country throughout his radio ministry. The Midwestern son of Irish stock was a member of the "one, holy catholic and apostolic Church" first, but a citizen of "the land of the free and the home of the brave" second. Sheen encouraged patriotism out of genuine affection for his country, but was also conscious of suspicions held by many Americans that Catholics were less than fully "American" because of their allegiance to Rome.

In the earlier years of the CH, Sheen's messages on patriotism were more focused on the latter problem. In a 1932 sermon, Sheen addressed those who accused the American Catholic Church of giving inadequate "tribute to America, inasmuch as her heart is across the sea, recognizing the Vicar of

---

[58]Sheen, *Crisis in Christendom*, 4, 6.

[59]Sheen, *Peace*, 30. Sheen repeatedly called for Catholics, Protestants, and Jews to devote themselves to daily "holy hours" in "prayer and meditation" during the war.

[60]Sheen, *One Lord: One World*, 3-8.

[61]Sheen, *Peace*, 145.

[62]Sheen, *War and Guilt*, 27.

Christ supreme in matters spiritual." He castigated such detractors by comparing them to the scribes and Pharisees who falsely accused Christ of "perverting our nation" before Pontius Pilate. Catholics, he assured, were doing anything but perverting the American nation, as they endeavored to live lives devoted to the Savior, and as they "rendered unto Caesar the things that are Caesar's, and to God the things that are God's." Moreover, he argued that Catholic Americans brought a stabilizing, unchanging morality that only added to the overall strength and stability of the country as a whole. In short, good Catholics were good patriots. Sheen closed the sermon by adapting a statement of his friend G. K. Chesterton: "Catholics will never love America because she is great, but America will be great because Catholics love her."[63]

In a 1937 broadcast, Sheen pointed to excessive "individualism" of many Americans, at one end of a spectrum, and forms of "collectivism" exhibited in fascism and communism at the other end. "Permit us here to suggest that the position of the Church is a golden mean between these two extremes," offered Sheen. He argued that the church both respected individual freedom, but also recognized the need for unity and community. Again invoking "render unto Caesar . . . render unto God" language, Sheen argued that the church and its members served to strengthen the things that America held dear.[64] The following year, in a sermon titled "Patriotism," Sheen began by noting that St. Thomas Aquinas, "the greatest philosopher of all times," placed patriotism under the umbrella of piety. "Once it is remembered that love of neighbor is inseparable from love of God," expounded Sheen, "it is seen that love of our fellow citizens is a form of piety." He then explained that "Catholics are taking religion so seriously in reference to our country," because "we take very seriously the Declaration of Independence which derives the rights of man from God." "It is our solemn duty as Catholics, therefore, to be conscious of our duty to America," while always remembering "the stars and stripes of Christ, by whose stars we are illumined and by whose stripes we are healed!" concluded Sheen.[65] With remarkable dexterity, he placed Thomas Aquinas, Catholic Americans, Thomas Jefferson,

---

[63]Sheen, *Manifestations of Christ*, 81-90. Chesterton had written, "Men did not love Rome because she was great. She was great because they loved her." See Gilbert K. Chesterton, *Orthodoxy* (New York: John Lane, 1908), 122.

[64]Sheen, *Our Wounded World*, 5-12.

[65]Sheen, *Justice and Charity*, 73-83.

and Jesus in league with one another to reinforce American ideals and strengthen the country.

As the global storm clouds of war darkened, Sheen shifted his rhetoric from a Catholic-centric patriotism to a more general appeal for patriotism. In a 1939 sermon, "Liberty and the Republic," Sheen fretted, "Patriotism is rapidly becoming a lost virtue," which he attributed to "a decline of religion." "As men cease to love God, they cease to love their neighbor," he explained. Americans needed to understand that "religion and tyranny grow in inverse ratio."[66] In 1941, Sheen stated that "it is important for us Americans to recall that the Declaration of Independence is also a Declaration of Dependence. . . . Not only does the Declaration of Independence affirm dependence on God, it also affirms dependence on law." He warned, "Given a freedom which is independent of God, independent of the moral law, independent of inalienable rights as the endowment of the Divine Spirit, and America could vote itself out of democracy tomorrow."[67] A few weeks later, Sheen went so far as to suggest a national "Day of Public Humiliation, Prayer and Fasting." Citing the precedents of several US Presidents, he called on Americans to realize that "the future of America depends on Americans' attitude toward God and the Cross of His Divine Son," and to commit themselves to confession of sin, fasting, and "a renewed sense of discipline for the sake of America under God."[68]

Yet even as Sheen wove religious concepts and love of country together, he also cautioned his listeners. In his 1942 "Faith in War-Time" sermon, he said, "The clay does not mould the potter, but the potter the clay. . . . We are not to attempt to fit Christianity into this war, but to fit this war into Christianity. Patriotism is part of religion, but religion is not part of patriotism." Having said that, Sheen concluded the sermon with a crusading spirit: "If we want a victory over our enemies, let us first get on God's side and then go out and knock the devil out of them, that they may be on God's side too!"[69]

As World War II continued, Sheen preached, "Men of good will must love America as a duty."[70] But the priest's loyalty to his homeland was not a blind

---

[66]Sheen, *Freedom and Peace*, 61-69.
[67]Sheen, *War and Guilt*, 87, 91, 93.
[68]Sheen, *War and Guilt*, 148-49.
[69]Sheen, *Peace*, 121, 128.
[70]Sheen, *One Lord, One World*, 30.

loyalty. "I love America," Sheen assured, but "not America right or wrong. If it is wrong, we will make it right." He added, "The end and purpose of our freedom must be justice, rooted in God."[71] While Sheen did not normally provide commentary on the prosecution of the war, he did feel that the United States had failed to live up to the appropriate standard of justice when it incinerated German cities from Allied bombers and dropped atomic bombs on Japan. He publicly expressed moral criticism about atomic bombing within months of their detonation.[72] Sheen was willing to challenge his CH listeners, most of whom were no doubt greatly relieved that the war was over, with the idea that America needed to rethink how it had ended. "Since we justified the bombing of cities because Hitler started it, shall someone justify the atomization of cities because we started it?" he queried, in a February 1946 broadcast. "Shall men who doubted that the Providence of God ruled the world now tremble at the new providences of man, who can destroy where God would not?"[73]

Generally speaking, Sheen steered clear of politics in all of his preaching, including in the sermons he delivered on the CH. He consciously considered himself apolitical and avoided commentary on candidates, political parties, or specific policy questions.[74] In this regard, he was quite different from his fellow priest-broadcaster, Rev. Charles Coughlin. When asked to compare his radio sermons to the highly political, often vitriolic radio addresses of Coughlin, Sheen was cautious in his reply. "There is a difference in the two. . . . Father Coughlin chooses to confine himself largely to the material. My sermons are confined to spiritual values. Which of the two is of the most benefit is, of course, a matter of opinion, but I will always assert the spiritual will out-weigh and out-last the material."[75] Even when Sheen addressed issues of social justice, personal or national morality, or the need

---

[71]Sheen, *Peace*, 37, 39.

[72]See Thomas C. Reeves, *America's Bishop: The Life and Times of Fulton J. Sheen* (San Francisco: Encounter, 2001), 161-62.

[73]Sheen, *Love on Pilgrimage*, 10.

[74]Reeves, *America's Bishop*, 92.

[75]Reeves, *America's Bishop*, 107. For a period, radio listeners did not seem to agree with Sheen's relative weighting of material vs. spiritual, as Coughlin's radio audience was estimated to have reached 40 million listeners, and for a time, Coughlin received more mail than any other person in America. Nonetheless, Father Coughlin's boisterous presence on the airwaves flamed out rather quickly. See Alan Brinkley, *Voices of Protest: Huey Long, Father Coughlin and the Great Depression* (New York: Vintage Books, 1983), 83.

for all to fulfill their "sacred obligation" to God and country, he avoided political allusions.

Early in his radio ministry, Sheen warned his audience about the perilous temptation of shifting to the modern, "new religion" that "must be social . . . political . . . worldly." The politicizing trend within religion required its adherents to "cease talking about the Kingdom of God and begin talking about the republics of earth." Why? "For the world problems, in need of a solution, are not religious, we are told, but economic and political." Sheen explained that this was precisely the temptation that Christ faced when Satan offered him "all the kingdoms of the world" if Jesus would bow down and "adore" him. "Satan tempted our Lord to make religion political by exchanging the Kingdom of God for the kingdoms of earth," explained Sheen. Further, without employing the term "Social Gospel," and without explicitly pointing to its liberal Protestant promoters, Sheen criticized the "new religion," that "must be social," as "Satan's challenge to . . . make religion center around the materialities of life."[76]

While acknowledging the desirability of sound national policies, Sheen cautioned against placing too much faith in the ability of governments to fix humankind's problems. Sheen devoted his 1938 series, "Justice and Charity," to addressing social issues, especially economic, and Christianity. Over several weeks, he acknowledged uneven distribution of wealth within capitalism, but also pointed out the unproductive demonization of each other by capital and labor. He began the series by promising, "This series of talks will not . . . appeal either to reactionaries or the revolutionists: it will seem traitorous to those who want Capitalism condemned as intrinsically wicked; and it will seem cowardly to those who want to see labor branded as irresponsible." Without ever advocating specific policy prescriptions, Sheen argued that Jesus had taught "us how to be capitalists without being exploiters, and how to be laborers without being Communists."[77] Over the years Sheen broadcast on the CH, he was never reluctant to condemn the excesses of capitalism, especially when the less privileged were exploited or overlooked; however, he was always vigilant about the dangers of alternative economic systems. In the end, he held that "the Church stands for

---

[76]Fulton J. Sheen, *The Eternal Galilean* (1934; repr., Garden City, NY: Garden City, 1950), 53-60.
[77]Sheen, *Justice and Charity*, 8-9.

Distribution through Charity and Justice," which could effectively sanctify even economics.[78]

The closest Sheen came to offering political commentary were his frequent, vocal attacks on communism, which were a constant throughout his priestly career. Even then, his opposition to communism had more to do with its atheistic components, its diminishment of individual autonomy, and a penchant for violence so prevalent under communist regimes, than with its underlying political ideas. Warning his listeners of the deceptiveness of communism's appeals during the Depression, Sheen stated, "Communism believes in starting with Equality, or the development of a homogeneous jelly-like state in which all men are equal because all are servants of the New Capitalism or Communism. They have had their 'Equality,' which is another name for tyranny, and it destroyed both Liberty and Fraternity."[79] "Communism," he explained, "is . . . not a reaction against Capitalism but the glorification of its worst features, and the ignoring of its better features."[80] Sheen admitted that with inequitable concentrations of wealth and privilege, and with the insecurity to which wage-earners were subjected, capitalism contained "accidental evil." "Communism, on the other hand, with its class-hatred and revolutionary technique of bitterness," was constructed from "essential evil."[81]

On multiple occasions during World War II, Sheen cautioned Americans against becoming complacent about the threat of communism, just because Russia had become a military ally. For example, notwithstanding a live war with the Axis Powers, in 1943 he warned, "There is one grave menace to our country and to the world which we may not ignore, and that is Marxian Socialism or Communism. It is rather soft-pedaled these days because of our alliance with Russia, but for no good reason." Russia and Communist supporters represented a "Trojan Horse" that could eventually threaten national and ecclesiastical security. Sheen presented the Russian model as one worthy of emulation: "Because she is on our side, Russia never feels impelled to go into ecstasies about the glories of democracy; neither do I see any

---

[78]Sheen, *Justice and Charity*, 51.
[79]Sheen, *Prodigal World*, 41.
[80]Sheen, *Prodigal World*, 24-25.
[81]Sheen, *Justice and Charity*, 5.

reason why, because Russia is on our side, we should go into ecstasies about Marxian Socialism."[82]

After the war, Sheen continued his barrage against communism. In a sermon on the seven deadly sins, he explained, "Envy is the sin of the *have-nots* as avarice is the sin of the *haves*. It regards anything *anyone else* has as being taken from self, and is sometimes called my 'right,' my 'cause,' or 'truth.' As avarice is the sin of capitalists, so envy is the sin of the Communists. Every Communist is a Capitalist without any cash in his pockets."[83] In 1950, with Cold War anxieties on the rise, Sheen attempted to respond to the mood of the times. "For 33 years Communism has been trying to convince the world there is no God. But it has succeeded in convincing the world there is a Devil." He then placed the situation in a broader drama: "In His Wisdom, God may be permitting our Western world that has become barren from its Godlessness, to be fertilized with the dung of Communism."[84]

Combining religious and patriotic fervor, Sheen exhorted his early Cold War–era listeners,

> It is our solemn duty as Christians to be conscious of our duty to America, and to preserve its freedom by preserving its faith in God against any group that would identify revolution with America; we must protest that there are stars in our flag and not a hammer and sickle, to remind us that destiny of human life is beyond the implements of daily toil—beyond the stars and the "hid battlements of eternity" with God. The Communists want the flag all red. We are willing to have a little red in it, but we want some white and blue in it too.[85]

As noteworthy as Sheen's prophetic utterances were, he was not the sole messenger that "crieth in the wilderness . . . make straight in the desert a highway for our God" (Is 40:3 KJV). From the very beginning of his radio ministry, Walter Maier raised his prophetic voice to his countrymen, often in themes similar to those of his Catholic counterpart. In his third network broadcast in 1930, Maier linked the future well-being of America with its

---

[82]Sheen, *Crisis in Christendom*, 24.
[83]Sheen, *Love That Waits*, 36.
[84]Sheen, *Rock Plunged into Eternity*, 79, 81.
[85]Fulton J. Sheen, *Light Your Lamps* (Washington: NCCM, 1947), 52-53.

fulfillment of what he considered its Christian calling. Invoking a historical political leader with a reputation for integrity, Maier declared, "No truer word has ever been uttered by human lips than this warning of Daniel Webster, 'If we continue in the teachings of the Bible, our country will continue to prosper; but if we and our posterity neglect its teaching, then no one can tell how sudden a catastrophe may overwhelm us and bury all of our profound glory in obscurity.'"[86]

In his Thanksgiving sermon later that year, Maier spoke of the need for gratitude to God: "We must give thanks because ingratitude is one of the most dangerous and deadly sins, especially for a nation that has enjoyed such an outpouring of blessings as we have." With the Depression worsening at an alarming rate, he reminded his listeners that "the American nation" was blessed "completely from the unlimited munificence of God by the purest exhibition of His divine grace." Maier speculated that Americans had forgotten this and "eat their three meals a day without a thought of God." Thus, this "neglect," this "spurned bounty of God invokes such visitations as the American nation has experienced during the past months." "Ingratitude and indifference" threatened to "dethrone the almighty God and ascribe our national greatness to our own resourcefulness and management and capabilities," and the perils were quickly becoming evident.[87]

Just as Sheen had lamented that modern humanity had "forgotten God," Maier regretted the current "forgetful generation." In a 1931 radio address titled "Our Generation of Moderns," he compared his contemporary Americans to the Israelites of the Old Testament, who after occupying the Promised Land through "God's merciful providence" in one generation, turned their back on God in the following "smugly self-satisfied generation." Maier then drew a parallel between the Israelite generations and American generations, contrasting "the Pilgrim Fathers" who "knew God . . . recognized His providential deliverance, the certainty of His judgment, and the boundlessness of his grace," and "this generation, this cynical, sophisticated, self-satisfied generation, which so largely knows not God . . . and prides itself in its ignorance." He concluded, "We are living in the greatest away-from-God movement that the country has ever known." "This forgetfulness"

---

[86] Maier, *Lutheran Hour*, 15.
[87] Maier, *Lutheran Hour*, 85-86.

of God and his Word had brought "supertragedy in our American life," as "we have brought upon ourselves the unenviable distinction of having broken more records in our departure from morality than any age in this country before us."[88]

Whereas Fulton Sheen's sermons occasionally *bordered* on jeremiads, Maier showed no reluctance to fully enter such oratorical territory. In an early 1935 sermon, Maier quoted Jeremiah himself: "O earth, earth, earth, hear the word of the LORD!" (Jer 22:29 KJV). Maier proceeded, "Perhaps no address of the entire Scripture is more impressive in its outward form than this triple repetition . . . and no appeal of Sacred Writ of more penetrating importance for our perplexed day." He then recounted how Jeremiah had uttered those words to an Israel nation experiencing "unparalleled crisis . . . days of devastation . . . that were soon to seal the doom of a profligate nation." Maier related this Old Testament situation to "the American nation, to the American churches, and to each individual American," all in the midst of the unparalleled crisis known as the Great Depression. "In spite of the lavish blessings showered upon us we have too often steeled ourselves stubbornly against the teachings of God's infinite wisdom." Maier then provided a narrative of his times:

> As a nation we became worshipers of self; we bowed down before the shrines of cold science; we cast the Word of God from us and substituted a selfish program for life that dethroned the Creator, exalted the ape, reduced man, made in the image of God, to the level of the brute, and choked off the hopes of the hereafter by heaping sarcasm upon every promise of the resurrection and every blessing of heaven. Men glorified the machine as a symbol of power; they preached and practiced doctrines which taught survival of the fittest and championed the eat-drink-and-be-merry ideal for life. . . . The calloused masses . . . chose the Barabbas of carnal godlessness in preference to the Savior of their souls. . . . And then we wonder why our glittering age of lavish luxury was cut off almost overnight, why this selfish, Bible-ridiculing, truth-denying, sin-loving system suddenly collapsed in the height of its heyday.[89]

---

[88]Walter A. Maier, *Lutheran Hour*, 256-60.

[89]Walter A. Maier, *Christ for Every Crisis: The Radio Messages Broadcast in the Second Lutheran Hour* (St. Louis: CPH, 1935), 30-33.

In a 1937 sermon during the week in which President Franklin Roosevelt would take the oath of office for his second term, Maier suggested that "the nation should echo" the closing line of the oath by praying, "Oh, help him, God!" While he intended no political commentary, Maier then cautioned, "Do not jump to the mistaken conclusion, now that the warm, softening rays of better times seem to shine upon us, that we can get along without God and thrive in opposition to His Word." Rather, he warned, "Unless God is with us as He was with our fathers; unless there is a reawakening of courageous, red-blooded Christian faith throughout this land, the worst may yet await us." Turning his gaze to the global scene, Maier then advised: "Let us not worry too much about what Hitler or Mussolini may do in Europe; let us not center our keenest concern on the Japanese and Chinese situation; right here in America, within our homes, we have problems, deep-rooted and decisive, which far outweigh any international issue." It was not that Maier wished to ignore trouble elsewhere on the planet. He only wished to call on average Americans to concentrate on a matter that they could control, which was "the task of making the American home a mighty part in the spiritual and moral foundation of a God-fearing, healthy, and happy nation."[90]

While the salvation of human souls was front and center for Maier, he was genuinely concerned about the welfare of the United States. Specifically, Maier railed against a range of aspects of contemporary culture:

> With marriage ridiculed, parenthood scorned, childhood left to entertain itself with newspaper comic strips, gangster movies, and crime broadcasts; with preachers bringing reproach to the name of the Church by conducting marriage mills, where drunken couples and runaway children can be made man and wife, or other preachers championing divorce, organizing birth-control clinics, making dance-halls of their parish-halls, with the American death-rate perilously close to the dropping birth-rate, we ought to realize that, as no nation in the past has been able to withstand the ravages of immorality and decay of the home, so this nation cannot escape disintegration unless it upholds domestic morality. Because this is a civic issue, of greater importance than many of the programs over which our legislators are engrossed; because any state, whether it is Christian or pagan, must seek to maintain the virtues

---

[90]Maier, *Fourth Lutheran Hour*, 205-6.

of purity and decency, the sanctity of the home and blessing of marriage, I ask all you public-spirited citizens, as your fellow-American, to take decisive action against every manifestation of immorality.

Maier concluded by imploring his listeners to organize and drive the purveyors of immorality from their communities.[91]

Maier continued to draw a linkage between the sinfulness of the country and its citizens and the ravages of the Depression. He opened the 1938 radio season by acknowledging the "swollen ranks of the unemployed" and of "wide-spread poverty," but claimed that the present "spiritual and moral crisis into which this nation has been hurled" was "incomparably more disastrous." More strikingly, Maier called this crisis "more destructive even than the coming world war which some leaders foresee." He regretted that the "prolonged years of personal reverses and money restrictions" had not brought "us penitently back to God." Rather, he noted that "easy morality, love of lust, gilding of sin, the trampling of those standards of right and wrong which God has imposed on every nation" were a "destroyer" that "hand in hand with . . . hatred of God . . . stalks through the land." Yet Maier assured his audience that "God's grace [was] even greater" than sin and vice. "Once more," he concluded, "I beg you: 'Be reconciled to God!'"[92] During the following spring portion of this same radio season, in a sermon titled "Darkness over the Earth," Maier again inventoried the "barrage of unbelief" and the numerous examples of the "moral darkness stigmatizing our age," and connected the dots to economic woes. "The beclouding sins are responsible for the tragedy that after ten years of the most wide-spread efforts for human relief and improvement the world has ever seen conditions in 1939 in many ways are not better than in 1929, in some respects definitely worse."[93]

As America's involvement in war moved from the possible to the likely, Maier preached on the need for national defense. While he told his audience to put their trust in God, he reminded them yet again that unfaithful churches, unbelief, immorality, and injustice "may help produce hard,

---

[91] Maier, *Cross from Coast to Coast*, 302.
[92] Walter A. Maier, *The Radio for Christ: Radio Messages Broadcast in the Sixth Lutheran Hour* (St. Louis: CPH, 1939), 3-4, 9, 15.
[93] Maier, *Radio for Christ*, 363.

bleeding days of internal strife and . . . war." While in no way downplaying external threats, Maier added, "In short, America needs to be defended against itself." He then provided the strategy for such defense: "Because no people can be weak with God on its side, the Christian cry in this crisis hour should be: Defend America by accepting Christ!"[94]

In his sermon on the Sunday following the attack on Pearl Harbor, Maier offered Jesus as the source of "unfailing solace, unchanging consolation, unfaltering assurance" in fearful circumstances. He provided a message of hope and assurance, yet reiterated that "spiritual defense is as vital as military defense." "The lessons of last week's attack," Maier explained, "showed us how destructive it is to imagine danger far off. Therefore, as God's Word calls out: 'America, turn to Jesus!'"[95] As World War II raged on, Maier lamented that more Americans were not moved to clean up their act, especially in light of such sobering, life and death realities. "At home sin-loving, self-seeking, pleasure-chasing have dropped to new low levels, as though there were no fields of battle in Italy and on Pacific islands, strewn with American dead. . . . The popular watchword is not 'Church, Home, Country,' but 'wine, women, and song'—and what kind of a song! . . . No wonder the war drags on!" Maier then drove home the national point with an individual query: "In the Savior's name I ask you today, my countrymen, are you on the Lord's side or on Satan's side? Are you helping to build a God-pleasing United States by accepting the Redeemer or are you dragging out this war by your rejecting Him?"[96]

In an early 1944 sermon, Maier flatly declared, "This war has come upon our nation partly as a punishment for American apostasy. No matter what the politicians tell you, Scripture assures you that every war is a visitation." He assured his war-weary audience, however, that "Christ will never fail anyone," and that "with Heaven's help you can ascend the summit of victorious faith, high above war and woe."[97] The following week, Maier noted that the consequences of apostasy could not only be seen in America, but in both allies and enemies:

[94]Maier, *For Christ and Country*, 45-50.
[95]Maier, *For Christ and Country*, 102-15.
[96]Walter A. Maier, *America, Turn to Christ!* (St. Louis: CPH, 1944), 140, 146.
[97]Maier, *Christ, Set the World Aright!*, 30, 35.

If Germany had kept Jesus first, in all likelihood there would have been no Nazism. If the Italians had kept Jesus first, there would have been no Fascism. If the Russians had kept Jesus first, there would have been no Communism. If France had kept Jesus first, there might well have been no national collapse. If Spain had kept Jesus first, there would have been no bloody civil strife. If England had kept Jesus first, it might not have been thrust into the war and brought difficulties which threaten its empire.

"What a price the world is paying for that mistake!" exclaimed the exasperated Lutheran.[98]

As Maier opened the 1946–1947 radio season, with World War II now concluded, his first sermon was titled "Must We Fight World War III?" He thanked the triune God, implored him for peace, and prayed for the president and national leaders. While highlighting the harsh realities of war and its aftermath, Maier asked his listeners to again turn to God, lest the Almighty's wrath bring worse things. "If day after day you go on as though there were no supreme Sovereign in heaven, who demands that all men should love, honor, serve, and obey Him . . . you will help bring World War III to America." To the unrepentant, he spoke with proleptic scorn: "Glorying in sin, rather than in the Savior from sin, you are the real wreckers of America, the ravishers of its youth, the breakers of its peace."[99] "Despite the war, which should have knocked sense into the nation," complained Maier in another sermon during this period, "domestic life in this country has dropped to the lowest depths in our nation's existence." "The ugly perversions of Sodom and Gomorrah are upon us; the ravages of vice and impurity which destroyed mighty world empires are about us."[100]

In response to such hubristic revolt against God, on several occasions during the latter half of Maier's broadcasting career, he explicitly called for national "days of humiliation." Echoing Fulton Sheen, though calling for such days more frequently and with greater fervor, Maier harked back to the centuries-old practice of setting aside specific days for national or community repentance. He specifically cited Presidents John Adams and Abraham Lincoln, who had requested that the nation "humble itself before

---

[98]Maier, *Christ Set the World Aright!*, 45-46.
[99]Walter A. Maier, *The Airwaves Proclaim Christ* (St. Louis: CPH, 1948), 1-11.
[100]Maier, *He Will Abundantly Pardon*, 111.

God." Just two weeks *prior* to the attack on Pearl Harbor, Maier asked, "Yet at a time when the need for humble, penitent supplication to the Almighty is greater than ever before. . . . Where are national days of humiliation?" He invited his listeners to "stand shoulder to shoulder" with him in awareness that the "plea in this perilous hour . . . must be: God make us penitent!"[101] In October of 1943, again citing Lincoln's precedent, Maier complained, "After a year and ten months of deadly war, we in the United States still have had no day of national humiliation before the Almighty. . . . America has not yet been on its knees before the Triune God, confessing its faults and faithlessness."[102]

After the war, Maier continued to decry licentiousness at home and spot threats from abroad. In 1947, Maier described how the Continental Congress had once "set aside a day of 'humiliation, fasting, and prayer,' for the purpose 'that we may, with united hearts, confess and bewail our manifold sins and transgressions, and by a sincere repentance and amendment of life, appease His righteous displeasure, and . . . obtain His pardon.'" Yet in the face of sin "many times higher than in the colonial era, America is so blinded by pride and self-righteousness that not once in the last twenty-five years has the nation been asked to drop to its knees in real repentance over our manifold sins." Maier asked how the nation could expect to "call Him to our side in any crisis tomorrow," in the face of this situation.[103] The following year, in a sermon that begged for both personal and national amendment, Maier again noted, "It is high time, past time, indeed, for a national day of humiliation and repentance in these United States. No one with the average quota of common sense can pick up a newspaper today without realizing we have come upon critical times."[104]

Notwithstanding Maier's stern admonishment of Americans, he was thoroughly American, demonstrating a consistent patriotism. The United States had been blessed by God with freedom, and Maier did not want his fellow citizens to take such blessing for granted. Maier positioned American freedom as an outgrowth of Christianity—the Christianity of the

---

[101] Maier, *For Christ and Country*, 57-59.
[102] Maier, *America, Turn to Christ!*, 134.
[103] Maier, *Global Broadcasts of His Grace*, 304.
[104] Maier, *Go Quickly and Tell*, 123-43.

Reformation in particular. Christian faith allowed one to proclaim, "I am free . . . from the tyranny of sin and hell . . . free in life and death, free for time and eternity!" He then expounded on the implications:

> That freedom spreads its blessings far and wide. Whenever the full Gospel of Christ is preached and believed it seeks to end the sway of ignorance . . . as it did in the days of the Reformation. . . . The separation of Church and State and the independence of each, the basic blessings of our American civic life, have come to us as a by-product of Christian liberty. The freedom of conscience, according to which men may worship unmolested by human interference . . . the free blessings of the American home, and the liberties that we have come to accept as our essential heritage,—these ultimately come from Christianity and from the Spirit of God.[105]

In a 1936 sermon commemorating the 419th anniversary of the Reformation, Maier wrapped the sixteenth-century events in distinctly American rhetoric, meant to reinforce the connection of Protestant and national ideals. "On October 31, 1517," explained Maier, "an Augustinian friar, Brother Martin, with swift, sure hammer-blows posted his Ninety-Five Theses, or religious propositions, which embodied the declaration of spiritual independence, the constitution of Christianity, and the emancipation proclamation of the soul's liberty for hundreds of millions . . . in all centuries since his day."[106]

Maier often pointed to what he considered to be America's Christian roots, going back to early European settlers. In his 1943 Thanksgiving broadcast, he began, "As we recall the Plymouth Pilgrims, who really gave America this national day of praise to the Almighty, we should discover a deep-rooted connection between their thankful recognition of the Almighty and the blessings they were permitted to enjoy." He then compared the New England settlements to less successful British settlements in Jamestown. While acknowledging that both groups suffered significant loss of life early on, he explained that the Massachusetts colony had succeeded as the Virginia settlement failed, even though the latter was "surrounded by more favorable circumstances." The "striking difference" was that "the Pilgrims had come to North America to worship God," and that these "pioneers knew

---

[105]Maier, *Christ for the Nation*, 46.
[106]Maier, *Fourth Lutheran Hour*, 36.

God and gave Him thanks," whereas "the Virginians" were driven by greed, and "gave the Almighty only a secondary place and did not learn to recognize Him fully."[107]

It was not uncommon for Maier to cite America's founding fathers, as well as subsequent national leaders, as keepers of the true faith. For instance, in a 1948 sermon on George Washington's birthday, Maier opened with a prayer that began, "God of our Fathers: With grateful hearts we praise Thee for the love which gave us Christian leaders, like Washington, the father of our country." He then described a book of Washington's handwritten prayers that had sold at auction in 1891. "Records no longer show the price paid; but, had it been sold for its weight in gold or diamonds, this would not outweigh the value of the lessons which these two dozen pages teach our country," assessed Maier. He noted that Washington's "reverent prayers, expressing a deep consciousness of sin, yet even more a victorious faith in the mercy of God's son, voicing a fervent supplication for family, friends, Church and State." The lesson was that if "America's most illustrious leader" was a "Christian patriot, kneeling in prayer," true patriots of subsequent generations should recognize the interconnectedness of faith and love of country.[108]

As the United States went to war, Maier added his patriotic voice to that of other Christian leaders. In the broadcast of the week following the Pearl Harbor bombing, Maier opened by praying for "the President, Congress, and all responsible for the nation's future course." He then quoted St. Paul's words, "If God be for us, who can be against us?" (Rom 8:31 KJV), reassuring his listeners, "May this divine truth strengthen the souls of millions throughout America as our beloved nation finds itself treacherously attacked." Maier added, "Earnest appeals are made to patriotism; and may the love for America now ring clear and true in every heart!"[109] In the following month, Maier delivered a radio address titled "Keep America Christian!" in which he argued, "Despite everything radicals may try to tell you, keep this basic truth firmly implanted in your mind: Our colonies, later the States, were settled by men and women who were Christians." He

---

[107]Maier, *America, Turn to Christ!*, 257-58.
[108]Maier, *Go Quickly and Tell*, 62-65.
[109]Maier, *For Christ and Country*, 102-3.

admitted, "Those early pioneers had their faults, of course, and I am not endeavoring to glorify something so far distant from us that its frailties cannot be seen, but for the most part, the people who built America were outstanding in their devotion to Christ." Looking back to the country's founding, while recalling the drafting of the Declaration of Independence, Maier noted, "In the early days of our War for Independence, although freethinkers sometimes occupied high places, an unmistakable Christian note rang through the official proceedings."[110]

Maier served as an advocate for a land of the free that could stand up to external threats. Just three weeks prior to the Japanese attack on Hawaii, Maier preached, "In a world of international greed, hatred, bloodshed, the United States should have a strong, complete defense." He stated that "every American Christian" was engaged in "earnest prayer . . . that our country be adequately protected and made too strong for successful attack by any foreign foe." He assured his audience, "The writers of the sacred Scriptures and the founding fathers were not pacifists; and neither should we be. . . . Christians of America . . . love this divinely endowed land, and they will work for it, save for it, fight for it, die for it. True followers of Christ are true patriots."[111]

Yet even while speaking as a patriot, and even as he spoke of the rightness of America's cause in time of potential and actual war, Maier was remarkably blunt in cautioning against nationalistic self-righteousness and in speaking of the faults of his nation. Sounding remarkably like Fulton Sheen, Maier declared, "Instead of super-patriots who shout, 'My country, right or wrong!' give us Christians who ask, 'O God, forgive us our wrongs and make us right!'"[112] In a 1939 broadcast, with Europe in violent chaos, he noted that it was the twenty-first anniversary of the end of World War I. Maier observed, "If the world had known then what it knows now, it would have realized that the little boy who mispronounced 'Armistice Day' as 'Our Mistake Day'

---

[110]Maier, *For Christ and Country*, 192-93. Maier went on to quote Christian commitments in the charters of Virginia, the Plymouth colony, Delaware, Maryland, the Massachusetts Bay Colony, Pennsylvania, Rhode Island, Connecticut, and New Hampshire, as pervasive evidence of America's Christian foundation.

[111]Maier, *For Christ and Country*, 45.

[112]Maier, *Peace Through Christ*, 59. In another broadcast, Maier voiced similar sentiments, only with more emphasis on personal responsibility: "Believers should . . . say, 'My country, right or wrong! May it always be right; but whenever it is wrong, may I do my utmost to make it right with God.'" See Maier, *Christ, Set the World Aright!*, 304.

unwittingly spoke the truth." He held Americans responsible for profiteering during that war, and for contributing to ongoing hatred. He also warned against the present-day "war-mongers in America," all too eager for another round of global bloodshed.[113]

In this same year, Maier commented that the "United States likes to think of itself as morally superior to other nations." The frank Lutheran broadcaster would not let his countrymen get away with this. "We look down on the cruel Nazi treatment of the Jews, yet how pharisaical this often is in the light of our own attitude toward the American Indian and our unfair discriminations against the Negro!" With subtle reference to popular radio priest Charles Coughlin, Maier continued, "Who in this audience, with the strong undercurrent of anti-Semitic agitation in our country and its support even from radio preachers, will deny that the flames of racial hatred can flare up within our own boundaries?"[114] Simultaneously skewering "racially superior" enemies abroad and racists at home, Maier quoted with approval a suggestion from a "Negro high-school student in Columbus" that war criminals "be punished by having their faces blackened and being forced to live as many American Negroes must exist." "That might be worse than quick death," Maier added, given the exploitation and mistreatment blacks experienced in the United States.[115] In 1944, with the country still embroiled in war, Maier condemned the "mania for dominion in our enemies." He then turned the tables, reminding his listeners, "Our own commonwealth was partially built on conquest." Maier continued in a tone uncommon for his time:

> We took this broad, blessed land from the Indian in exchange for cheap whisky, gaudy beads, and firearms. With a few notable exceptions we repeatedly cheated, spoiled, and demoralized the red man. Then, not satisfied, we hired hunters to steal tens of thousands of black men and women from the coasts of Africa, to throw them into the markets of the South, and make them slaves to the lash and the lust of their owners. We sent armies to tear five eighths of Mexico . . . from the hands of those who in turn had torn it from the Apaches, Comanches, and other Indians. Now, we are urged to police the

---

[113]Maier, *Peace Through Christ*, 25-27.
[114]Maier, *Peace Through Christ*, 58.
[115]Maier, *Rebuilding with Christ*, 146.

earth, and in plain language that means to maintain militarism and the "might makes right" policy indefinitely throughout the world.[116]

After the war, Maier continued to hold his country accountable for what he considered national sins. The radio pastor was particularly critical of the use of the military means that ended the war. In reference to the atomic bomb, Maier warned, "The Frankenstein horror we have created will continue to haunt us." He lamented that his quick, postwar call for "the destruction of all atomic munitions factories and the disavowal of atomic research for destruction" had been "ridiculed."[117] With disdain Maier commented, "We actually think that we are great when one of our atomic bombs takes 78,150 lives at Hiroshima, when a quarter of a million human beings, including aged and invalid, infants and mothers, are destroyed in Dresden . . . in a single night."[118] In another broadcast, he flatly stated, "When the atomic bombs dropped on Japanese cities, a new, but not pleasant, page in the American record began. . . . We must kill and kill and kill until our enemies beg for peace."[119] In a particularly unsettling 1947 sermon, Maier quoted extensively a newspaper correspondent's observations after a recent visit to a school in Hiroshima. The reporter had seen "thumbs or fingers . . . burned away by the bomb," children with "only one eye or faces that looked as though they had been sliced by a white-hot knife," others with missing and "patchily growing" hair, all of which made the victims "look like little ghost gnomes from hell." After sharing this report, Maier expressed the need for national repentance: "With such brutal instruments of wholesale massacre the United States fought the last war—may God forgive us!"[120]

While unafraid to criticize his country's leaders on moral matters, Maier, like Sheen, eschewed partisan political commentary. In his 1930 University of Virginia address, "The Jeffersonian Ideals of Religious Liberty," which Maier's son and biographer considers "a key to [Maier's] political thought," Maier presented Thomas Jefferson as the embodiment of the "two kingdoms" spirit of the princes who signed the Augsburg Confession in the sixteenth

---

[116]Maier, *Christ, Set the World Aright!*, 346-47.
[117]Maier, *Airwaves Proclaim Christ*, 252. On another occasion, Maier referred to the atomic bomb as "the Frankenstein of frightfulness." See Maier, *Let Us Return unto the Lord*, 245.
[118]Maier, *He Will Abundantly Pardon*, 80.
[119]Maier, *Airwaves Proclaim Christ*, 49.
[120]Maier, *Global Broadcasts of His Grace*, 34.

century.[121] While acknowledging that he "certainly [did] not . . . share [Jefferson's] religious convictions," he lauded Jefferson for "emphasizing the spiritual realm of the Church and insisting upon its clean-cut aloofness from political issues."[122] Maier proceeded to take his fellow clergy to task for "breaching" the "Wall of Separation." He cited as a travesty a list of advertised, political sermon topics ranging from an assessment of Mussolini to regulations on streetcar ventilation.[123]

In the following years, Maier watched the radio rise of the highly political Father Charles Coughlin with increasing wariness. Not only did Maier disapprove of someone providing political commentary from the pulpit (physical or ethereal), but he also worried that such activism could reflect poorly on radio preaching in general. He initially resisted denouncing Coughlin for fear that such would be misinterpreted as anti-Catholicism on the part of a Lutheran cleric. Nonetheless, in 1935, he wrote an editorial protesting "against the interference of a Roman Catholic priest in the political affairs of the nation." In a speech a year later, Maier explicitly mentioned Coughlin and suggested that the Catholic Church either officially approve or reject Coughlin's political activities.[124]

Maier willingly prayed for the president, Congress, and other political leaders, but nearly always avoided speaking about public policy.[125] One of the few exceptions, which came up on more than one occasion, was his assessment of the destruction of large amounts of surplus potatoes not long after the war under an Agriculture Department policy. He lashed out on this specific governmental program because he considered it unconscionable for a federal agency to execute a "philosophy of scarcity" to drive up prices, at the same time that "European children" were "digging through the garbage pails at our military stations." Maier warned that a nation guilty of such

---

[121]Paul L. Maier, *A Man Spoke, A World Listened* (New York: McGraw-Hill, 1963), 128; Walter A. Maier, *The Jeffersonian Ideals of Religious Liberty: Address Delivered at the University of Virginia at Charlottesville, Va., August 9, 1930* (St. Louis: CPH, 1930), 7.

[122]Maier, *Jeffersonian Ideals*, 15.

[123]Maier, *Jeffersonian Ideals*, 17.

[124]Maier, *A Man Spoke*, 187-88. The Catholic Church eventually did silence the rabble-rousing Coughlin.

[125]Notwithstanding his avoidance of commentary on specific policies or politicians, Maier did urge participation in the political process, telling his listeners before the 1940 national election, "We should have a 100-per cent vote, particularly by the Christian citizenry." See Walter A. Maier, *Courage in Christ* (St. Louis: CPH, 1941), 14.

"wanton waste" would "have to pay a full penalty," "unless the Almighty is merciful."[126] This may have been a public policy issue, but for Maier it possessed considerable moral gravity.[127]

Like Sheen, Maier did not consider stands against communism to be a breach of the "Wall of Separation," for many of the same reasons. He was equally vocal in denouncing "godless" communists, on radio and in editorials, well before the emergence of the Cold War.[128] Maier was also an outspoken opponent of fascism, especially as he saw it in his ancestral Germany, once its odious realities became apparent. Fascism was a false, "substitute Gospel" that equated to "worship of the state," and "a totalitarianism which put the individual conscience under state control."[129] Fascist and Communist dictators "feverishly" removed "the line of demarcation separating Church and State" and threatened to "extinguish the torch of liberty that towers as a distinctive beacon of our freedom."[130] Upon the death of the fascist Mussolini, Maier preached, "When you see Mussolini's corpse brutally beaten after death and the body of his mistress executed with him, learn from this hideous spectacle that the fury and folly of Fascism springs from minds which exalt themselves above God's Law."[131]

Maier saw communism as the biggest threat to America. In his first year on TLH, Maier cautioned that "though the center of world Communism may be several thousand miles away . . . the same tragedies that have provoked the curses of groaning millions may be repeated in our fair land if the thankless unbelief and boastful materialism that has engulfed Russia inundates our country."[132] He asked Americans to pray to God that "He would spare us this communistic ruin."[133] In 1939, he worried that there were more communists "in the United States today than there were in Russia when that country turned Red," and that they were currently targeting "the

---

[126]See Maier, *Airwaves Proclaim Christ*, 287; *Global Broadcasts of His Grace*, 36.

[127]Maier called for Americans to share their resources with the "food-less, destitute masses in Europe and Asia," adding, "Don't think it patriotic to starve women, children, aged, and invalids!" See Maier, *Global Broadcasts of His Grace*, 30.

[128]Harriet E. Schwenk, "Dr. Walter A. Maier's Undeviating Stand Against Atheistic Communism," *Concordia Historical Institute Quarterly* 23, no. 2 (July 1950): 49-58.

[129]Maier, *Christ, Set the World Aright!*, 304.

[130]Maier, *Christ for Every Crisis*, 22.

[131]Maier, *Let Us Return unto the Lord*, 73.

[132]Maier, *Lutheran Hour*, 87.

[133]Maier, *Christ for the Nation*, 29.

unemployed and disgruntled worker" in an attempt to convince them that "the world will never be better until capitalism is destroyed and all possessions, as all families, have become common property. Yet, if you look at the crimson chaos in Russia, you will conclude that atheistic Communism must come from the same hell to which it leads."[134]

While Maier saw numerous problems with communism as a political system, his primary concern was its imbedded theological hostility. In a 1947 broadcast he sought divine help: "May the Holy Spirit give us the farsightedness and the insight to realize that in Communism, as it spreads over our world, we are confronted by the biggest and the best organized advance of atheism history knows."[135] Years earlier, Maier had warned, "A Red victory in our country would mean the hellish reality of closed, desecrated churches, and a deposed, persecuted clergy." While a "small group of preachers will be spared," in the event of "the Stars and Stripes" being "pulled down to make way for the Hammer and Sickle," they would no doubt be "Modernists who heap scorn on God's Word and Christ's atonement." America, as his listeners knew it, would cease to exist.[136]

Yet Maier gave his audience hope, in true pastoral fashion, by assuring them that their sovereign God would prevail. In a 1948 sermon titled "Heaven's Hammer and Sickle," he noted that "God's hammer blows are sometimes delayed;" however, "in His own good time . . . His hammer and His sickle combine to destroy all persistent rebels against His grace. Atheist Communism is doomed."[137]

Accountability was an important theme of Walter Maier's and Fulton Sheen's radio preaching. They stressed to their listeners the need for a Savior due to their accountability for sin before a holy God. But their emphasis on accountability went beyond just the individual, to the nation as a whole. Linking holy writ with current events and modern culture, Sheen's and Maier's prophetic voices called America to repentance and prayer. In tones

---

[134]Maier, *Radio for Christ*, 196.
[135]Maier, *Global Broadcasts of His Grace*, 97.
[136]Maier, *Peace Through Christ*, 38.
[137]Maier, *Go Quickly and Tell*, 238.

reminiscent of the Old Testament prophet Jeremiah, they attributed national calamity to modern unbelief and prevalent sinfulness, warning of greater manifestations of God's wrath if the country failed to amend its ways.

Yet during trying times, they also offered hope and encouragement to somber listeners. They modeled and urged deep (though hardly blind) patriotism, reminding their audience of America's special role in God's providence.[138] They assured their fellow citizens that their Maker and Redeemer had not abandoned them during the Depression, they affirmed the rightness of the nation's cause in war, and they condemned the godlessness of America's foes. But while Maier and Sheen did their part to lift up the nation, they boldly held America accountable for what they considered national sins ranging from racism to war tactics. While shunning partisan politics, they called on political leaders as well as ordinary citizens to strive for a higher standard. And they cautioned against self-righteousness, noting that the sins of America were not all that different from those of her enemies.

And week after week, millions tuned in, apparently finding solace in the striking combination of salvation and accountability, for themselves and their country.

CHRISTIAN COMMON GROUND/LUTHERAN AND CATHOLIC TOUCHPOINTS

Sheen and Maier attempted to reach audiences well beyond the confines of their respective denominations. The gospel was for all who would hear, and they both were committed to presenting it in verbiage that would have broad appeal and be easily understood. While *Catholic* and *Lutheran* were labels attached to their respective "Hours," the orthodoxy they both espoused, and the narrative content of their sermons, usually downplayed denominational distinctiveness. The messages they delivered on such important topics as scriptural authority, the atonement, justification, sanctification, repentance,

---

[138]Maier's and Sheen's assertion of a distinctly American role in God's providential plan was balanced by their boldness in taking America and Americans to task for their sinfulness and self-righteousness, and tempered by their caution against "America right or wrong" patriotism. It should be noted, however, that while American/Christian exceptionalism was nothing new when they went on the air, their broadcast reach likely amplified such conceptions within the minds of many Americans. Future manifestations of these ideas (e.g., forms of Christian nationalism, conflation of political parties with Christian identities), sans their dire warnings of national and personal depravity, would likely have been disappointments to Sheen and Maier.

and prophecy were based on Christian doctrines more than specific Catholic or Lutheran doctrines. Though both speakers held different theological beliefs on a number of particulars, their sermons conveyed to non-Catholic Christians and non-Lutheran Christians that the Jesus of whom this priest and this pastor spoke was the same one they knew. As importantly, for the non-Christian this same Jesus was presented in an accessible way that required no "inside" information or vocabulary. Detailed discussions of Lutheran or Catholic positions on the ontological substance of the Eucharist, or the regenerative nature of baptism, or formal liturgical practices, or synergism in divine election, as important as they may have been in denominational settings, were just not productive in spreading the message of salvation over network radio.

In her fine essay on TLH and its founding speaker, historian Tona Hangen noted that "Maier rarely mentioned his denomination's name and referred to Martin Luther hardly at all, or indirectly as 'the great Reformer of the Church.'"[139] While it is true that he limited his references to Lutheranism, and it is also true that he sometimes referred to Luther other than by name (e.g., "the Great Reformer and Restorer," "the friar of Wittenberg"), to say that he referred to Luther "hardly at all" is an overstatement. What is more, he usually did so by name. When doing so, however, Maier presented Luther as an expositor of scriptural Christian truths, or as a leader of the broader Protestant Reformation, rather than as the founder of a sect or denomination. He cited the sixteenth-century churchman as a restorer of the doctrine of justification and expounder of pure grace, as a champion of "supreme liberty," as a foreseer of modernist heresy, as a loving family man rocking his baby, as a robust hymn writer, as a devout man of prayer, and as a bearer of the Protestant standard of *sola scriptura*.[140] On occasion, Maier drew parallels between Luther and American leaders, such as George Washington and Abraham Lincoln.[141]

---

[139]Tona Hangen, "Man of the Hour: Walter A. Maier and Religion by Radio on the *Lutheran Hour*," in *Radio Reader: Essays in the Cultural History of Radio*, ed. Michele Hilmes and Jason Loviglio (New York: Routledge, 2002), 119.

[140]See Maier, *Peace Through Christ*, 7; *Lutheran Hour*, 203; *Christ for the Nation*, 40-42; *Cross from Coast to Coast*, 114; *Radio for Christ*, 114-15; *Peace Through Christ*, 134; *Rebuilding with Christ*, 12; *America, Turn to Christ!*, 206-7.

[141]Maier noted similar disappointments experienced by Luther and Washington when their respective followers abused hard-won freedoms. See Maier, *Peace Through Christ*, 316. He noted

Additionally, Maier avoided the potential for creating a sectarian hue to his mention of Luther by frequently speaking of non-Lutheran historical church leaders as exemplars of the faith. His sermons made it clear that Luther and he were in the same universal church as other important churchmen, like John Wyclif, John Huss, William Tyndale, William Coverdale, John Hooper, John Foxe, Richard Baxter, John Bunyan, John Wesley, George Whitefield, John Newton, David Brainerd, Timothy Dwight, Charles Spurgeon, D. L. Moody, and David Livingstone, just to name a few.[142] Amazingly, Maier even spoke approvingly of Horace Bushnell, the nineteenth-century American cleric often referred to as the "father of American theological liberalism," as "the doubter" who became "an ardent disciple, a powerful preacher."[143]

Maier also cultivated pandenominational mutuality by quoting, or telling stories associated with, hymns in his sermons. Though he occasionally quoted texts from obscure hymns, the majority would have been broadly recognized by most Protestants. Reinforcing theological points in his sermons, he wove in popular hymns of European and American origin, more of which were written by non-Lutherans than Lutherans. While some-times quoting just a single line, and on other occasions reciting an entire verse or two, Maier's utilization of hymn texts as homiletic components was extensive. A survey of his published radio sermons reveals that he quoted hymns and, occasionally described hymn writers, at least 150 times over his twenty years of network radio preaching. Maier employed the texts of no fewer than seventy *different* hymns on those occasions. Interestingly, the hymn from which he quoted most frequently, beginning with the very first TLH broadcast in 1930, was "Just as I Am, Without One Plea"—a non-Lutheran hymn that Billy Graham would later use as his standard invitation

---

the parallels of Luther and Lincoln as they both championed "truth and right" and experienced the "burden of solitude" as they "defied a world arrayed" against them. See Maier, *Cross from Coast to Coast*, 320.

[142]See Maier, *Christ for the Nation*, 20 (Wyclif, Tyndale, Coverdale); *Radio for Christ*, 339 (Huss); *Cross from Coast to Coast*, 261 (Hooper); *Rebuilding with Christ*, 45 (Foxe); *Cross from Coast to Coast*, 55-56 (Baxter); *Peace Through Christ*, 343 (Baxter); *Cross from Coast to Coast*, 237 (Bunyan); *Fourth Lutheran Hour*, 264 (John Wesley); *Let Us Return unto the Lord*, 200 (Whitefield); *Cross from Coast to Coast*, 291-92 (Newton); *Airwaves Proclaim Christ*, 153 (Brainerd); *He Will Abundantly Pardon*, 142 (Dwight); *Lutheran Hour*, 219 (Spurgeon); *He Will Abundantly Pardon*, 163-64 (Moody); *For Christ and Country*, 268 (Livingstone).

[143]Maier, *He Will Abundantly Pardon*, 222.

hymn at the close of his evangelistic crusade events and broadcasts.[144] The second most quoted hymn was Luther's "A Mighty Fortress Is Our God."[145] Maier even quoted the prolific blind nineteenth-century hymn writer Fanny Crosby, and commended her devout acceptance of God's will in her life.[146] This was noteworthy in that although Crosby's hymns (e.g., "Blessed Assurance," "Safe in the Arms of Jesus," "Pass Me Not Oh Gentle Savior") were quite popular with non-Lutherans, especially revivalistic types, they generally did not appear in Lutheran hymnals.

In his 1947 Reformation Day sermon, Maier characteristically mentioned Luther's consistent call for repentance. In this sermon titled "A Thousand Voices for Our Redeemer's Praise!" he then spoke admiringly of Methodist founder and hymn writer Charles Wesley. Maier described Wesley's hymn, "Oh, for a Thousand Tongues to Sing My Great Redeemer's Praise," as "one of the outstanding hymns among his 6,500." Remarkably, he proceeded to observe that TLH was the unforeseen answer to this "hymned prayer"—an answer that Wesley could never have imagined. "By divine mercy," Maier explained, "we actually have a thousand radio voices, a thousand stations, each a million times stronger than the human voice, with which to proclaim the glory of Jesus Christ. . . . This broadcast, the first in radio history ever to attain this goal, now uses more than a thousand marvelous mechanical tongues to invite sinners to their Savior."[147] The proclamation by the most visible American Lutheran in the first half of the twentieth century that his radio program was the answer to an eighteenth century Methodist founder's prayer was of no small significance.

Maier did employ Luther in one noticeable way that would have felt distinctly Lutheran to Lutheran listeners, yet more broadly Christian to non-Lutherans. On several occasions he quoted from Luther's Small Catechism,

---

[144]See Maier, *Lutheran Hour*, 52; *Christ for Every Nation*, 229; *Courage in Christ*, 231; *Victory Through Christ*, 268; *Rebuilding with Christ*, 56; *Jesus Christ Our Hope*, 32; *Airwaves Proclaim Christ*, 39, 262; *Global Broadcasts of His Grace*, 87; *One Thousand Radio Voices for Christ* (St. Louis: CPH, 1950), 230.

[145]See Maier, *Lutheran Hour*, 22; *Fourth Lutheran Hour*, 65; *Radio for Christ*, 19, 117; *Peace Through Christ*, 141; *For Christ and Country*, 56; *America, Turn to Christ!*, 195-96; *He Will Abundantly Pardon*, 54.

[146]See Maier, *Cross from Coast to Coast*, 294; *Courage in Christ*, 198; *Christ, Set the World Aright!*, 132.

[147]Maier, *One Thousand Radio Voices for Christ*, 83-84.

usually his confessional explanation regarding the second article of the Apostles' Creed, concluding with the Reformer's common declaration, "This is most certainly true." Maier usually attributed such quotations to Luther, but he did not explicitly refer to them as part of his catechism.[148] The term *catechism* may have been off-putting to non-Lutherans, either because they were unfamiliar with it or because they associated it with denominational indoctrination. Many Lutherans, on the other hand, would have learned the Small Catechism in their youth, and would have recognized the words and known their source immediately, thereby identifying Maier as one of their own. Lutheran and non-Lutheran Christians, however, would have generally accepted the theology articulated in this catechetical excerpt.

References to Lutheranism itself were relatively infrequent, and even then Maier went out of his way to avoid assigning any superiority to his denomination, other than as a legitimate bearer of Christian orthodoxy. He did, however, speak of denominations from time to time—usually in a manner meant to break down barriers and promote unity within the one true faith. While excluding "Christ-rejecting" churches that "know only a caricature of our Lord," Maier celebrated in his 1939 Good Friday sermon that "never do Christians, Protestants and Catholics, Lutherans and Reformed, in organized church-bodies and independent groups, seem closer to each other than in this Holy Week." He continued, "How glorious and God-pleasing if in reality there could be only one Church . . . over the world inwardly agreed in the full acceptance of every Scripture truth, bound together in an absolute unity of the Spirit."[149] Earlier in that same radio season, Maier described Heaven: "Where the ten thousand times ten thousand worship with God in holiness, there will be no denominations and conflicting creeds. . . . In the glory of heaven all who trusted in Christ and penitently came to His cross

---

[148]For examples, see Maier, *Lutheran Hour*, 61, 70; *Christ for the Nation*, 44; *Peace Through Christ*, 212; *For Christ and Country*, 41-42; *Christ, Set the World Aright!*, 49-50; *Jesus Christ Our Hope*, 6; *Victory Through Christ*, 214-15; *Airwaves Proclaim Christ*, 78.

[149]Maier, *Radio for Christ*, 371-72. With a bit of subtle humor, Maier continued by inviting his listeners to imagine "if there were, for example, no Northern Baptists, Southern Baptists, Primitive Baptists, Free-will Baptists, Duck River Baptists, Two-Seed-in-the-Spirit Baptists; no Roman Catholics, Greek Catholics, Old Catholics, Holy Eastern Orthodox Catholics, Polish National Catholics; no Missouri Synod Lutherans, American Lutherans, United Lutherans, Augustana Lutherans, Free Lutherans;—instead all followers of Jesus, completely united in the same reverence for their Savior."

for forgiveness, in whatever Church they worshiped here on earth, in one united faith will sing His praise."[150] In a sermon titled "Do You Believe in Jesus Christ?" Maier described the necessary faith in the Savior's divine and human natures, his atoning work, and his eternal sovereignty. He then declared, "If you have this faith, wholly, sincerely, reverently, then, whatever your denomination—Protestant or Catholic, Lutheran or Reformed, Low-Church or High-Church—you are a Christian."[151]

In a 1943 Pentecost sermon, Maier explained that the events described in the New Testament book of Acts occurred when early "disciples and the believers, only 120 together . . . assembled . . . 'all with one accord.' No denominational differences split their ranks." He responded, "O God, we plead, give us more spiritual unity in a day when the churches are thrown into opposing camps, when one group often despises the other with a hatred that insults Christ!" He assured his audience that Christ himself "pleads for spiritual unity."[152] Always eager to strengthen the Church catholic, Maier encouraged his believing listeners to stand firm. "I know that churches have their faults, but I also know that all other institutions on earth combined have not produced even a small part of the blessings which Bible-loving, Christ-exalting, Cross preaching congregations have given billions of believers."[153]

From the time he entered the airwaves, Fulton Sheen's primary purpose was the winning of souls for Christ. That urgent calling, along with a number of aforementioned core theological tenets shared with many Protestants, enabled him to demonstrate common purpose with many Protestants who tuned in each week to hear him. Additionally, recall that Sheen was intentional about putting Catholicism in a positive light to non-Catholics, whether Protestant or unaffiliated, without openly proselytizing. Thus, the priest was careful to craft radio addresses that would be broadly understood and accessible, combining winsomeness, intellectual substance, and

---

[150]Maier, *Radio for Christ*, 128.
[151]Maier, *Victory Through Christ*, 214-15.
[152]Maier, *America Turn to Christ!*, 118-19.
[153]Maier, *He Will Abundantly Pardon*, 43.

doctrinal clarity on essentials, in a way intended to capture the interest of Catholics and non-Catholics alike.

While Sheen made it clear that he was indeed a loyal Catholic, he often used the more generic terms *church* or the *mystical body of Christ*, even when he meant the Roman Catholic Church. He also relied on the general term *Christianity* in many addresses. Since Protestants considered themselves part of Christ's church and part of Christianity, this avoided exclusionary interpretations of what Sheen said. He only rarely mentioned non-Catholic denominations. In one of the few exceptions to this, in a 1944 sermon titled "Call to Unity," he noted that "a few decades ago Christianity's struggles were more in the nature of a civil war; that is, religious rivalries and contentions existed between sects within the great body of Christendom itself." "For example," Sheen explained, "between Methodists and Presbyterians, Lutherans and Anglicans, and in a broader way between Jews, Protestants, and Catholics," this "civil war" had occurred. "Christianity," he noted, "was no longer engaged exclusively in a civil war," because it was now "face to face with an invasion, an incursion of totally alien forces who are opposed to all religion and all morality, whether it be Jewish or Christian." Placing contemporary realities in a longer historical narrative, Sheen explained, "The wars of religion of the seventeenth century have become the wars against religion of the twentieth century."[154] In short, unbelief was more insidious than varied belief, and godly people could not afford to retreat into sectarian ghettos.

Notwithstanding Sheen's carefulness to avoid denominational divisiveness, he was not always successful due to his high view of historical Christian doctrines and of his ecclesiological foundations. One striking example occurred in 1947. *Time* magazine reported, "When Fulton J. Sheen described the devil to his radio audience, Unitarians were quick to note that Fulton Sheen's Satan sounded like nothing so much as a good Unitarian." This prompted Unitarian minister Pierre van Paassen to publicly rant against Monsignor Sheen, the Catholic Church, and their obsolete "obscurantisms," which no doubt confirmed for Sheen that he was striking the appropriate dogmatic tone.[155] Sheen continued to counter liberal modernist

---

[154]Sheen, *One Lord: One World*, 4.
[155]"Religion: Liberalism Lives," *Time*, March 17, 1947.

churches and church leaders such as Unitarians and van Paassen, but only doctrinally, not by name.

Though he consistently spurned denominational references, it was not uncommon for Sheen to speak broadly of "Protestants, Catholics, and Jews." There was an implied acknowledgment of a common faith between Protestants and Catholics in the lordship of Jesus Christ, and a common allegiance to the God of Abraham among these three faith groups. This was particularly apparent in Sheen's wartime and postwar calls for "a daily Holy Hour by Jews, Protestants, and Catholics." He began calling for a daily "Holy Hour," which was to be dedicated to prayer, meditation, spiritual reading, and acts of devotion, in his first broadcast after the Pearl Harbor attack. "The Jews and Protestants can make it in their homes, or in their synagogues and churches. Catholics should make it in the presence of Our Divine Lord in the Blessed Sacrament," Sheen instructed.[156] A few weeks later Sheen preached, "We must make ourselves worthy of our objectives; and how can we do that except by each Jew, Protestant, and Catholic, according to the light of conscience, living close to God and His Divine Son Jesus Christ, that we may catch a spark from the Flame and rekindle the embers that had already burnt low." He went on with the enthusiasm of a football coach giving a locker room pep talk to his team: "You know as well as I do there is only one way for America to win. . . . But how shall we get God on our side, unless we first get on His? All right, then! The Holy Hour tomorrow morning! Jews, Protestants, and Catholics!"[157]

Whereas Walter Maier often held up historical figures from across the Christian (especially Protestant) landscape, Sheen referred to historical Christian leaders relatively infrequently. Occasionally, he listed exemplary men and women of the church that would have been particularly recognizable to Catholic listeners, such as Vincent de Paul, Don Bosco, Boniface, Augustine of Canterbury, Cyril, Patrick, Francis of Assisi, Clare, Teresa of Avila, Dominic, Ignatius Loyola, Francis Xavier, Therese of Lisieux, Bernadette, Thomas à Becket, John of the Cross, Francis de Sales, Gertrude, and Catherine of

---

[156]Sheen, *Peace*, 10-11.
[157]Sheen, *Peace*, 55-56. For other examples of Sheen's call for a daily "Holy Hour" exercised by Protestants, Catholics, and Jews, see Sheen, *Peace*, 75, 103, 110, 119; *Crisis in Christendom*, 7; *You*, 122; *Love That Waits*, 65.

Sienna.[158] While he made it clear that such figures were worthy of admiration and imitation, Sheen typically only mentioned them briefly, and did not expound in any detail on their accomplishments. More commonly, Sheen mentioned great historical thinkers, both Christian and pagan, as might be expected from a trained philosopher. They ranged across the centuries, from before Christ to contemporary times, and included Socrates, Plato, Aristotle, Seneca, Augustine of Hippo, Virgil, Bernard, Thomas Aquinas (a favorite of Sheen's), Bonaventure, Dante, Shakespeare, Goethe, Pascal, Dostoyevsky, Samuel Johnson, Jacques Maritain, and G. K. Chesterton (a friend). Although Sheen indicated that such intellects supported Christian truths, either generally or specifically, he did not expound on their thought in detail. Even for the many in his audience who were unfamiliar with these philosophers and thinkers, Sheen's perceived erudition and the authority of his Christian message were likely enhanced by these references. What is more, the strong implication was that all capital-T Truth, regardless of its discoverer, was compatible with the teaching of the "one true church" that Sheen represented.

In her well-researched biography of Fulton Sheen, historian Kathleen L. Riley notes that a "point in Sheen's favor was the fact that he sounded like a genuine evangelical."[159] In his unrelenting advocacy of historical, orthodox doctrine, in opposition to liberalism and modernism, this was indeed true. Additionally, Sheen sermonized in a way that was appealing to non-Catholics as well as Catholics. Nonetheless, a consistent listener of the CH would not likely have mistaken Sheen for an evangelical in particular, or a Protestant generally. While Sheen was catholic in attitude, he was unabashedly Catholic in fact, and he made no secret about that in his broadcasts. If anything, the extensive common theological ground Sheen established with non-Catholics, along with his disarming reasonableness and likeability, earned him the right to speak in distinctly Catholic ways at opportune times. Sheen was thoughtful in picking his spots.

In a 1932 sermon titled "The Church and the Times," he spoke of the church standing firm against a corrosive modernity, only to be "robed in the garment

---

[158]For examples, see Sheen, *Fullness of Christ*, 15, 46, 86-87; *Peace*, 82-83; *Crisis in Christendom*, 32; *Love That Waits*, 63.
[159]Kathleen L. Riley, *Fulton J. Sheen: An American Catholic Response to the Twentieth Century* (Staten Island, NY: St. Paul's/Alba House, 2004), 82.

of a fool." Sheen described several "fools" employed in the work of the church, including "devout nuns . . . who leave the lights and glamours of the world for the shades and shadows of the Cross, where saints are made," and priests who "practice celibacy in a world which has gone mad about sex."[160] Occasionally, he spoke of Catholic religious orders, as in 1935 when he spoke of various paths by which one could live "The Christian Life." The range of devout orders could accommodate "the most varied personal inclinations":

> A Francis who loves the poor may become a Franciscan; a Clare who loves the needy may become a poor Clare; a Teresa who loves penance may become a Carmelite; a Dominic who loves study and preaching may become a Dominican; an Ignatius who loves spiritual action may become a Jesuit; a Paul who loves the Passion of Christ may become a Passionist; a Paul who loves preaching the Gospel may become a Paulist; a Vincent who loves orphans may become a Vincentian; and so on for the hundreds of communities within the Church.[161]

In a later sermon, Sheen commended "the contemplative orders of the Church" such as "Trappists, Carmelites, Poor Clares and dozens of others with gifted souls who enter into a life of reparation, not because they want to save *their own* souls, but because they want to save your soul and mine."[162]

Sheen's strong devotion to Mary, the "Blessed Virgin," "Our Lady," was often apparent. He presented her as a person worthy of adoration, emulation, and devotion. Mary's own "beautiful devotion" to her "Divine Son" made her "the loveliest of all the lovely mothers of the world, the paragon of maternity, and the prototype of motherhood." In addition to bearing Jesus's physical body, Sheen explained, "Mary is the Mother of the Mystical Body of Christ, the Church."[163] In a 1945 radio sermon, he noted that "every single broadcast I give is dedicated to Our Lady, in the hope that as the sponsor of each broadcast she may bring her divine Son into your souls."[164] Anticipating non-Catholic consternation about excessive devotion to Mary, he explained that "all favors come to us from Jesus through her;" however, to

---

[160]Sheen, *Manifestations of Christ*, 91-96.
[161]Sheen, *Fullness of Christ*, 86.
[162]Sheen, *Love That Waits*, 90.
[163]Sheen, *Fullness of Christ*, 114-15.
[164]Sheen, *You*, 113.

clarify Sheen added, "There is no question here of confusing Our Lady and Our Lord; we venerate Our Mother, we worship Our Lord."[165]

In a 1950 sermon titled "Our Blessed Mother," he made a striking appeal for critics of Catholicism to rethink their wariness of devotion to Mary. Sheen began, "There is only one mother in the history of the world of whom men have spoken unkindly. . . . How tongues have slandered and how pens have splattered that lovely and beautiful Mother of Jesus!" As he proceeded, he reiterated her divinely appointed role in the life of the Savior, and noted the high esteem in which Jesus himself held her. Sheen then asked his listeners, "Suppose when I was invited into your house I completely ignored your mother, failed to greet her on entering, and never once addressed a word to her about you whom I claimed as a friend? . . . But must not Our Divine Lord suffer the same bitter disappointment when we refuse to show some respects to His Beloved Mother?" For those still firm that Christ alone deserved a Christian's devotion, Sheen concluded with another poignant question: "I have never found that anyone who loved my mother, loved me less, have you?"[166] Sheen shared his hope "that on the last day, when we go before God for judgment, we shall hear Him say the most consoling words of all, and the pledge of our eternal salvation: 'I've heard My Mother speak of you.'"[167]

While always reinforcing that allegiance to the pope did not conflict with allegiance to America, from time to time Sheen felt the need to speak of the papacy. In a 1935 sermon named "The Vicar of Christ," he explained why it was necessary for there to be "a visible head or a primate" after Jesus's ascension into heaven. He spoke of the appropriateness of Catholic polity, in light of God's providential oversight, and concluded by explaining that St. Peter was indeed the foundational "rock" of the church. Sheen expressed a desire that "we, the other living stones, might build upon him as the

---

[165]Sheen, *Prodigal World*, 96-97.

[166]Sheen, *Rock Plunged Into Eternity*, 129-38.

[167]Sheen, *Light Your Lamps*, 107. Sheen's eloquence and tenderness when speaking of Mary no doubt moved both Catholics and non-Catholics, even if many of the latter would have still resisted Sheen's level of adoration and devotion. Occasionally, however, Sheen's rhetoric may have left Protestants and other non-Catholics scratching their heads, such as when he described Mary as "a living ciborium, a monstrance of the Divine Eucharist, the Gate of Heaven through which a Creator would peer upon creation, a Tower of Ivory up whose chaste body He was to climb 'to kiss upon her lips a mystic rose.'" See Sheen, *You*, 32.

immutable rock, compacted together in the bonds of faith, hope and charity."[168] When the pope came under criticism during World War II, Sheen noted that many were asking, "Why does not your Church do something about the war?" He rhetorically countered, "Well, why did you not pay attention to the red light before the auto struck you? Did you accept Leo XIII's warning over fifty years ago, about Liberalism leading to collectivism and socialism?"[169] In a 1942 sermon, "Papacy and Peace," he again responded to those who accused Rome of doing too little to end the war: "I find it somewhat amusing to hear those who do not believe in the Holy Father as the Vicar of Christ, condemn him for not acting as the Vicar of Christ." Sheen went on to explain: "Christ did not give to Peter the keys to Caesar's palace, or to Wilhelmstrasse, the Kremlin, or the Quirinal. He gave to him only the keys of the Kingdom of Heaven."[170]

While constantly reinforcing common ground with non-Catholics on key doctrinal Christian points, Sheen addressed "Catholic" topics with Catholics and non-Catholics alike, when he felt it appropriate. In addition to the subjects just described, he spoke of the sacrifice of the mass, of being in the presence of the Lord via the Eucharist, of seven sacraments, of praying the rosary, and of the mystical body of Christ, without making them primary or oft-repeated themes.

Over a twenty-year period, millions of people tuned in every week to hear Walter Maier on TLH and Fulton Sheen on the CH. What they had to say kept their ethereal congregants, across the country and around the world, huddled around their radio sets. In the midst of increasing individualism and uncertain opinions, many wanted to hear words of immutable authority. In the midst of rising modernity, many wanted to hear affirmation of traditional orthodoxy. In the midst of national and international strife, many wanted to hear a message of providential stability and hope, even if it came with blunt admonition. In the midst of religious fragmentation, many wanted to hear words creating a shared Christian community. Maier and

[168]Sheen, *Fullness of Christ*, 31-40.
[169]Sheen, *War and Guilt*, 28.
[170]Sheen, *Peace*, 70-74.

Sheen delivered messages that provided just these elements. In 1931, the *Boston Pilot* reported Sheen's own comments about his weekly CH addresses: "The Christian finds a thrill in the monotony and 'repetition,' because he has a fixed 'goal,' while a pagan of today finds repetition monotonous because he has never decided for himself the purpose of living."[171] He could just as well have been speaking of Maier's TLH broadcasts. Their theological content was indeed "monotonous" in the sense Sheen described, as it came from an unchanging God. Seldom was it presented, however, in what listeners considered a monotonous way.

With eloquent confidence they confirmed the reliability of scriptural authority, reaffirmed the necessity for (and the validity of) Jesus Christ's atoning blood, promised the universal availability of God's grace, urgently called for sanctified personal lives and national repentance, established common ground across traditional Christian groups, urged patriotism while holding patriots to their ideals, and promised that God's providential hand was guiding the affairs of the world, notwithstanding the messiness of the times. While articulating these overarching themes, they demonstrated a broad knowledge of developments in economics, politics, academia, medicine, science, literature, popular entertainment, and society as a whole, which further enhanced the relevance of their messages.

While they both were accused occasionally of speaking above listeners' heads, they enjoyed their greatest popularity with common men and women. In fact, even though Maier and Sheen were well-educated men and academics by profession, they went out of their way to craft messages that were accessible and moving. Though a biblical scholar who prepared his expository preaching by reading Scripture in its original Hebrew and Greek, Maier virtually never referred to the original texts in his broadcasts. While it was not uncommon for Sheen to use Latin phrases in his sermons, he usually provided the translations for the listener. On the few occasions when they did indeed speak with overly lofty vocabulary, the effect likely only increased the authority they communicated to their audiences.

In the content of their sermons, several topics deserve special mention. Sheen and Maier considered godly families to be the building blocks of

---

[171]*Boston Pilot*, January 9, 1931.

society, and they reinforced this conviction frequently. They urged fathers to provide stable family leadership, and mothers to care for their homes and nurture their children. They counseled repentance and reconciliation in cases of infidelity or harmful behavior. As for children, Maier and Sheen urged them to respect their parents, and shun the common urge to "sow" their "wild oats." Unconfessed sin, after all, could land one in hell in the event of one's unexpected demise. Both preachers urged husbands and wives to take the biblical instruction to "be fruitful and multiply" to heart. They railed against birth control, with Maier being considerably more vocal on this topic than both his Catholic radio counterpart and his Protestant clerical peers. Birth control, in his opinion, represented a shirking of societal duties, a rejection of familial fulfillment, and a thwarting of God's will.[172] Abortion also came under fire, for these reasons in addition to its taking of an unborn life.

Maier and Sheen also connected with their audiences as they spoke of societal ills plaguing American life. They acknowledged the prevalence of alcohol abuse and urged those afflicted to turn their addictions over to God. They cautioned against the allure of gambling and extramarital sex. They both warned of the perils of a life of crime, quoting current crime statistics, while invoking the authoritative name of J. Edgar Hoover on numerous occasions. Maier, in particular, also spoke of the damning sin of suicide with some regularity. Sheen and Maier were both aware of the shortcomings of both the country and the church in matters of race. Both were remarkably critical of the treatment of minorities, especially black people, in America. They urged the church to recognize the equality of all men and women before God, and pleaded for social reform in society, without prescribing specific policies.

Maier and Sheen were educators who were often critical of the academy. While both made it clear that they were supporters of academic inquiry, scientific discovery, and liberal education, they inveighed against those who used these endeavors to undermine belief in almighty God and in Christian

---

[172]Sheen had plenty to say against birth control, especially in light of official church teaching; however, Maier was unrelenting in his attacks on birth control throughout his career. In addition to preaching against it in sermons, he often addressed it in *The Walther League Messenger*, of which he was editor from 1920 to 1945.

orthodoxy. They took humanistic optimists, liberal theologians and philosophers, and atheistic scientists to task, while highlighting members of the
academic community who retained their faith commitments. Sheen and
Maier were particularly vocal about the threat of Darwinian evolution to
Christian teaching. Though early in his radio career Sheen allowed that
evolutionary theories were not definitionally in conflict with church
doctrine,[173] he was disturbed by the way such theories often disallowed a
providential overseer. Over his radio ministry, he criticized evolutionary
theory repeatedly. In addition to atheistic assumptions he perceived to be
imbedded in many of these theories, Sheen disliked the humanistic confidence that evolution would lead to human perfectibility.[174] From the beginning, Maier also vehemently opposed evolutionary theories, for much
the same reasons as Sheen. Additionally, Maier voiced strong consternation
about their impact on morality over time.[175]

Finally, although they had plenty to say about society and the church,
Maier and Sheen gave partisan politics a wide berth. By doing so they
avoided potentially alienating radio listeners, and prevented distracting
"noise" from interfering with their biblical messages. What their sermons
lacked in partisanship they made up for with the sturdy truth claims of
Christianity, as they understood them. At a time when liberal Protestants
like Harry Emerson Fosdick argued, "What one says on the air must be
universal, catholic, inclusive, profoundly human," Sheen and Maier talked
about universal love and inclusive hope, but claimed that such were made
possible by the exclusive work of Christ.[176] They were indeed catholic, but
with an urgent message that they presented as profoundly divine.

---

[173]See NCWC News Service, "Dr. Sheen Gives Evolution Theory Stand of Church," April 12, 1930.
Sheen Archives, Rochester, "Press Clippings, 1930–1935" file.

[174]An example: "We must be prepared to be told a thousand times over that we are . . . benighted
fools. . . . We are a race of darkened minds because we do not know that evolution has proven
original sin a myth; that we are ignorant because we do not know that science has dispensed
with Providence, with God, and with Christ." Sheen, *Manifestations of Christ*, 105-6.

[175]An example: "Humanity is not an accident, a chemical coincidence, but it is God's supreme
masterpiece, created after a counsel of the divine Trinity. . . . If there is nothing divine in man,
if he is only a refined form of the beast, then all the ideals of clean, constructive living are shattered." Maier, *Lutheran Hour*, 67-68.

[176]Fosdick as quoted in Quentin J. Schultze, "Evangelical Radio and the Rise of the Electronic
Church, 1921–1948," *Journal of Broadcasting & Electronic Media* 32, no. 3 (Summer 1988): 298.

Chapter Eight

SPAN OF SIGNIFICANCE

THE IMPACT OF MAIER AND SHEEN ON NETWORK RADIO

Most of us restrain our hearts in silence,
Sadly knowing all that language mars,
But you can take the golden words from heaven
And string them into sentences like stars!

JAMES L. DUFF

To the "Big Gun" of the Lutheran Hour, Dr. Walter A. Maier,
with my best wishes and prayers, and my admiration for
the accuracy of his long-range fire—Sincerely in Christ.

REV. PAUL G. JACKSON

FOR TWENTY YEARS, FULTON Sheen and Walter Maier took to the air-waves on their *Catholic Hour* (CH) and *The Lutheran Hour* (TLH) radio programs. For twenty years, they delivered their weighty messages of

---

James L. Duff was a Los Angeles coffee broker who sent a poem to "Father Sheen." The second epigraph is from a handwritten inscription on a photograph sent to Walter Maier from Paul G. Jackson, the pastor of Calvary Baptist Church, Brewer, Maine, who held a weekly Christian broadcast of his own on local radio station WABI.

traditional, Christian orthodoxy with urgency and fervor, in the midst of an unprecedentedly calamitous era. And for twenty years, from coast to coast, week after week, millions tuned in to listen. The impact was significant.

PASTORS OF THE AIRWAVES

Maier and Sheen both believed that they were called by God to serve as pastors—spiritual "shepherds" of human "flocks" loved by Jesus. These Lutheran and Catholic clerics devoted their careers to this role. Like most pastors, they evangelized, admonished, exhorted, warned, encouraged, counseled, and comforted their congregants. Yet unlike most pastors, Sheen and Maier were not confined to a geographic parish or a specific group of denominational adherents. They were indeed pastors—pastors of the airwaves—who were invited into the homes of their "parishioners" by the turn of a radio dial. A confluence of the stressful times in which they lived, new and enhanced technology, the emergence of mass culture via network radio, the combination of perceived intimacy with, and authority of, radio personalities, in tandem with Maier's and Sheen's gripping delivery of their messages, enabled these two radio preachers to unlock greater potency of the centuries-old pastoral "office of the keys" across the nation and beyond.

By all estimates, millions of loyal listeners tuned in to Sheen and Maier each week. Detailed data does not exist, however, to enable precise audience tallies. In 1940, *Time* vaguely noted that Sheen "counts his hearers in millions," adding that he makes "religion sensible and attractive to great masses."[1] In that same year, on the tenth anniversary of the CH's launch, the NCCM estimated that Sheen's audience had reached at least 17.5 million. Their methodology involved multiplying an assumed ratio of total program listeners to the subset of listeners who wrote letters, times the amount of mail Sheen received during a specific week. The NCCM employed a multiple that had been estimated in the 1939 "Princeton Radio Research Project."[2] When Sheen spoke on a Sydney radio station during a 1948 trip to Australia, a local

---

[1]"Monsignor's Tenth," *Time*, March 11, 1940, 60-61.
[2]Edward J. Heffron, *Ten Years of the Catholic Hour* (Washington, DC: NCCM, 1940), 5. The 17+ million audience estimate is cited by recent historians of Sheen's radio ministry. For examples, see Kathleen L. Riley, *Fulton J. Sheen: An American Catholic Response to the Twentieth Century* (Staten Island, NY: St. Paul's/Alba House, 2004), 67; Timothy H. Sherwood, *The Preaching of Archbishop Fulton J. Sheen: The Gospel Meets the Cold War* (Lanham, MD: Lexington Books, 2010), 13.

Catholic newspaper reported that Sheen's "voice . . . claims an audience of 15 million, whenever it is heard over the N.B.C. network in the United States."[3] Whatever Sheen's listener base was at any point in time, it was quite large by national radio standards, either religious or secular; however, estimates of CH audience size were spotty and inconsistent.[4]

Also in 1940, the admittedly biased NCCM publication *Catholic Action*, assessed that "the current series by Monsignor Sheen," which had generated more listener correspondence than any prior series, "is undoubtedly the most popular religious series ever given on radio."[5] The less-biased radio industry periodical *Radio Varieties* described the CH as "the world's largest year-round religious broadcast," marveling that it had achieved that status on sustaining time.[6] The following year, CH's home network, NBC, published a commemorative booklet celebrating fifteen years of religious broadcasting on the nation's oldest and largest radio chain. The piece provided an overview of NBC's religious programming history that included brief statements of appreciation by the network's clerical mainstays, Harry Emerson Fosdick, Jonah B. Wise, and Sheen. Franklin Dunham, director of religious programs for NBC, personally sent a copy of the booklet to the star CH speaker. Inside the cover he wrote the following note: "To Monsignor Sheen: Who brings the largest audience to a religious program in the history of American broadcasting. With devotion, Franklin Dunham, Easter 1941."[7] While this inscription is obviously short on statistical data, it

---

[3]"Cardinal Spellman Arrives: Mgr. Fulton Sheen on War Danger," *The Catholic Weekly* 7, no. 322 (April 29, 1948): 1.

[4]Two examples, both from 1950, are noteworthy. *Pageant* ran a flattering feature on Sheen, in which it referred to him as a "cherished" NBC "star." It marveled at his twenty year "spellbinding" run on the network and his popularity with the radio public, yet stated his audience at a rather precise "3,601,600." See George Frazier, "Fulton J. Sheen: Unprofitable Servant," *Pageant*, June 1950, 38-46. A March issue of *Catholic Action* presented CH's audience at approximately 4 million. See *Catholic Action*, "March 5: Catholic Hour Milestone," March 1950, 18. Neither article states the methodology for its estimates. In that there were never indications that CH's listenership was declining, it is unclear why these estimates were so much lower than the aforementioned 1940 and 1948 estimates.

[5]"Ten Years of the Catholic Hour," *Catholic Action*, March 1940, 23.

[6]Aileen Soares, "The Catholic Hour," *Radio Varieties* 3, no. 1 (January 1940): 3. The article noted that Sheen was "that well-loved inspiring figure" who presented "a message of dignity and simple sincerity" that was "never over the heads of the radio audience."

[7]This booklet, *The Word of God: Fifteen Years of Religious Broadcasts; The National Broadcasting Company—1926-1941*, with Dunham's inscription, can be found in the Sheen Archives, Diocese of Rochester, "Memorabilia" files, "1941" folder.

does provide a noteworthy general assessment of Sheen's listener draw by a network executive.

For the remainder of the decade, references gauging Sheen's CH audience size typically presumed it to be significant, but lacked precision. For instance, in December of 1940, *Catholic Action* quoted "prominent Protestant writer" Stanley High as saying that "no other strictly religious program has a comparable following" to the CH.[8] A 1945 *Time* article concluded that Sheen was "probably America's best-known priest," given his "audience of millions for his Sunday preaching on NBC's Catholic Hour."[9] In 1947, a feature story on Sheen in the *St. Louis Post-Dispatch* noted, "There are few voices more familiar to the listening public today than that of Monsignor Fulton J. Sheen," who was heard on "the Catholic Hour and his radio listeners are in the millions," extending "beyond this country . . . to nearly every nation on the globe."[10] In the same year, a feature in *Look* magazine on Sheen's "spiritual zeal" for "saving souls" focused on his concern for "millions of men and women."[11] In a similarly general tone, *Time* called Sheen "the Roman Catholic best-known to most US citizens," due to his "annual broadcasts . . . [that] have long been among the most popular on the air."[12]

More frequent efforts were made to estimate audience size for Maier's TLH. This was likely due to a variety of factors, the most important being that TLH had to pay for its airtime, while the CH was the beneficiary of NBC's sustaining time. As would be expected, the Lutheran Laymen's League (LLL), under whose sponsorship TLH operated, paid particular attention to audience penetration. Minutes of the LLL's Lutheran Hour Operating Committee noted that during the peak of radio's popularity in the late 1940s, an average of seventy radio sets out of one hundred would be turned on, at some point, during a typical Sunday in the United States. They reported that of those seventy sets, "four, sooner or later, tuned into 'The Lutheran Hour.'"[13]

---

[8]"The Catholic Radio Bureau," *Catholic Action*, December 1940, 25.
[9]"Religion: Reconversion," *Time*, October 22, 1945.
[10]Dickson Terry, "His Voice Is Known to Millions," *St. Louis Post-Dispatch*, March 31, 1947.
[11]Gretta Palmer, "Why All These Converts? The Story of Monsignor Fulton Sheen," *Look*, June 24, 1947, 36-40.
[12]"Religion: To the Hierarchy," *Time*, June 4, 1951.
[13]Fred Pankow and Edith Pankow, *75 Years of Blessing and The Best Is Yet to Come: The History of the International Lutheran Laymen's League* (St. Louis: International Lutheran Laymen's League, 1992), 88.

In other words, according to LLL research, with biases of its own, nearly 6 percent of Sunday radio listeners in America heard TLH.

The popular press often provided assessments of Maier's audience numbers, especially during the 1940s. As early as 1938, however, in an article on Maier's public denunciation of the Federal Council of Church's "radio monopoly," *Time* stated that the "distinction" of being "radio's most popular religious broadcast . . . belongs to . . . the Lutheran Hour," which its editors contrasted with the major network, sustaining-time religious programs.[14] In a 1943 piece, *Time* declared that "the Lutheran Hour is a personal triumph" for the "dynamic, hearty Dr. Maier," with its twelve million listeners in the United States, and many others "from all parts of the world."[15] The following year, William F. McDermott reported in *Collier's* that the Lutheran "radio parson" reached a global audience of fifteen million, as he "preaches to the equivalent of the entire US population every two months."[16] In 1945, *Sunday* magazine noted that TLH's listener base was "professionally estimated at 15 million," and that his national "Hooper rating" indicated "more listeners than any other religious program tested."[17]

In another 1945 article, which highlighted the vastness of religious radio's presence, reporter-turned-radio columnist Ben Gross asserted that 35 to 40 million Americans "draw religious inspiration and solace from the air." He explained that "some gospel spellbinders of the kilocycle lanes have bigger audiences than the Bob Hopes, Jack Bennys, and Charlie McCarthys," as well as "Frank Sinatra." Gross went on to name several prominent radio preachers, but concluded, "More people each week tune in Dr. Walter A. Maier . . . than listen to any top comedian, singer or other entertainer. He is Number One among the radio evangelists." The article further claimed that TLH's worldwide monthly audience, including network and transcription broadcasts, totaled "a staggering . . . 60 million listeners."[18] While Gross's

[14]"Religion: Maier vs. the Council," *Time*, April 11, 1938.

[15]"Lutherans," *Time*, October 18, 1943, 48.

[16]William F. McDermott, "Old-Time Religion Goes Global," *Collier's*, May 6, 1944, 50. The *New York Times* obituary for Maier in 1950 also noted that "every two months [Maier's] cumulative audience was the equivalent of the population of the United States." See "Dr. Maier is Dead; Radio Preacher, 56," *New York Times*, January 12, 1950, 27.

[17]Donald E. Hoke, "He Throws Inkwells on the Air—Part I," *Sunday*, April 1945, 13-14.

[18]Ben Gross, "The World's Largest Congregation," *Pageant*, February 1945, 119-23. Two years earlier, *Coronet* magazine published an article also suggesting that Maier's radio audience (along

assessment of Maier's relative popularity appears generous, it is noteworthy that a leading secular entertainment commentator made such bold claims about the conservative Lutheran minister's radio following, especially in comparison to household name personalities.[19]

In 1947, the *Christian Herald* presented Maier's audience as twenty million each Sunday, which it claimed made Maier "the 'preaching-est preacher' in all the world today, and doubtless of all time." His "impassioned sermons" reached six hundred million in a radio season.[20] In a lengthy feature article on Maier in June of 1948, the *Saturday Evening Post* declared that "Doctor Maier . . . hold[s] something big. . . . His radio gospel encircles the globe" as it is "heard by 20 million persons . . . fifty-two times a year."[21]

A limited number of references were made to the ratings of the CH and TLH in articles about Sheen and Maier. This may seem odd given that network performers "lived or died" by their ratings, the most influential of which during the late 1930s and most of the 1940s were "Hooperatings" produced by C. E. Hooper, Inc. (Bob Hope famously grumbled that "a Hooperating is an ulcer with a decimal point.")[22] Due to a variety of reasons, however, standard radio ratings were of less value for programs like the CH and TLH than they were for typical, commercially sponsored shows, and were especially flawed as assessors of aggregate audience size. First, ratings did not cover the entire population of listeners, as surveys focused on urban areas with station affiliates of the three major networks. Second, Hooperatings were primarily aimed at assessing appeal of *network* programs. As a result of these two factors, not only would a portion of Maier's and Sheen's audiences in less populated areas be ignored, but so would listeners of the

with that of California radio preacher Charles E. Fuller) exceeded audiences of Charlie Mc-Carthy and Bob Hope. The columnist explained that "these men of faith number . . . their followers by tens of millions." See William F. McDermott, "America Goes Back to Church," *Coronet*, May 1943, 3.

[19]Ben Gross was primarily known as the influential radio critic of the *New York Daily News*. Gross possessed considerable knowledge of, and personal familiarity with, radio entertainers and their programs. His memoirs reveal no particular affinity for, or interest in, religious broadcasting, which makes his trumpeting of Maier's popularity all the more noteworthy. See Ben Gross, *I Looked and I Listened: Informal Recollections of Radio and TV* (New York: Random House, 1954).

[20]William F. McDermott, "Twenty Million Hear Him Preach," *Christian Herald*, March 1947, 43.

[21]Hartzell Spence, "The Man of the Lutheran Hour," *Saturday Evening Post*, June 19, 1948, 17, 88.

[22]Jim Ramsburg, *Network Radio Ratings, 1932–1953: A History of Prime Time Programs Through the Ratings of Nielsen, Crossley and Hooper* (Jefferson, NC: McFarland and Company, 2012), 18.

significant number of nonnetwork stations that broadcast TLH and the CH using transcription discs. It should be noted that C. E. Hooper himself cautioned against using ratings as a "measurement of the *total* audience." Rather, he explained that they should be used primarily as a "tool" for program advertisers to use in assessing "comparative" audience interest, "from program to program and from month to month."[23] Additionally, because rating services were primarily in business to serve commercial clients, they generally ignored unsponsored (i.e., sustaining) programs. Thus, while Maier's TLH was sponsored by the LLL (albeit for noncommercial purposes), and did receive a Hooperating (however flawed it may have been), Sheen's CH did not receive a published rating, as it was an NBC sustaining program. This is not to say that networks never commissioned ratings on their sustaining programs, but such ratings were not usually made public.[24]

Another indicator of the breadth of Maier's and Sheen's pastorates is the number of radio stations over which their programs could be heard. When Maier inaugurated TLH on CBS in 1930, thirty-six stations in the larger cities of the country, plus two shortwave outlets, broadcast the program.[25] Station coverage increased dramatically in the late 1930s through growth of the Mutual network, introduction of transcription technology for non-network broadcasters, increased popularity of the program, and international expansion.[26] One hundred seventy-one stations broadcast the 1939–1940 season of TLH, of which 72 used transcription techniques. Total stations jumped to 374 the following year, of which 310 were domestic outlets and 64 were foreign broadcasters.[27] To provide scale for this level of distribution, it should be noted that at this time baseball's World Series, which communications scholar James Walker states "commanded the nation's

---

[23]C. E. Hooper, "Lifting the Veil from the Radio Audience," *Printers' Ink Monthly* 42, no. 6 (June 1941): 37.

[24]For background information on radio ratings, see Hugh Malcolm Beville Jr., *Audience Ratings: Radio, Television, and Cable*, rev. student ed. (Hillsdale, NJ: Lawrence Erlbaum Associates, 1988), 1-27; Ramsburg, *Network Radio Ratings*, 14-21; Frank Stanton, C. E. Hooper, A. M. Crossley, and L. D. H. Weld, *How Radio Measures Its Audience: Four Discussions by Research Authorities* (New York: Columbia Broadcasting System, 1939).

[25]Paul L. Maier, *A Man Spoke, A World Listened* (New York: McGraw-Hill, 1963), 115.

[26]After its initial radio season on CBS, TLH moved to the Mutual Broadcasting System.

[27]Pankow and Pankow, *Best Is Yet to Come*, 56; Tona Hangen, "Man of the Hour: Walter A. Maier and Religion by Radio on the Lutheran Hour," *Radio Reader: Essays in the Cultural History of Radio*, ed. Michele Hilmes and Jason Loviglio (New York: Routledge, 2002), 120.

largest radio stage," was broadcast on only 238 stations nationwide, when the Yankees played the Reds in the 1939 "Fall Classic."[28] By the 1948–1949 radio season, 1,100 stations worldwide broadcast TLH, of which 598 were US stations. The following year—Maier's last—ABC carried TLH, in addition to the Mutual network, transcription outlets, and foreign stations, taking the total to 1,236. At that point, TLH was broadcast in 36 languages, from 55 countries, and could be heard in 120 nations.[29]

In 1930, when the CH was first broadcast on NBC, it went out over twenty-two network stations, located in seventeen states and the District of Columbia. NBC had offered the program to seventy-three stations, but only these twenty-two stations chose to carry it.[30] By the following radio season, however, fifty NBC affiliates offered the CH, and the number would continue to grow.[31] Also in 1931, the CH began developing an international audience, through a shortwave station in Schenectady operated by General Electric Company, which could be heard in Canada, Europe, Cuba, Africa, Hawaii, the Philippines, and South America.[32] Near the end of the decade, the NCCM reported that the CH had "the largest network of a year-round religious broadcast in the world," with eighty stations in thirty-nine states.[33] In 1940, the number of stations including the CH in their programming reached 106, as NBC grew and additional stations picked up the program.[34] In December of that year, the NCCM began making transcription recordings of Sheen's CH addresses available to local sponsors, to be broadcast on local, non-NBC stations. By February of the following year, over forty stations in twenty-six states and Ontario inaugurated such transcription programming.[35] When

---

[28]James R. Walker, *Crack of the Bat: A History of Baseball on the Radio* (Lincoln: University of Nebraska Press, 2015), 97, 111.

[29]Maier, *A Man Spoke*, 347-48; Hangen, "Man of the Hour," 120; Pankow and Pankow, *Best Is Yet to Come*, 77.

[30]*A Nationwide Audience for God* (Washington, DC: NCCM, 1940). This promotional booklet can be found in the "Catholic Hour I" file, "History" folder, Sheen Archives, Rochester, NY.

[31]"Catholic Hour Now Broadcast Each Sunday from 6 to 6:30 P.M., Eastern Standard Time," *N.C.W.C. Review*, December 1931.

[32]"Cosmopolitan Audience of the Catholic Hour," *N.C.W.C. Review*, April 1931; Joseph M. Tally, "The Catholic Hour—Outstanding Work of the N.C.C.M.," *Catholic Action*, May 1933, 10.

[33]"Month by Month with the N.C.W.C.," *Catholic Action*, April 1939, 14.

[34]"The Catholic Radio Bureau," *Catholic Action*, November 1940, 30.

[35]See map labeled "Radio Programs of the National Council of Catholic Men," dated February 1, 1941, "Memorabilia Files," "1941" folder, Sheen Archives, Rochester, NY; "Canal Zone to Hear Sheen Transcriptions," *Catholic Action*, 26.

Sheen left the CH in 1952 to redirect his airwave homiletics to television, the CH was broadcast via 127 domestic stations, located in forty-two states, the District of Columbia, and Hawaii.[36]

As mentioned in chapter two, mail volume was a key indicator of the reach of radio programs in the 1930s and 1940s. Mail generated by Sheen and Maier clearly demonstrated a broad, engaged listener base. Reporters often marveled at the amount of correspondence each received. On CH's third anniversary, the NCCM boasted, "Great numbers of letters have been received from interested listeners—thousands of whom are non-Catholics, not a few, ministers."[37] By the end of that radio season, three thousand letters per month were coming to NCCM's mailbox.[38] The volume steadily increased with the number of stations broadcasting the CH, and with Sheen's ever-growing popularity. In 1940, the NCCM commented that "the worth of any broadcast can be measured, to a large extent, by its audience mail." They reported that mail received had reached a new peak during Sheen's current series at twenty-eight thousand letters per week—"an incredibly large figure for a non-controversial religious program."[39] A "small booklet of prayers" that Sheen offered to his listeners in his first broadcast of that year generated 111,000 requests during the month of January alone.[40] In March of that year, *Time* noted that Sheen received three to six thousand letters a day, in addition to letters sent directly to the NCCM. The editors added that 1.75 million copies of his radio talks had been sent out since the CH went on the air.[41] At this point, Sheen had two full-time secretaries to handle personal mail, and an additional staff of twenty clerks, employed by the NCCM, to handle the bulk of his incoming mail.[42]

A 1947 *Look* feature on the Monsignor explained, "Until four years ago— when he stopped keeping count—his mail ran to 742,227 letters in the

---

[36]Fulton J. Sheen, *The Life of Christ* (Washington, DC: NCCM, 1952), 110.

[37]"Catholic Hour's Third Anniversary," *Catholic Action*, March 1933.

[38]Thomas C. Reeves, *America's Bishop: The Life and Times of Fulton J. Sheen* (San Francisco: Encounter Books, 2001), 81.

[39]"Ten Years," 23.

[40]"The Catholic Radio Bureau," *Catholic Action*, February 1940, 19.

[41]"Monsignor's Tenth," 60-61.

[42]Reeves, *America's Bishop*, 110.

nine-months' period of the college year. It is now very much larger."[43] In 1950, the NCCM stated that the CH audience had sent in roughly four million letters in the twenty years since the program's inception. While this included mail produced by all CH speakers, the writer highlighted Sheen's particular popularity with correspondents.[44] Later that year, when Sheen gave up his faculty position at CUA to become national director of the Society for the Propagation of the Faith (SPF), *Newsweek* mentioned his "specially-equipped office designed to handle as many as 1,000 letters a day."[45] In 1952, after Sheen concluded his CH presence, *Time* noted that Sheen had "a staff of 30 helpers," assisting with SPF responsibilities, and presumably, correspondence.[46] Months later, a *Collier's* feature on the bishop mentioned "an experienced clerical staff of about 35 women" that assisted with the "tremendous and continuing number of letters he receives," totaling thousands per week.[47] Although this latter article spoke of mail resulting from Sheen's recently begun television program, it seems reasonable to assume that the "experienced" staff had been in place during his CH radio presence, which concluded in the previous year.

Whereas Sheen had not always been precise in recording mail volume, Maier and the LLL were more meticulous in their accounting of listener-generated epistles. In 1930, the first year that TLH was on the air over the CBS network, the program produced record mail volume for a religious broadcast. Though TLH was aired for only nine months on CBS, more mail was sent to its New York headquarters concerning TLH than in response to any other network program. By another measure, after only one-half year on the air, Maier received more mail than did *all* the programs sponsored by the Federal Council of Churches over the NBC network (the nation's largest) that entire year, even though such programs enjoyed nine times as much air time as TLH.[48] While mail received totaled fifty-seven thousand in this first season (1930–1931), it climbed to seventy thousand in the first

[43]Palmer, "Why All These Converts?," 39. It should be understood that this figure included all letters received by Sheen, not just mail generated by his radio ministry.
[44]"March 5: Catholic Hour Milestone," *Catholic Action*, March 1950, 18.
[45]"Sheen the Evangelist," *Newsweek*, September 25, 1950, 85.
[46]"Microphone Missionary," *Time*, April 14, 1952, 79.
[47]Howard Cohn, "Bishop Sheen Answers His Fan Mail," *Collier's*, January 24, 1953, 22-24.
[48]Maier, *A Man Spoke*, 125.

full radio season after TLH returned to the air in 1935, notwithstanding that it had moved to a smaller network.[49] The annual rate of mail had increased by over one hundred thousand during the 1939–1940 radio season to 176,508. Maier reported that "almost 13,000 letters have come to headquarters during a single week, almost 3,500 in one day." He noted that "at the season's height, it is necessary to employ a clerical force of twenty-five workers," which "does not include my own staff, engaged exclusively in answering personal and problem mail."[50]

In early 1945, *Pageant* noted that the broadcast employed "from 30 to 55 clerks and stenographers . . . to assort and answer his mail, which at times becomes an engulfing torrent of 25 thousand letters a week."[51] The tally for this radio season ending a few months later was 340,000.[52] In March 1947, the *Christian Herald* explained that "four million people have written letters to Dr. Maier" since he went on the air, and that "it takes 70 women to handle the mail," which arrived at a pace of "as many as 8,000 [letters] in a single day."[53] The following year, a *Saturday Evening Post* profile noted that Maier's clerical staff handling correspondence had reached one hundred persons— a number repeated a few months later in the periodical *Radio and Television Life*.[54] In his 1948 critical examination of the Federal Council of Churches (FCC), Ernest Gordon pointed out that even though the FCC reaped the benefits of "close to a monopoly of free time" from major networks, Maier and TLH "receives 30,000 letters a week—three times the mail of all FCC programs together."[55] By the time Maier died in January 1950, his annual incoming mail had risen to over five hundred thousand letters.[56]

Even more than the sheer volume of mail, the content of listener correspondence demonstrated the genuine pastoral role Sheen and Maier filled for thousands of members of their radio flocks. In his memoirs, Sheen

---

[49]Hangen, "Man of the Hour," 120.

[50]Hangen, "Man of the Hour," 120; Walter A. Maier, *Peace Through Christ: Radio Messages Broadcast in the Seventh Lutheran Hour* (St. Louis: CPH, 1940), vii.

[51]Gross, "World's Largest Congregation," 119-20.

[52]Hangen, "Man of the Hour," 120.

[53]McDermott, "Twenty Million Hear Him Preach," 46.

[54]Spence, "Man of the Lutheran Hour," 89; Judy Maguire, "The Lutheran Hour," *Radio and Television Life* 18 (October 31, 1948): 34.

[55]Ernest Gordon, *Ecclesiastical Octopus: A Factual Report of the Federal Council of the Churches of Christ in America* (Boston: Fellowship Press, 1948), 89-90.

[56]Hangen, "Man of the Hour," 120.

mentioned with a sense of tenderness the "hundreds of thousands of letters of soul-searching and reaching out for Divinity which came to our office." He explained, "I personally answered as many as I could." Regardless of whether he responded himself or not, Sheen "felt that he owed it to the writers to destroy their letters" after they had been read, in light of his sacred, priestly duty toward these corresponding "parishioners."[57] While some wrote simply to request copies of his addresses, a greater number wrote with more substantive content and inquiries. They asked for explanations of Catholic doctrine and guidance on personal matters.[58] "The varieties of human despair brought to Monsignor Sheen are beyond number," observed *Look* magazine, when discussing his mail flow. "Very often practical and financial help is needed, as a first-aid measure." Sheen's daily mail, noted the author, "includes an average of 50 appeals on marriage problems alone," and "each of these receives a personal answer."[59] He also went out of his way to personally send a kindly response to the relatively modest number of "hateful" letters, many of which revealed more hostility toward God than to Catholicism or him. These latter types represented an evangelistic opportunity for Sheen, as he observed, "these souls may be like Saul who hated ignorantly."[60] It was not uncommon for the radio priest to dictate some two hundred replies to correspondents on a daily basis.[61]

In addition to those seeking counsel, thousands of listeners wrote to share how Sheen's messages had touched or influenced them. In 1940, the NCCM summarized what its staff had gleaned from countless letters received:

> The bulk of . . . [the] mail shows that the Catholic Hour['s] . . . influence is profound. It has educated consciences; it has strengthened wills; shown many, faced by pain or despair or monotonous enslaving routine, the purpose of existences. Repeating again and again the law of love of God and neighbor . . . dispelled misconceptions of Catholic teaching and practice, and increased good will among the citizens of the nation. . . . It has . . . brought the saving Christian truths to many who *could not* hear them in any other way . . . and

---

[57]Fulton J. Sheen, *Treasure in Clay: The Autobiography of Fulton J. Sheen* (New York: Image Books/Doubleday, 1980), 76.
[58]Dickson Terry, "His Voice Is Known to Millions," *St. Louis Post-Dispatch*, March 31, 1947.
[59]Palmer, "Why All These Converts?," 39.
[60]Riley, *Fulton J. Sheen*, 68.
[61]Reeves, *America's Bishop*, 110.

has reached some who *would not* hear them in any other way. . . . It has brought comfort and consolation to many plagued with misfortune. . . . It has provided counsel and information to many confused and perplexed. . . . The Catholic Hour has brought individuals closer to Christ and to Christian principles.[62]

From time to time, the NCCM published excerpts from letters received by Sheen in *Catholic Action*. Such excerpts excluded specific confessions of individual sins or struggles, inquiries relating to spiritual concerns or doctrinal questions, and requests for prayers or guidance. Rather, excerpts were published to demonstrate the broad, uplifting appeal of the CH—to serve as miniature endorsements of the CH speaker as pastor and teacher. The geographic origin of the letters was stated, but the identity of the writers was omitted. Particular delight seemed to be taken when letters of non-Catholics praised the edifying nature of Sheen's messages. For example, a non-Catholic "Philadelphia layman says: 'Just a word of appreciation for the great service rendered me through your radio sermons.'"[63] In 1941, the editors quoted at length an enthusiastic letter from an Illinois plumber, a portion of which read,

> I love and respect truth and wisdom regardless of the source. I am not of the Catholic faith. I was raised Lutheran. I can truthfully state that I have never heard more common sense, truth and wisdom uttered from the lips of a man than was uttered by you in your splendid and noble address. . . . Your message will do much good to cure the ills and evils of our nation. . . . Our nation needs your message . . . and needs to live up to its wonderful teachings.[64]

The editors often quoted writers who had accepted the Catholic faith for the first time, or returned to it, as a result of the program. They also quoted those who spoke of comfort provided by Sheen's words, as they endured suffering or heartache.[65] The NCCM shared supportive correspondence from non-Catholic clergy, especially as demonstrated in a 1942 article devoted entirely to such letters. The editors applauded the "generous spirit and broad understanding" of the appreciative Lutheran, Presbyterian, Methodist,

---

[62]"Ten Years of the Catholic Hour," 23.

[63]"Ten Years of the Catholic Hour," 23.

[64]"Transcribed Program Elicited This Letter," *Catholic Action*, April 1941, 26-27.

[65]For examples, see "From Our Mail Bag," *Catholic Action*, March 1942, 23; "From Our Mail Bag," *Catholic Action*, February 1943, 23; "Radio Mail Box Gleanings," *Catholic Action*, September 1949, 17.

Baptist, Evangelical Reformed, and generically "Protestant" ministers from the United States and Canada, along with a rabbi from North Carolina, who had praised Sheen's "splendid Catholic Hour sermons." Some correspondents promised to share his homilies with other church leaders within their spheres of influence.[66] In a subsequent column, an excerpt from a letter from a Brooklyn rabbi praised the CH for "disseminating religious culture and preaching true and sublime fundamental doctrines of religion, faith, and tolerance." Demonstrating a remarkable spirit of ecumenism, the rabbi concluded with a blessing: "May God strengthen your hands and lend his support to the sublime task in which you are engaged."[67] Pastors of various stripes affirming Sheen as pastor was noteworthy endorsement indeed.

Like Sheen, Walter Maier took his individual pastoral duties toward radio correspondents quite seriously, though he seems to have gone about it in a more systematic way. From the beginning of TLH broadcasts, mail poured into Maier's St. Louis office, both confirming his pastoral role and seeking his pastoral counsel. Many writers sent letters of affirmation and support (including financial support), and others wrote simply requesting a copy of specific sermons. Many shared redemptive personal narratives that were an outgrowth of Maier's sermons, including suicides halted at the last minute and extramarital rendezvous stopped short.[68] Yet thousands more confessed temptation and wrongdoing, sought advice and prayer, and asked questions relating to Scripture, doctrine, and the church. Maier's son recalls that "probably no category of effort commanded more of Father's time than answering problem mail. Even with staff counseling assistance, he . . . [dictated] late into . . . evenings."[69]

As previously mentioned, TLH continually invited listeners to write letters to the program, often offering inexpensive, inspirational gifts such as cross lapel pins or small pictures, in addition to copies of the week's sermon. But Maier went further in his pastoral efforts, while also respecting the role of local parish ministers. The closing announcements of the weekly broadcasts extended an invitation: "If you have no church affiliation and are

---

[66]"From Our Mail Bag," *Catholic Action*, July 1942, 26.

[67]"From Our Mail Bag," *Catholic Action*, February 1946, 23.

[68]Spence, "Man of the Lutheran Hour," 88.

[69]Maier, *A Man Spoke*, 172. By "problem mail" Maier was referring to mail from writers experiencing some personal struggle or problem.

troubled by a spiritual problem, Dr. Maier will be glad to advise you."[70] The announcer assured the listeners that their letters seeking counsel "will be regarded as a personal, sacred trust."[71]

Through the end of his ministry, Maier in-sisted on personally answering one hundred to two hundred letters per week.[72] Certain letters describing particularly urgent personal prob-lems or needs were passed on to Lutheran pastors in the geographic area of the letter writer for more personal assistance. On oc-casion, Maier even went so far as to prepare a sermon for a single letter writer, and then tele-phoned that person to urge him or her to listen to his upcoming broadcast. Maier's clerical staff handled the remaining bulk of his mail. While

Figure 8.1. A mailman delivering correspondence to Maier as Hulda looks on, October 1943

responses to correspondents varied in their level of personalization, over the years Maier developed standardized tracts or texts to respond to four hun-dred different problems, questions, and situations, thereby enabling him and his staff to respond situationally and quickly.[73]

A review of these prepared responses demonstrates just how seriously Maier and his staff took their pastoral responsibilities to letter-writing lis-teners. An internal TLH correspondence guide emphasized that the "problem-solution paragraphs" on file were "to be used only for Lutheran Hour Correspondence Work," and were "a privileged possession entrusted only to such who carry the delicate responsibility of answering problem mail." The guide further instructed, "These paragraphs are not to be re-copied for general distribution," nor were they to "be made available to 'some good friend.'" Topics were alphabetically cataloged and covered an amazing range, including anger, the Apocrypha, baptism of the insane, bobbed hair,

---

[70]See "Continuities" from broadcasts of *The Lutheran Hour*, Lutheran Hour Archives, St. Louis. The announcer often added the words "as he has thousands of others," or "at no charge," or "freely and confidentially," at the end of this invitation.

[71]For an example of the "personal, sacred trust" reference, see the "Continuity" for November 9, 1941, in "Continuities" from broadcasts of *The Lutheran Hour*, Lutheran Hour Archives, St. Louis.

[72]Maguire, "Lutheran Hour," 34.

[73]Spence, "Man of the Lutheran Hour," 89; Hangen, "Man of the Hour," 128.

Catholics attending Lutheran churches, drunkards, gambling, insurance policies, Judas, interracial marriage, masturbation, Millerites, predestination, soul sleep, suicide, water (holy), and worry (needless). Responses were remarkably gracious in tone, easy to understand, and often supported arguments or advice with scriptural references. It was not uncommon for TLH responses to encourage personal contact with a local pastor.[74]

From the beginning of TLH broadcasts, Maier considered correspondence as a means to extend his pastoral care and as an affirmation of his evangelistic and pastoral impact for supporters of his program. Thus, in the annual publication of his radio sermons in book form, Maier often included excerpts from letters.[75] Such letters indicated the place of origin, but excluded names and initials of the letter writers. Excerpts were often limited to one to three sentences, though some were quoted at greater length. In his book of 1930 radio sermons, Maier included a dozen pages of quotations from letters.[76] By the late 1940s, he sometimes included over sixty or seventy pages of excerpts.[77] To demonstrate the global and ministerial breadth of listener responses and to aid the interested reader, Maier grouped letters in categories, such as "Brought to Christ by the Broadcast," "Blessed by Baptism," "Repentant, Renewed, Restored," "Protestant Clergy and Laity Acclaim Broadcast," "Roman Catholic Endorsement," "Broadcasting to the Armed Forces," "The Gospel Penetrates Prison Walls," "Sick and Shut-In," "Christ's Help for the Troubled," "Negro Listeners Appreciate Our Broadcast," "Tasmania," "Bolivia," and "France." Just as Sheen had celebrated non-Catholics tuning into the CH, Maier expressed sincere appreciation that Catholics and non-Lutheran Protestants found inspiration and solace in TLH.

As their ministries flourished via radio networks Sheen, Maier, and their loyal listeners adopted correspondence as a means to personalize mass-mediated pastoral relationships. These radio pastors offered access to the

---

[74]M. L. Heerboth, ed., "Answer Guide for Correspondence," found in "International Lutheran Laymen's League" Collection, box: "Lutheran Hour. Correspondence. Guide for Answers to Lutheran Hour Correspondence," CHI, St. Louis.

[75]Maier's sermons from TLH were published each year, in one or two volumes, by CPH, St. Louis.

[76]See Walter A. Maier, *The Lutheran Hour* (St. Louis: CPH, 1931), 311-23.

[77]See Walter A. Maier, *The Airwaves Proclaim Christ: Radio Messages of the First Part of the Fourteenth Lutheran Hour* (St. Louis: CPH, 1948), vii-lxix; Walter A. Maier, *One Thousand Radio Voices for Christ: Radio Messages for the First Part of the Fifteenth Lutheran Hour* (St. Louis: CPH, 1950), 375-453.

unique combination of intimacy and authority with anonymity. Said another way, the very public proclamation of religion enabled a very personalized privatization of religion for those who desired it. To be sure, other radio preachers generated and responded to significant correspondence of their own.[78] But the letter writing of Maier's and Sheen's listeners, and the manner in which this priest and this minister responded, broadened their "pastorates" in the most dramatic and often life-changing ways.

RETHINKING THE RELIGIOUS GREAT DEPRESSION

When describing a "National Preaching Mission of the Federal Council of Churches," launched in the midst of the Great Depression to "help sweep the country back to God," historian Martin Marty curtly summarizes, "The mission was a dud."[79] The rather depressing reality for America's religious leaders was that such an assessment applied to most religious enterprises of the Depression era. When the stock market crash of 1929 plunged the United States into a devastating economic downturn, the "American Religious Depression" was already well underway, according to historian Robert Handy's famous summary. Handy primarily focused on the broad decline of Protestant leadership and influence during the period from the mid-1920s to the mid-1930s, as a time when "the general disillusionment of the postwar decade" met "the great knife of depression" that "cut deep into church life." He pointed to "a serious decline in missionary enthusiasm and conviction," growing negativity toward religion in modern thought, disruptive "cultural cross-currents," and shifting theological commitments, in addition to economic burdens, as contributors to the religious depression. Handy had

---

[78]In the 1920s, radio preaching pioneer Paul Rader received thousands of letters a month, requiring dedicated secretarial support. See James L. Snyder, *Paul Rader: Portrait of an Evangelist (1879–1938)* (Ocala, FL: Fellowship Ministries, 2003), 151. In his memoirs, Harry Emerson Fosdick mentioned letters "from all sorts of places and from all imaginable human situations," generated by his *National Vespers* program on NBC. See Fosdick, *The Living of These Days: An Autobiography* (New York: Harper & Brothers, 1956), 223-25. Letters were a regular part of Charles E. Fuller's *Old-Fashioned Revival Hour* program. Each week, Fuller's wife read a sampling of their abundant radio-response correspondence, especially those letters that bore "witness to what the Lord has done." In the mid-1950s, Grace Fuller published a book of excerpts of letters received that she considered "the most interesting and edifying" of "testimonies." See Mrs. Charles E. Fuller, *Heavenly Sunshine: Letters to the "Old-Fashioned Revival Hour"* (Westwood, NJ: Fleming H. Revell, 1956).

[79]Martin E. Marty, *Modern American Religion, vol. 2, The Noise of Conflict: 1919-1941* (Chicago: University of Chicago Press, 1991), 253.

much less to say about Roman Catholics during the Depression, but noted that they did not have a hegemonic perch from which to fall like Protestants did, and that they were not immune to the negative economic and religious environment in which they lived.[80] Nonetheless, as Robert Moats Miller summarized, "Churches suffered along with the rest of the nation," as "memberships dropped, budgets were slashed, benevolent and missionary enterprises sent adrift, ministers fired, and chapels closed."[81]

America's "Religious Depression" occurred in defiance of the expectations of churchmen and students of the past. In his 1937 study of American religion in the Depression, Samuel Kincheloe explained, "Some religious leaders actually hailed the depression with rejoicing since they had the idea that previous depressions had 'driven men to God' and felt that the time was overdue for men again to be reminded of the need to let the spiritual dominate the materialistic order." Even in the latter half of the Depression, Kincheloe noted that church leaders still retained "an expectancy that men would be compelled to turn to religion."[82] In the words of Lutheran scholar Theodore Tappert, however, "this hope was soon blasted." He concludes that "no evidence" emerged of "a general deepening of spiritual life," and "the rate of the church's growth was retarded."[83] More recently, historian Jon Butler noted that while "economic depression might be thought a very natural support to religion," the "deep personal suffering experienced in the Great Depression challenged American optimism individually and collectively; organized religion everywhere discovered that economic catastrophe brooked little spiritual exceptionalism."[84]

Yet Maier and Sheen, two of the most popular "pastors of the air," whose network programs were anything but "duds," were in fact examples of remarkable "spiritual exceptionalism" during the Depression and the

[80]Robert T. Handy, "The American Religious Depression, 1925–1935," *Church History* 29, no. 1 (March 1960): 3-16.

[81]Robert Moats Miller, *American Protestantism and Social Issues, 1919–1939* (Chapel Hill: University of North Carolina Press, 1958), 63.

[82]Samuel C. Kincheloe, *Research Memorandum on Religion in the Depression* (1937; repr., Westport, CT: Greenwood, 1970), 1-2.

[83]Theodore G. Tappert, "Lutherans in the Great Economic Depression," *Lutheran Quarterly* 7 (May 1955): 145.

[84]Jon Butler, "Forum: American Religion in the Great Depression," *Church History* 80, no. 3 (September 2011): 575.

following decade. While their extensive listener bases do not invalidate Handy's general description of a religious depression, their national roles as sober, yet uplifting preachers and pastors complicate, and partially offset, the story of religious decline. What is more, the supposedly unmaterialized religious awakenings expected during these trying times may have occurred after all, albeit in an unexpected way, over an unexpected medium, to a greater extent than previously recognized. Providing pastoral care to radio audiences comparable in size to audiences for whom top network stars provided entertainment, in an era when radio listening was at its peak, would indeed represent an incidence of spiritual exceptionalism. In short, at a time when Americans were expected to turn to religion, many did—by turning the dials on their Philcos.

In his 1980 article "Fundamentalist Institutions and the Rise of Evangelical Protestantism," historian Joel Carpenter accepted the "prevailing opinion" of Handy and others that "Protestantism suffered a depression" in the 1930s, but he accepted it only so far as it applied to historically dominant, mainline denominations. He explained, "In singular contrast to the plight of major denominations, fundamentalists and other evangelicals prospered," during this period. Carpenter noted that such prosperity occurred, "as popular fundamentalist alienation toward old-line denominations reached new heights." Though efforts by fundamentalists and evangelicals to "cleanse the denominations of liberal trends had seemed to fail," they successfully withdrew from these previously undisputed bodies of American religious leadership to develop "their own institutional base from which to carry on their major purpose: the proclamation of the evangelical gospel." While Carpenter cites certain parts of this conservative thrust that were far from hidden, including religious broadcasting, these efforts were generally decentralized, and often separatist by design.[85]

Carpenter complicates a straightforward, broadly accurate narrative of religious declension during the Depression era, previously put forth by Handy and others. Interestingly, the successful radio ministries of Sheen and Maier complicate Carpenter's own depiction, even as they confirm significant portions of it. Sheen and Maier enjoyed great popularity preaching

---

[85]Joel A. Carpenter, "Fundamentalist Institutions and the Rise of Evangelical Protestantism, 1929–1942," *Church History* 49 (January 1, 1980): 62-75.

traditional orthodox Christian messages about such topics as the virgin birth, blood atonement, the wages of sin, repentance, forgiveness, and divine miracles. This content and the urgency with which it was spoken sounded quite similar to that of the fundamentalists and evangelicals Carpenter presents as flourishing during this period. What is more, the medium mastered by Maier and Sheen also aligned with the general evangelical upswing. "More than any other medium," Carpenter observed, "radio kept revivalistic religion before the American public."[86] In their own distinct ways, Maier and Sheen called for revival on the radio. They did so via Christian programs that spanned the country and much of the world.

Yet unlike the fundamentalist and evangelical activities described by Carpenter, Sheen's and Maier's ministries did not arise in response to theological shifts within their denominations. While their sermons were crafted to avoid sectarian narrowness, they were not in conflict with the doctrinal positions of their respective ecclesiastical bodies—"old-line" bodies whose roots went back centuries in Europe. What is more, the CH and TLH were successful evangelistic enterprises that enjoyed a level of autonomy, but were anything but independent from their denominations. They purposefully operated under the general auspices of their church bodies, and more directly under organizations (i.e., the NCCM and the LLL) sanctioned by these bodies. Even the programs themselves identified with their denominations by including *Catholic* and *Lutheran* in their names.

Furthermore, though Maier and Sheen often sounded similar to their fundamentalist contemporaries, they hailed from denominations not typically considered fundamentalist, at least not by the common terminology of the first half of the American twentieth century. Lutherans and Catholics were often wary of American revivalism as practiced by fundamentalists and evangelicals. Lutherans and Catholics held to a high level of "confessionalism" associated with subscription to historical Christian creeds. Lutherans and Catholics rejected the dispensationalist eschatology that had become a driving force within American fundamentalism. And Lutherans and Catholics placed greater emphasis on sacraments of the church as a means by which God extended grace, than did most of their fundamentalist

---

[86]Carpenter, "Fundamentalist Institutions," 72.

and evangelical counterparts. In sum, Sheen and Maier actively contributed to the conservative, evangelistic upsurge described by Carpenter, though they did so without engaging in separatist enterprises, and while continuing to reside within centuries-old denominational bodies not known for evangelistic innovation.

Maier and Sheen served in an important pastoral capacity for millions of radio listeners. They were learned academics who spoke of the things of God with gravitas, yet they generated huge popular followings. While historians may be right in spotting a decline in American religiosity during this period, Sheen and Maier were able to at least partially offset this trend via their network pulpits. The messages of these two radio preachers were traditional and orthodox, but were in a new form, via a new medium. Americans turned to them as trusted pastors at a time when they were looking for answers. As historian Andrew Finstuen explains, "The Great Depression, World War II, and the cold war provided the context for the renewed relevance of sin and evil in America."[87] In his book *Original Sin and Everyday Protestants*, Finstuen proceeds to demonstrate the proclivity of average Americans to engage with leaders bearing pastoral and theological authority on substantive societal and theological topics in the mid-twentieth century and the decades preceding. Maier and Sheen possessed this type of authority through education and ecclesiastical office, which was only enhanced by the credibility and accessibility provided by radio.

SHEEN TO CATHOLICS; MAIER TO LUTHERANS

Another major outcome deserves emphasis, which both resulted from and augmented the triumphs of Sheen and Maier. That is the validation their success brought to the Roman Catholic Church in America and the Lutheran Church, especially its Missouri Synod branch. In the case of the Catholic Church, Sheen overcame generations of anti-Catholic sentiment to make Catholicism less theologically and ethnically foreign, and proclaimed

---

[87]Andrew S. Finstuen, *Original Sin and Everyday Protestants: The Theology of Reinhold Niebuhr, Billy Graham, and Paul Tillich in the Age of Anxiety* (Chapel Hill: University of North Carolina Press, 2009), 2.

it as fully congruous with American ideals. Sociologist of religion Will Herberg noted that during this period "American Catholicism" had "successfully negotiated the transition from a foreign church to an American religious community," and was "now part of the American Way of Life." He explained, "The new status of the Catholic Church . . . is reflected in the fact that today it speaks to, and is heard by, the entire nation, and not merely as its own community, as was frequently the case in the past." What evidence of this does Herberg provide? "Fulton Sheen, though appareled in a bishop's cassock, is followed by a vast radio audience consisting of many non-Catholics as well as Catholics."[88]

Figure 8.2. Distinctly attired in his clerical garb, Fulton Sheen addresses an extended audience via multiple microphones in the 1930s

Equally important, Catholics themselves felt validated by Sheen's popularity on the radio and later on television. They effectively took ownership in his success. Just as actor Ramon Estevez took the name Martin Sheen out of admiration for the priest after the latter had become a television star and a bishop, many Catholics wanted to be associated with his name in his radio days.[89] Historian James O'Toole credits Sheen's success "in the realm of popular culture" with firmly placing Catholics in the "American mainstream."[90] It was *their* priest who was so popular on the radio week after week, across the nation. It was *their* priest featured in *Look* magazine with his celebrity converts. It was *their* priest who

[88]Will Herberg, *Protestant, Catholic, Jew: An Essay in American Religious Sociology* (Chicago: University of Chicago Press, 1960), 160-61.

[89]Early in his acting career, Estevez asked Fulton Sheen for permission to adopt his last name, which Bishop Sheen granted. See Sheen, *Treasure in Clay*, 69.

[90]James M. O'Toole, *The Faithful: A History of Catholics in America* (Cambridge, MA: Belknap Press, 2008), 196.

authored a seemingly endless stream of popular books on the Christian life. It was *their* priest who leveraged his network radio success into an Emmy-winning television show. It was *their* priest who would become universally recognized, from the top of his violet zucchetto to the bottom of his flowing ferraiolo. And his twenty years of *Catholic Hour* prominence was key to it all.

While it is impossible to know the exact split of Sheen's listeners between Catholics and non-Catholics, one-third of Sheen's mail was from non-Catholics, the vast majority of which was positive.[91] Sheen's eloquent sermons demonstrated that the doctrinal divide between Catholics and Protestants was not quite as gaping as previously assumed. This not only broke down barriers with non-Catholic listeners, but aided local Catholics in their relationships with their neighbors. On the tenth anniversary of the CH's first broadcast, *Catholic Action* took special note of what audience mail revealed about the program: "By telling simply and clearly what Catholics are, what they believe and how they worship, it has shown them to many of their non-Catholic neighbors in a new light, dispelled misconceptions of Catholic teaching and practice, and increased good will among citizens of the nation."[92] This was especially powerful for Catholics in communities that had modest Catholic populations, as in many southern locales. A 1942 letter from a Catholic in Mississippi captures the impact of the CH and its speakers, of which Sheen was the star:

> The logic of Catholic Hour speakers, the program's broad Christian spirit, its promotion of a common front against spiritual indifference have broken through the long standing wall of prejudice against our faith. More and more my neighbors, who know little of our beliefs, are now eagerly listening to the Catholic Hour. Just recently the head of _____ College, himself a Protestant minister, said he had listened regularly to the Catholic Hour for five years. The cashier of our bank told me what an inspiration it was to him to listen to the broad and tolerant views of our Catholic leaders heard in the Catholic Hour. . . . I could give you a great many more instances of reaching people who never were in a Catholic Church, some of whom actually believed we Catholics did not believe in God. . . . What I know is this, that you have made

---

[91]Fulton J. Sheen, *Treasure in Clay: The Autobiography of Fulton J. Sheen* (New York: Doubleday, 2008), 75, 381.

[92]"Significance of Audience Mail," *Catholic Action*, March 1940, 23.

it much easier for us Catholics living in towns where only a small number of people are Catholic.[93]

Sheen built community both within American Catholicism and between Catholic and non-Catholic Americans. Even though Catholics represented the largest single group of Christians in the United States when Sheen first took to the airwaves, Catholics themselves often felt isolated even in the midst of their own church body. Within individual towns and city neighborhoods, Catholics were often divided by national heritage or ethnicity. The spoken word during masses may have been in Latin, but the conversations between Catholics in pews exhibited no such universality. The inhabitants of the next Catholic parish over, be they Polish, or Irish, or Italian, or German, could feel nearly as "other" as the Baptists down the street, if you did not share their national or provincial heritage. As Herberg observed, the "story" of "Catholicism in America" was "that of a foreign church, or rather a conglomerate of foreign churches."[94] Sheen helped Catholics recognize and celebrate their common membership in the Church of Rome on American soil, and thereby amalgamated, at least to a significant extent, the disjoint components of the "conglomerate." His ministry of the air was more effective in accomplishing this than that of many a frustrated bishop who had tried to do so on the ground. In his examination of Catholicism in popular culture during the Depression and World War II, Anthony Burke Smith summarizes Sheen's role within the lives of fellow Catholics:

> His participation on the *Catholic Hour* represented an important project of cultural formation, crafting an imagined community of American Catholicism in the thirties and forties out of religious devotionalism and moral theology. . . . Sheen's rise to popularity on the *Catholic Hour* indicates that new medium of radio . . . helped Catholics imagine themselves as part of a transethnic Catholic community in America.[95]

---

[93]Quoted in "From Our Mail Bag," *Catholic Action*, March 1942, 23. Note that the editors of *Catholic Action*, in what appears to have been an act of reciprocal graciousness, omitted the name of the college at which the Protestant minister served as leader—presumably to shield him from the criticism of fellow Protestants that may not have been as appreciative of *Catholic Hour* broadcasts.

[94]Herberg, *Protestant, Catholic, Jew*, 136.

[95]Anthony Burke Smith, *The Look of Catholics: Portrayals in Popular Culture from the Great Depression to the Cold War* (Lawrence: University Press of Kansas, 2010), 129.

As for community making beyond those who went to mass on Sundays, Sheen contributed much. The theology he espoused did not seem as heretical as what Protestant listeners would have assumed. As a matter of fact, it often sounded a lot like what they heard from their own ministers. What is more, notwithstanding the doctrinal sturdiness of Sheen's sermons, there was an inviting warmth and logic to what he said. His radio messages made it easier for non-Catholics to conclude that if those Catholics with whom they worked or saw at the grocery store believed the things that Monsignor Sheen did, perhaps they were not so peculiar after all. Additionally, the patriotic tone of many of Sheen's messages enhanced the image of Catholics as worthy fellow citizens. Jesuit church historian Mark Massa summarizes this best: "Sheen made Catholicism look both friendly and American—a religion of people worried about their crabgrass, like their Methodist neighbors."[96]

Sheen's impact within American Catholicism was amplified by his ability to attract attention. In addition to his exposure over a national radio network, Sheen was a tireless preacher, lecturer, and public speaker. While maintaining faculty status at Catholic University of America (CUA) until 1951, he annually participated in over 150 speaking engagements. These

Figure 8.3. A father and daughter stop in front of a Loyola University Forum poster announcing Sheen's upcoming speaking engagement in the 1940s

included a recurring series of Lenten sermons at the highly visible pulpit of St. Patrick's Cathedral in New York, countless lectures and speeches at schools,

---

[96]Mark S. Massa, *Catholics and American Culture: Fulton Sheen, Dorothy Day, and the Notre Dame Football Team* (New York: Crossroad, 1999), 101.

Figure 8.4. Sheen speaks before a packed house during one of his many public speaking engagements across the country during the 1930s

colleges, societies, and parishes, and public addresses at large Catholic gatherings where he rallied crowds of up to forty thousand to live out their faith and support Catholic causes. Both the Catholic and secular press enthusiastically reported on his peripatetic oratorical exploits.[97]

Perhaps without knowing it, Sheen was fulfilling the aspirations that had been expressed for CUA, his faculty home, by John Hennessy, bishop of Dubuque, as the university was taking shape in the late 1880s. The Iowa prelate had written, "I feel a deep interest in the success of the grand undertaking which will, I hope, be the means of advancing the interests of religion in this country even beyond our most sanguine expectations."[98] All of this only added to Sheen's fame and favor with the public, especially among Catholics, further augmenting his influence. The frequency with which he was away from Catholic University, however, created tension with certain of his academic colleagues. Some expressed displeasure that his consistent absences prevented him from fully serving as a "teacher and trainer of men."[99] Admittedly, there was likely legitimacy to these complaints. Nonetheless, given the favorable publicity Sheen's activities away from the classroom

---

[97]Massa, *Catholics and American Culture*, 89; Smith, *Look of Catholics*, 134-36. A review of press clippings in the Sheen Archives, diocese of Rochester, reveals remarkably extensive coverage of Sheen's addresses. Editors quoted Sheen's addresses and sermons at length and often printed full interviews and biographical information.

[98]John Tracy Ellis, *The Formative Years of the Catholic University of America* (Washington: American Catholic Historical Association, 1946), 281.

[99]Riley, *Fulton J. Sheen*, 14-16.

generated for the university, and the positive light they cast on the Catholic faith, envy over the popular professor's celebrity may well have played a role in such criticism as well.

As for the Lutherans, Maier triumphed over the relative obscurity associated with their non-Anglo ancestry and doctrinal sectarianism, and brought them toward the mainstream. This was no mean feat, as the Lutheran situation was markedly more complex than meets the eye. While American Lutheran families hailed from multiple locales in Europe including Scandinavian countries, most traced roots to Germany. Maier's denomination, the Lutheran Church–Missouri Synod (LCMS), was distinctly German in heritage, as indicated by its original name, Deutsche Evangelische-Lutherische Synode von Missouri, Ohio, und anderen Staaten (the German Evangelical Lutheran Synod of Missouri, Ohio, and other States).[100] Maintaining the German language in worship, education, and theological literature was a core element of LCMS identity even in the early part of the twentieth century.

World War I placed many Lutherans under suspicion and even disdain as anti-German hysteria swept America. Outsiders assumed that German-speaking Lutherans were sympathizers of the Kaiser. Some congregations experienced mob violence and others endured various forms of discrimination.[101] Yet even as LCMS members proved themselves loyal to the American war effort, they struggled with how tightly to hold onto their historical German identity. Historian Frederick Luebke observes, "In few German-American churches was the identification with the German government so weak and the retention of German language and culture so strong as in the Lutheran Church–Missouri Synod, the largest and most conservative of

---

[100]"German" was not dropped from the denomination's name until 1917, in the midst of World War I, when representatives from across the synod voted in convention to change the name. (Congregations ratified the change the following year.) The name was officially changed to the less cumbersome the Lutheran Church–Missouri Synod during the body's 100th anniversary in 1947. See Mary Todd, *Authority Vested: A Story of Identity and Change in the Lutheran Church–Missouri Synod* (Grand Rapids, MI: Eerdmans, 2000), 105, 259.

[101]Various laws against the German language were enacted in twenty-six states, which would not be declared unconstitutional until 1926. See Don Heinrich Tolzmann, "The Role of the German Language in the Missouri Synod: A 75th Anniversary Perspective," *Concordia Historical Institute Quarterly* 82, no. 2 (Summer 2010): 119-20.

German Lutheran organizations in the United States." From the beginning of hostilities, LCMS commentators were conspicuously neutral on the war in synodical publications. As would be the case with Maier when World War II raged, LCMS spokesmen were not timid about pointing out the particular sins of each of the belligerent nations in World War I.[102]

The experiences surrounding World War I, a genuine desire for broader evangelistic impact on American religious life, and the natural drift of its members toward the language in which they functioned when not at church, moved the LCMS toward broader employment of English in their ecclesiastical activities. Nonetheless, the change was gradual. It is noteworthy that when the LCMS celebrated the seventy-fifth anniversary of existence in 1922, the synod's press, Concordia Publishing House (CPH), produced a commemorative book of essays in German, but not English.[103] Interestingly, of the seventy-eight titles published by CPH in the 1920–1922 period, 76 percent were in English.[104] In looking back on this period, Lutheran historian Alan Graebner comments, "Not a few Missouri Synod Lutherans (both pastors and laymen) were yet unsure whether it was their Synod's . . . duty to care for Americans of non-German background."[105] Maier held no such reservations. Beginning in the 1920s, especially through his writing in the *Walther League Messenger*, he urged Missouri Synod Lutherans to more fully integrate: "Let's Discover America!" so that America could "discover Missouri." He boldly told them to abandon their "inferiority complex," their "German complex," and "work for the upbuilding and strengthening of the two greatest institutions in the world, the American Government and the Lutheran Church."[106]

---

[102]Frederick C. Luebke, *Bonds of Loyalty: German Americans and World War I* (DeKalb: Northern Illinois University Press, 1974), 102.

[103]Tolzmann, "Role of the German Language," 119-20. This linguistic foot-dragging is captured by a story about an old Lutheran who was asked whether God could understand English. After thinking for a minute, the old man replied, "Ja, God understands English, but He doesn't like it." See Mark Granquist, *Lutherans in America: A New History* (Minneapolis: Fortress, 2015), 239.

[104]Alan Niehaus Graebner, "The Acculturation of an Immigration Lutheran Church: The Lutheran Church—Missouri Synod, 1917–1929" (PhD diss., Columbia University, 1965), 148.

[105]Alan Graebner, "KFUO's Beginnings," *Concordia Historical Institute Quarterly* 37, no. 3 (October 1964): 90.

[106]Dean Way Kohlhoff, "Missouri Synod Lutherans and the Image of Germany, 1914–1945" (PhD diss., University of Chicago, 1973), 167-70.

The decades from the turn of the century to Maier's commencement of network broadcasts were indeed transitional for the LCMS, especially regarding language usage. During this period, Missouri Synod Lutherans occupied the periphery of American Christianity—both in their own eyes and in the eyes of outsiders. LCMS congregations holding *one or more* worship services in English per month stood at only 4 percent in 1900. World War I played a significant role in prompting more parishes to add English services, as this percentage, which had climbed to only 15 percent by 1916, reached 76 percent by 1919.[107] Yet 1925 was the first full year in which *total* worship services conducted in English exceeded those conducted in German within the denomination.[108] In 1929, the year before Maier began TLH, 67 percent of LCMS schools provided religious instruction in English only, but 29 percent still taught in both English and German.[109] In 1930, subscribers to the LCMS's German language periodical, *Der Lutheraner*, outnumbered subscribers to its English language magazine, *Lutheran Witness*, 31,000 to 28,000.[110]

Finally, it should be noted that LCMS pastors were steeped in German, especially as they thought about and expressed their faith, through their training at synodical seminaries. At Concordia Seminary in St. Louis, where Maier was trained for pastoral ministry and had become one of its professors in 1922, lectures were in German or Latin in the early 1900s, except for those by the sole faculty member designated the "English" professor. A shift to more courses in English occurred during the 1920s, but it was not until shortly after 1930 that Concordia offered more courses in English than in German.[111] The denomination's other seminary, Concordia Theological Seminary in Springfield, Illinois, held out until 1930 before offering its first course in English, and slowly deemphasized German over the following decade.[112]

---

[107]Graebner, "Acculturation of an Immigration," 149.

[108]Graebner, "Acculturation of an Immigration," 151.

[109]Graebner, "Acculturation of an Immigration," 116.

[110]Graebner, "Acculturation of an Immigration," 145.

[111]Carl S. Meyer, *Log Cabin to Luther Tower: Concordia Seminary During One Hundred and Twenty-Five Years. Toward a More Excellent Ministry, 1839-1964* (St. Louis: CPH, 1965), 138-43.

[112]Erich H. Heintzen, *Prairie School of the Prophets: The Anatomy of a Seminary, 1846–1976* (St. Louis: CPH, 1989), 128-30. In 1976, the LCMS relocated Concordia Theological Seminary from Springfield to Fort Wayne, Indiana, where it still provides pastoral training and theological education.

As if language and cultural barriers were not isolating enough, Missouri Synod Lutherans tended to their theological fences in such a way as to confine themselves to a rather sectarian existence. The LCMS considered itself to be the embodiment and protector of "confessional Lutheranism" in North America. Absolute subscription to the sixteenth-century Lutheran Confessions, as contained in the *Book of Concord*, was at the core of their Christian commitment.[113] Such Lutherans were careful to argue that the confessions were not above or equal to Scripture, but that they were a pure and accurate exposition of God's Word. Because of their confessionalism, Missouri Synod Lutherans resisted joint worship and formal ecclesiastical fellowship with Christians who did not share completely such beliefs. LCMS members may well have been willing to acknowledge non-Lutherans as fellow Christians, but they considered coming together around "altar and pulpit" with Christians who were not in complete doctrinal agreement to be the dilutive practice of "unionism."

Concerns about unionism were not based on a desire to keep others out, but were focused on assuring the unadulterated survival of distinctly Lutheran theology within the church—theology its adherents were convinced was divinely mandated. The term *unionism* originated in nineteenth-century Germany, as a disapproving description of Frederick William III's attempt to meld Lutheran and Reformed Christians into a single evangelical church. This so-called Prussian Union was announced in 1817, followed by various forms of political persuasion and coercion to achieve its objective in the decades that followed. Confessional Lutherans considered a forced ecclesiastical union between two parties that did not share complete doctrinal harmony to be a dangerous compromise of the very faith they held as the foundation of their church in the first place. A key factor in the decision to immigrate to the United States in the 1840s by many of the Saxons who would eventually form the LCMS was the fear that the German government would step up pressure to accept the Union and erode historical Lutheranism.[114]

---

[113]The Lutheran confessions contained in the *Book of Concord* are the three Ecumenical Creeds of the early church (i.e., Apostles,' Nicene, Athanasian), the Augsburg Confession, the Apology of the Augsburg Confession, Luther's Small and Large Catechisms, the Smalcald Articles, the Treatise on the Power and Primacy of the Pope, and the Formula of Concord.

[114]Walter A. Baepler, *A Century of Grace: A History of the Missouri Synod, 1847–1947* (St. Louis: CPH, 1947), 10-13.

Thus, from its founding the LCMS was highly sensitive about doctrinal differences within Christianity and treated opportunities to actively engage with other churches, at both denominational and local levels, with considerable wariness.

So while American Lutherans proudly traced their roots to Martin Luther, the Reformation, and the igniting of the broader Protestant movement, they found themselves on the outskirts of a Protestant-dominated America in the early decades of the 1900s. This was due to German culture and language within their churches, and unwavering devotion to the Lutheran Confessions, particularly within the LCMS. Both factors contributed to a sectarian existence, even if that was not the intent. Other American Christians did not know quite what to make of their Lutheran brethren. Walter Maier and TLH changed that in no small way. By being the first conservative Protestant preacher to gain regular access to network audiences, Maier was able to attract and retain moderate and conservative Christian listeners, as well as spiritual seekers. His "no-holds-barred" presentation of Scripture, combined with his eloquence and intelligence, gained respect for himself and for Lutheranism. As Sheen had done for Catholics, Maier established substantial common ground with the broader Christian community. Huge amounts of mail attested to listenership from nearly every type of church affiliation, as well as no affiliation. In the 1940 publication of his sermons, Maier noted that "contrary to the opinion of many, the greater part of the correspondence does not come from those affiliated with my Church." As evidence, he noted that an "investigation of some thirteen hundred letters received during a certain period at Station WCAE, Pittsburgh, revealed that only fifty-five were written by members of my communion."[115] Also like Sheen, Maier exhorted his listeners to sincere patriotism. Whereas Sheen helped quell common concerns about Catholic loyalty to the Vatican, Maier further dispelled suspicions that Lutherans were beholden to a bellicose *Deutschland*.

It is interesting to note that the establishment of credibility beyond Lutheran circles opened the path for Maier to expand internationally, via unexpected channels. When fundamentalist Clarence Jones, former assistant to Chicago radio evangelist Paul Rader, returned from his Protestant

---

[115]Maier, *Peace Through Christ*, viii.

missionary radio venture in Ecuador in 1939, he heard Maier on the radio. Notwithstanding Maier's Lutheran affiliation, Jones decided that his sermons

were sufficiently biblical and appropriately "undenominational." He offered airtime on HCJB in Quito, "The Voice of the Andes," which reached most of Latin America.[116] Maier accepted and TLH commenced an expeditious global expansion. By 1947, Maier's broadcasts were reaching seventy-one countries, while his LCMS denomination had missionaries in only eighteen of those countries.[117] By the time of Maier's death, TLH was heard in 120 countries, in thirty-six languages.[118]

Not unlike Catholics and Sheen, Lutherans acquired a sense of validation through Walter Maier's popularity and the "Lutheran" name on his program—a sense they acquired from the beginning of TLH broadcasts. Graebner recalls, "To be part of

Figure 8.5. Maier addresses an assembly of 10,000 on Lutheran Day at the New York World's Fair, August 3, 1940

a denomination with a national network broadcast was heady stuff for a laity only a dozen years from the calumny of World War I." In 1931, the *Lutheran Laymen's League Bulletin* trumpeted, "The *Lutheran Hour* has 'registered' OUR Church with the American public." "It cannot be denied," several LCMS pastors noted, "that our members suffer from an 'inferiority complex,' as they consider the standing of our Church with that of sectarian churches that were more in the public eye." Now, these Lutherans were "taking pride in the fact that they belong to a church which was carrying on its work in such a manner."[119] Maier led Lutherans, especially of the LCMS variety, out

[116]Paul L. Maier, *A Man Spoke*, 177-78. For a more complete history of HCJB and Clarence Jones, see Timothy H. B. Stoneman, "Preparing the Soil for Global Revival: Station HCJB's Radio Circle, 1949-59," *Church History* 76, no. 1 (March 2007), 114-55.

[117]Walter A. Maier, *Let Us Return unto the Lord* (St. Louis: CPH, 1947), vii.

[118]Maier, *A Man Spoke*, 393-94.

[119]Alan Graebner, *Uncertain Saints: The Laity in the Lutheran Church–Missouri Synod, 1900–1970* (Westport, CT: Greenwood, 1975), 132.

of their ethnic and ecclesiastical enclaves. He affirmed the appropriateness of using English to preach the gospel from Lutheran pulpits. And he deepened a sense of belonging for Lutherans that invited their entry into the broader Christian and civic communities. In a 2008 presentation to the American Academy of Religion, Maier's son Paul recalled that an oft-repeated refrain had been "[Walter Maier] put the Lutheran Church on the American map."[120]

To stoke Lutheran pride and broader support for TLH, Lutheran Hour Rallies were held in major and mid-sized US and Canadian cities. Never leaving these important events to chance, Maier and TLH staff produced a meticulous set of guidelines for local religious leaders to use as they considered, planned, and hosted rallies.[121] Maier's energetic, missionary-minded preaching was the marquee attraction, first with a live TLH broadcast from the rally, and later in a more free-flowing address to the attendees. Rallies were well-publicized in advance, drawing crowds as large as 27,500 souls, many of whom had the opportunity to participate in the program as members of mass youth or adult choruses. Civic leaders and celebrities often added to the pageantry. These events generated enthusiasm, strong financial support, and considerable positive media coverage.[122] Maier and other prominent speakers stressed the blessings already produced by TLH, and how supporters could share in that success. After Maier led a 1948 rally at the Hollywood Bowl, the *Los Angeles Times* reported that local ministers celebrated that "for the first time . . . all branches of Lutheranism in this area gathered in one place to hear Dr. Maier, in whose sermons they could all find union."[123] In crowds composed of Christians, many of whom belonged

---

[120]Paper by Paul L. Maier, "Walter A. Maier (1893–1950)," as part of a session titled "Fathers and Sons: The Influence of Evangelists Walter A. Maier, Percy Crawford, Merv Russell, Jack Wyrtzen, and Charles Woodbridge on Fundamentalism in the 1930s, 1940s, and 1950s," Annual Meeting of American Academy of Religion, Chicago, Illinois, November 3, 2008. (Copy of paper provided by Paul L. Maier.)

[121]See "Lutheran Hour Rally Guidelines" (undated), WAM Collection, CHI, St. Louis, MO, box 6, file 54. This document includes objectives, doctrinal statements, event financing, promotional plans, music guidelines, decorating recommendations, programming rules, preferable times of day for rallies, handout materials, techniques for maximizing "the Rally Collection," and organizational checklists.

[122]For example, *Time* magazine referred to the October 1943 Lutheran Hour Rally, which was held in Chicago, as "the biggest religious event of the year." The *Chicago Tribune* covered the event on its front page. See Pankow and Pankow, *Best Is Yet to Come*, 62.

[123]"Maier, Lutheran Radio Hour Preacher, Passes," *Los Angeles Times*, January 12, 1950, 20.

Figure 8.6. A large crowd gathered to hear Maier speak at a Lutheran Hour Rally in Portland, Oregon, 1946

to the LCMS—a denomination not known for flashiness—the highly visible rallies yielded considerable goodwill.[124]

Yet despite this goodwill and the overall effectiveness of Maier's contributions to Lutheranism, he was not without detractors within his church body. While he enjoyed broad support from clergy and laity, Maier encountered criticism from a modest number of vocal "ultra-orthodox" observers, from various locales.[125] Critics usually framed their opposition around theological concerns, especially Maier's use of synergistic sermon language when

---

[124]Maier, *A Man Spoke*, 232-35, 329-30. While many Lutherans attended Lutheran Hour Rallies, Maier found it particularly gratifying when non-Lutherans participated in these events, especially in communities with small Lutheran populations. See Walter A. Maier, "Foreword," in "Lutheran Hour Rally Guidelines" (undated), WAM Collection, CHI, St. Louis, MO, box 6, file 54. TLH was not the only gospel radio program to hold large, highly publicized rallies. Charles Fuller and Grace Fuller of the *Old-Fashioned Revival Hour* held rallies around the United States on par with Maier and TLH. See Joel A. Carpenter, *Revive Us Again: The Reawakening of American Fundamentalism* (New York: Oxford University Press, 1997), 140.

[125]Maier, *A Man Spoke*, 259-60.

inviting listeners to "choose Christ," and his supposed engagement in unionism when interacting with non-Lutheran groups.

At the denominational level, confessional watchdogs made note whenever Maier spoke at pan-Christian events, especially if anything resembling joint worship or prayer occurred. Those who detected unionism in Maier's participation at such events lodged complaints with the president of the LCMS, either directly or through other, regional synodical leaders. Maier and LCMS President John Behnken enjoyed a cordial relationship, according to Maier's son, Paul.[126] What is more, Behnken was a supporter of TLH ministry, having been involved in religious broadcasting early in his career.[127] Nonetheless, correspondence between Maier and Behnken reveals that the harping from the antiunionism complainers did create tension in their relationship. Though Behnken genuinely cared about Lutheran orthodoxy, he also cared about Maier and his ministry. In letters between the two, Maier appears frustrated that Behnken does not fully appreciate the public, pan-Christian nature of his role, and Behnken appears exasperated that Maier is not more sensitive to the controversy this highly visible, nontraditional role causes for the head of his denomination.[128] The complexity of their relationship was displayed in one particularly difficult exchange on an allegation of unionism in 1945. Behnken wrote, "You know that I have always 'played ball' with you. I have tried to be very fair. I have defended you wherever I could. . . . However, I shall not continue to offer excuses when you resort to such practices."[129] Less than a month later, however, and with the matter still under discussion, Behnken sent a handwritten letter that closed with a seemingly heartfelt expression of concern for Maier's health, a suggestion that he get more rest, and a prayer for his strength.[130] Behnken chose not to take formal action against Maier. Five years later at Maier's

---

[126]Phone interview with Paul Maier by author, May 16, 2013.

[127]John W. Behnken, the president of the Lutheran Church–Missouri Synod 1935–1962, had embraced radio as an evangelistic tool early in his own career. As a young pastor in Houston during the mid-1920s, he frequently took to the airwaves to preach the gospel. See Alan Graebner, "KFUO's Beginnings," 82.

[128]See correspondence with John W. Behnken, WAM Collection, CHI, St. Louis, box 1, file 17.

[129]J. W. Behnken to Walter A. Maier, dated April 26, 1945, WAM Collection, CHI, St. Louis, box 1, file 17.

[130]J. W. Behnken to Walter A. Maier, dated May 22, 1945, WAM Collection, CHI, St. Louis, box 1, file 17.

funeral, Behnken preached about the TLH speaker in laudatory tones: "We recognized in the departed a child of God . . . whom the Lord had graciously endowed with special gifts and talents." The LCMS president's voice quivered with emotion.[131]

Just as some fellow faculty members criticized Sheen at CUA, a few faculty members at Concordia Seminary found fault with their radio-preaching colleague. Maier maintained friendly, supportive relationships with most of his faculty colleagues, but some grumbled that his radio addresses and related activities were not distinctly Lutheran enough. They, too, objected to perceived synergistic invitational language and to supposed unionistic fellowship with non-Lutherans. Paul Maier recalls that Concordia Seminary President Ludwig Fuerbringer was appreciative of Maier's ministry, but his successor Louis Sieck was much less so.[132] Faculty member Theodore Graebner resisted publishing information about the LCMS's most visible outreach mechanism, TLH, in the denomination's lay magazine, *The Lutheran Witness*, of which he served as editor.[133] When a seminary student inquired during a class whether Maier's request for "prayers and continued support" from his radio listeners equated to unionism, Professor Theodore Engelder curtly answered, "I don't listen to the Lutheran Hour."[134]

In that Missouri Synod Lutherans always have been notorious for their doctrinal rigidity, it is likely that some genuine theological concerns existed with certain faculty colleagues.[135] Yet given the obvious success of TLH— success that accrued to the benefit of Lutheranism and traditional Christianity—jealousy may have also played a part in the disapproving glances

---

[131]I am grateful to Gerald Perschbacher for sharing an audio recording of the January 14, 1950 funeral service for Walter A. Maier, from the Lutheran Hour Archives, St. Louis. The words quoted above differ slightly from the published version of Dr. Behnken's funeral remarks, as found in "Christ, Your Matchless Advocate," network memorial address by John W. Behnken, in *The Dr. Walter A. Maier Memorial Booklet* (St. Louis: The Lutheran Laymen's League, 1950), 52-59.

[132]Paul L. Maier, interview with author, May 16, 2013.

[133]Paul L. Maier, email exchange with author, October 10, 2013.

[134]E. Theodore Bachmann, "Missouri and Its Relations to Other Lutherans: Some Observations on the Shaping and Exercise of Conscience," *Concordia Historical Institute Quarterly* 45, no. 2 (May, 1972): 162.

[135]Paul Maier continues to defend his father's Lutheran orthodoxy against his few detractors. For a succinct, yet forceful theological response to the charges of unionism and synergism, see Paul L. Maier, "Walter A. Maier (1893–1950): Sixty-Five Years into the Historical Record," *Concordia Journal* 41, no. 4 (Fall 2015): 329-34.

directed at Maier. Paul Maier commented, "My father worked under a continuous green glow"—from the eyes of certain colleagues, "green" with envy.[136] Fulton Sheen would have been able to relate.

Maier and Sheen: Broader Impact

In summarizing America's faith climate in the wake of World War II, historian Sydney Ahlstrom describes a "generalized kind of religiosity," in which a rather bland "faith in faith" provided "peace of mind and confident living . . . in the 'Age of Anxiety.'"[137] While this may have applied to much of the population, it does not describe the kind of religion espoused by Sheen and Maier, and sought by their millions of listeners. With radio ministries spanning the Great Depression, World War II, and the beginning of the Cold War, these popular clerics guided Americans through what could be referred to as a "continuum of anxiety." And they did so with a Christianity not designed to feed a bland sort of spiritual appetite. While Maier's and Sheen's impact on their respective denominations, and perceptions of their denominations, were significant, their impact within American Christianity and society more broadly was as remarkable. In a new era of mass communications, these professional academics became popular public figures that generated significant followings.

Celebrity and celebrities. From the early days of their ministries, both Sheen and Maier were often quoted and covered by the press, including the secular press. With weekly radio exposure, numerous other speaking and preaching engagements, and publishing for popular audiences, they achieved a level of celebrity of their own, and became comfortable in the company of celebrities. While neither was shy about being in the limelight, Sheen was the more visible within celebrity circles. This was in large part due to his New York and Washington presence and his natural ability (and inclination) to attract attention. Such attention would grow to even greater heights when Sheen moved to television in the 1950s, but radio propelled him onto the national stage. In 1936, then entertainment columnist Ed Sullivan wrote that Sheen was "the greatest orator I'd ever heard." Sullivan had

---

[136]Paul L. Maier, interview with author, March 23, 2013.
[137]Sydney E. Ahlstrom, *A Religious History of the American People*, 2nd ed. (New Haven, CT: Yale University Press, 2004), 955.

a few facts wrong in his blurb, however, and in his syndicated "Broadway" column a number of days later, he sought to clarify under the subheading, "To Rt. Rev. Fulton Sheen:"

> Dear Dr. Sheen: The other day, in listing my all-time preferences, I rated you as the greatest orator I'd ever heard. Since then, the mail has been burdened with letters pointing out that you are not a Jesuit, that your name is *spelled* S-h-e-e-n, and that you are a Professor of the Philosophy of Religion at Catholic University. But, at least, I had one fact straight . . . you ARE the greatest speaker I'd ever heard, and Jesuits should feel pleased that I assumed that only their order could produce one like you. Sincerely, ED. S.[138]

This piece is noteworthy for three reasons. First, the homiletic delivery gifts of a Catholic priest were not normally the subject of a Broadway columnist's musings, even on a slow day in show business. Second, misstated attributes of such a priest would not have been expected to prompt numerous readers of an entertainment column to send corrective letters to the writer. And third, after only six years on the CH, Sheen's name appeared in the same column as that of actor Bert Lahr, Broadway entertainer and radio personality Sophie Tucker, and opera singer Gladys Swarthout—and it did not appear out of place.[139] Yet while Sheen's popular presence may have been on par with entertainment celebrities, no attempt was made to reduce the substance of who he was or what he said to a form of entertainment. In 1941, Walter Winchell concluded his syndicated "On Broadway" column by recommending "Monsignor Fulton J. Sheen" to his readers. The gossip commentator suggested that they write Sheen for a free copy of his latest booklet, "especially if you're bigoted." He even provided Sheen's address.[140] Later in the decade, Ed Sullivan again lauded Sheen in his "Little Old New York" column, citing his sustained attacks on communism. Sullivan claimed that he was no longer invited to certain parties, because of his habit of taking reprinted, anticommunist radio sermons of Sheen and handing them out to "parlor-pinks of that era."[141]

---

[138]Ed Sullivan, "Broadway," *Washington Post*, January 10, 1936, 12. Sheen had saved this syndicated column. See Sheen Archives, Rochester, New York, "Press Clippings" files, 1936 folder.
[139]Sullivan, "Broadway," 12.
[140]Walter Winchell, "On Broadway," *Daily Mirror*, January 15, 1941.
[141]Ed Sullivan, "Little Old New York," *Daily News*, August 5, 1948.

Other high-profile persons paid attention to the Catholic broadcaster. In 1939, Hollywood couple Maureen O'Sullivan and John Farrow were so moved by a CH sermon that they sent a Sunday telegram to Sheen to "respectfully offer our congratulations on your masterly address this afternoon."[142] Later that year, President Franklin Roosevelt sent Sheen a letter thanking him for his "fine Christmas message," and extending his "heartiest greetings and good wishes for many blessings."[143] In 1940, Harry Emerson Fosdick's patron, John D. Rockefeller Jr., dropped Sheen a note thanking him for sending his book titled *Freedom Under God*. Rockefeller promised to read it "with much interest—first, because I was so moved by your sermon, 'The Two Tombs,' and, secondly, because I have since had the pleasure of meeting the author."[144] Nothing bolstered Sheen's celebrity stature more, however, than his gift for bringing about notable conversions to Catholicism through his ministry.

Stories of Sheen's convert making often appeared in the press. Already in 1934, in obituaries for prominent attorney and Herbert Hoover campaign manager Col. Horace Mann, major newspapers noted that Mann and his wife had been baptized into the Catholic faith after listening to Sheen's CH broadcasts. Mann's conversion had been seen as significant, given his leading role in coordinating attacks on the Catholic Democratic candidate Al Smith in southern states, during the 1928 presidential election.[145] Many more conversions occurred in the years to follow. By 1947, Sheen's conversion record was worthy of a feature article in *Look* magazine, "Why All These Converts?" The piece noted that the priest's quest for souls was not confined to the rich and famous, describing his proclivity to engage strangers on the street, "the obscure . . . of all races and incomes," and millions over the airwaves. But it highlighted his conversions of noted columnist Heywood Broun, violist Fritz Kreisler, corporate leader Henry Ford II, outspoken leader of the American Communist Party Louis Budenz, and Congresswoman Clare

---

[142]Telegram from Maurine [*sic*] O'Sullivan and John Farrow to Monsignor Fulton Sheen, dated January 29, 1939, Sheen Archives, Rochester, "Correspondence A–P" file, "O" folder.

[143]Letter from Franklin D. Roosevelt to Fulton J. Sheen, December 27, 1939, Sheen Archives, Rochester, "Correspondence Q–Z," "R" folder.

[144]Letter from John D. Rockefeller Jr. to Monsignor Fulton J. Sheen, May 16, 1940, Sheen Archives, Rochester, "Correspondence Q–Z" file, "R" folder.

[145]See "Col. Horace Mann Dead in Nashville," *New York Times*, March 16, 1934; "Mann, Hoover Aid in South, Is Dead at 65," *Washington Post*, March 15, 1934.

Boothe Luce. Yet Sheen made it clear that "priests do not convert." "The Grace of God converts," he explained, "it is sunlight, necessary if plants and souls are to grow." Priests "are merely the gardeners, hoeing the earth a bit and watering the roots. It is God who drops the seed."[146] Notwithstanding Sheen's expression of horticultural humility, *Look*, along with *Time*, *Newsweek*, and countless other publications, gave him the credit for bringing high-profile persons (and others) into the Catholic fold.[147]

Even Maier took note of Sheen's evangelization of the well-known. In his voluminous files, he kept a newspaper clipping about the CH speaker's conversion of communist Louis Budenz, having underlined several sentences, including one in which Budenz credits Sheen with helping him finally see that communism "aims to establish a tyranny over the human spirit." Maier also kept an article about Sheen's officiating at the wedding of Henry Ford II to Anne McDonnell in Southampton. He underlined the paragraph explaining that Ford had been baptized and received his first communion during the two days prior to his wedding, after Sheen had "tutored the young Ford in the Catholic faith."[148]

Sheen also maintained relationships with celebrity Catholics who were not converts. Most notably, Hollywood star Loretta Young became a close personal friend in 1940. After listening to Sheen and the CH, she and John Wayne's wife, Josephine, came to hear him preach at St. Patrick's Cathedral in New York on Good Friday. Once she met Sheen, Young thought of him as "a superstar." Young and Sheen visited each other many times over the coming years, in person and by phone, and Sheen served as confessor and adviser to her and fellow household name actress, Irene Dunne.[149] Sheen's

---

[146] Gretta Palmer, "Why All These Converts?," 36-40. Adding further irony, after his conversion Budenz became an economics professor at the University of Notre Dame, and later at Fordham University.

[147] For examples, see "Religion: Converter in Wax," *Time*, May 6, 1946; "How to Win a Convert," *Time*, July 12, 1948. "Sheen the Evangelist," *Newsweek*, September 25, 1950, 85.

[148] WAM Collection, Concordia Historical Institute, St. Louis, box 25, folder 13. In addition to noticing well-known Sheen converts, TLH personnel monitored CH-prompted "conversions" in general. During a 1937 LLL board of governors meeting, it was reported that a survey of pastors indicated that at least 134 people "were gained for the church" through TLH broadcasts, which they noted compared favorably to the fifty-one converts to Catholicism reported by the NCCM, for the same season. (See "Minutes of the L.L.L. Board of Governors' Meeting, held April 10, 1937," Lutheran Hour Archives, St. Louis.)

[149] Reeves, *America's Bishop*, 135-37.

relationships with other entertainers, politicians, and business leaders continued throughout his years on radio, and thereafter. The publicity generated by celebrity converts and society movers and shakers undoubtedly added not only to his own celebrity, but also to his appeal as a churchman and moralizer. After all, if the likes of Ed Sullivan, Henry Ford, and Clare Luce were persuaded to follow Sheen's spiritual counsel, the common listener could easily conclude that he or she ought to pay attention to what the CH preacher had to say.

The Midwestern-based Walter Maier did not actively pursue or maintain the same breadth of glamour-set relationships. Nonetheless, his radio presence, press following, preaching appearances, and well-attended Lutheran Hour Rallies provided him with celebrity recognition of his own. A 1948 *Saturday Evening Post* feature on Maier marveled that "a night club singer in Panama, a dance-band drummer in Ecuador, [and] a trumpet player in a Los Angeles honky-tonk" all had sent autographed photos to the Lutheran cleric, requesting that he return the favor.[150] Paul Maier recalls that he and his older brother "had fun growing up as WAM's sons," given the recognition, respect, and celebrity treatment the Maier family enjoyed, wherever they went.[151] Maier interacted with a number of political leaders on various occasions. Governor Henry F. Schricker of Indiana, a Lutheran and friend of Maier, appeared at Lutheran Hour Rallies. Vice President Alben Barkley and other national politicians sent personal greetings on the Maiers' silver wedding anniversary in 1949.[152] At the conclusion of World War II, US Army General Mark W. Clark wrote a letter to Eugene Bertermann, Maier's radio director, acknowledging "Divine Guidance for the accomplishment of our purpose" and "the victory granted us" as an answer to "prayerful petitions" of "thousands of Americans." Clark granted permission for his letter to be quoted on the air.[153] Admirals William Halsey and Chester Nimitz also wrote to express gratitude for the spiritual role of TLH during the war.[154]

---

[150]Spence, "Man of the Lutheran Hour," 89.

[151]Interview of Paul Maier by author, May 16, 2013.

[152]Maier, *A Man Spoke*, 234, 343-44.

[153]Letter from Mark W. Clark, General, USA, Commanding to Eugene R. Bertermann, dated May 17, 1945, WAM Collection, CHI, St. Louis, box 1, file 21.

[154]Maier, *A Man Spoke*, 228.

Maier also caught the attention of a few Hollywood players. During the 1938–1939 radio season, his staff was surprised to receive a letter from the president's office of Warner Brothers Pictures. Harry Warner had written, "Enclosed herewith please find my contribution to your most worthy program, and I wish you an abundance of success in appreciation of your good work."[155] The Jewish studio executive apparently found something appealing in what he heard from the Lutheran broadcaster. Several Hollywood performers wrote Maier and contributed to the broadcasts, including actress Adeline Reynolds (*Going My Way*) and dancer/actress Vera-Ellen. During a 1948 Lutheran Hour Rally at the Hollywood Bowl, popular character actress Agnes Moorehead made an appearance. She addressed the crowd of twenty thousand with a moving message about divine love, for "one world of one blood . . . one world, God's world," after which a "Parade of Nations" representing one hundred countries demonstrated TLH's global ministry.[156]

Figure 8.7. Print advertisement featuring Maier speaking at the Hollywood Bowl

---

[155]Maier, *A Man Spoke*, 176. Paul Maier states that the letter was signed "E. M. Warner." This appears to be a mistake or a typo.
[156]Maier, *A Man Spoke*, 330.

Moorehead was likely drawn to Maier for multiple reasons. First, his messages fit with the religion she had been brought up on, as the daughter of a fundamentalist Presbyterian clergyman. Second, her father was known as a spellbinding preacher, whom she described as a "great man with a magnificent voice," who "could quote great swatches from the Bible. . . . He was quite a showman." The Reverend Moorehead, whom Agnes revered, had died suddenly at his pulpit during a 1938 worship service.[157] Perhaps Maier reminded the actress of her father. Third, Moorehead, who had been named "Best Actress" by the New York Film Critics in 1942, had begun her acting career on radio, working with Orson Welles.[158] Of all people, she would have appreciated Maier's gifts for reaching a radio audience. And she wanted others to embrace the biblical messages he preached over the same airwaves she had used to entertain.

One well-known personality brought attention to Maier that was anything but welcome. In a 1949 edition of Eleanor Roosevelt's "My Day" syndicated column, the former first lady made a disparaging remark about Maier that stunned him and other readers. Roosevelt had read information that falsely connected Maier with ultrarightist, anticommunist groups associated with Lawrence P. Reilly and Gerald L. K. Smith, and misstated his views.[159] In her column, she lumped Maier in with Reilly, Smith, and their ilk, stating that Maier was "a somewhat fanatic fundamentalist who shortly before V-E Day was still insisting that the Germans were a bulwark against Communism!"[160] The day after the article appeared across the country, Maier fired off a letter to Hyde Park, which was released to the press, demanding that she "publicly . . . withdraw your derogatory statements," not only because the "vast Lutheran Hour radio audience, estimated at 20,000,000 people, made up of members of all denominations, will bitterly

---

[157]Charles Tranberg, *I Love the Illusion: The Life and Career of Agnes Moorehead* (Albany, GA: BearManor Media, 2007), 11-13, 54.

[158]Tranberg, *I Love the Illusion*, 46-86. Moorehead received the best actress award for her role in the film *The Magnificent Ambersons*.

[159]Lawrence Reilly was a former seminary student of Maier's who had formed the Lutheran Research Society to combat "enemies of religion." The Society had no actual affiliation with any Lutheran denomination or organization. Both Reilly and Gerald L. K. Smith quoted Maier on occasion, when it suited their purposes, much to Maier's chagrin. See Maier, *A Man Spoke*, 265-68.

[160]Eleanor Roosevelt, "My Day," *St. Louis Post-Dispatch*, September 9, 1949.

resent this branding epithet," but also because "the Bible has stern warnings against those who wreck reputations and seek to destroy good names." Maier stated that he was indeed "fundamental" in his "unswerving" loyalty to "the cross of our Lord Jesus Christ," but "emphatically" denied "being fanatic"—a term he considered dangerous and "border[ing] on libelous." He invited her to find his "wide and unsparing" denunciations of "Hitlerism" by reviewing his sermons, which were in print. Maier reminded Roosevelt that her late husband had "thought enough of me" to seek his counsel on a "Supreme Court issue." "I feel that you are serving destructive services by such scurrilous attacks," Maier scolded, but he softened his message by acknowledging that she likely acted "unwittingly."[161]

The importance that other Christian leaders placed on Maier's reputation and stature quickly became evident in the reaction to Roosevelt's column. James DeForest Murch, editor and manager of the *United Evangelical Action*, wrote TLH promising to counter the negative publicity by publishing a "strong editorial endorsement of Dr. Maier" in their next issue. He added, "The Lutheran Hour is rendering a magnificent contribution to the evangelical cause and we are with you one hundred per cent."[162] Fellow religious broadcaster H. M. S. Richards of *The Voice of Prophecy* wrote Maier "to encourage you in your work," in light of Roosevelt's labeling him a "fanatical fundamentalist." Richards, a Seventh-day Adventist, summarized, "If there is anyone in America to whom that name is not appropriate, it certainly would be your kind self."[163] Even fundamentalist Presbyterian Carl McIntire came to Maier's defense, writing a corrective letter to Roosevelt less than a week after the offending "My Day" was published.[164]

Eleanor Roosevelt published a retraction on December 10. She acknowledged that her previous comments on Maier had been based on what "appears to" have been "entirely erroneous information, or rather" she admitted

[161]Letter from Walter A. Maier to Eleanor Roosevelt, dated September 10, 1949, WAM Collection, CHI, box 11, file 17.

[162]Letter from James DeForest Murch to Eugene R. Bertermann, dated September 22, 1949, WAM Collection, CHI, box 11, file 15.

[163]Letter from H. M. S. Richards to Walter A. Maier, dated September 14, 1949, WAM Collection, CHI, box 11, file 15.

[164]Letter from Eugene R. Bertermann to Carl McIntire, dated September 21, 1949, WAM Collection, CHI, box 11, file 15. In this letter, Bertermann thanks McIntire for his letter of September 15, and for his "kindness in writing as you did to Mrs. Eleanor Roosevelt."

that she had perhaps "misread the information." She stated, "One of his friends who feels strongly that I have done him an injustice has asked me to state that I made this mistake, and I am more than glad to do so." Roosevelt concluded by mentioning Maier's Lutheran Hour program, and expressed concern that "any misunderstanding of his position might hurt his spiritual leadership." Maier immediately issued a statement of gratitude for the retraction, also thanking "the thousands of friends and newspapers throughout the country which wrote in protest . . . against Mrs. Roosevelt's patently unfounded charges." He closed in a tone of grace: "Now that the matter has been brought to this happy conclusion, I thank Mrs. Roosevelt for her courageous, straight-forward statement and wish her a joyous Christmas season in Christ."[165]

One final observation regarding Sheen's and Maier's broadly recognized fame must be made. Neither of these clerics was the first preacher to acquire celebrity status. (The eighteenth century's George Whitefield and the nineteenth century's Dwight Moody come to mind.) However, the national and global reach of their broadcasts provided them with a level of fan support previously inconceivable for religious leaders. While their stout theological commitments and reliable moral compasses allowed them to carry out their ministries with apparent integrity, they (along with their religious broadcasting peers) set the stage for future religious broadcasters to build their own celebrity status, not all of whom proved as scrupulous as Maier and Sheen.

---

[165]Telegram from Eugene R. Bertermann to Paul Gustafson, *Milwaukee Sentinel*, WAM Collection, CHI, box 11, file 15. Eleanor Roosevelt managed to offend the *Catholic Hour* in her "My Day" column as well, though less egregiously. In her October 10, 1944 column, she referred to "a new NBC radio series, known as Eternal Light, and sponsored by the Jewish Theological Seminary." Roosevelt commented that the program "is unique in that it is the first broadcast religious program which is not a religious service." In response, while making it clear that they "in no wise wish[ed] to belittle the program called Eternal Light," the NCCM pointed out that the CH had been on the air for fifteen years, and "is not a broadcast of a religious service." "It is the endeavor of the N.C.C.M. to produce . . . a program which avails itself of modern radio technique, rather than one that simply presents a religious service. . . . While the Catholic Hour should remain always a religious program—religious in content and atmosphere—it should nevertheless be presented as a radio program rather than a religious service." Apparently "religious service" was too parochial or pedestrian sounding for the NCCM. See "Some Notes on Catholic Radio Programs," *Catholic Action*, November 1944, 18.

God and country. Sheen and Maier vocally opposed general, doctrinally flimsy religiosity. Yet while their preaching persuasively presented specific orthodox Christian beliefs, it also contributed to the strengthening climate of civil religion in America during the 1930s and 1940s. In most instances, they avoided explicit political commentary, but called for patriotism and higher morality on personal and national levels. Their coast-to-coast radio ministries, under Catholic and Lutheran banners, also brought their de-nominations from America's periphery to its civic and Christian main-streams. In turn, this likely contributed to a greater sense of national religious cohesion during stressful times.

In a 1952 Fulton Sheen cover story issue, *Time* noted that "Bishop Sheen is a unique product of two unique historical forces—the Roman Catholic Church and the United States. . . . Into the making of Fulton Sheen went St. Paul and Thomas Jefferson."[166] In her biography on Sheen, Kathleen Riley cites his 1951 speech to the National Confraternity of Christian Doctrine titled "God and Country" as the "exemplary summary of Sheen's views on Catholicism and Americanism." In that address, Sheen responded to the anti-Catholic rhetoric of Paul Blanshard and others, which accused Catholics of insufficient patriotism and loyalty to the nation, and of desiring the blending of church and state. Sheen pointed to the Creator as the author of the American freedoms boldly stated in the Declaration of Independence. He called for a "Declaration of Dependence" whereby Americans would again acknowledge that "prosperity and peace were associated with obedience to God's laws." Yet Sheen unequivocally avowed that Catholics were good citizens who were loyal to and fully accepted the First Amendment, which guaranteed freedom of religion. He concluded by imploring that "no more lies" be told about American Catholics regarding these positions.[167]

As discussed in previous chapters, Maier delivered a headline-producing speech titled "The Jeffersonian Ideals of Religious Liberty," at the University of Virginia in 1930. Maier aligned Jefferson's thinking with the "two kingdoms" compartmentalized mindset of the Augsburg Confession's

---

[166]"Microphone Missionary," 72.

[167]Riley, *Fulton J. Sheen*, 208-14; See also Kathleen Riley Fields, "Bishop Fulton J. Sheen: An American Response to the Twentieth Century" (PhD diss., University of Notre Dame, 1988), 340-43.

signatories in 1530, and lauded the founding father for separating the spiritual superintendence of the church from the realm of politics.[168] Sheen may have been the embodiment of the apostle Paul and the third president, but Maier personified a melded Luther and Jefferson. In so doing, they demonstrated their belief in the compatibility of their denominations, genuine Christian faith, and American ideals.

These two clerics used their radio programs as the primary platforms from which to espouse their ecclesiastical and national commitments. They did so via other complementary avenues as well. One such remarkably similar endeavor was their presumably coincidental decisions to author and distribute pocket-sized prayer booklets during World War II—Maier's *Wartime Prayer Guide* and Sheen's *The Armor of God*.[169] Maier's sixty-plus-page booklet was a *Lutheran Hour* publication and was offered to TLH listeners. It was provided "not to take the place of your own intercessions . . . it is rather to serve as a guide for your petitions." Specific prayers were provided for those who were in service ("A Christian Soldier's Prayer Before Battle"), for those interceding for loved ones in military service ("A Prayer for a Sweetheart in the Armed Forces," "A Prayer for Air Men," "A Prayer for Those Missing in Action"), and for other needs in time of war ("For Wartime Traveling," "For Civil Authority," "For Deeper Trust in Wartime"). Understandably, Maier also included "A Prayer for Wartime Radio Mission," requesting divine assistance to "defeat any evil plan to restrict or remove our Gospel broadcast!"[170] Demands from home and abroad forced several printings of the booklet, with several hundred thousand copies eventually distributed.[171]

In the introduction to his *The Armor of God*, Sheen explained, "This prayer booklet is for soldiers, sailors, marines, coast guard, for all fighting

---

[168]Walter A. Maier, *The Jeffersonian Ideals of Religious Liberty: Address Delivered at the University of Virginia at Charlottesville, Va., August 9, 1930* (St. Louis: CPH, 1930).

[169]Walter A. Maier, *Wartime Prayer Guide* (St. Louis: The International Lutheran Hour, 1942); Fulton J. Sheen, *The Armor of God* (New York: J. Kenedy, 1943). An abridged version of Sheen's booklet is currently in print as Fulton J. Sheen, *Fulton Sheen's Wartime Prayer Book* (Manchester, NH: Sophia Institute Press, 2003). In addition to the popularity Sheen's wartime prayer book enjoyed in the 1940s, the Archbishop Fulton John Sheen Foundation continues to distribute the booklet to US military personnel around the world. To date, it has given away over 200,000 copies. See fultonsheen.blogspot.com/2011/09/wartime-prayer-books.html.

[170]Maier, *Wartime Prayer Guide*, 32.

[171]Maier, *A Man Spoke*, 223-24.

forces at home and abroad . . . and for civilians at home: for all who live in a world at war, that through our prayerful lives God may grant us victory and give the world His peace and justice." He also pointed out, "This book is not made up exclusively of prayers, because prayer consists not in the saying of words but in the lifting of our heart and mind to God."[172] While Maier's booklet was nondenominational in content, Sheen's had a distinctly Catholic flavor. It was dedicated "To Mary, Mother Immaculate," and included devotions to "The Blessed Mother," as well as traditional Catholic prayers. Sheen included brief, uplifting commentaries, inspirational snippets, Scripture readings, quotes from well-known Catholics (e.g., St. Ignatius Loyola, Cardinal Newman), and his own prayers. An abridged version of Sheen's prayer book, *The Shield of Faith*, was published on the same day as *The Armor of God*, and offered free of charge to all CH listeners who requested one. To maximize readership, the NCCM announced that the booklets would be available in bulk, on a "cost plus handling and postage charges" basis, which totaled only pennies per copy, to priests and others who wished to distribute it broadly.[173] While it is unclear how many copies were printed and distributed, in full or abridged form, it is certain that the demand was significant. Sheen's and Maier's pastoral roles now included the equipping of prayer warriors in time of war.

After the cessation of hostilities, important trips abroad by both Maier and Sheen represented two additional parallels in the ministries of these radio preachers. In 1947, Maier joined a delegation of cultural leaders, at the request of the US War Department, to visit Europe and advise the Allied military government for Germany on educational and religious matters. During a briefing in Berlin, Maier was instructed to survey the state of the postwar church in Germany, and prepare recommendations on what should be done in the area of religious broadcasting, which had been halted under Hitler. After meeting with Allied military officials and German religious and civic leaders, Maier submitted his findings: "Report and Recommendations on Religious Broadcasting in Germany." He called for religious broadcasts to fill the spiritual void caused by destroyed churches and a shortage of

---

[172]Sheen, *Fulton Sheen's Wartime Prayer Book*, vii.
[173]"Msgr. Sheen Compiles 'The Shield of Faith,'" *Catholic Action*, March 1943; www.bishopsheen today.com/books-videos/books/.

clergy. Maier recommended immediate establishment of Lutheran, Catholic, and Jewish programs, noting the "particular importance" of Jewish broadcasts, in light of Nazi treatment of Jews and their places of worship. Seeing the devastation of his ancestral Deutschland was nearly overwhelming to Maier, especially as he witnessed gaunt, starving women and children. In addition to providing his recommendations on the country's religious state, Maier returned to the United States and redoubled his efforts to augment war relief from American Christians.[174]

The following year, Sheen flew in the opposite direction, as the monsignor accompanied Francis Cardinal Spellman on a lengthy trip to Asia and Australia. This fifty-two day, 43,000 mile journey both confirmed Sheen's stature and further augmented his visibility. Both Sheen and Spellman were struck by the former's celebrity reception, nearly everywhere they went. The CH's reach and its star speaker's popularity seemed to have no bounds. During the trip, Sheen delivered over two hundred speeches, lectures, and sermons.[175] Additionally, as a famous broadcaster, local radio stations frequently invited him to speak over their airwaves. After a spur-of-the-moment radio appearance in Sydney, an appearance for which Sheen had not prepared, a local broadcaster, John Dunne, declared, "In all my years in radio I have never heard anything to equal this."[176] Apparently, Dunne was not the only one to notice. In Sheen's diary from the trip he noted, "The Protestant ministers declare me 'the greatest menace that has yet visited Australia.'" "Menace to what?" queried the monsignor.[177] It seems that his whirlwind tour did not give Sheen adequate time to win over non-Catholics as he had done in the United States. In Singapore, Sheen acknowledged the still-visible marks of war bombing, but complimented the positive spirit and unity of local Catholics. The next day, the *Straits Times* marveled that "one of America's most popular broadcasters . . . used no script."[178] During the trip, notwithstanding whatever awkwardness Sheen's competing attention

---

[174]Maier, *A Man Spoke*, 319-22.

[175]Reeves, *America's Bishop*, 186-96.

[176]"Cardinal Spellman Arrives: Mgr. Fulton Sheen on War Danger," *The Catholic Weekly*, Thursday, April 29, 1948, 1.

[177]Sheen diary from Asia-Pacific trip with Cardinal Spellman, Sheen Archives, Rochester, "Correspondence Q–Z" file, "Diary Fulton J. Sheen May–June 1948" folder.

[178]"Monsignor Sheen on Co-operation," *The Straits Times (Singapore)*, May 22, 1948.

may have generated, Spellman commented that Sheen was "doing more than any archbishop or any bishop to make the Faith known and loved. He is one of the most truly apostolic souls of our times. He has the ear of Catholics; he has the ear of non-Catholics."[179]

Like Maier in Europe, Sheen got to see up close the devastation of war in Asia. It left him with a deeper sense of the need for Christian compassion and evangelistic missions. During a Tokyo dinner hosted by Supreme Allied Commander Douglas MacArthur, the general provided several reflections that pleased Sheen. MacArthur said that he wished he "had 800 Catholic missionaries for every one I have now," adding the "the world struggle is not economic or political but religious and theological."[180] The general made an impression on the priest, and that was apparently mutual. A few weeks later, MacArthur wrote to thank Sheen for sending him a book on communism, and stated that "the indelible influence of your visit to Tokyo is still vivid." He asked Sheen to return for a longer stay.[181]

Politicians. Though avoiding political activity themselves, Maier and Sheen did interact with people involved in the political arena. As mentioned, Maier developed a friendship with Indiana Governor Henry Schricker. As a Lutheran and as a civic leader, Schricker was a visible supporter of Maier and TLH. On November 5, 1941, one month before the Pearl Harbor attack, Maier led the US House of Representatives in an opening invocation, acknowledging the "lowering clouds of bloody conflict" gathering "swiftly and ominously." He prayed that God would "keep these legislators keenly mindful of the vital truth that our national preeminences are neither automatic nor irrevocable." Maier closed by beseeching God to "keep the will of the Congress in harmony with Thy divine will."[182] In 1948, Maier accepted an invitation from Carroll Reece, chairman of the Republican National Committee, to serve as a chaplain for the national convention. Speaker of the House and convention chairman Joseph W. Martin introduced Maier on the convention floor to deliver the invocation. In addition to praying that

---

[179]Sheen, *Treasure in Clay*, 143.

[180]Sheen diary from Asia-Pacific trip with Cardinal Spellman, Sheen Archives, Rochester, "Correspondence Q–Z" file, "Diary Fulton J. Sheen May–June 1948" folder.

[181]Letter from Supreme Commander Douglas MacArthur to Monsignor Fulton J. Sheen, dated August 13, 1948, Sheen Archives, Rochester, "Correspondence A–P" file, "M" folder.

[182]*Congressional Record*, 77th Congress, 1st Session, 1941, 87, pt. 8: 8537.

God would guide the delegates in choosing "a man of prayer, a man of faith, a man of Christ," he asked the Almighty to grant all present "a deep sense of genuine repentance for our many individual and national sins."[183]

Sheen had a few political relationships of his own during his CH years. In his memoirs, he mentions calling on Franklin Roosevelt at the White House, though he did not claim a close relationship.[184] When the *Boston Globe* featured an article on Sheen in 1936, FDR's postmaster general and chairman of the Democratic National Committee James A. Farley sent a congratulatory note. The letter from a fellow Irish-American was brief, but warm, and was casually signed "Jim."[185] The priest's vocal, persistent anti-communism occasionally led to shared podiums with local and national leaders, such as New York Mayor Fiorello LaGuardia and Secretary of Agriculture Henry Wallace. Even with his anticommunist rhetoric, Sheen was cautious to avoid becoming linked to controversial anticommunist politicians such as Senator Joseph McCarthy.[186]

The radio priest was asked to deliver the opening prayer in the House of Representatives on March 30, 1948. Sheen decided to "break with tradition" and rather than pray, he instructed the members of Congress that they should pray. They were to pray because "we have forgotten God; we have imagined in the deceitfulness of our hearts that all our blessings were produced by some superior power and wisdom of our own." He called for humility and confession of "national sin," and reminded them of the biblical precedent of God using less-than-virtuous foreign powers as "the rod and staff of His anger." Sheen closed by boldly urging the legislators to individually "pledge . . . to spend at least 30 minutes a day in prayer" so that "our beloved country" would "grow in peace, victory, justice, and happiness."[187]

Sheen's closest association with a politician was his sincere mutual friendship with former New York governor and unsuccessful candidate for the presidency Alfred E. Smith.[188] In a number of personal letters to

---

[183]Maier, *A Man Spoke*, 328-29.

[184]Sheen, *Treasure in Clay*, 85-87.

[185]Letter from James A. Farley to Monsignor Fulton J. Sheen, dated May 4, 1936, Sheen Archives, Rochester, "Correspondence A–P" file, "James Farley" folder.

[186]Riley, *Fulton J. Sheen*, 112, 174-76; Reeves, *America's Bishop*, 232.

[187]*Congressional Record*, 80th Congress, 2nd Session, 1948, 94, pt. 3: 3701-2.

[188]Beginning in 1933, Smith served on the board of trustees at the Catholic University of America, where Sheen was a member of the faculty. See Warren H. Willis, "The Reorganization of the

Sheen, Smith reveals a dedication to listening to Sheen's CH program and a personal affection.[189] In one note, he indicates that "all the family" was "patiently waiting to hear you again on the radio." In another, Smith mentions hosting a "radio party" during which he and his guests had listened to Sheen. In December of 1938, Smith sent Sheen a rather humorous letter complaining that he did not know what to give the priest as a Christmas present. He enclosed a check and instructed Sheen to buy something he liked and "hang a little tag on the package" that said, "With love and best wishes from Al and Katie." In 1937, Sheen accompanied Mr. and Mrs. Smith on a highly publicized trip to Europe that included a private papal audience for the ex-governor and the monsignor. Upon their departure, Catholic University's *The Tower* gushed, "The eyes of the nation followed a ship as it left New York harbor today, for it bore two of the greatest personages of the Roman Catholic Church in the United States."[190]

Figure 8.8. Reflecting a comfortable friendship, Sheen looks at political leader Al Smith while at the Catholic Summer School of America in Cliff Haven, New York, 1937

While Sheen and Maier had little interest in dabbling in public policy matters, and were leery of even giving the impression of political involvement, their stature as religious leaders led to interactions with a number of political figures. Even if limited in frequency, political relationships that brought about such exposure as praying on the floor of Congress or traveling to Europe with the former presidential nominee only further contributed to the credibility the listening public projected onto them.

Catholic University of America During the Rectorship of James H. Ryan (1928–1935)" (PhD diss., Catholic University of America, 1971), 144.

[189]Letters from Alfred E. Smith to Fulton J. Sheen, dated April 13, 1933, December 6, 1933, January 3, 1935, January 17, 1936, September 15, 1936, Sheen Archives, Rochester, "Correspondence" file, "Alfred E. Smith" folder.

[190]"Father Sheen and Al Smith Sail Today for Europe," *The Tower*, May 17, 1933.

The Red Menace. For Maier and Sheen, even with their similar commitments to a "wall of separation" between church and state, a stronger church meant a stronger America, and a stronger America meant a stronger church. This mutuality of well-being was featured prominently when it came to fighting communism. The virulent attacks these radio preachers directed at "the Reds" focused on theological and ideological issues, but highlighted important complementary roles that churchmen, statesmen, and common citizens were to play. In addition to speaking against godless Marxism on their radio programs, both men frequently opined—in person and in print— on the topic. Maier's private secretary of twenty-one years recalled in 1950 "his clear, consistent view of the menace of Red Communism's objectives and tactics, especially while the USSR was our ally. . . . When it was especially popular to support Soviet policies, he proclaimed fearlessly."[191]

In a radio interview in New Jersey six months before his death, the first question posed was, "Dr. Maier, what would you say is the most burning and vitally important question confronting our country today?" Maier gave an impassioned reply: "The steady and unbroken increase throughout the world of atheistic Communism . . . the Red rebellion against God is going on from triumph to triumph." He acknowledged failed diplomatic efforts, but also blamed left-leaning church leaders in America. "Unless Almighty God intervenes and the Christian people of the world wake up to their responsibilities," he warned, the potential for "Red ruin" of the world, including the United States, would be realized.[192]

Sheen was even more unrelenting on the subject. In 1937, he claimed that his outspokenness had earned him the rank of "public enemy no. 1" on the Kremlin's "black list." Newspapers reported that this list contained "100 principal enemies of Communism in the United States," and that Sheen had heard a shortwave radio broadcast in which the announcer promised, "We will never be satisfied until we have [Sheen's] head rolling in the gutter." During subsequent speaking engagements, the priest repeatedly quipped, "That's the strange thing about Christianity. In order to get a martyr's crown

---

[191]Harriet E. Schwenk, "Dr. Walter A. Maier's Undeviating Stand Against Atheistic Communism," *Concordia Historical Institute Quarterly* 23, no. 2 (July 1950): 49.

[192]"Radio Interview 'Question and Answer' Program on WJLK, Asbury Park," dated July 16, 1949, WAM Collection, CHI, St. Louis, box 6, file 19.

you've got to lose your head, and then you have no place to put the crown."[193] However real the actual threat was, the situation heightened the drama and added to the perceived gravity of Sheen's crusade.

During the war, Sheen also expressed concern about intertwining the interests of the United States and the West with those of the Soviet Union. The postbellum Iron Curtain only confirmed his assumptions regarding communist motives, and increased his fervor. In addition to anticommunist preaching, speech making, and article writing, Sheen published a thoughtful book titled *Communism and the Conscience of the West* in 1948. It became one of his more popular publications, receiving positive reviews from secular and religious writers.[194] Sheen dedicated the book to "Mary, Gracious Mother-Heart of the World's Saviour, in prayerful hope of the Conversion of Russia." He analyzed communism philosophically, with thoughtfulness and characteristic grace. In his preface, the monsignor sounds the alarm: "As Western civilization loses its Christianity it loses its superiority." He surveyed the flaws of communism, but attributed them, at least in part, to Western liberalism taken to an extreme, in which "progress" was measured "by the height of the pile of discarded moral and religious traditions."[195]

The *New York Times* described Sheen's book as an "exceedingly careful and accurate analysis of the philosophy of communism and an equally careful and devastating analysis of historical liberalism," presented with a "refreshing and necessary" tone of "passion."[196] The journal *World Affairs* declared Sheen's work "a magnificent analysis of the present world struggle," explaining that "the demoniac attempt to control each individual soul is . . . the only way Communism can remain in force." It concluded, "This brilliant Christian logician brings us the answer—and the antidote."[197] The Canadian *International Journal* said that the book was written by "a man of great intellectual charity." "There is no bitterness in the indictment," it

---

[193]See Sheen, *Treasure in Clay*, 90; Riley, *Fulton J. Sheen*, 156; "Sheen Welcomes Brotherhood Idea: Quotes Pope in Support of Proposal; 'Proud' He's on Red Death List," *New York Journal*, March 2, 1938; "Msgr. Sheen Accepts Hate of Communists: Catholic Leader, Here for Dinner, Doesn't Mind That They Rate Him as Public Enemy No. 1," *Pittsburgh Press*, February 28, 1938.

[194]Riley, *Fulton J. Sheen*, 164-68.

[195]Fulton J. Sheen, *Communism and the Conscience of the West* (Indianapolis: Bobbs-Merrill, 1948).

[196]Quoted in Riley, *Fulton J. Sheen*, 66, 167.

[197]F. D., review of *Communism and the Conscience of the West*, *World Affairs* 111, no. 2 (Summer 1948): 132.

explained, "but a great wisdom, that encourages the reader to keep on, to enter into his own soul, to ask himself what he can do to discharge his responsibility before God and man."[198] In the *American Bar Association Journal's* review, the writer promised, "Americans who are looking for guidance, and for ways and means, to combat Communism in the United States will find in this book material that should lead them to a good deal of thinking." He summarized, "Monsignor Sheen makes his challenge to the sluggish conscience and decadent religious faith of the West—the materialism, the positivist and relativist philosophy, the *laissez faire* liberalism that discarded God and the absolutes of law and morality," which when "carried to extremes" leads to communism.[199]

Maier and Sheen were ardent anticommunists who opposed the twentieth-century descendants of Marx on theological and philosophical grounds. To those flirting with communistic ideas, they offered a rhetorical cold shower. For those anxious about communistic threats, they provided reinforcement. Maier and Sheen believed that communism was a threat to the American way of life and to the faith to which they had dedicated their lives. They preached and exhorted that it was the duty of Christians to oppose communistic encroachment, wherever it threatened, and they did so over multiple channels. Yet it was their prominent radio presence that not only served as the *primary* channel for such messages, but also lent national credibility as they addressed communism in person and in print. By so doing, they not only energized Christians, but contributed to America's Cold War consensus in substantive ways. Maier did this until he died in 1950, and Sheen went on to oppose communism on television and through other media for an additional two and a half decades. But it all grew from radio platforms that they built and mastered.

Casting wide nets. In a 1938 banquet speech in New York, Harry Emerson Fosdick derisively compared "sectarian religion," by which he meant traditional, doctrinally firm Christianity, to a ten-year-old boy who found out that there was to be a solar eclipse and sold tickets for ten cents to the

---

[198]Joseph Ledit, review of *Communism and the Conscience of the West*, *International Journal* 4, no. 1 (Winter 1948–1949): 81.

[199]W.L.R, review of *Communism and the Conscience of the West*, *American Bar Association Journal* 34, no. 6 (June 1948): 494.

naive boys in the neighborhood to watch it from his backyard. "Religion," he added, "is a cosmic matter."[200] Yet even with strong commitments to the orthodoxies of their traditional, European-rooted denominations, Sheen and Maier pointed to cosmic wonders while allowing the millions in their audience to see them from their *own* back yards. By so doing, they created common ground and made common cause with a wide range of Christians.

Sheen without borders. Sheen had a habit of thinking beyond the boundaries of whatever "territory" he found himself occupying. In 1935, he shared his vision for the Catholic University of America (CUA) with a "Visiting Committee of Bishops." He called for CUA to play a broader role in the life of the nation. Everything that he said to them, Sheen explained, "revolves about one fundamental idea, namely, the *primacy of the spiritual.*" The university's "task" was "integrating the supernatural with the natural, of infusing human knowledge with the divine, of complementing our knowledge of things with our knowledge of God, of making all things Theocentric." He assured the bishops, "The best way" to "keep apace with the times" was "to save the times."[201] Apparently Sheen's vision for CUA mirrored his vision for the *Catholic Hour* and his ministry as a whole.

As mentioned previously in this chapter, Sheen's CH broadcasts broke down perceived barriers between Catholics and their Protestant neighbors. Non-Catholics perceived Catholics to be less foreign, both as citizens and as Christians, as each week Protestants in droves turned on NBC to hear a *priest*, of all things. But it was more than a matter of curiosity that drew in Protestant listeners. It was often a genuine desire to reap what he was sowing. Feedback from non-Catholics demonstrated that Sheen's impact on them was powerful. Sheen and the NCCM were particularly gratified when clergy expressed support. A Baptist minister from New York wrote, "Never have I heard more reasoned addresses. . . . The Right Reverend Msgr. Sheen is doing a tremendously important national service."[202] A non-Catholic clergyman from Michigan wrote, "The 'Catholic Hour' has been a delight to me

---

[200]"The Church of the Sky" (New York: Federal Council of the Churches of Christ in America, 1938), 33.

[201]Willis, "Reorganization of the Catholic University," 255-57. Emphasis original.

[202]"Excerpts from letters received in response to Msgr. Sheen's addresses of January 9 and 16, 1938," Sheen Archives, Rochester, "Correspondence A–P" file, "N" folder.

for a long time. May God continue to make it a blessing to many."[203] A Protestant pastor from Illinois commented, "Like everyone else I listen to all kinds of drivel over the radio but—all is NOT drivel. I want to thank Monsignor Sheen for the addresses I hear him make . . . every Sunday," which the correspondent especially appreciated since "Sundays with me are busy days." He went so far as to say that "I can endorse everything [Sheen] said yesterday, even his remarks concerning the Church and the Bible." From California, another Protestant minister praised Sheen, "Your program today was truly inspired. The material presented by Father Sheen was exceptional. . . . I think your program does more to promote real thinking in America than any other program on the radio." He concluded with the ultimate endorsement: "If you don't mind, may I use your thoughts as I ascend the lectern myself?"[204]

Non-Catholic laypersons also expressed appreciation. The president of a Nebraska bank wrote, "As a Protestant, I wish to add my congratulations. . . . It seems to me that our country is sorely in need of just such constructive counsel at this time." A railroad agent from the South commented, "Notwithstanding the fact that I am a Protestant, I am sufficiently broadminded to appreciate the wonderful lectures [Sheen] has given over the radio. Anyone who has failed to hear them has missed a great deal of benefit to any American citizen." A non-Catholic New Yorker promised to listen to all future broadcasts, adding, "I wish the whole troubled world might have heard that address and been comforted and inspired as I was by Monsignor Sheen."[205] The Protestant periodical *The Southern Methodist Layman* editorialized that Sheen was "one of the greatest preachers of this generation," and suggested to its readers that "if any of your brethren are ever given to criticize our Catholic brethren, you should" recommend that they read "the 14 sermons recently delivered by Monsignor Sheen."[206] A Pennsylvania Protestant wrote, "I candidly admit I receive much religious instruction and inspiration from the 'Catholic Hour.' It is a wonderful course of religious

---

[203]"From responses to Msgr. Sheen's first talk" (undated), Sheen Archives, Rochester, "Correspondence A–P" file, "N" folder.

[204]"The Catholic Radio Bureau," *Catholic Action*, February 1941, 25.

[205]"From responses to Msgr. Sheen's first talk" (undated), Sheen Archives, Rochester, "Correspondence A–P" file, "N" folder.

[206]"Msgr. Sheen Lauded by Methodist Paper as 'Great Preacher,'" *The Catholic Week*, May 19, 1944.

instruction."[207] *Catholic Action* enthusiastically reported that a "wife of a former Vice President of the United States had written the CH to say, 'I have been a member of a Protestant church many years but I get much help from Father Sheen's sermons.'"[208] A letter to the editor of the *Detroit News* expressed appreciation to local radio station WWJ for "giving the public the rare spiritual treat of listening to the magnificent, unrivaled sermons of that brilliant scholar, Monsignor Fulton J. Sheen." The writer concluded by stating, "I am becoming Catholic just as soon as this illustrious church will receive me into the fold." It was signed, "Former Lutheran."[209] Walter Maier may not have approved.

In 1939, Sheen took note when a conservative Presbyterian businessman from Pittsburgh sent him a copy of his self-published critique of the social gospel.[210] In the eighty-eight page booklet, Alexander Fraser interprets social gospel teachings to be contrary to Scripture and, therefore, misguided. He quotes Sheen twice—once positively and once negatively. Fraser praises Sheen for taking the position that institutions (e.g., banks, political bodies) and resources (e.g., land, money) possessed no intrinsic moral value themselves. He quotes, "Father Sheen has well said . . . 'We point the sword of blame at *things*, only because we have not the courage to run it into our own hearts.'"[211] However, Fraser argues that Sheen "errs in his otherwise sound practical application of the Christian ethic" when the priest declared that "workers . . . do more to create social wealth than those who merely clip coupons."[212] According to Fraser, those "clipping coupons" (i.e., investors) indeed contributed much to overall economic well-being, especially in a country still suffering an economic depression. Yet the devout Presbyterian industrialist's concern was primarily theological, and he felt a kinship with the Catholic radio preacher. In a handwritten inscription, Fraser wrote, "To the Rt. Rev. Msgr. Fulton J. Sheen, whose gospel of the cross of Christ has

---

[207]"Non-Catholic Letters 20 Percent of Total," *Catholic Action*, March 1940, 24.

[208]"The Catholic Radio Bureau," *Catholic Action*, February 1941, 25.

[209]"Detroit News—April 29, 1941, Thanks WWJ," Sheen Archives, Rochester, "Correspondence Q–Z" file, "Unable to Identify, Undated, Etc." folder.

[210]Alexander Fraser, *The Social Gospel and the Bible: A Business Man Turns to His Bible to Learn the Truth Concerning the Social Gospel* (Pittsburgh: Self-published, 1939).

[211]Fraser, *Social Gospel and the Bible*, 33.

[212]Fraser, *Social Gospel and the Bible*, 70.

sounded over all this land and has warmed uncounted thousands of hearts. Alexander Fraser."[213]

To be sure, not all Protestants embraced Sheen and his preaching. There were, after all, still theological differences of consequence between Catholics and Protestants and others. What is more, after generations of Catholic distrust, even a priest as eloquent and likable as Sheen could not win over everyone. Nonetheless, he won over more than both Catholics and non-Catholics would have thought possible prior to his grasp of an NBC microphone.

The CH was Sheen's primary pan-Christian engagement from 1930 to his departure from radio in 1952. While he had many acquaintances, interactions, and friendships with non-Catholics, his ecclesiastical activities, numerous and significant as they were, were mainly within his denomination. Toward the end of his radio ministry in 1950, as an outgrowth of the visibility he had gained on radio, Sheen was appointed the national director for the Society of the Propagation of the Faith, which required him to leave his faculty position at CUA. When asked why he was willing to leave a well-established academic post to lead a mission organi-

Figure 8.9. Sheen interacting with crowd at UCLA, October 12, 1940

zation, he demonstrated his broad aspirations for service and Christian outreach: "I have pushed out the classroom walls, and now I can embrace the

---

[213]Booklet with inscription found in Sheen Archives, Rochester, "Memorabilia" file, "1939" folder.

whole world."[214] At the time, *Ave Maria* observed that "the Monsignor's parish is the world and his parishioners the peoples of the world."[215]

Speaking engagements, especially within academic or civic settings, often involved non-Catholic participants in addition to Catholic attendees. As a prolific author of books, pamphlets, articles, and columns, Sheen found other ways to speak to people of a variety of faith commitments.[216] Such would also be the case when Sheen moved to television in 1952, becoming a network star with his program *Life Is Worth Living*.

One additional Sheen engagement is worthy of mention. In 1973, the seventy-eight-year-old archbishop was invited to speak before twenty thousand young people and three thousand counselors during a pan-Lutheran youth gathering at the Astrodome.[217] Sheen served as keynote speaker for the multigenerational All Saints Festival during one of the conference's evening sessions. The printed program referred to him as "one of the most respected elder statesmen of the Christian church."[218] Robed in his episcopal splendor, Sheen delighted the youthful audience by introducing himself as "Cock Robin."[219] After the event, a local Lutheran pastor wrote a letter to the one of the gathering's organizers, Richard Bimler, in which he applauded "exposing young people to" a "diversity of ideas." He complained, however, that the ideas expressed by most of the speakers "were heavily weighted in the leftist direction," reflecting the times a bit more than he liked. Mentioning the historical Lutheran-Catholic conflicts from the time of the Reformation, the pastor added what he considered an ironic note: "I thought

---

[214]As quoted in Archbishop Edward T. O'Meara's homily delivered at Sheen's funeral, December 13, 1979, Sheen Archives, Rochester, "Memorabilia" files.

[215]As quoted in Riley, *Fulton J. Sheen*, 234-35. Riley notes that the Society for the Propagation of the Faith, a global Catholic mission organization, supported 300,000 missionaries, 150,000 schools, 26,000 hospitals, 400 leper colonies, and 5,000 orphanages worldwide during Sheen's tenure as head of its American branch.

[216]Over a period of fifty-four years Sheen authored sixty-six books and published sixty-two booklets, pamphlets, and printed radio sermons, in addition to writing countless articles and newspaper columns in the secular press and in religious publications. Over two million copies of radio addresses were published in twenty-four booklets, in at least ninety press runs and reprint editions. See Reeves, *America's Bishop*, 2; "Media Contributions and Awards of Fulton J. Sheen: A Chronology," Sheen Archives, Rochester, "Memorabilia" file, "Personal" folder; Sheen, *Treasure in Clay*, 385-90.

[217]This youth gathering was cosponsored by the Lutheran Church–Missouri Synod, the American Lutheran Church, and the Lutheran Church in America.

[218]Personal files of Richard Bimler, Bloomingdale, Illinois.

[219]Interview with Richard Bimler by author, July 27, 2013.

that Fulton Sheen was one of the best witnesses we had at the gathering."[220] One can only speculate as to whether Sheen saw the irony as well, or whether he thought of fellow radio crusader Walter Maier as he approached the Lutheran-sponsored microphone.

Maier without borders. Walter Maier broke down barriers between Lutheranism and the rest of American Christianity through his radio ministry. This not only produced the aforementioned shift of Lutheranism toward a more mainstream presence, but it allowed Maier to reach a large cross-section of non-Lutherans in his preaching and ecclesiastical work. Interestingly, a seemingly detrimental turn of events likely enhanced the reach of his broadcast ministry. Recall that in the early days of TLH, Maier had hoped to gain access to network sustaining time. When access to NBC's free religious airtime was denied, Maier had settled for purchasing time on the smaller CBS network. While TLH withdrew from CBS after one season due to depleted funds, CBS would go on to launch its own sustaining time religious programming under the name "Columbia Church of the Air," featuring multiple preachers, from varying denominations. While CBS executives were open to having Lutheran clerics participate in this program, they objected to Maier, even in light of his experience and early success on their network, because they preferred "someone less aggressive and pugnacious" in demeanor. When Maier was told of CBS's concerns, rather than modify his style or homiletic content, he committed himself to finding another network and paying for on-air access, and the global success of TLH followed.[221] Without this series of events, Maier may have ended up with only occasional radio exposure, with less control of content and less ability to develop a broad, consistent following.

The multifaceted audience Maier garnered over the coming years would be evidenced in national surveys conducted periodically by TLH, to understand their audience better. For instance, in 1947, Director of Radio Eugene R. Bertermann sent a summary of their most recent survey to key supporters. The survey had been sent to random TLH listeners and generated 1,706

---

[220]Letter from Richard F. Wagner to Rich Bimler, dated September 10, 1973, Richard Bimler's personal files, Bloomingdale, IL.
[221]E. Clifford Nelson, *Lutheranism in North America, 1914–1970* (Minneapolis: Augsburg, 1972), 60-61, 67.

responses, from listeners in forty-five states, the District of Columbia, and Canada. Roughly 80 percent of respondents reported listening to TLH broadcasts "regularly" or "frequently." Half of those submitting a survey were not Lutherans, with broad distribution across denominational lines. Interestingly, the largest listener groups (after Lutherans) were those classified as "other" (11 percent) and Baptists (10 percent), followed by Methodists (9 percent) and Presbyterians (5 percent). Most were regular or frequent church attenders.

In rather un-Lutheran fashion, the survey had inquired about the number of conversions that had resulted from Maier's broadcasts.[222] The 1,706 respondents reported 483 conversions within their families, and 470 conversions, of which they were aware, outside their families. The report stated that these statistics "represent a startling total of 953 saved through the broadcast Word." TLH also asked about known conversions "through other religious broadcasts," of which 111 faith commitments were reported. Responses to other questions indicated that 43.5 percent of TLH listeners read their Bibles more frequently, and 20.6 percent participated in Holy Communion more often as a result of the broadcasts. Demonstrating the program's multigenerational impact, 10.5 percent of households reported greater Sunday school attendance. Finally, TLH asked those surveyed to list other network religious programs to which they listened "frequently," in order of preference. While 72 percent gave no response, of those that did, the most common response for "first choice" after TLH was Charles Fuller's *Old-Fashioned Revival Hour* (16.2 percent). 1.2 percent of those who answered this question named the CH as their top alternative to TLH.[223]

This survey is important for two reasons. First, the responses indicate engagement with an audience that expanded well beyond Lutheranism. Second, the composition of the survey, with its request for data on conversions and altered behaviors, and with its inquiries on denominational

---

[222]Lutherans are often reluctant to keep statistics on conversions due to their assumptions about the inability for anyone other than God to truly know if someone is "converted," and to avoid giving the appearance that the work of the Holy Spirit can be measured by empirical data. That said, they are more willing to track outward actions, such as baptisms, communion participation, and professions of faith.

[223]"Blessing upon Blessing: A Report on the Lutheran Hour Questionnaire," with cover letter from Eugene R. Bertermann, dated June 30, 1947, WAM Collection, CHI, St. Louis, box 7, file 20.

affiliations and alternative religious broadcast affinities, indicates that TLH leadership, including Maier, thought of themselves as part of a larger American Christian landscape—especially the broader evangelical segment.

As was the case with the CH, TLH took note of correspondence from clergy and laypersons of other faith traditions, including Catholics. At the beginning of Maier's TLH ministry, the Catholic chaplain of Michigan State Prison in Jackson wrote, "I want you to know that I appreciated greatly the soundness of your doctrine and the beauty of your diction. It is to be regretted that the whole world couldn't have been blessed with the same privilege which was mine on that night." Acknowledging that they were of different faith traditions, the chaplain concluded, "The message you gave to the radio audience . . . was such as to break down all barriers. . . . The crucified Christ of whom you spoke so beautifully died for all alike and I want you to know that I deem it a great privilege to have the opportunity of listening to your message."[224] Maier responded two weeks later, thanking the Catholic priest for his "very cordial and enheartening note," saying that "if the radio activities would result in nothing more than a better mutual understanding among all who confess the glorious name of Christ . . . this alone would make the effort worthwhile." He added, "While I am not of your faith and conviction, I appreciate among other things, the bulwark that the Roman Catholic Church has erected toward the inroads of modernism and materialism."[225]

In the publications of Maier's radio sermons, excerpts of the thousands of letters he received included many from Catholics. For example, a New Yorker wrote, "If souls can't be saved by your fine way of preaching the Gospel, then there is no hope for them. We are Catholic, but we are for every good worker out to save souls with the great message." From Indiana, a correspondent declared, "I am a Catholic, but I get as much good out of your sermons as I do from those in my own church." A young man from New Jersey explained that he lived with an aunt and uncle who "are Roman Catholics also." After listening to TLH, however, he wished to become a

---

[224]Letter from D. J. Quillan to Walter Maier, dated April 4, 1931, WAM Collection, CHI, St. Louis, series 1, subseries A, box 1, file 33.

[225]Letter from Walter A. Maier to D. J. Quillan, dated April 17, 1931, WAM Collection, CHI, St. Louis, series 1, subseries A, box 1, file 33.

Protestant minister. "Will you please send me the address of a Lutheran boarding school which isn't so far from where I live?" he inquired.[226]

Maier generated additional Catholic attention through his editorials in *The Walther League Messenger*, his speaking engagements, and from TLH broadcasts. In 1933, the *Western Catholic* newspaper in Quincy, Illinois, published a column titled "Our Lutheran Friend." Referring to Maier, it opened, "There's a Lutheran gentleman whom we would like to meet, greet and congratulate." It praised Maier in glowing terms for labeling "notorious faith wreckers" who "sit high in the council of academic distinction." His sharp criticism of "collegiate immorality," "common indecency," and "unbelief and practical atheism," in American education, elicited a "Bravo Professor Maier!" from the columnist. Ironically, the editors used their endorsement of Maier's position as a reason why their readers should send their children to Catholic schools, "where Christ reigns and where Mary Immaculate is loved."[227] Years later, the editors of *Our Sunday Visitor*, in an editorial complaining that Maier had mischaracterized certain Catholic positions in a recent *Walther League Messenger* column, added this remarkable advertisement: "We seldom miss listening to Dr. Walter Maier, who speaks over a radio network embracing more than five hundred stations every Sunday. We believe that he has done an incalculable amount of good in his defense of the moral law, of right living, and of the divine inspiration of the Scriptures."[228] Maier had a way of leaving a lasting impression. In 1965, Maier's successor as the *Lutheran Hour* Speaker, Oswald C. J. Hoffmann, had occasion to call on Boston's Richard Cardinal Cushing. Cushing recalled with appreciation that when he had taken an unpopular position in support of legal bans on birth control devices, earlier in his Catholic episcopacy, "I was supported in my position by a Lutheran down there in Missouri. His name was Walter Maier."[229]

---

[226]Walter A. Maier, *Rebuilding with Christ* (St. Louis: CPH, 1946), xvi, xvii.

[227]"Our Lutheran Friend," *The Western Catholic* (Quincy, IL), September 1, 1933.

[228]"Lutheran Opposition Surprises Us," *Our Sunday Visitor*, May 20, 1945. In the previous year, in a universal appeal for prayer, *Our Sunday Visitor* reported approvingly, "The Lutheran Hour, 'Born of zeal to bring Christ to the nation,' and supported by the gifts of both rich and poor, has carried a message to almost the entire world, Sunday after Sunday, throughout the period of the war. See "A Reader Wants Universal Prayer," *Our Sunday Visitor*, October 1, 1944.

[229]Oswald C. J. Hoffman, *What More Is There to Say but Amen: The Autobiography of Dr. Oswald C. J. Hoffman* (St. Louis: CPH, 1996), 210-11.

While many Catholic laypersons tuned in to hear the only Lutheran cleric most of them would ever hear, and many Catholic clergy respected Maier, the Lutheran's greatest impact was across American Protestantism. In addition to the thousands of letters arriving daily from Lutheran listeners, those from non-Lutheran Protestants demonstrated something more than perfunctory auditing of his broadcasts. Maier's sermons provided encouragement and inspiration to orthodox clergy. A Christian Reformed pastor in South Dakota expressed his gratitude: "Your practical, yet orthodox approach is certainly stimulating, especially when there is so much of the pagan philosophy of Liberalism expounded over the radio." Another cleric from Kalamazoo wrote, "I am a young orthodox Christian Reformed minister. I can assure you I go into my pulpit Sunday evenings with a new courage having received reinforcement from your noonday broadcast." A Disciples of Christ pastor in Fort Wayne declared, "I am pleased that there is a truly representative Protestant voice on the air . . . truly religious and inspiring and challenging." A Presbyterian from Oregon simply exclaimed, "What a preacher! What a true message! . . . Our Lord is richly blessing you."[230]

The laity was as appreciative. In addition to the aforementioned letters seeking pastoral counsel, thousands wrote in simply to express their gratitude to Maier, to offer him their encouragement, or to send a donation to support the radio ministry. "Since the age of twenty-one, I was a Communist atheist," wrote a Californian. "I listened to you six years ago and have ever since. You changed my entire outlook, thank God!" A Presbyterian from Pennsylvania spoke in words that a Missouri Synod Lutheran would have celebrated: "My former pastor is a stickler for doctrine, but he certainly does endorse your program and has repeatedly urged us to tune in." A janitor in a Methodist church wrote to say that he hurried home after services to hear TLH, since the preacher at his church "does not preach the Bible." From New York, a man explained, "I listened to your radio broadcast tonight. . . . Boy, did it strike home! It hit me on the top of the head and instead of knocking me out it brought me to my senses." He was thankful that Maier's words were going to make him a better father and husband. A mother in Ohio simply

---

[230]Walter A. Maier, *Christ for Every Crisis: The Radio Messages Broadcast in the Second Lutheran Hour* (St. Louis: CPH, 1935), 154-58.

wrote, "My little girl and I have been brought to Christ through your earnest religious broadcasts."[231]

From his earliest days as editor of the *Walther League Messenger* and public speaker, Maier built a reputation as a vocal foe of unbelief, which added to his reputation and stature as he built a radio presence around the world. Only months before he began his first TLH season, in a widely reported speech at a gathering in Ocean Grove, New Jersey, Maier warned of the consequences of growing unbelief in America.[232] Shortly thereafter he received an invitation from the Atheist Society of Chicago. "Having noticed your attack on the Atheists in the newspapers," the handwritten letter stated, "I have the honour . . . to send you a challenge to debate any of our speakers on any subject you may choose to oppose us." In addition to an attached list of potential debaters, the writer stated, "I can secure . . . even the well-known Clarence Darrow to defend us."[233] Maier jumped at the chance to debate Darrow. When the press began reporting on the pending debate, the Atheist Society admitted to Maier that they "had made no definite arrangement with Mr. Darrow and he was much displeased by this unauthorized publicity."[234] Maier wrote to express his displeasure, and though other debating opponents were offered, an Atheist Society debate did not occur.[235] Nonetheless, even having one's name mentioned in the national press as a potential debater against Darrow enhanced Maier's reputation as a Protestant defender of the faith.[236]

Maier held other defenders of the faith in high regard, as well. Though he did not appear to have had a close relationship with famed Presbyterian

---

[231] Walter A. Maier, *He Will Abundantly Pardon: Radio Messages of the Second Part of the Thirteenth Lutheran Hour* (St. Louis: CPH, 1948), x-xxxi.

[232] Maier, *A Man Spoke*, 130-31.

[233] Letter from James E. Even to Walter A. Maier, dated August 11, 1930, WAM Collection, CHI, St. Louis, box 1, file 10.

[234] Letter from James E. Even to Walter A. Maier, dated September 4, 1930, WAM Collection, CHI, St. Louis, box 1, file 10.

[235] Letter from Walter A. Maier to James E. Even, dated September 5, 1930, WAM Collection, CHI, St. Louis, box 1, file 10; Maier, *A Man Spoke*, 133-34. Paul Maier states that Darrow's refusal to debate, "albeit defensible since he had not issued the challenge," was "one of the great disappointments in Walter's life."

[236] A dissenting opinion came anonymously from "An Atheist" at Stanford University, who wrote Maier, "Say Man, Don't make an *Esel* of yourself. Clarence Darrow has more brains in his little finger than *all you Ministers*." Anonymous letter to Maier (undated), WAM Collection, CHI, St. Louis, box 1, file 10.

J. Gresham Machen, he clearly respected the intellectual fundamentalist. When Machen was engaged in theological battles at Princeton and within the Presbyterian Church in the mid-1930s, Maier wrote him a word of encouragement, saying, "I certainly view the situation sympathetically with you."[237] He also appears to have requested additional information on the ecclesiastical proceedings, which Machen sent.[238] Shortly after Maier's death in 1950, one of Machen's former Westminster Seminary students, Raymond M. Meiners, sent his condolences to Maier's widow. He recalled how he and his fellow students were devastated when their mentor, Machen, had died unexpectedly in 1937. In their grief, the Presbyterian seminarians attended a Lutheran Hour Rally in Philadelphia. Meiners and his colleagues waited to meet Maier, and he recalled, "I have never forgotten his words of encouragement as we looked forward to the uncertain future. He said that even though . . . Dr. Machen had been taken from us, we should not lose heart, but rather take courage in the faithfulness of God and plant our feet firmly in His word of Truth."[239]

As J. Gresham Machen had experienced, Maier's preaching of traditional Christian doctrine, in the face of modernist shifts within mainline Protestantism, attracted for him the label *fundamentalist*—a moniker that could be meant as a term of derision or as a confirmation of theological soundness. Maier welcomed this label, but preferred a lower-case *f* on his brand of fundamentalism. He considered certain doctrines to be "fundamental," including "the deity of Christ, His virgin birth, resurrection, and Second Advent; the inspiration and authority of the Bible; and certainly also the cardinal Reformation emphasis on justification by faith."[240] His dogged sermonizing on these core beliefs earned him the respect of fundamentalists, which he reciprocated, notwithstanding different views on such issues as sacramental efficacy, societal engagement, educational virtue, and the potential for a bottle of beer to damn one's soul. More importantly, his

---

[237]Letter from Walter A. Maier to J. Gresham Machen, dated March 13, 1935, WAM Collection, CHI, St. Louis, box 1, file 129.

[238]Machen-Maier correspondence, WAM Collection, CHI, St. Louis, box 1, file 129; see also box 9, file 10.

[239]Letter from Raymond M. Meiners to Mrs. Walter A. Maier, WAM Collection, CHI, St. Louis, series 1, subseries B, box 3, file 8.

[240]Milton L. Rudnick, *Fundamentalism & the Missouri Synod: A Historical Study of Their Interaction and Mutual Influence* (St. Louis: Concordia, 1966), 98; Maier, *A Man Spoke*, 213.

worldwide evangelistic efforts brought not only their admiration, but emulation. In the end, Maier became known as the LCMS's "only ambassador to Fundamentalism."[241] Upon Maier's death, the *Christian Fundamentalist*, a publication of the World Christian Fundamentals Association, placed Maier's picture on its front page, and reprinted in its entirety his radio sermon, "You, Too, Should Be a Fundamentalist." The editor declared Maier's death "a national calamity," and celebrated that the Lutheran had declared himself a "Fundamentalist." "This should put iron in the blood and concrete in the backbone of young preachers and give them the courage of their convictions," wrote the editor.[242]

As the highly engaged evangelical movement emerged from withdrawn fundamentalist quarters in the 1940s, Maier established relationships with many of its leaders. He was held in particularly high regard by the first president of the National Association of Evangelicals (NAE), Harold John Ockenga. In a 1979 interview, Ockenga recalled that the formation of the NAE "was sparked" by a reaction to attempts by the FCC to block evangelicals from having access to radio airwaves. "Well, that would have hit men like Charlie Fuller, who had his broadcast, and Walter Maier, who had a big broadcast of about 900 stations, and lesser people like Donald Grey Barnhouse and myself," explained Ockenga. He referred to Maier as "the spokesman of the Lutheran Hour, and he was a great one, too!"[243] In a 1960 *Christianity Today* article, Ockenga stated that Maier was one of the leading "fundamentalists . . . steadfast to Christ and biblical truth regardless of cost" who "were well-known to me personally."[244]

Ockenga regularly invited Maier to speak at evangelical functions, and they became good friends.[245] In a noteworthy example of mutual support

---

[241]Rudnick, *Fundamentalism & the Missouri Synod*, 103-13.

[242]"You, Too, Should Be a Fundamentalist," *The Christian Fundamentalist* 7, no. 2 (June 1950): 1-12.

[243]Recorded interview of Harold John Ockenga by James A. Hedstrom, Wheaton College Billy Graham Center Archives, Collection 629.

[244]Harold John Ockenga, "Resurgent Evangelical Leadership," *Christianity Today*, October 10, 1960, 11-15. Ockenga described Maier as "fundamentalist" in his doctrinal positions, but viewed him as a fellow evangelical.

[245]Paper by Paul L. Maier, "Walter A. Maier (1893–1950)," as part of a session titled, "Fathers and Sons: The Influence of Evangelists Walter A. Maier, Percy Crawford, Merv Russell, Jack Wyrtzen, and Charles Woodbridge on Fundamentalism in the 1930s, 1940s, and 1950s," Annual Meeting of American Academy of Religion, Chicago, November 3, 2008. (Copy of paper provided by Paul L. Maier.) Maier recalls that when he visited Ockenga's Park Street Church as a

and respect, Maier spoke at a week-long evangelistic conference at Ockenga's Park Street Church in Boston, in October 1945. At the conclusion of the week, Maier was scheduled to hold a Lutheran Hour Rally at the Boston Garden. In the August prior to these events, the New England Fellowship, an evangelistic organization formed to "publish, broadcast, preach and teach the fundamentals of the Christian faith" and in which Ockenga was involved, sent a letter to all pastors within a fifty mile radius of Boston.[246] The purpose of the letter was to encourage involvement of every church in the region in promoting the upcoming "great Lutheran Hour Rally." "This Rally can make a tremendous impact on New England and be a great testimony," wrote the Fellowship's executive director, Franklin Ellis. He asked each pastor to appoint a "key person in your church" to "be my contact man," so as to coordinate publicity for the Rally, and enlist choir members and ushers for Maier's event. Below his signature Ellis included the phrase "In essentials unity—in non-essentials liberty—in all things charity."[247]

While the LCMS did not join the NAE, Maier and TLH were actively involved in the formation of the National Religious Broadcasters (NRB) in 1944, under NAE auspices. He and his radio director, Eugene R. Bertermann, were charter members of the NRB, and served on its initial board of directors.[248] The NRB was the leading organization in providing a united

---

Harvard undergraduate, Ockenga "made a big deal out of my being WAM's son." Interview of Paul L. Maier by author, May 16, 2013. Whatever affinity Ockenga held for Walter Maier, he did not hold for Maier's Catholic counterpart, Fulton Sheen. At a 1945 convention of the NAE, Ockenga revealed a sharp anti-Catholic mindset as he attacked the US government's decision to appoint diplomats to the Vatican. Addressing the delegates, he described this development as "a sinister portent in America, the activity of an alien political philosophy in American affairs, which is greater than Communism itself." In a backhanded compliment to Sheen's broad appeal, Ockenga added, "The political activity of the Roman Catholic Hierarchy is doubly dangerous, because Americans are unaware that the philosophy of Monsignor Fulton J. Sheen may involve a change in American culture almost as fundamental as that of Josef Stalin." Even granting that the extent of Stalin's ruthlessness had not fully come to light in America by 1945, the words of Ockenga are strikingly harsh. See "Boston Pastor Charges Catholic Church Seeks Control of Government," *Boston Daily Globe*, Friday, May 4, 1945.

[246] New England Fellowship described in Garth M. Rosell, *The Surprising Work of God: Harold John Ockenga, Billy Graham, and the Rebirth of Evangelicalism* (Grand Rapids, MI: Baker Academic, 2008), 89-90.

[247] Letter from Franklin F. Ellis to "Fellow Pastor," dated August 3, 1945, G. Christian Barth files, Concordia Theological Seminary, Fort Wayne. I am grateful to Lawrence R. Rast Jr., president of Concordia Theological Seminary, for calling this correspondence to my attention.

[248] James DeForest Murch, *Co-operation Without Compromise: A History of the National Association of Evangelicals* (Grand Rapids, MI: Eerdmans, 1956), 72-81. Eugene Bertermann went on to serve

voice for evangelical broadcasters and assuring their consistent access to America's airwaves.

Maier's relationships extended to another leading institution within American fundamentalism and evangelicalism—Wheaton College. In 1940, the west suburban Chicago campus's annual Washington Banquet was canceled by President V. Raymond Edman, who encouraged the students to donate what they would have spent on the social event to a Christian relief fund for Finnish and Chinese Christians in war areas. Taking the banquet's place was an informal event in the college's chapel, with Maier as the guest speaker.[249] Edman must have liked what Maier had to say, because in 1944 he invited the Lutheran to preach at one of the college's chapel services. "We are often reminded of your last visit . . . and your helpful and stirring message,"

wrote Edman, adding, "We are eager that [our present students] have this opportunity for your personal ministry among us." He closed the letter, "We are grateful to the Most High for the strong and effective testimony which He has committed to you, and are trusting Him for His continued guidance and rich blessing to be upon it."[250] Teaching obligations kept Maier from accepting, but he

Figure 8.10. Maier preaching in Pierce Chapel at Wheaton College in the mid-1940s

thanked Edman for "the encouraging lines you have written about our work," and offered to come later in the semester.[251]

Edman was pleased to welcome Maier as the chapel speaker later that year, when he came to campus to preach on Reformation Day (October 31).

as NRB president from 1957 to 1975. He continued to serve as a board member and secretary until his death in 1983.

[249]Paul M. Bechtel, *Wheaton College: A Heritage Remembered, 1860–1984* (Wheaton, IL: Harold Shaw, 1984), 132.

[250]Letter from V. R. Edman to Walter A. Maier, dated January 12, 1944, WAM Collection, CHI, St. Louis, series 1, box 2, file 59.

[251]Letters from Walter A. Maier to V. R. Edman, dated January 18, 1944, and January 21, 1944, WAM Collection, CHI, St. Louis, series 1, box 2, file 59.

Months later, the college president asked Maier to serve as commencement speaker for the 1945 graduating class, and to teach in the school's summer session "with some pertinent reemphasis and interpretation of the Protestant Reformation." Edman added, "In a day of deepening apostasy we need a new appreciation of Martin Luther's stand for the Scriptures and the truth of God."[252] Maier reluctantly turned down the invitation due to an abundance of speaking engagements he had already accepted.[253] The busy Lutheran did agree to serve as keynote speaker for the college's February 1950 Washington Banquet, but died in January. Edman commented, "Few men in the century have stood so earnestly, staunchly, and eloquently for the Lord."[254] The significance of the president of an evangelical, fundamentalist citadel like Wheaton repeatedly inviting a Missouri Synod Lutheran cleric to preach, and the noteworthiness of such a Lutheran leader eagerly accepting such invitations, must be recognized.

Unrelated to his friendship with Raymond Edman, Maier developed a relationship with the man who would go on to become Wheaton College's most famous alumnus. In 1944, the young Billy Graham was serving as pastor of the Village Church in Western Springs, Illinois, in the western suburbs of Chicago. When Maier addressed the West Suburban Men's Fellowship Group, the unknown Graham approached him and asked if he would speak at his nearby church. Maier agreed, which Graham never forgot. Years later, he told a crusade audience in St. Louis, in the presence of Maier's son and widow, "The fact that the great Dr. Maier took time from his crowded schedule to address the little flock of a struggling young pastor left an indelible impression on me."[255] So did Maier's address to the fellowship group. Graham wrote him later that year, saying, "We look back with great joy upon your ministry in our midst. . . . The men were thrilled with the exemplification of Christ and rebuked by the fearless denunciation of sin." He invited Maier to address the

---

[252]Letter from V. R. Edman to Dr. Walter A. Maier, dated February 3, 1945, WAM Collection, CHI, St. Louis, series 1, box 2, file 59.

[253]Letter from Walter A. Maier to Dr. V. R. Edman, dated March 26, 1945, WAM Collection, CHI, St. Louis, series 1, box 2, file 59.

[254]"Broadcaster Dies of Heart Attack," *The Wheaton Record*, January 12, 1950. This brief article in Wheaton College's student newspaper mentions that Maier had visited the campus several times. Note: I am grateful to Keith Call, special collections assistant at Wheaton College, for bringing this article to my attention.

[255]Maier, *A Man Spoke*, 357.

group again on October 31, in celebration of the anniversary of Luther nailing the Ninety-Five Theses to the Castle Church door in 1517.[256] Maier agreed in a warm reply, and later sent Graham a book of his radio addresses.[257] After Graham left parish ministry to work for Youth for Christ International, he sent Maier another letter recalling their previous time together, and asking for his prayers. Graham closed the letter, "Thanking you for the kindness and sweetness you have shown in the many things you have done for us, for the great ministry that God has given you from coast to coast, I am sincerely yours in Christ."[258] Graham was about to rise to national and international prominence as the twentieth century's most influential evangelist. Historian Robert Handy would later observe that Maier was the "missing link" between Graham and evangelist Billy Sunday of an earlier generation.[259]

When Maier was on his deathbed, Graham sent multiple telegrams of concern.[260] When he died a few days later, Graham heard the news over a radio station in Boston, where he was conducting his Boston Garden Crusade. Harold John Ockenga was in attendance and wired, "Great loss in homegoing of Dr. Maier and expressed by 5,500 Christians meeting in revival . . . under Billy Graham. . . . Announcement moved many to repentance."[261] In his autobiography, Graham remembered, "I was so jolted that I knelt in my hotel room and prayed that God might raise up someone to take his place on the radio." This occurrence, followed by unsolicited encouragement from several evangelicals, led to Graham's commencement of a radio ministry, and the launch of his *Hour of Decision* program.[262] A few years later, Graham would

---

[256]Letter from William F. Graham to Walter Maier, dated July 25, 1944, WAM Collection, CHI, St. Louis, series 1, subseries A, box 1, folder 80.

[257]Letters from Walter A. Maier to William F. Graham, dated August 16, 1944 and October 21, 1944, WAM Collection, CHI, St. Louis, series 1, subseries A, box 1, folder 80.

[258]Letter from Billy Graham to Walter Maier, dated September 17, 1946, WAM Collection, CHI, series 1, subseries A, box 1, folder 80.

[259]Richard J. Shuta, "Walter A. Maier as Evangelical Preacher," *Concordia Theological Quarterly* 74, nos. 1–2 (January/April 2010): 5.

[260]Maier, *A Man Spoke*, 357.

[261]Paul L. Maier, "Walter A. Maier & Billy Graham," *Decision*, June 1981, 4. This same issue of *Decision*, a publication of the Billy Graham Evangelistic Association, featured an article, "A Man for the World: Walter A. Maier," composed of excerpts from Maier's prose. The editors noted, "Most probably, Dr. Maier was the first American churchman whose published works exceeded 15,000 printed pages."

[262]Billy Graham, *Just as I Am: The Autobiography of Billy Graham* (New York: HarperCollins, 1997), 176–81.

look back at the career of Maier and describe the Lutheran as "the greatest combination of preacher and scholar that America has thus far produced in this century."[263]

As the 1940s drew to a close, Maier's influence showed no sign of waning. Presbyterian Philadelphia pastor and radio preacher Donald Grey Barnhouse invited Maier to choose and edit a dozen sermons of Martin Luther, and record them in his "Portable Church Services" audio tape series. Maier enthusiastically agreed.[264] In addition to his weekly radio appearances, and his multiple speaking engagements and rallies, his writing production had reached nine hundred magazine articles, thirty-one books, and abundant devotional material, with more in process.[265] While most of his books were compilations of his radio sermons, he also published a popular marriage guide, *For Better Not for Worse: A Manual of Christian Matrimony*. First printed in 1935, this incredibly long treatment exceeded five hundred pages and went through multiple print runs and revisions until Maier's death.[266] His thorough scholarly commentary on the Old Testament book of Nahum was published posthumously in 1959. Ever eager to expand the base of TLH supporters, Maier decided at the end of 1949 to begin publishing a brief monthly newsletter targeted at boys and girls. Titled *The Junior Broadcaster*, the first issue went out in January 1950, with Maier on the cover, and an invitation from the radio preacher to read future editions to learn how to help "bring Christ to the nations." Unfortunately, Maier died that month, and the February issue began, "Dear Junior Broadcaster: Dr. Maier is in heaven."[267]

Maier's untimely death stunned Christians across the country and around the world. Lutheran leaders came together in mourning. Christian

---

[263] As quoted in a McGraw-Hill print advertisement promoting Maier's 1963 biography, *A Man Spoke*, written by his son, Paul L. Maier. The quote is repeated in Maier, "Walter A. Maier & Billy Graham," 4. Published thirteen years after Walter Maier's death, *A Man Spoke* sold some 80,000 copies in the first two years after its release. It is currently in its fifteenth printing, with roughly 200,000 copies in print. Email exchange between Paul L. Maier and author, January 24, 2016.

[264] "Great Sermons on Tape," *Time*, December 17, 1951, 73. Maier died before he was able to complete this project.

[265] "A Man for the World," *Decision*, June 1981, 4.

[266] Walter A. Maier, *For Better Not for Worse: A Manual of Christian Matrimony* (St. Louis: CPH, 1935). One reviewer wrote, "It should be in every Church or Sunday School library and deserves a place in every public library." See Winter 1940–1941 clipping from *Christianity Today*, WAM Collection, CHI, St. Louis, box 5, file 4.

[267] See Eugene R. Bertermann Papers, Concordia Historical Institute, St. Louis, box 4, file 1.

broadcasters and other leaders, especially evangelicals, sent messages of sympathy to Maier's family and associates.[268] Newspapers around the world reported the shocking news. In a genuinely touching show of respect, fundamentalist preacher Charles E. Fuller, whose radio program *The Old-Fashioned Revival Hour* rivaled TLH in audience size, paid tribute to Maier during his broadcast, just days after the Lutheran's death.[269] In a lamenting tone, Fuller said to his radio audience,

> When word came to me that Dr. Walter Maier of *The Lutheran Hour* radio broadcast had suddenly departed to be with Christ, it came as a great shock. I'm sure we all feel what a great loss his home-going, especially at this time in the world's history, is. Dr. Maier was a modern Jeremiah, a "Weeping Prophet," warning this sinful generation to turn to God. Dr. Maier, a prince among preachers, though his warning voice is stilled, will long be remembered, especially by those who have been converted under his faithful ministry. He will be greatly missed by countless thousands over the world. And, may we who remain be faithful, and occupy till Jesus comes.

Fuller then asked his studio audience to sing "Shall We Gather at the River?"[270]

St. Louis television station KSD-TV asked for permission to televise Maier's funeral, which Mrs. Maier granted. The plan was for KSD-TV to transmit the services to the NBC network, making Maier's funeral the first nationally televised funeral in United States history. Although the signal was successfully fed to Chicago, a technical problem prevented its relay to New York and the network. Viewers in the greater St. Louis area watched the solemn proceedings.[271]

Summary

Through eloquence and erudition, preparation and sensitivity, political and denominational-specific rhetorical restraint, all the while maintaining

---

[268]For examples, see "Dr. Walter A. Maier Memorial Edition," *Bringing Christ to the Nations: The Lutheran Hour News*, Lent-Easter Edition, 1950, Lutheran Hour Archives, St. Louis.

[269]Fuller had sent a telegram to Maier on hearing that he had been hospitalized. The message assured Maier that Fuller and his staff were praying for "your speedy recovery and continued ministry over the air." See Western Union telegram from Charles B. Fuller [sic] to Walter Meier [sic], dated January 6, 1950, WAM Collection, CHI, St. Louis, series 1, subseries A, box 1, folder 74.

[270]Audio recording from transcription disc of *The Old-Fashioned Revival Hour*, broadcast January 15, 1950. I am grateful to Read Burgan of Lake Linden, Michigan, for providing me with this recording, from his personal collection.

[271]Maier, *A Man Spoke*, 367-68.

doctrinal firmness, Fulton Sheen's and Walter Maier's preaching inspired their listeners and kept them tuning in week after week. Their network audiences rivaled, and often exceeded, top entertainment programs. Yet what they provided was far more than mere entertainment. They preached from, and expounded on, what they and their ethereal parishioners considered to be the Word of God. Additionally, while thousands may have turned to these radio preachers with cynicism or by accident, many found it impossible to turn off the programs once they started listening and ultimately embraced their life-changing messages. The confluence of stressful national and personal times, emerging mass media via network radio, and their dedicated, innovative approach to pastoral ministry empowered Sheen and Maier to serve a genuinely pastoral role for millions of people seeking solace and counsel.

As they did so, they also brought their respective denominations, which had functioned on the periphery of American Christianity, into the mainstream. Catholics and Lutherans enjoyed the legitimacy brought by Sheen's and Maier's broad popularity. In the eyes of outsiders, their Catholic and Lutheran neighbors became a bit closer—their theology seemed less suspect, their ecclesiology and worship seemed less threatening, and their ethnic elements seemed less foreign. During their twenty years on the radio, Maier and Sheen not only reached millions of listeners across geographic and denominational borders, but their visibility, their perceived theological soundness, and their personal commitments to serving God's people, allowed them to leverage their radio ministries to produce a broader impact. Through teaching, speaking, preaching, and writing, these clerics made their presence known. In turn, other leadership opportunities emerged, enabling Sheen to serve broader Catholic missions and objectives and Maier to forge relationships with key evangelical leaders within the Protestant community.

Maier's and Sheen's forward-thinking approach to ministry sparked an interest in both about the emerging medium of television. In 1940, Sheen conducted what a summary in his archives chronicles as the first religious service ever broadcast on television.[272] The Easter service was conducted in NBC's studios, under the sponsorship of the NCCM. The advent of

---

[272]"Media Contributions and Awards of Fulton J. Sheen: A Chronology," Sheen Archives, Diocese of Rochester, "Memorabilia" file, "Personal" folder.

television appears to have awed Sheen. A newspaper reported Sheen observing that "it was fitting that the first message of the first religious television broadcast in the history of the world should 'be a tribute of thanks to
God for giving to the minds of our day the inspiration to unravel the secrets
of the universe.'"[273] Eight years later, Maier celebrated with his TLH supporters that "our radio mission entered the field of television," as New Year's
Day and Good Friday services were televised on an experimental basis over
KSD-TV, St. Louis. NAE leader and historian James DeForest Murch
credited Maier with conducting "the first televised service of worship in
history" with these telecasts.[274] (Murch was either unaware, or chose to
ignore, that Sheen had broken this barrier previously.) Maier died before he
could fully embrace television as an evangelistic tool. Sheen, on the other
hand, moved from radio to network television in 1952, and made himself
into a star of the new broadcast medium.

Maier's success on national radio and his interest in TV likely did influence
the LCMS's entry into television. In 1952, a drama series, *This Is the Life*,
began a multidecade syndicated run. The program dramatized Christian
responses to the challenges of modern everyday life. Upon the fifteenth anniversary of this program, Fulton Sheen wrote to Eugene Bertermann, Maier's former radio director who had become head of the LCMS's television
productions, to offer encouragement. Acknowledging the success of the
Lutheran-sponsored television show, Sheen wrote, "Because you have
brought Christ closer to the people, I express my gratitude and my congratulations." He wished Bertermann "every blessing."[275]

It was a fitting word from one of the era's great radio preachers concerning the legacy of the only other radio voice that matched his confessional orthodoxy and wide appeal on the airwaves.

---

[273]See "First Religious Broadcast" clipping from unidentified newspaper, Sheen Archives, Diocese
of Rochester, "Press Clippings" file, "1940" folder.

[274]Walter A. Maier, *Go Quickly and Tell: Radio Messages for the Second Part of the Fifteenth Lutheran
Hour* (St. Louis: CPH, 1950), ix; Murch, *Co-operation Without Compromise*, 81; Maier, *A Man
Spoke*, 347.

[275]Letter from Fulton J. Sheen to Eugene R. Bertermann, dated July 29, 1966, Sheen Archives,
Diocese of Rochester, "Correspondence A–P" file, "B" folder.

Epilogue

TUNING IN TO RELIGIOUS RADIO

IN HIS LENGTHY, impressive history, subtitled *The American People in Depression and War*, David M. Kennedy speaks of the powerful impact of radio in the 1930s and 1940s. Kennedy observed that radio—a vehicle offering "a wondrous, newfangled technology"—produced dramatic "political and social effects." More specifically, "The new medium swiftly developed into an electronic floodgate through which flowed a one-way tide of mass cultural products that began to swamp the values and manners and tastes of once-isolated localities." Further, "radio assaulted the insularity of local communities," and "catalyzed the homogenization of American popular culture," as "tens of millions of Americans regularly gathered around their radio receivers."[1] Yet in what one reviewer rightly described as this "monumental book" that devoted "over nine hundred pages, some six pounds" to providing "towering narrative history in the grand style, describing the most momentous era in the twentieth-century United States," something important was left out.[2] Kennedy virtually ignores the role of *religious* radio, and even religion in general, as a cultural force during this tumultuous period. The only radio preacher he discusses is the controversial Father

[1]David M. Kennedy, *Freedom from Fear: The American People in Depression and War, 1929–1945* (New York: Oxford University Press, 2005), 228-29.
[2]*Freedom from Fear* description from Harvard Sitkoff, "Review of Books," *American Historical Review* 105, no. 3 (June 2000): 954-55.

Charles Coughlin, though he appropriately presents him as primarily a political rabble rouser rather than as a religious leader.[3]

With due respect to the excellence of Kennedy's work, he, along with most
historians of the 1930s and 1940s, as well as even radio historians, ignore or
give only passing simplistic attention to religious broadcasters during this
era. When religious radio is mentioned, often only Father Coughlin or
Aimee Semple McPherson appear—the former for his political harangues,
and the latter for her flamboyant persona and highly visible personal
scandals. Yet while Coughlin and McPherson generated significant followings, they were hardly representative of the whole of religious broadcasting during this era. When they are accepted as such, we receive a
distorted portrayal of the times. When religious radio is ignored entirely, the
distortion is even more pronounced. As the last chapter demonstrates, religious broadcasters such as Fulton Sheen and Walter Maier carried significant cultural force. They spoke to millions of people about matters temporal
and eternal, with recognized authority and perceived, personal proximity.
To leave them out of the national history is to accept an incomplete narrative
that diminishes or disregards the importance of such larger-than-life figures
in the lives of millions of people during this era.

Coast-to-coast broadcasting, especially as facilitated via network hookups,
dramatically changed American culture. Radios, which had not existed at
the turn of the twentieth century, suddenly became a part of most Americans' *daily* lives. Radio receivers evolved swiftly from crude "crystal" sets
assembled by enthusiasts to pieces of furniture manufactured by craftsmen,
and became the new "hearth" around which families gathered. In the midst
of a proliferation of program offerings, citizens turned on their radios to
hear comedy, variety, drama, music, sports, information, instruction, and
news broadcasts. They also chose to include religious broadcasts in their
listening habits, which was neither a casual afterthought nor an accident. As
Americans embraced new forms of entertainment and information available
through new technology, they also clung to old-time religion delivered
through the new medium this technology empowered.

---

[3]Kennedy, *Freedom from Fear*, 227-33. Kennedy does briefly mention Aimee Semple McPherson,
but only as a "melodramatic revivalist" in Los Angeles, not as a religious broadcaster (224).

While religion was part of broadcasting lineups from the advent of commercial radio, it was far from a homogeneous component. Already in 1922, Paul Rader brought a passionate revivalism to the airwaves, at Chicago Mayor William H. "Big Bill" Thompson's request. Over the mayor's crude city hall station, Rader opened by declaring that "one hundred thousand sinners within the sound of my voice today must be saved." He went on to broadcast over numerous radio stations well into the second half of the 1930s.[4] A contemporary of Rader who occupied the other end of the theological spectrum, New York pastor S. Parkes Cadman began *National Radio Pulpit* in 1923.[5] Cadman preached a liberal ecumenical Protestantism in a nonsensational fashion, avoiding revivalistic rhetoric or methods.[6] As the 1920s progressed, religious broadcasting expanded significantly, exhibiting a variety of styles and content—a trend that continued during the following two decades. Network broadcasters, clergy on local stations, and radio stations operated by religious organizations for the sole purpose of evangelistic outreach, all took to the airwaves.

In addition to the sheer amount and variety of religious programming during this period, the cultural significance of religious radio was especially highlighted by the large followings and personal stature acquired by leading network preachers. In the 1930s and 1940s, in addition to Maier and Sheen, several such preachers became household names as their broadcasts further demonstrated the breadth of listener appetite. Harry Emerson Fosdick brought a brand of antifundamentalist progressivism to millions of homes over NBC's *National Vespers*, earning him the title "Modernism's Moses."[7] Although not broadcast on a major network, Aimee Semple McPherson could be heard across much of the country as she preached her "Foursquare Gospel" from Angelus Temple in Los Angeles, via her own station, KFSG. McPherson combined glamour, entertainment, faith healing (which she invited listeners to receive by placing their hands on their radios), revivalistic

---

[4]James L. Snyder, *Paul Rader: Portrait of an Evangelist* (Ocala, FL: Fellowship Ministries, 2003), 139-43; Tona J. Hangen, *Redeeming the Dial: Radio, Religion, & Popular Culture in America* (Chapel Hill: University of North Carolina Press, 2002), 43-50.

[5]Michael Edgar Pohlman, "Broadcasting the Faith: Protestant Religious Radio and Theology in America, 1920–1950" (PhD diss., The Southern Baptist Theological Seminary, 2011), 12.

[6]Fred Hamlin, *S. Parkes Cadman: Pioneer Radio Minister* (New York: Harper & Brothers, 1930), 92-93, 113-15, 134-36.

[7]Pohlman, "Broadcasting the Faith," 24.

preaching, humor, and organizational skills, in a fashion that attracted loyal listeners, and propelled her to a position of religious leadership unheard of for females during this era. Even when scandal eventually surrounded McPherson, many of her admirers continued to look to her for religious guidance and a sense of hope.[8]

Also broadcasting from southern California, Charles Fuller generated a radio following that surpassed Sheen's and even rivaled Maier's. Fuller, who first preached over the radio in 1924, started regularly broadcasting over a hookup of Pacific Coast stations as the 1930s began. By the latter part of that decade, Fuller's *Old-Fashioned Revival Hour* was heard coast to coast through the MBS and transcription broadcasts on independent stations.[9] By 1943, Fuller had become Mutual's top broadcaster, generating 50 percent more revenue than the next largest secular customer.[10] The *Old-Fashioned Revival Hour* was one of the few religious programs that actually was an hour in duration. The fundamentalist Fuller delivered a warm, folksy broadcast, which he described as "the old songs and the old Gospel which is the power of God unto salvation," while eschewing discussions of "politics or plans for fixing up the world, much as it needs fixing."[11] In addition to extensive hymn singing by his musical staff and the studio congregation, Fuller's wife, Grace, read a sampling of letters from listeners each week. A solid sermonizer, Fuller offered prayers and a simple, biblical sermon promising salvation through faith in Jesus Christ. As with any revival, each program ended with an invitation for members of the radio audience to "accept Jesus." Fuller's program was long on nostalgia and short on the militancy often associated with the dispensationalist fundamentalism to which he subscribed. His broadcasts covered much of the globe and his popularity lasted into the 1960s.

Other religious broadcasters built up significant audiences during the 1930s and 1940s, via networks, regional hookups, and transcription

---

[8]The "Foursquare Gospel" consisted of "Jesus, the only Savior, Jesus, the Great Physician, Jesus, Baptizer with the Holy Spirit, Jesus, the coming Bridegroom, Lord and King." See Edith L. Blumhofer, *Aimee Semple McPherson: Everybody's Sister* (Grand Rapids, MI: Eerdmans, 1993), 191.

[9]Daniel Fuller, *Give the Winds a Mighty Voice: The Story of Charles E. Fuller* (Pasadena, CA: Fuller Seminary Press, 2008), 113-16.

[10]Mark Ward Sr., *Air of Salvation: The Story of Christian Broadcasting* (Grand Rapids, MI: Baker, 1994), 55-56.

[11]Fuller, *Give the Winds a Mighty Voice*, 122.

recordings. They included Norman Vincent Peale from New York City on the *Art of Living*, Theodore Epp from Lincoln, Nebraska on *Back to the Bible*, H. M. S. Richards Sr. from Los Angeles on the *Voice of Prophecy*, M. R. De Haan from Grand Rapids on *Radio Bible Class*, Donald Grey Barnhouse on a weekly program from his Tenth Presbyterian Church in Philadelphia and later on *The Bible Study Hour*, T. Myron Webb from Tulsa on *The Bible Fellowship Hour*, Paul Myers as "First Mate Bob" from Beverly Hills on *Haven of Rest*, Peter Eversveld from suburban Chicago on *The Back to God Hour*, and Percy Crawford from Philadelphia on the *Young People's Church of the Air*, to name only a few. Even two religious bodies that many considered beyond the pale of orthodox Christianity, the Jehovah's Witnesses and the Church of Jesus Christ of Latter-day Saints (Mormons), acquired network access. Jehovah's Witnesses launched their own radio station in Brooklyn in 1924, and by the early 1930s had cobbled together a "wax network" of several hundred stations through the distribution of transcription recordings of their religious program.[12] From Salt Lake City, *Music and the Spoken Word*, featuring the 325-voice Mormon Tabernacle Choir, went on the air in 1932 and has remained there ever since.[13]

Religious broadcasts, in sum, provided an undeniably significant component of all radio programming throughout the entire United States (and beyond) during the "Golden Age of radio." They attracted massive, loyal audiences, and helped millions of Americans find a religious anchor during a period of unprecedented national and international upheaval. Religious radio contributed to the cultural life of the country at a time when culture itself, including its religious elements, was under siege. In short, the story of religious radio should not be marginalized or left out of the history of these times if we are to more fully understand this period as it actually developed.

When radio emerged as a source of entertainment and information in the 1930s, religion did not seem out of place on the air any more than it did elsewhere in society. Even if religion, and Christianity in particular, was in a state of flux during this period, it was not all that surprising that the novelty

---

[12]Christopher H. Sterling, ed., *The Concise Encyclopedia of American Radio* (New York: Routledge, 2010), 386. "Wax network" referred to multiple stations playing transcription discs, rather than participating in an actual network hookup.

[13]Hal Erickson, *Religious Radio and Television in the United States, 1921–1991: The Programs and Personalities* (Jefferson, NC: McFarland & Company, 1992), 133.

of an Aimee Semple McPherson, the ecumenical, doctrinally relaxed preaching of a Harry Emerson Fosdick, or the earnest, yet comfortable fundamentalism of a Charles E. Fuller drew listeners to their radio sets. What would have been much harder to predict was that a priest and a pastor, from denominations perceived as residing on America's religious periphery, would become two of the most popular radio broadcasters—and not just religious broadcasters—of the medium's most powerful era.

The Catholic Fulton J. Sheen and the Lutheran Walter A. Maier were extraordinary religious spokesmen, on an extraordinary medium, at an extraordinary time. They harnessed fertile minds, exceptional erudition, awareness of the times, powerful communications skills, and unwavering Christian conviction—and all deployed to call the souls of listeners and the soul of a nation to repentance and godliness. They put forth a sturdy doctrinal presentation of the Christian faith in response to the erosion of traditional orthodoxy that they observed in modernism, humanism, and skepticism. They offered hope for those experiencing twentieth-century problems through an ancient faith in a God who created, redeemed, and sanctified those who only believed. They contributed to the cultural, ecclesiastical, and civic lives of millions of Americans in ways that drew attention from a wide range of contemporary observers, both secular and religious. As societal, economic, intellectual, military, and religious forces threatened to diminish adherence to, and the role of, orthodox Christianity and even religion itself, the Reverend Doctors Maier and Sheen led the counteroffensive. Many enlisted—by turning a radio knob.

FIGURE CREDITS

Figure 3.1. Walter A. Maier on baseball team. Image courtesy of Concordia Historical Institute, St. Louis, Missouri

Figure 3.2. Rev. Walter Maier as World War I American military chaplain. Image courtesy of Concordia Historical Institute, St. Louis, Missouri

Figure. 3.3. Walter A. Maier after receiving his PhD from Harvard University. Image courtesy of Concordia Historical Institute, St. Louis, Missouri

Figure 3.4. Dan Sullivan, Charles Hart, and Fulton Sheen on St. Viator College Debate Team, 1914–1915. Photograph courtesy of Diocese of Rochester Archives

Figure 3.5. Fulton Sheen and fellow student at St. Paul Seminary. Photograph courtesy of Diocese of Rochester Archives

Figure 3.6. 1932 sketch of friends G. K. Chesterton and Fulton Sheen by British artist Fred A. Farrell. Image courtesy of Diocese of Rochester Archives

Figure 4.1. Promotional photograph of Monsignor Sheen at the NBC radio microphone. Photograph courtesy of Diocese of Rochester Archives

Figure 4.2. Promotional photograph of Rev. Maier at the Mutual radio microphone. Image courtesy of Concordia Historical Institute, St. Louis, Missouri

Figure 5.1. Fulton Sheen with Father William Finn on the *Catholic Hour*. Photograph courtesy of Diocese of Rochester Archives

Figure 5.2. Walter Maier delivering a *Lutheran Hour* sermon in the radio studio wearing a T-shirt. Image courtesy of Concordia Historical Institute, St. Louis, Missouri

Figure 5.3. Fulton Sheen working at his desk in his Washington, DC, residence. Photograph courtesy of Diocese of Rochester Archives

Figure 5.4. Walter Maier with paper clips. Image courtesy of Concordia Historical Institute, St. Louis, Missouri

Figure 8.1. Mailman delivering correspondence to Walter Maier. Image courtesy of Concordia Historical Institute, St. Louis, Missouri

Figure 8.2. Sheen behind podium with flowers. Photograph courtesy of Diocese of Rochester Archives

Figure 8.3. Father and daughter looking at Sheen poster. Photograph courtesy of Diocese of Rochester Archives

Figure 8.4. Fulton Sheen speaks before a large audience. Image courtesy of Diocese of Rochester Archives

Figure 8.5. Maier at World's Fair Lutheran Day. Image courtesy of Concordia Historical Institute, St. Louis, Missouri

Figure 8.6. Lutheran Hour Rally in Portland, Oregon. Image courtesy of Concordia Historical Institute, St. Louis, Missouri

Figure 8.7. Print advertisement featuring Maier at the Hollywood Bowl. Image courtesy of Concordia Historical Institute, St. Louis, Missouri

Figure 8.8. Sheen looking at Al Smith. Photograph courtesy of Diocese of Rochester Archives

Figure 8.9. Sheen at UCLA, 1940. Photograph courtesy of Diocese of Rochester Archives

Figure 8.10. Maier preaching in Pierce Chapel at Wheaton College. Courtesy of Buswell Library Archives & Special Collections, Wheaton College, Illinois

INDEX